FAMILY LIFE IN

19TH-CENTURY AMERICA

Recent Titles in
Family Life through History

Family Life in 17th- and 18th-Century America
James M. Volo and Dorothy Denneen Volo

Family Life in 19th-Century America
Marilyn Coleman, Lawrence H. Ganong, and Kelly Warzinik

FAMILY LIFE IN

19TH-CENTURY AMERICA

AMERICA

JAMES M. VOLO
AND DOROTHY DENNEEN VOLO

Family Life through History

GREENWOOD PRESS
Westport, Connecticut • London

Library of Congress Cataloging-in-Publication Data

Volo, James M., 1947-
 Family life in 19th-century America / James M. Volo and Dorothy
Denneen Volo.
    p. cm. — (Family life through history, ISSN 1558-6286)
  Includes bibliographical references and index.
  ISBN-13: 978–0–313–33792–5 (alk. paper)
  ISBN-10: 0–313–33792–6 (alk. paper)
 1. Family—United States—History—19th century.   2. United States—
Social conditions—19th century.   I.   Volo, Dorothy Denneen, 1949–   II.
Title.   III.   Title: Family life in nineteenth-century America.
HQ535.V65 2007
306.850973′09034—dc22   2007018352

British Library Cataloguing in Publication Data is available.

Library of Congress Catalog Card Number: 2007018352
ISBN-13: 978–0–313–33792–5
ISBN-10: 0–313–33792–6
ISSN: 1558–6286

First published in 2007

Greenwood Press, 88 Post Road West, Westport, CT 06881
An imprint of Greenwood Publishing Group, Inc.
www.greenwood.com

Printed in the United States of America

The paper used in this book complies with the
Permanent Paper Standard issued by the National
Information Standards Organization (Z39.48–1984).

10 9 8 7 6 5 4 3 2 1

Contents

Introduction

Parents should instruct their children in the Scriptures. Should bring them up in the nurture and admonition of the Lord. Should also teach them to be sober, chaste, and temperate, to be just to all and bountiful to the poor as they have opportunity and ability. Parents should govern their children well; restrain, reprove, correct them as there is occasion.[1]

—Benjamin Wadsworth
A Well-Ordered Family (1719)

Family

Family was the primary mechanism by which 19th-century children passed to successful adulthood acquiring the skills, the values, and the philosophies of their forbearers, their community, their church, and their nation. The knowledge gained by the experiences of childhood, the acquisition of formal or informal occupational training, and the formation of adult values were all intimate functions of the family. The family served to transmit cultural ideals, societal standards, and political awareness through succeeding generations. A well-ordered family also helped to mitigate the sometimes wild fluctuations in the levels of agricultural success, economic stability, and personal security that affected family members in an organized and distinctive way.

Modern historians have suggested that by the beginning of the 19th century several complex factors had worked together to undermine the family household of colonial times. Among these were the waning of traditional church authority and the rise of emotionalized religions, revivalism, evangelicalism, and camp meetings; the growth of industrial manufacturing and regional consumerism and the subsequent weakening of the traditional farmland economy; the challenge to parental authority posed by public school and by the growing body of secular officials and agencies within the community; and the loss of patriarchal influence in the afterglow of enlightened thought and republican principles. The challenge to families represented by the secession crisis and the Civil War should not be underestimated. Yet Victorian-era families in America seem to have lived in well-ordered and structurally sound homes.

The 19th-century idealization of the American family home as a place of gathering and foundation of community bordered on the reverence accorded a sanctuary in some circles. In 1864 self-improvement advisor and child-rearing author, John F. W. Ware noted some of the impending threats to the traditional family home, and he warned, "[Our] English ancestors . . . [were] an in-door people. . . . Make this whole nation an out-of-doors people, teach them to find their amusement, their happiness, away from home, in gardens, in cafes, in the streets as it is in France and Italy, and it would be as difficult to maintain our Republic as it has been to establish one in Paris and Rome. . . . [W]e should all be grateful that we have so pure a model as the ideal Anglo-Saxon home."[2]

It is important for the reader to keep in mind the limitations created by such ethnocentric attitudes when considering the words and deeds of different classes of persons in the 19th century. Nonetheless, it seems safe to suggest that the functions of the family, as perceived by those living at the time, can be separated into several general themes: *religious, economic, educational, societal,* and *supportive.* These several functions of the family, which will be discussed in detail later, allowed each family member to adapt to the outside world and overcome the peculiar challenges of life. Each of these themes took on a different level of significance as the 19th century progressed. At times they were seemingly subverted by the larger historical issues of the day such as abolition, secession, or civil war; but all five continued to characterize the overall purposes of the family through-out the period.

The *religious function* was thought to be the key to a well-ordered 19th-century family. For children in particular, family religious instruction remained uniquely important because it was thought that they received religious training at home at an earlier age and in a more appropriate manner than any formal religious training institution could have effectively done. As Ware notes, "The Divine Mind seems to have laid broadly and deeply the foundations of an institution [the family] which should satisfy the wants of the most uncultured, at the same time that it should be capable of stretching itself out so to satisfy the highest aspirations of the most refined."[3] The antebellum period was characterized by a grassroots upwelling of evangelical sentiment and a Second Great Awakening of religious fervor among the established religious communities. In many cases formal church membership among traditional Protestants rose to historic highs.

However, many of the immigrants to America were highly sectarian in their beliefs. Irish immigrants, in particular, introduced an ever-increasing Roman Catholic presence into a largely Protestant urban population that was ill disposed to accept them. There were also a number of new religious sects that became popular in this period (among them Mormons, Campbellites, Shakers, Rappites, Fourierists, Unitarians, and Universalists). These sects tended to be more narrowly focused on discrete principles than the more traditionally organized churches, and their doctrines generally rejected formalized ceremonies and traditional religious organizations for a more popularized format. Some of these, like the Mormons, affected the social and economic characteristics of the wider community while others were mere splinter groups or cultural curiosities.

Sectarian groups were often self-led or formed around a particularly charismatic leader, while organized churches generally had a trained authoritarian ministry and a long-standing dogmatic tradition. It was thought that young women were particularly susceptible to being led astray by these novel religions, unconventional doctrines, and celebrated preachers. Ware notes, "No words can describe the mischief that has been so largely done in these latter days, by those who have laid themselves out, to lead away our young women from their home faith." Nonetheless, many religious sects initiated at the dawn of the century—the Methodists and the Mormons, for instance—eventually evolved into remarkably well-organized and authoritarian churches, each with its own set of sophisticated and discrete doctrines.[4]

As a method of religious instruction and a means of religious support, the family supplied an ethical atmosphere based on the particular tenets of its religion or sect that helped to maintain its core beliefs. It was thought that core religious beliefs would "touch and control the home life in all its relations," and any compromise in this regard between a husband and wife was considered injurious to the maintenance of family order. "To make home life happy and united, one faith should run through it—father, mother, children, after the same way worshipping [God] the Father." For this reason, should the young couple differ in religious belief when engaged to marry, the woman was expected to defer to the man's faith before marriage—the women's judgment in this area being thought "but scant proof" against temptation. "The family is no sooner begun, and children become old enough to ask questions and receive the simpler rudiments of religious knowledge, than the difficulty assumes a still graver aspect." Family religious traditions and training, on the other hand, continually reinforced the practice of worship even outside the formal settings of Sabbath Day worship.[5]

The *economic function* of the family was primarily one of providing the daily necessities of life to every person. Family members were fed, clothed, and sheltered in a manner commensurate with the social and economic status of their household. For a frontier family experiencing subsistence living, meeting this function required the cooperation of all its members. Yet a single well-aimed bullet could provide a month's meat, and a well-tended garden plot insured greens, herbs, and tubers for the table. For the families of tradesmen, laborers, or craftspersons residing in a more urban setting, the availability of food and shelter was all but assured at a level undreamed of in colonial times. Yet the young American economy remained filled with imponderable dangers, uncertain trends, and erratic governmental policies that might threaten the family's ability to purchase sustenance or provide a roof over its head. This was particularly true for immigrants, blacks, and others living on the lowest rungs of the economic ladder. Although family farming would remain the major source of income for a majority of Americans into the early 20th century, maintaining a residence in the city or commuting to work from the newly forming suburbs was a new experience for most people. Moreover, manufacturers enforced extended daily schedules on factory workers, making them put in long hours to earn a living wage. Both the commute and the long hours took a great deal of time from meaningful interactions among family members.

A man was expected to provide an income for his wife and children through his own work, but brothers, sisters, and grandparents living in the household were expected to lend their assistance to the realization of the annual funds sufficient to meet the needs of the entire household. This activity was part of the social contract as it had been understood since colonial times, and it remained a part of the fabric that bound and maintained families in the 19th century. Although the nation as a whole remained largely rural, 19th-century America experienced a remarkable growth in both its urban population and its industrial workforce. In many cases whole cities were springing forth from the countryside. The tendency of men to go to work in the cities or labor in the factories for a daily wage or a salary rather than to work in a home-based shop or in the fields surrounding his home did very little to change these responsibilities. "Let a single member of a household forget or neglect his duties to the other members of it, and the home fails."[6] Except in the most affluent of circumstances, even preteens and adolescent children were considered an essential part of the family workforce either helping in the barnyard, hoeing in the garden patch, and plowing in the farm fields; or selling newspapers, clearing garrets, making deliveries, and laboring in the mills beside their city-dwelling parents.[7]

The *educational function* of the family was one by which parents (and grandparents) transferred their values and skills to the next generation. All facets of family life, not just occupational training, were involved in this process. The overheard conversations among adults, the way they lived, the way they dealt with others in the community, and the way they carried out their own daily duties were of particular importance for instructing children by example. It was often essential to the well-being of the family, possibly even to its survival, that children perform any task correctly. Formal education, as in a schoolroom setting, was just coming into its own during the period and universal public education was evolving as an institution. Both sectarian and nonsectarian education exhibited remarkable growth, and a number of comprehensive school systems were created on the state and municipal levels. Although the aims of both public and parochial education were firmly linked to training young citizens for their civic, social, and intellectual responsibilities, no educational leader before 1860 would have placed these goals above the principal one of moral training. Disciplines based on the Ten Commandments, the recitation of common prayers, and the reading and copying of passages from scripture suffused the classroom, the curriculum, and the culture of the 19th century. Unfortunately, the schools generally valued extremes of austerity and conformity as foundations of proper education, and a rigid uniformity took hold that valued subject matter more highly than creativity.

Most 19th-century Americans seemed positively impressed by public schools, but Southern aristocrats, social conservatives, and sectarian groups (especially the Roman Catholics and the Pietist sects) distrusted institutionalized public instruction. Public schools were thought to overemphasize both Northern cultural norms and the liberal opinions held by social reformers. In 1860 Timothy Titcomb, an author of self-improvement books and a self-appointed authority on "prominent questions which concern the life of every thoughtful man and woman" found public education "a curse to all the youth whom [it] unfits for their proper places in the world. . . . Every boy and girl is taught to be something in the world, which would be very well if being something were being what God had intended they should be; but when being something involves the transformation of what God intended should be a respectable shoemaker into a very indifferent and slow minister of the Gospel, the harmful and even the ridiculous character of the instruction becomes apparent."[8]

Tax support for public schools was always an issue. Early school laws in Massachusetts (1789) and New York (1812) legalized the public school district but required tuition of all who could pay. Prior to 1825 public school advocates avoided the property tax as a sources of funds. Lotteries were extensively used to calm public resistance. Permanent school funding, in the form of land grants, was recognized in the Northwest Ordinance of 1785. However, the right of taxation for the purpose of public education was realized in the Pennsylvania School Law of 1834 and a Massachusetts law of 1837. Other state and Federal laws slowly incorporated the concept that public education should be paid for by the "people at large."

Significant among these was the Morrill Act of 1862 (a Federal act passed in the absence of representation from the South) that provided funds to the "land grant colleges" of each state. A second Morrill Act was passed in 1890 to carefully define the use of these funds.

This dichotomy of opinion regarding public education affected a regional pattern of non-public development that ranged from in-home schooling by the hearthstone to full-fledged sectarian universities. A number of denominational schools and school systems were developed during the 19th century. Prominent among these were the schools established by Catholics, Lutherans, Quakers, and Jews. The development of Catholic schools was generally spurred by the virulent anti-Catholicism of mid-century. The movement began as a series of parish schools and grew to include a vast number high schools and colleges generally located in major cities of the Northeast. The Lutherans were strongly committed to religious education and organized an extensive system of parochial schools governed by their various synods throughout the United States. By the end of the century, for instance, the Missouri Synod alone operated more than 1,700 schools. The Quakers supported education for all races and classes, and operated many schools that reflected their views. For the most part these were absorbed into the public elementary schools as that movement gained acceptance among the general public. Jewish education was varied, but generally rejected the maintenance of separate institutions. They developed instead a variety of schools that reflected the diversity of culture among Jewish immigrants. These included Congregational Day Schools (German Jews), Sunday Schools (Reform Jews), and Yeshivas (Russian Jews).[9]

The *societal function* focused on the maintenance of the family's social position in the community, which was often considered "of first and lasting importance" for parents. This applied especially to the choice of marriage partners by one's children. The continued success of middle- and upper-class families was thought to ultimately rest on the "fitness" of the prospective couple for each other and for their work. The decision of who to marry may have been the most difficult to settle without resorting to "fancy, or passion, or property, or position, or caprice, or custom, or convenience." Yet many of these factors were prominent considerations at the onset of the process. Ware notes, "When we reflect that the selection [of a spouse] is often made, and the future determined, at a time when we consider no habit or principle of character fixed [in our children], one may almost marvel that a Divine wisdom should have left the matter to individual decision." While most persons believed that freedom of choice in this area was a cornerstone of a contented marriage, they allowed that the greatest precautions needed to be taken in the matter. A marriage was not to be based on "the mad freak of passion, or the stupid bargain of convenience or of gold." Young adults were expected to take a reasonable span of time for the prudent exercise of choice among qualified marriage prospects, and parents were enjoined to "circumscribe" the freedom of a child's acquaintances so that the risk of "accidental attachments" to a person "of whose character and antecedents they know absolutely nothing" might be avoided. Most parents admonished their children to choose their day-to-day associates from among their own social class, and they frowned on anything other than necessary business dealings or unavoidable discourse with any others. Yet overmanagement and blatant maneuvering—the "deliberate and pitiful making of matches for their children" that has come to characterize 19th-century parents—was thought by most persons to endanger the future happiness of a prospective couple.[10]

Finally, as part of its *supportive function* the family provided emotional, social, and financial assistance as well as physical protection to each member of the household and, sometimes, to the wider community of relatives. The role of each individual in the family was somewhat better defined during the 19th century than at present, but the consequences of

Although the 19th-century family home became more female-dominated as the period continued, a man's place became more authoritarian. Here a father, book in hand, enjoys the warmth of a family gathering, surrounded by his loved ones and his possessions.

faulty parenting were not so well understood as they may be today. It was thought that the mature wisdom and disciplined governance of the father differed from the tender affection and nurturing heart of the mother. Ideally the father headed the household with stern guidance and loving care; and the mother provided comfort in good times and sympathy and understanding in the face of difficulty.

The presence of children provided emotional support for parents and guaranteed caring aid in their old age. In order for the family to be perfectly constituted, it was thought that the children must be of both sexes. Ware produced a description of this dynamic that was more than satisfactory in capturing 19th-century thought in this regard. "There are affections that can only be called out, influences only to be exerted, proportion and finish to character only to be attained, where both boys and girls grow together in the home. The fathers who are growing old without a daughter's clinging affection, the mothers who pass their prime without a son's chivalric devotion; the brothers who come up rude, unpolished, and untamed for want of a sister's gentleness—shy, awkward, and ill at ease; the sisters who have never felt the proud, encouraging protection of a brother's love—each and all have lost from their life an element to completeness, and the home, happy and bright as it is, is shorn of a great glory."[11]

Many observers at the time considered the family-centered Anglo-Saxon home of the Northern upper classes "an institution which was not only sanctioned but created by God," one which could only be "dishonored at a fearful cost to the manhood and integrity of the race." The perfect constitution of the family was reached only when parents, daughters, and sons, sisters and brothers, clustered beneath the common familial roof. Although the so-called Culture of Domesticity put women in charge of the operation of their households, during no former time in American history was the ideal of a man's home as his castle so strongly held.[12]

Nineteenth-century society endowed men with considerable power within this family setting. The very term *husband*, derived according to Ware from *houseband*, showed that his principal duty was "to bind together the household . . . be he merchant, mechanic, or the man of profession."[13] The concept of the urban home as "an enclosure" or "a sacred center" made most families remarkably nuclear in composition. Only the parents and their children lived under a common roof. Although the family group was often surrounded by unrelated domestic help or even a slave or two, these were commonly ignored as persons and treated more like animated household furnishings. Extended family structures were much less common in the 19th century than in colonial times, but they did exist, mainly on the frontiers, in the South, or in immigrant conclaves. Through the machinery of a vastly improved communications network (mail, telegraph, railroads, etc.), the kinship community living outside the immediate familial home could provide support, and uncles, aunts, grandparents, and cousins were available for daily counsel, economic assistance, and emotional underpinning in times of trouble.

However, in a wildly expanding nation, the call of cheap land, personal freedom, or stirring adventure caused many young men and women to leave the confines of their parental homes and stretch the bonds of family support. Those who left the sanctuary of the kinship community, as did many of the families that chose to emigrate to the American West, exchanged the support of family and friends for exposure to possible economic ruin, moral temptation, or physical danger. Possibly for this reason many emigrants traveled in family groups, uprooting married sons, daughters, and grandchildren when making a move. It was not unusual for a single kinship group to occupy a dozen separate wagons in the same emigrant train. Barring such unanimity of choice, many families chose to emigrate in sequence. Known as a serial migration, one small part of a family might lead the way to a new region where it became established to be followed later by other waves of migrating kinfolk. In this manner the family maintained its support structure.

The power structure within the 19th-century family—particularly that of the middle classes—was a tiered system of obligations and responsibilities among family members. Ware noted, "You will see that all harmonious action is the result of compromise, that there has everywhere to be an accommodation of forces . . . a system of checks and balances. . . . The man or woman who attempts to act without [compromise] will make a miserable failure, [and] must become either a selfish tyrant or an abject slave."[14] Husbands claimed and exercised authority over their wives and children, but they usually deferred to their spouses in matters of nurturing and maintaining the physical well-being of children to a greater extent than during the previous century. Nineteenth-century women retained their traditional authority over childbearing matters, but fathers felt free to discipline their children and to advise their wives with regard to any matter—sometimes to the point of being condescending. Women were thought to be too indulgent and too affectionate in nature to effectively govern their children, yet they were given great authority over servants and slaves.

Nonetheless, as the 19th century progressed, there was a shift in the power structure of the family brought about from both within and without the household. Women, under the umbrella of the "Culture of Domesticity," took an increasing role in directing household matters; schoolteachers (even female ones) were given expanded authority over the instruction of children (especially in the teaching of secular knowledge); physicians and other health care experts extended their influence over the care and well-being of children; and self-proclaimed men of the cloth espoused new and unfamiliar religious doctrines—many sprung from the very soil of America. Young women, and young men to a lesser extent, realized a new source of financial independence as they found income-producing work in the mills and manufactories of an industrial-ized society where they were no longer tied to the family home, farm, or business. Yet the family remained the foundation stone of the American Republic even as it passed through the crisis of the Civil War. In 1864 Ware noted of the family, "Probably no other thing has so much to do with making the man, and shaping his destiny. . . . It is the place he finds himself when he comes into the world; it is the place he goes from when he goes from it, and every intermediate stage—youth, manhood, age—receives from it the strongest influences and incentives."[15]

The life and character of American families and family members in the 19th century is the focus of this book. In particular the interaction of par-ents and children, the methods of parenting, and the molding of young lives in a variety of settings common to the period have been analyzed. The roles of fathers, mothers, children, and other members of the family household such as slaves and servants have been detailed. A comparative study of all the disparate family groups in America during the period with regard to these principles would be most interesting, but it would be so far-reaching as to be well beyond the scope of a work of this size. With these limitations in mind, there has been a tendency among researchers and historians to polarize discussions of this sort around Northern and Southern families, rural and urban families, or rich and poor families as did the commentators of the time. This leaves a great deal of unplowed middle ground for which there is very little disaggregated data. Yet, good historical research should raise questions even if they cannot be imme-diately answered. It is by this means that meaningful contributions to understanding are made.

The authors have included a number of unconventional sources in their research. John F. W. Ware (1864), for instance, was part of the burgeon-ing corps of self-help advisors and home-life improvement authors, who took advantage of the increased efficiency and lower cost of printing and publishing during the 19th century to expound on the principles of family structure and order. Other authors included in this category are Lydia Child (1831), Catherine Beecher (1850), Timothy Titcomb (1861), T. L. Haines and Levi W. Yaggy (1876), J. Clinton Ransom (1889), and Gaillard Hunt (1914), a spread from Child to Hunt of more than eight decades of observation and commentary on the 19th-century home and family. This book relies heavily on their thoughts about family, society, and culture.

Included as well are the comments of better-known journalist, diarists, and other observers who lived during the period such as Mary Chesnut, Susan Morgan, Elizabeth Bacon Custer, Thomas H. Burrowes, Richard Henry Dana, Francis Parkman, Jacob A. Riis, and George Templeton Strong. The observations of a number of children have been referenced, among them Francis Marion Watkins (10 years old), Albert Dickson (13), William Bayly (13), and Tilly Pierce (15).[16] Although the perceptions of urban dwellers are among those most commonly available in secondary sources dealing with the 19th century, those settlers and emigrants on the frontier have also been included in this work. As the words of commentators writing from the perspective of the 19th century, they must be taken in the context of all its commonly held racial, social, and ethnic prejudices, and readers should be aware that they do not necessarily reflect the opinions of the authors.

Like the previous study by the same authors concerning colonial family life in the 17th and 18th centuries, this work includes a basic historical background of the 19th century: the Antebellum Period, the Civil War and Reconstruction, and the postwar period of Manifest Destiny. Although the Civil War remains the critical historical event of the period, the authors have taken care not to over-emphasize its place in this work. Each chapter attempts to detail the lives of fathers, mothers, children, servants, and slaves against this background. Since this is a reference work designed by the authors to be user-friendly, each part has been written to stand alone and bring the reader to closure within an individual chapter.

The work relies heavily on the record established in diaries and journals, personal letters, church documents, newspapers, and published material contemporary with the period. These are included in the text where appropriate. On the other hand, the names of modern historians and commentators have been largely left in the chapter endnotes in order to increase the readability and flow of the text. Through the investigation of these sources and through reference to studies in American social and demographic history, many valuable insights have been gained, and a number of areas for further study have been identified. The authors—devoted historians and teachers for four decades—hope that they have extricated the germ of truth from these and other sources without distorting a genuine picture of family life in 19th-century America.

Notes

1. Wadsworth quoted in Leonard Pitt, ed., *Documenting America: A Reader in United States History from Colonial Times to 1877* (Dubuque, Iowa: Kendall/Hunt Publishing Co., 1989), 228.

2. John F. W. Ware, *Home Life: What It Is, and What It Needs* (Boston: William V. Spencer, 1864), 24–25.

3. Ibid., 27.

4. Ibid., xxiii

5. Ibid., xxi.

6. Ibid., xiv.

7. Alvin E. Conner, *Sectarian Childrearing: The Dunkers, 1708–1900* (Gettysburg, Pa.: The Brethren Heritage, 2000), 119.

8. Timothy Titcomb, *Lessons in Life: A Series of Familiar Essays* (New York: Charles Scribner & Co., 1861), 112.

9. Francesco Cordasco, *A Brief History of Education* (Totowa, N.J.: Littlefield, Adams & Co., 1970), 128–129.

10. Ware, *Home Life*, 28–29.

11. Ibid., 34.

12. Ibid., viii.

13. Ibid., 37.

14. Ibid., xiv–xv. For a more detailed analysis of family functions, see Conner, *Sectarian Childrearing*, 111–140.

15. Ware, *Home Life*, vii–viii.

16. Besides Ware, prominently included (in order of publication) are Timothy Titcomb, *Lessons in Life: A Series of Familiar Essays* (New York: Charles Scribner & Co., 1861); George E. Woodward, *George E. Woodward's Architecture and Rural Art*, vols. 1 and 2 (New York: by author, 1868); T. L. Haines and Levi W. Yaggy, *The Royal Path of Life; or, Aims and Aids to Success and Happiness* (Chicago: Western Publishing House, 1876); J. Clinton Ransom, *The Successful Man in His Manifold Relations with Life* (New York: J. A. Hill & Co., 1889); Gaillard Hunt, *As We Were: Life in America, 1814* (1914; repr., Stockbridge, Mass.: Berkshire House Publishing, 1993); Francis Marion Watkins as told to Ralph Leroy Milliken, "The Story of the Crow Emigrant Train of 1865," in a 1935 pamphlet reprinted by *The Livingston Chronicle*, January 1937; George Templeton Strong, *The Diary of George Templeton Strong* (New York: Macmillan Co., 1952); C. Vann Woodward, ed., *Mary Chesnut's Civil War* (New Haven: Yale University Press, 1981).

Part 1

The 19th Century: An Overview of America

1

The Background of 19th-Century America

Remembering the "Good Olde Days"
—first used in 1844 by Philip Hone, Mayor of New York

A Century of "Isms"

The forces of industrialization, reform, expansion, and warfare walked hand in hand during the 19th century. Often they passed along singly, providing a glimpse at some discrete facet of American life. At other times they crashed together simultaneously, devastating all that had been there and leaving behind almost unrecognizable consequences. Driven by these forces, America went through a period of national maturation during the antebellum years and came apart during the Civil War. The process involved changes in governance, justice, economics, finances, industry, manufacturing, communications, travel, agriculture, social structure, and family order, among others.

Antebellum observers noted the prevalence in American speech, newspapers, and publications of "isms." *Modernism* seems to be the catch-all term used by historians today when referring to the period, but urbanism, abolitionism, feminism, humanitarianism, reformism, commercialism, and others filled the consciousness of the 19th-century public. The ideals of traditionalism, Americanism, and nativism seem to have come to loggerheads with the shifting patterns of political republicanism and social pluralism in mid-century over the prospect of increasing immigration. With the Civil War prominent among the pivotal historical events of the century, sectionalism, racism, secessionism, and radicalism are commonly thought to have prevailed; but nationalism, militarism, and expansionism, in many fields—geographical, social, political, scientific, and economic—were equally influential in forming the character of the period. Different groups of people manipulated these "isms" for a variety of reasons, but the fact that large segments of the 19th-century population believed in them and chose to follow them suggests that the "isms" had real meaning.

Cultural and social changes were sweeping the cities of America during the 19th century. Industry and urbanization had moved the North toward a more modern society with an unprecedented set of novel cultural values, while the South had essentially lagged behind in the traditions of the 18th century. Historians have noted that the differences between the "Folk Culture" of the South and the "Modern Culture" of the North fueled the broad-based reform movements of mid-century and may have also ignited the turmoil over state sovereignty and slavery in a form of a "Culture War." The debate surrounding these questions, driven by an intensely partisan press, "not only aroused feelings of jealousy, honor, and regional pride, but raised fundamental questions about the future direction of the American society."[1]

Reformism

The atmosphere of the American nation before the Civil War was one of youthful vigor, and much of its energy was directed toward reform movements. Half a dozen causes were prominent during the period, but scores of lesser-known reform ideals abound. Although the abolition of slavery is often thought to be the leading reform cause in 19th-century America, it was actually less popular among reformers in the first half of the century than its prominence during the Civil War would suggest. The major concern raised by a British visitor to the United States in the 1850s identified "women's employment" as "the most delicate and difficult problem presented by modern civilization." Each reformer seemed a self-directed zealot on a special mission—some for generosity, some for learning, some for justice, some for freedom, and some for self-aggrandizement. These were men and women largely drunk on ideals; and they took "an intense delight" in the clash of rival schools of social thought.[2] William Fletcher, who would go on to fight on the side of secession in the Civil War, observed, "Both North and South seemed to be swayed by the demagogue."[3]

Helped by liberal newspapermen like Horace Greeley, who scattered his ranting editorials across the North, the reformers experimented impartially with religion, education, free love, birth control, abortion, criminal codes, temperance, capital punishment, public housing, labor, Utopian socialism, feminism, vegetarianism, and world government. "In a world where there is so much to be done," wrote one reformer, "I felt strongly impressed that there must be something for me to do." It did not help the reform causes that their proponents were sometimes wildly extreme, comically impractical, or fiercely uncompromising. Ralph Waldo Emerson, no enemy of reform, proclaimed that there was "not a reading [educated] man but has a draft of a new community in his waistcoat pocket." Much of the individual fervor and personal commitment pent up in 19th-century reformers is lost on modern-day students who have grown accustomed to impersonal government programs and massive philanthropic agencies dealing with the most pressing needs of social reform.

Reformers were absolute in their belief in the efficacy of the cures they espoused and demanded immediacy in their implementation. Most were people who saw their own ideals as the single true path for all of society. They attempted to affect these changes through the state and territorial constitutions and the state and Federal courts, but they showed no hesitation in calling for the dissolution of the old governmental structure, if it were deemed necessary to carry out their plans. "A new type of despotism" emerged from the imperative to reform. Although it was based on intellectual and emotional forces rather than on physical compulsion, the reform movement, in many of its guises, was willing to suppress personal liberty, tradition, and even constitutional principles to correct the social ills in America. William Lloyd Garrison actually called for the dismantling of the U.S. Constitution as a means of eradicating slavery.[4]

The mixing of traditional folkways with the reform vision of many Americans caused social influence, political authority, and the traditional concepts of family to become uncertain, unstable, and somewhat ambiguous. Nowhere was this more clear than in the contrast between the sections of the country in the antebellum period. Reform, modernize, and improve became the watchwords of the North; while maintain, reinforce, and defend were those of the South.

Urbanism

The most obvious modern element in Northern society was the rapid growth of its urban centers as more and more people flocked to the cities to find work in the factories that blossomed along the inland waterways of Massachusetts, Connecticut, and Rhode Island. Teeming factory cities sprouted from the rural countryside in less than a decade. The water- and steam-driven factory machines of Lowell and Lynn, created to facilitate the production of consumer products like store-bought clothing, hats, and shoes, filled the wharves of Boston with ready-to-wear items. Northern port cities like New York, Philadelphia, Boston, Salem, and Newport soon outstripped Southern port cities in terms of the volume of their trade in manufactured items. The cities of Charleston, Savannah, Mobile, and Baltimore continued to serve as outlets for the agricultural produce of the South, while steamboats joined the river cities of Pittsburgh, Cincinnati, Memphis, Natchez, Lexington, and Louisville and the farmlands of the central part of the country to the markets of the world through the gateway ports of New Orleans, Mobile, and Galveston.

Westward expansion along the growing system of canals and the successful navigation of the Western rivers by steamboats made a number of inland ports equally important. St. Louis, in particular, served as a central hub for river traffic. Located on the Mississippi River near the junction of the Ohio and the Missouri, St. Louis benefited from its connections with both the states of the Midwest and the Western territories of the Great Plains and Rocky Mountains. Only the Civil War blockade of the Mississippi River strangled its continued growth. By 1840 Buffalo, Cleveland, Chicago, Milwaukee, Syracuse, Rochester, and Detroit had emerged as important cities serving the Great Lakes Region. Buffalo, at the western terminus of the Erie Canal, underwent a remarkable transformation from a frontier trading outpost to a virtual metropolis in just a few decades. Detroit had been a disappointment as a fur trading post to its French founders in the 17th century, but it took on a revitalized importance as a commercial center as emigrant farmers entered the region.

Although many towns grew because of their proximity to canals, rivers, or lakes, others grew because of the spread of railroads. Lowell, Massachusetts, was the first manufacturing town to have its own railroad connection to the Atlantic coast, and Boston was the terminus for no fewer than seven major railroad lines stretching from the interior. Chicago grew with the aid of the railroads that extended from its center like a web of tracks in all directions. The antebellum rivalry between St. Louis and Chicago shifted the existing pattern of trade with the Western territories toward the North, and the aggressive railway and canal construction from the Northeast to the Midwest during the 1840s stretched the flow of interstate commerce from a predominately north-south direction into a west-east orientation. All of this development disadvantaged the Southern port cities, particularly New Orleans, which prior to mid-century had entertained most of the commerce of the region through the outlet of the Mississippi River. Even the Great Chicago Fire of 1871 could not reverse this tend.[5]

In the 1830s, New York City (population: 800,000), aided by the success of the Erie Canal that joined the waters of the Atlantic-flowing Hudson River to those of the Great Lakes, emerged as the financial center of the nation, surpassing Philadelphia (population: 560,000) as the nation's largest city in terms of population and the value of trade that passed through it. Brooklyn (population: 270,000)—still a separate municipality from New York City before the construction of its famous bridge in

1883—was the nation's third-largest city, surpassing older colonial giants like Baltimore, Boston, and New Orleans in size by 1860. This made the immediate area surrounding Manhattan Island one of the most densely populated and commercially productive in all the Western world. In 1860 there were more than 135 persons per acre living in New York City alone. By way of comparison Boston had a population density of 83, Philadelphia 80, and Pittsburgh 69.[6]

In 1800 the entire United States had been an essentially rural country. Fewer than 6 percent of its population of 5 million lived in towns with populations larger than 2,500. Only Philadelphia and New York had populations greater than 25,000. All but one of the nation's 20 largest cities were ports, and that one, Lancaster, was served by nearby Philadelphia on the Delaware River. Nonetheless, river ice in winter often blocked the passage to the Atlantic Ocean from Philadelphia, the largest colonial port in terms of the volume of its trade, insuring the continued importance of Norfolk, Baltimore, and New York as ports of entry and departure.

The first half of the 19th century witnessed a vast internal migration from the coasts to the farmlands of the interior Midwest. Ironically as the number of family farms increased nationwide, so did the population of the major cities. Waves of immigration from northern Europe and Ireland supported the increase in urban population. By 1850, the population of the country had risen to 23 million, and more than 30 percent of these had settled into the towns larger than 2,500 persons. Although three-quarters of the population was still involved in agriculture, the expansion of commerce and industry had also drawn almost 2 million factory workers into towns that were both old and new. The urban portion of the population grew from approximately 9 percent in 1830 to almost 20 percent in 1850, thereby becoming the fastest-growing demographic in America prior to the Civil War.[7]

The number of towns having more than 10,000 persons increased from 6 to more than 60 in less than half a century. Almost a dozen cities crossed the 100,000 mark by 1860, and the regions centered on New York and Philadelphia housed more than 1 million persons each. Cities as distinct as Providence and Chicago were experiencing similar rates of growth if not the same absolute numbers. A number of small coastal towns became booming cities by mid-century in response to America's rise to maritime greatness in the clipper ship era. Boston, Salem, Portland, and New Haven, for example, were all active coastal trading cities in 1850. Salem, a town best noted today for the witch trials of the 1690s, was among the top five seaports in the nation with respect to the value of the trade that passed through it annually. Nathaniel Hawthorne lived there and worked for a time as a clerk in the customs office. His "House of Seven Gables" overlooked the wharves of the old town filled with decorative items entering New England from China and the Far East.

The cities that had been the largest at the end of the 18th century remained so in the 19th century and experienced the greatest rates of population growth. The notable exception among these was San Francisco, which experienced phenomenal growth due to the discovery of gold in California in 1848. Prior to that event the sleepy Pacific coast town had less than 1,000 residents, yet by 1852 there were 36,000 and by 1860 more than 56,000. With the exception of San Diego far to the south, there was no other good harbor along the entire California coast with better connections to the gold fields and the interior West. Steamboats routed themselves up the Sacramento, the San Joaquin, and lower Feather Rivers, and coasting vessels connected San Francisco to northernmost California, the Oregon Territory, British Columbia, and Alaska. The discovery of the gold fields heightened the demand for a fast passage to the Pacific by clipper ship. Seamen reaching San Francisco would "jump ship" for a miner's claim in the interior, often leaving dozens of vessels stranded in the harbor for lack of crew to man them.[8]

The average physical size of American cities also increased from less than a one-mile radius to that of four or five miles. The development of public horse-drawn trams, known as *horsecars,* made daily commuting from such a distance possible, but most Northern men were willing to make the half-hour walk from their homes to their place of work in order to save the fare. Southerners did not share this characteristic of Northern males, choosing to ride astride their horse for even short distances.

Moreover, America's fastest-growing cities were often growing up as well as outward. The six-story Adelphi Hotel, built in New York in 1827, was the city's first skyscraper, and the Boston Exchange Hotel, built in 1830, sported eight floors. Two- and three-story structures with dressed stone, brick, or cast iron façades became common sights in the older urban districts, often replacing buildings of wood. Shops and workplaces were sometimes located on the lower floors and residential quarters could be found in the back or on the upper floors. Called apartment houses, or flats, these dwellings initially accommodated three or more sets of tenants, living and cooking independently from one another, usually on different floors or in a basement apartment. Each apartment usually had its own toilet and bathing facilities.[9]

Tenements

Northern cities were generally characterized by a well-defined business district and a manufacturing area within easy access of the railroad tracks or other transportation hub such as a waterfront or canal. This area was usually surrounded by lower-class residences, the style of which often became characteristic of whole parts of the city known loosely as neighborhoods. A style of row housing (the brownstone dwellings of Manhattan's East Side, for example) was developed in most major cities so that many people (related by race, language, or ethnicity) lived near each other and near their work. These neighborhoods were sometimes referred to by descriptive sobriquets such as Hell's Kitchen, the Back Bay, China Town, or Germantown, among many others. Some of these names continue in use today. One of the worst and most crime-ridden ethnic neighborhoods was Five Points in New York City, named for the conjunction of streets at its center.

Ethnic neighborhoods were often characterized by buildings known as tenements, which were usually viewed in a negative connotation by the upper classes of urban society. Before they decayed into slums and ghettos, these buildings had accentuated the appearance of uniformity and equality among their residents, at least as viewed from the street; but they were quickly abandoned by the better-heeled segments of the population for free-standing homes in the 19th-century equivalent of the suburbs. Unscrupulous landlords often subdivided the living space in urban dwellings into separate living areas with little regard for space, light, or ventilation. Tenement residents, like apartment dwellers, had separate family quarters, but they often shared toilets and baths. Rents were determined by the size of the living space or their location in the building with lower amounts demanded for those on upper floors or in the rear. Monthly rates in New York City averaged between $5 and $6 for a single room with a cooking area, and so many living units were created that a landlord could realize a monthly profit of $600 from some buildings.[10]

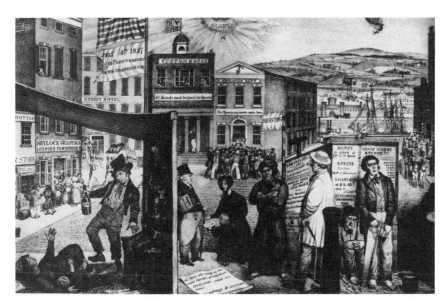

A period illustration noting all the ills of urban living. Although drunkenness, sexual deviancy, and the specie crisis are obvious to us today, much of the symbolism is lost to the modern eye.

The growing number of poor and uneducated persons in the cities soon turned the older tenements and apartment buildings from acceptable, if crowded, residences into ethnically segregated slums and ghettos. (See Table 1.1 for statistics on the tenement problem.) These were described as "crazy old buildings, crowded rear tenements in filthy yards, damp basements, leaking garrets, shops, outhouses, and stables converted into dwellings, though scarcely fit to shelter brutes, [the] habitations of thousands of our fellow-beings." This was largely an unfortunate consequence of social and ethnic prejudice combined with unchecked levels of immigration and population growth. In 1889 more than 350,000 persons entered New York City. More than 100,000 came from England, Scotland, and Ireland; 75,000 came from Germany; 31,000 from Poland and Russia; 29,000 from Italy; 16,000 from Hungary; and 5,400 from Bohemia.[11]

One had only to walk through an ethnic ghetto or slum to discover the overwhelming atmosphere of social decay and moral degeneration—a condition Southerner apologists quickly pointed to as evidence of the failure of modern Northern society. "The city," wrote Martha Lamb, an observer during the 1835 to 1845 period, "was a general asylum for vagrants and young vagabonds." Even the reformers believed that the standard of living among these ethnic city dwellers had to be improved if the squalor of the tenements was not to become a permanent feature of American cities. Juvenile crime, in particular, increased at a frightful rate, and even the interposition of the Children's Aid Society and similar philanthropic organizations failed to stem its growth. The perpetuation of such social ills was ascribed at the time to a lack of public will in implementing the appropriate cures, which the reformers thought they had clearly identified. Yet the dire predictions were borne out by the subsequent decades of urban poverty even in the face of best efforts by governmental and private agencies.[12]

Table 1.1 General Statistics: The New York Tenement Problem

	Total
Lost children found in the street	2,968
Sick and destitute cared for	2,753
Found sick in the streets	1,211
Number of pawnshops	110
Number of cheap lodging houses	270
Number of saloons	7,884

Source: Jacob A. Riis, *How the Other Half Lives: Studies among the Tenements of New York* (New York: Charles Scribner's Sons, 1890).

Many Americans could not escape the view that the decay and degeneracy of cities was due to the immigrants themselves who seemed to tolerate—if not frequent—taverns, beer halls, saloons, dance halls, gambling establishments, and houses of ill repute with amazing disregard for traditional American standards of conduct. A tone of condensation and disdain quickly entered the rhetoric of the reformers, and many attributed widespread social nonconformity among immigrants to social degradation, rather than to differences in ethnic character. They, therefore, incorrectly directed their campaigns against the foreign-born instead of toward the correction of social injustice in the American system. Tenements were degraded and crime-ridden, and many reformers, altruistic in their goals, often came to blame the degradation and crime of the overcrowded slums and ghettos on the tenants rather than on their environment. Dr. John H. Griscom, the health inspector for the city of New York, blamed the dilapidated condition of urban housing "on the recent influx of hordes of ignorant, poverty-stricken immigrants, which were flooding the city; and placing a heavy strain on the sanitary facilities."[13]

Early statistics on the absolute number of tenement dwellings are not readily available because no one at the time saw a need to separate them out from other multi-family dwellings. However, Riis reports that by the time of the Civil War the tremendous waves of immigration into the city had brought the number of tenement dwellers up to almost 500,000 people just on the island of Manhattan. By 1888, the number of tenement buildings was recorded as 32,000, and the number of their inmates had tripled to 1.5 million. The death rate among tenement dwellers in 1869 was more than 28 percent (13,285 deaths). In 1888 the death rate had fallen to 25 percent, but the absolute number of deaths (24,842) had almost doubled. The number of deaths among children was not reported as a separate statistic.[14]

Suburbs

The former residents of the city centers, composed mainly of aspiring middle- and upper-class families, moved to the fringes of the cities, built innovative balloon-framed homes of five, six, or more rooms, and established community parks and tree-lined streets to remind themselves of a more romantic and pastoral past. They hoped thereby to assure a more idyllic setting for the future of their children than the urban slum. Today we would call their communities suburbs.

The development of urban green areas also became a central theme of city planning in the years after the Civil War. Public parks soon became the primary outward manifestation of a desire to develop user-friendly open spaces where urban dwellers and townsfolk might commune with nature. Both the poet, William Cullen Bryant, and the writer, Washington Irving, struggled to protect open areas from unrestricted urban development, and they were instrumental in saving a large and potentially valuable portion of Manhattan Island in a semblance of its natural state before the sprawling city overtook it. This was to become Central Park, the most extensive and elaborate public space project of the century. In 1857 Frederick Law Olmstead was appointed superintendent of the Central Park project, and, thereafter, he and his associates also designed Prospect Park in Brooklyn; Riverside Park in Manhattan; the city parks of Hartford, Boston, and Louisville; and the grounds around the nation's newly restyled capitol in Washington, D.C.

Ethnic and Racial Bigotry

The lower classes of the North were exceedingly poor and composed, in large part, of immigrants. Being foreign-born, they were generally denied the vote even under the newly relaxed qualifications. A growing sense of politics as usual, out of touch with the pulse of the people, and dedicated only to entrenched interests allowed new political parties to form with intriguing agendas designed to insure the defeat of the old party candidates.

Among these were the anti-immigrant, anti-Catholic Nativists who rose very rapidly to prominence, gaining traction in several Northern states at

The focus of many park and natural areas became the town bandstand with its fancy decorative work. Here the community celebrated its holidays and military victories, and heard its election speeches.

the local level but failing to carry their message of pure Americanism and anti-Catholicism to an accepting national audience. Nativist propaganda was widely promulgated throughout the nation, and even those who disagreed with Nativist positions were well aware of them. They were strongly supported by some of the finest established families of the North but had few adherents among Southerners, who were generally more tolerant of Catholics than Northerners. Southern cities had many established populations of native-born citizens with French and Spanish Catholic backgrounds. Nativism appeared intermittently and under the guises of several "All American" movements that targeted immigrants, the best known being the Know-Nothing Party.[15]

Between 1820 and 1860 the three major countries of origin of immigrants in the order of their numerical importance were Ireland, Germany, and Great Britain. These three countries supplied 85 percent of all immigrants to the United States in the antebellum period. By mid-century more than half of the residents of New York and Boston were foreign born. In Philadelphia this rose to 30 percent of the population, but major concentrations of Irish and German immigrants could be found in all three cities. San Francisco, Cincinnati, St. Louis, and Milwaukee also had large groups of foreign-born residents. Moreover, several Southern cities including Charleston, Mobile, Richmond, Nashville, and New Orleans supported a large proportion of free white immigrants as laborers or skilled help.

Many of the poorest immigrants were Irish Catholics. The Irish were the first truly urban group in America, living in crowded slums rife with crime, drunkenness, and disease, and experiencing severe religious prejudice at the hands of the Protestant majority. The Irish, who came during the Irish Potato Famine of 1845–1849, were also the only immigrant group in which females outnumbered males. With men leaving the rural regions of Ireland to find work in the cities "women had less of an opportunity to marry, encouraging them to emigrate as well." Advertisements for help were often followed by signs stating, "Irish Need Not Apply." It is ironic that the new modernism in Northern society allowed for the simultaneous existence of two seemingly contrary but equally strong sentiments based on race—radical anti-slavery and severe ethnic prejudice.[16]

The Germans tended to separate themselves from traditional America by moving away from the cities into more rural agricultural areas in Pennsylvania and the upper Midwest. By this means they avoided being the targets of overwhelming prejudice and achieved a far greater social solidarity than any other group of immigrants up to that time. Nonetheless, as they generally followed a European Sabbath tradition, Germans hurried home from their religious observances to a convivial afternoon in music halls and beer gardens that violated the more sober American concept of proper conduct on the Lord's Day. In this way they became the particular target of Sabbatarian groups and temperance crusaders.[17]

One of the striking features of 19th-century cities was the widespread presence of blacks among the population. The distinction between free blacks, black servants, and black slaves quickly blurred, especially in the South. Nonetheless, free blacks maintained an unseen but not inconsiderable presence in many major cities of the North. They seem to have preferred to live in an urban setting and were twice as likely to reside in cities than slaves, who were primarily agricultural workers. In cosmopolitan areas free blacks found opportunities for employment, exposure to black culture and religion, and the company of other freemen. While most served as wage laborers or craftsmen, a few black men have been identified as owning property, shipping and transportation concerns, manufactories, and shops; but the majority of free blacks were women who worked for wages primarily as domestic servants, laundresses, bakers, market sellers, or prostitutes. A few black women independently kept shops, ran boarding houses, or served as nurses and midwives among their own race.

The institution of race-based slavery required absolute control of blacks be they bondsmen or freemen. However, the dictates of urban living made it difficult for whites to supervise an entire race every minute of the day, as they attempted to do on isolated plantations. Southern cities responded to this circumstance by restricting the activities of all blacks, free and slave, instituting formal segregation in housing and excluding blacks from all public accommodations. The majority of free blacks lived on the margins of poverty in Northern cities, but they were subject to detention and questioning by the authorities without cause everywhere.

Mob Behavior

Beginning about 1833 and continuing through the remainder of the decade, there were almost 100 riots reported in several major cities throughout the country. About half of these incidents, characterized by the violence rather than the decorum of their assemblies, involved reactions to increasing pressure from anti-slavery activists. "Liberty was not the fashion for the moment, so the American government came in for condemnation because it had not power enough, especially in the executive branch."[18] In New York, Boston, Philadelphia, Utica, and Cincinnati, mobs broke up abolition meetings, tormented free blacks, and razed buildings in black neighborhoods. Yet any trivial incident could instigate a violent civic disorder, and many citizens, alarmed at the breakdown of law and order, refused to go into the streets after dark. New York diarist George Templeton Strong called the atmosphere of the streets a "rowdyism." This particular characteristic of 19th-century life seems to have been most prevalent in urban areas where both restraint and subtlety were conspicuously absent from many public gatherings.[19]

In 1831 an English actor in New York, who was reported to have made anti-American statements, was forced from the stage with hisses and boos on one night and driven from the theater during the following performance by a shower of rotten fruit, eggs, and sundry missiles. Philip Hone, a wealthy New York diarist, recorded the incident. Hone also recorded the violence that visited the city's municipal elections in 1834. "A band of Irishmen of the lowest class came out . . . [and] there was much severe fighting and many persons were wounded and knocked down." In the same year New York experienced the Stonecutter's Riot, one of the most violent of public mêlées, brought about by the city's decision to use convict labor instead of free workers to cut the marble for several municipal building projects. The protesting stonecutters were quickly outnumbered by a mob that turned from the initial purpose of the protest to attack a group of free blacks and white reformers at an abolition meeting. Hone noted that gangs of young men were stalking the streets in the Bowery, on Canal Street, and near the infamous Five Points neighborhood. Several houses and a church were destroyed. It took 3,000 militia to quell the disturbances.[20]

In 1835 William Lloyd Garrison was dragged through the streets of Boston by a mob of anti-abolitionists, and in 1837 abolitionist newspaper editor Elijah Lovejoy was killed during a riot in Alton, Illinois. So pervasive was the rancor engendered by the outrages prosecuted by anti-abolition forces that Connecticut passed legislation in 1836 banning anti-slavery lecturers from church pulpits. Anti-temperance riots ran a close second to those associated with abolition with the remainder equally divided among a series of causes, including reactions to Catholics, immigrants, and employers. A study of newspaper accounts from the period 1833–1837 suggests that more than 60 of these reactionary incidents took place in New England with Massachusetts, Connecticut, and New Hampshire being first, second, and third in hosting 17, 16, and 13 mob-style riots, respectively. [21]

These outbreaks of violence were no spontaneous upwelling of emotion. The rowdies were members of established gangs in many cities, and the forces behind the rioters were usually organized to systematically attack the increasingly common reform gatherings such as anti-slavery, anti-poverty, and temperance. These appealed largely to the sentiments of middle-class women and children and hoped to influence public opinion in their favor. The established social order—composed mostly of male voters of property, substance, and social position—viewed such tactics as a great danger threatening to envelop American society, and they were willing to take to the streets to stop them. By making direct appeals to women and children, activists were attempting to bypass the domestic authority of fathers and husbands, as well as the political leadership of the city fathers, and the social prominence of all members of the elite classes. Moreover, many of those antagonistic to reform movements considered them "foreign and . . . alien" to America, having been imported from similar campaigns in England supported by British philanthropists. This aspect of the reform movement as a conspiracy was considered to be particularly focused on America because British supporters of reform in the United States had not fostered efforts in European nations afflicted with similar social ills.[22]

It was paranoid, or at least fanciful, for Americans to think that the abolition movement was an insidious foreign stratagem or Tory plot hatched by British politicians, noblemen, and money barons to destroy the American republic and economy. Yet the idea caught the imagination of many anti-abolitionists, especially among those Jacksonian supporters who regularly overreacted to any criticism of the United States coming from British sources. The concept received considerable support in 1834, however, when the American Colonization Society—itself under attack by the forces in favor of immediate emancipation and racial amalgamation—identified the abolitionists as pawns of foreign agents in a widely circulated pamphlet and repeated these claims at its annual meeting in New York City. The American Colonization Society was a respected organization formed in 1817 to encourage free blacks to return to Africa. The initial meeting was held in no less a prestigious place than the chambers of the House of Representatives. Among its founders were Henry Clay, Andrew Jackson, Francis Scott Key, and other notables from both the North and South. The society found support from all sections of the country and from both slavery and anti-slavery advocates.

Social Mobility

Americans of the period were acutely aware of the need to create a stable and cohesive society. Yet the people of America were among the most mobile and diverse on earth. Geographically, socially, and economically, Americans (and those immigrants who wished to be Americans) were dedicated to change, movement, and progress. This may have been the most durable and common of American traits, but it was a difficult quality to circumvent when trying to form a unified national persona. Moreover, 19th-century Americans were innately diverse in terms of their ethnic backgrounds, employment, social class, education, language, customs, and religion. The creation of solidarity out of such variety was a vital task for a new society, and reasonable Americans knew that both the individual and the group were important parts of the process.[23]

In the mobile 19th-century world, emigration and resettlement were more common than in other periods. Moving to a sparsely settled frontier region heightened a parent's concern for personal and family safety. Added to the very real threat of attack by Indians, bushwackers, bandits, or venomous snakes were common farm accidents, indispositions, nutritional deficiencies, bad water, and difficult childbirths—all capable of striking without warning, but still a part of the fabric of ordinary life.[24] Even common sicknesses were made more threatening by distance from friends, kin, and established "patterns of care." Warnings about these fill the period guidebooks, military reports, physicians' articles, and private letters of the period.[25]

Similarities and differences were both sources of national strength, and neither could be cultivated alone at the expense of the other without stifling the process. The great flaw in the work provided by historians of the antebellum period was that they could not explain how the geographic sections of the nation could share so many important cultural and political characteristics and still be mutually antagonistic to the point of shedding blood. The actual causes of the Civil War are both sophisticated and multidimensional, and any discussion along these lines inevitability remains totally academic. Yet it is clear that the nation did not go to war because of slavery any more than it did over disputes involving temperance, urbanization, poverty, politics, or economics. Possibly historians should look to the cumulative effect of all the various disputes as a cause of the war.

Temperance

Temperance was as politically divisive in 19th-century America as any other social issue. In colonial times the consumption of alcoholic beverages by persons of all ages was accepted because they were served in lieu of fresh, potable water and were thought to have a prophylactic effect in preventing a wide range of diseases. Wine, beer, brandy, rum, and other liquors were common items stocked in the colonial family's pantry. The drinking of mildly alcoholic beverages was also embedded in the customary sociability of family events and in the relaxed atmosphere of the lunch or supper breaks during the workingman's day—the quintessential example being the traditional daily ration of grog given to sailors and other mariners. The public drinking traditions of the colonial period continued into the early national period and helped to fuel popular support for the Whiskey Rebellion of 1794, which tested the resolve of the new Federal government over the issue of the excise tax. Thereafter, whiskey became a symbol for some of the deeper divisions between classes, including its association with crime, prostitution, unemployment, poverty, spousal abuse, the abandonment of children, sexual dysfunction, and general ill-health.

Many of the first temperance reformers were factory owners and captains of industry with Federalist sympathies. These men initially banned whiskey and other strong liquors from their workplaces and their homes for political reasons, but they created a divide between themselves and their working-class employees that spilled over into the wider society. The lower classes retained their love of public drinking as a symbol of their resistance to a declining social respectability and to the increasing commonality of deplorable working conditions. The consumption of alcohol was also seen as symbolic of an autonomous social life away from the proscribed behaviors demanded at the factory or office. Thereby temperance became a defining characteristic of wealth and position for those middle-class citizens aspiring to increased social respectability.

The 1820s saw the formation of a number of middle-class temperance organizations allied to the evangelical movement that were as hostile to wealthy drinkers as they were to lower-class ones. "Progressing from tactics of moral suasion and conversion to firings, boycotts, and political campaigns to outlaw drink," these reformers converted thousands of ordinary citizens to new ideas about temperance and its link to social standing. Anti-drinking supporters attended picnics, marched in parades, and held prayer meetings. By the 1840s many native-born working-class Americans took up the cause of temperance to separate themselves from the unyielding drinking habits of immigrant Irish and German laborers.[26]

Meanwhile, the Whig Party, in search of issues that might buoy its success at the ballot box, undertook to make temperance into a vehicle for political gain. The Whigs began to campaign among the electorate for coercive temperance, and it drew on traditional Protestant churchgoers, nativists, mechanics, professional men, factory managers, and their families to support the anti-drinking movement. In response the Democratic Party offered a refuge to the newly enfranchised among the immigrant Irish and German working classes, as well as distillers, tavern owners, mariners, and small retailers, thereby polarizing much of the population. The result was particularly destructive as opposing groups collided in the streets of urban America. In the 1830s mob action bordering on riots became all too frequent in American cities. The confrontations, similar to those engendered by anti-abolitionists, became too heated to be controlled by the political parties with anti-immigrant, pro-temperance riots occurring in Boston, Baltimore, Philadelphia, St. Louis, Louisville, and other cities.

Abolitionism

No reform movement is more closely associated with the sectionalism of the antebellum period than the abolition of slavery. Those who identified themselves as abolitionists generally crusaded for the immediate social and political equality of all blacks in the United States. Contrary to the common Southern perceptions of abolitionists, however, the more provocative tactics and strategies of the emancipation radicals rarely had any effect outside of New England. Anti-slavery, as a wider movement, was far too decentralized and subject to too many local variations, to march in lock step behind the radicals.

Attacks on slavery in the early years of the Republic had been based upon the ideals set forth in the Declaration of Independence and the incompatibility of slavery with the concept that: "All men are created equal." Many Americans freed their slaves during and immediately after the American Revolution. Those blacks that fought in the Revolutionary army or navy won their personal freedom and became entitled to a Federal pension from Congress. A large number of Southerners spoke about the end of slavery in abstract terms, but took no action to end it. Others were sufficiently dedicated to its ultimate eradication to provide after their death for the private manumission of their slaves—a formal emancipation process controlled by law. Yet early opposition to immediate emancipation, including that of politicians as diverse as Thomas Jefferson and Abraham Lincoln, was based largely on the concept that the inherent inequality in the races would prevent their living in peace and prosperity together. There was rarely expressed any allegiance to slavery as an institution except in the rhetoric surrounding the turmoil over states' rights.

While many Northerners were against slavery, they were also remarkably prejudiced against blacks. They were averse to having them live in their communities and inclined to leave the issue of universal emancipation alone. The treatment of blacks in Northern states was often brutish, and black freemen were despised and treated with contempt. Any plan for a general abolition of slavery had to deal with the touchy problem of free blacks living in a white-dominated, racist society where many whites feared the amalgamation of the races through widespread miscegenation. This led many sympathetic whites to fear for the ultimate welfare and safety of a free black population suddenly foisted on an unfriendly America.

The majority of the proponents of emancipation looked to the concepts of gradualism and colonization, rather than the immediatism, inclusion, and amalgamation proposed by the radicals to relieve the supposed incongruities of the races living peacefully together. Gradual emancipation legislation in many Northern states provided that children born as slaves were freed on attaining maturity (age 25 years), having been given a skill or education in the interim so that they might provide for themselves. Similarly formed legislation had quietly obliterated slavery throughout the New England states by mid-century, the last being Connecticut in 1848. Private parties among anti-slavery proponents favored the removal of free blacks to colonies established far from the Americas. The African city of Monrovia was founded as a "freemen's colony" in 1821 in this manner. Less dramatic suggestions were also made to remove free blacks to the Indian Territories, Florida, the Caribbean Islands, and Central America.

There was a growing recognition, however, that slavery was a great moral and social evil that must be ended soon. However, it was also true that slavery had become uneconomical for smaller planters and industrialists. Free white immigrant labor was more efficient economically.

As early as 1816, several Southern states, Virginia, Georgia, Maryland, and Tennessee included, had asked the Federal government to procure a site for colonization by free blacks, and they had jointly petitioned for Federal financial aid to offset the monetary loss involved in emancipating their slaves. The British government had successfully indemnified its slaveowners in the West Indies for their loss when the Atlantic slave trade was ended in 1808, but a similar arrangement was not possible in antebellum America either financially or politically.

As an alternative to integration, African colonization was very popular politically. At mid-century, it was estimated by the proponents of colonization that through this means slavery could be abolished by 1890. One more generation born into slavery would live to see its end. During the debates with Stephen A. Douglas in 1858, Abraham Lincoln had expressed both support for colonization and a belief in an inherent inequality among the races. True to his word, in 1862 one year before the Emancipation Proclamation, President Lincoln signed a Congressional appropriation for $100,000 for the purpose of encouraging black colonization. A minority of free blacks espoused great interest in their African homeland, yet a larger number were interested, not in Africa, but in other areas outside the United States. Black colonizationists often mentioned Canada, Central America, and Haiti as possible alternative sites for black emigration.

Nonetheless, the radical abolitionists demanded immediate, unreimbursed emancipation, and integration of freed blacks into white society, not gradualism and separation. They felt that no price, including bloodshed, war, or disunion, was too great to pay in the cause of ending slavery and racial prejudice. Active participation in the cause and face-to-face confrontation with slaveowners was held in high esteem among these abolitionists; and many traveled to the South to speak out at meetings, denounce slavery proponents, and conduct escaping slaves along the Underground Railroad. The radical abolitionists berated the gradualists and colonialists as being less than completely dedicated to the cause of emancipation, and they went so far as to suggest that such persons were actually serving as covert supporters of slavery by allowing free blacks to remain among them only as "inferior beings."

With no solution to the perceived problems of free black participation in white society, and faced with economic ruin if forced to forfeit their considerable investment in black labor, Southerners turned away from any moderate attitudes they may have possessed and toward a total defense of Southern society against any disruption from without. Impelled by a growing body of public opinion in the North that slavery must be abolished at all costs, Southern apologists launched an equally militant defense of the institution of slavery portraying it as a positive good—a civilizing and caring medium for blacks who would otherwise revert to the brutality of their African origins. The impracticality of blacks being quickly and painlessly integrated into the fabric of American society in the antebellum period can best be measured by the resistance to racial integration seen in the post-1865 South after a costly and painful war had forced immediate emancipation upon it.

Summary

Nineteenth-century families had to deal with enormous changes in almost all of life's categories. The first generation of 19th-century Americans was generally anxious to remove the "Anglo" from their Anglo-Americanism. The generation that grew up in Jacksonian America matured during a period of nationalism, egalitarianism, and widespread reformism. Finally, the generation of the pre-war decades was innately diverse in terms of its ethnic backgrounds, employment, social class, education, language, customs, and religion. Among the persistent problems of this period were a growing sense of sectionalism, an emotional and uncompromising factionalism, and a lack of political restraint that ultimately led to civil war.

Americans had no doubts about their own ability to master their environment, to encourage economic growth, to reform the ills of society, and to resolve the problems associated with raising a family in a changing world. They were acutely aware of the need to create a stable and cohesive society , but they were also dedicated to change, movement, and progress. The creation of solidarity out of such variety was a vital task for a new society.[27]

Notes

1. Richard H. Sewell, *A House Divided: Sectionalism and the Civil War, 1848–1865* (Baltimore: Johns Hopkins University Press, 1988), xi.

2. Faithful quoted in Marion Tinling, ed., *With Women's Eyes: Visitors to the New World, 1775–1918* (Norman: University of Oklahoma Press, 1993), 120.

3. William A. Fletcher, *Rebel Private: Front and Rear* (1908; repr., New York: Meriden, 1997), 2.

4. Don E. Fehrenbacher, *The Era of Expansion, 1800–1848* (New York: John Wiley & Sons, 1969), 98.

5. Howard P. Chudacoff and Judith E. Smith, *The Evolution of American Urban Society* (Upper Saddle River, N.J.: Pearson-Prentice Hall, 2005), 81.

6. Ibid., 66.

7. Ibid., 71.

8. Rodman Wilson Paul, *Mining Frontiers of the Far West, 1848–1880* (New York: Holt, Rinehart & Winston, 1963), 49.

9. James Volo's grandparents, Genaro (Jimmy) and Ermina (Emma) Volo, were grocers in New York who lived and raised their family behind such a small store on East 215th Street in the Bronx.

10. In Manhattan, the suburbs of the 1850s began at the southern end of what would become Central Park.

11. Jacob A. Riis, *How the Other Half Lives: Studies among the Tenements of New York* (New York: Charles Scribner's Sons, 1890), Appendix, "Statistics Bearing on the Tenement Problem."

12. Ibid., 3.

13. Roy Meredith, *Mathew Brady's Portrait of an Era* (New York: W. W. Norton & Co., 1982), 22.

14. Riis, *How the Other Half Lives,* Appendix.

15. Its most recent political iteration was during the 1960 Nixon-Kennedy campaign.

16. Hasia R. Diner, *Erin's Daughters in America: Irish Immigrant Women in the Nineteenth Century* (Baltimore: Johns Hopkins University Press, 1983), 24.

17. Fehrenbacher, *Era of Expansion,* 100.

18. Gaillard Hunt, *As We Were: Life in America, 1814* (1914; repr., Stockbridge, Mass.: Berkshire House Publishing, 1993), 33.

19. Page Smith, *The Nation Comes of Age,* vol. 4 (New York: McGraw-Hill Book Co., 1981), 748.

20. Ibid., 746–747.

21. Leonard I. Richards, *Gentlemen of Property and Standing, Anti-Abolition Mobs in Jacksonian America* (New York: Oxford University Press, 1970), 40.

22. Ibid., 62.

23. Russel B. Nye, *The Cultural Life of the New Nation, 1776–1830* (New York: Harper & Row, 1960), 148–149.

24. The term *Indians* has come under scrutiny in recent years from Native American and Indian rights activists, and some authors have resorted to using terms like *Native American, Amerindian, indigenous peoples,* or *First Nations* when referring to Indians. The authors are aware of controversy surrounding the term, and are sensitive to the feelings of others. However, *Indian* was the term used during period and, in the absence of a consensus as to an alternate, they have decided to use the period-specific term where appropriate. The authors have determined, nonetheless, to correct any insulting or pejorative terms used in period documents or journals with reference to persons regarding their ethnicity or racial heritage.

25. Conevery Bolton Valencius, *The Health of the Country: How American Settlers Understood Themselves and Their Land* (New York: Basic Books, 2002), 4–5.

26. Chudacoff and Smith, *Evolution of American Urban Society,* 75.

27. Nye, *Cultural Life of the New Nation,* 148–149.

Part 2
Family

2

The Family

I went out into the streets. . . . and the show impressed me with great
horror . . . to huddle men together in fifteen layers, one atop of the
other.
　　　　—Rudyard Kipling, on his visit to the tenement district of Chicago

Family Statistics

Researchers generally have demographic data for families during the
19th century, but the statistics are neither as complete nor as articulate
as modern researchers would like. Although the first official census
of the United States was taken in 1790, the early Federal government
was principally interested in sampling the growth, structure, and
redistribution of the population. The collection of vital data (birth,
death, marriage statistics) was generally left to state and local agencies.
Although some large cities had registered similar data in the previous
decade, Massachusetts, in 1842, was the first state to initiate the continuous recording of births, deaths, and marriages. Nonetheless, as late
as 1865 the New York State Census was limited to obtaining "data for
determining the natural increase of the population in this state among
the various classes."[1]

Infant mortality and life expectancy figures were not kept by the
Federal government until 1850. Almost all statistics in this period reflected
institutionalized racism and were kept in terms of whites, colored, and
slave. For whites there are compilations of data concerning absolute birth

rates, fertility, infant mortality, and life expectancy for the entire century and beyond. The same data does not begin for blacks until 1850, and much of it is averaged or otherwise questionable. Not until 1933 were the vital statistics for entire nation recorded with any precision.[2]

If the year 1850 is taken as a center date for the period under consideration, some of the limitations of the census data become obvious. In the 1850 census, all individuals were assigned to "families" that were defined solely by their joint occupation of a dwelling place. The 19th-century definition of a *family dwelling* was clearly broader than the current meaning of the term, literally including every structure from a teepee to a penitentiary. The term *family* could thereby denote a single person living in a tent or cabin, several persons living together in a more conventional home, or even several dozen unrelated persons living in a boarding house, hotel, military barracks, or hospital.

More than 10 percent of the total population counted in 1850 resided in multi-family dwellings that were counted as single units in the sample. This high frequency of group living, when compared to the 18th century, demonstrates the increased use tenements, boarding houses, hotels, and other large institutional domiciles with which the government researchers were simply not ready to deal. British author Rudyard Kipling described the city tenements in Chicago, "I went out into the streets, which are long and flat and without end. . . . I looked down interminable vistas flanked with nine, ten, fifteen-storied houses, and crowded with men and women, and the show impressed me with great horror. Except in London . . . I had never seen so many white people together, and never such a collection of miserables . . . to huddle men together in fifteen layers, one atop of the other."[3]

The chief liability of the census techniques used in 1850 was that in sampling by dwelling the number of individual family observations was greatly reduced, and the resulting data may have become clustered for low-income groups more than for upper-income ones. Moreover, data for "colored," or black families "were usually more under-registered" than for whites. This may also be true to a lesser extent for immigrants as opposed to native-born families.[4] Perhaps households should have been distinguished by some other characteristic such as a common source of support; a blood relationship; or even by separate cooking facilities, sleeping quarters, or entrances.

Recent historical research, however, has begun to sift through the data to present a more dynamic and precise picture of family structure. An analysis of common surnames allows researchers to discriminate among blood kin and disaggregate the statistics, thereby relieving the limitations somewhat; but these methods do not answer the questions concerning family structure that census takers do today. For instance, the disappearance of maiden names through marriage (especially where marriage records are unavailable) renders extensive kinship reconstruction almost impossible when the census is used as a sole source of data.[5] Moreover, there were many unsettled people in 19th-century America. It has not yet been determined whether these constituted a "propertyless, floating population" of those who moved about constantly, a series of successive waves of emigrant families moving onto the frontiers, or an occupationally mobile core of "persisters" who generally returned to their home communities after completing a task elsewhere. Nonetheless, with these limitations in mind some generalizations can be made about the 19th-century family, and secondary sources of family and population study can be tapped to provide both a qualitative and quantitative analysis.[6]

Household Structure

Families can take on many functional and acceptable forms, and a wide diversity of household structures could be found in America. It must be remembered that statistical data provides only a snapshot of family living without duration. It is precisely the correlation of individual time (birth, childhood, youth, adulthood, and old age) with family time (courtship, marriage, the birth of the first and the last child, the empty nest, the death of a spouse) that can provide a more meaningful framework for the study of family. While each family has discrete characteristics, in general they can be condensed into a handful of archetypes with real families falling into a gray region between the black-and-white features of particular types. In this regard it is necessary to define some terms before continuing. Of all the general forms of family structure social historians normally include these four among those found in America: *nuclear families, extended families, stem-nuclear families,* and *clan-like families.* Each of these familial structures has its own peculiar characteristics.

The true *nuclear family* was composed of a married couple living with their children under the same roof and apart from all other relatives. A *stem-nuclear family* occurred when a son married, moved with his bride (or vice versa) into their parents' home, and raised the next generation there creating a three-generation homestead. In 1850 the absence in the data of married or unmarried children in the home more than 20 years of age is pronounced, signaling perhaps the rarity of this form.[7]

An *extended family* structure, much like the nuclear one for individual parents and minor children, was a matter of living arrangement. In the 19th century, to the extent that non-nuclear adults were present, they were likely to be limited to a single farm worker, a domestic servant, or a female relative such as a widowed mother or unmarried sister living in the household while being bathed in the reflected protection of close and loving relations. Post-adolescent sons were expected to move out of the home, but daughters who remained unmarried into their adult years were often given the position of companion to their fathers if they were widowers.[8] Once again the data from the period suggest that the presence of non-related persons vastly outnumbered those cases of related but non-nuclear persons of this sort.[9]

In the *clan-like family* structure, the basic unit of habitation was clearly nuclear, but the members of each clan claimed a common ancestry, usually carried a common name, and, most important, recognized a common identity beyond the bounds of the nuclear family that was largely unaffected by any daily living arrangement. It was the acknowledged continuity and maintenance of ancestry that defined the clan. This form was extremely rare in the North during the period under consideration, but Southern and frontier families often continued to evince this structural pattern. Moreover, solitary residence–single living in a distinctly separate dwelling, not boarding or lodging—was practically unknown in the 19th century except on the most isolated fringes of civilization as among miners, mountain men, or missionaries.[10]

Most 19th-century American households were clearly nuclear in structure and remarkably similar in size. Although this pattern varied slightly across urban, rural, and ethnic lines, the variations were minimal. Some researchers considered the tendency of 19th-century Americans to form and maintain simple nuclear families of approximately a half-dozen members to be "overwhelming." Moreover, the household structure of many urban immigrants from Europe was also clearly nuclear, but they tended to show a greater extension in urban environments than in rural ones. Nonetheless, family structures were often more flexible than they are sometimes presented. Any imbalance created in the nuclear family living in an industrialized and urbanized environment may have "resulted from the breakup of the family as an economic partnership, a fragmentation caused by separation of place of work from place of residence and by the spread of a wage and money economy." The husband's added importance as a wage earner may also have prompted wives, particularly newlywed ones, to form extended ties with their own parents (especially their mothers), as a counterforce to men's increased "power prerogatives."[11]

The family expanded and contracted at different stages of its life cycle, and the members of the household responded and reacted when the web-like strands of their individual life changes pulled at each other. As the years passed and the family life cycle lengthened, these familial ties tended to weaken or adjust. Within these variations, it is safe to say that 75 to 80 percent of households were clearly nuclear within the urban environment. A young married couple might live with their parents for a brief time until they found separate quarters but rarely would the arrangement continue beyond the birth of their first child. Once established in their own residence, these households rarely changed in composition. Among those newlyweds yet without children about one in five took in a relative or a boarder. Yet with the arrival of their first child, about half the households with relatives as lodgers expelled them. Ironically, the vast majority of such households did not expel their boarders.[12]

Native-born migrants, newly arrived in a city or frontier community, initially settled themselves as heads of nuclear households, or boarded temporarily in the homes of strangers. Research indicates that approximately 44 percent of newcomers to cities set up their own households directly upon arrival, and as few as 12 percent lived with blood relations. This leaves a sizeable group (also 44 percent) that needed to make other living arrangements in boarding houses, rooming houses, or commercial hotels. Many of these were single men or young women in the transitional stage between their parents' household and their own.[13]

Vital Data

Having explored the alternative living styles of a minority of Americans, it is time to discuss further the most common form of family living, the nuclear family. Some historians attribute the dominance of the nuclear family during this period to the consequences of industrialization or a trend toward female domesticity. Yet it has been established that this household structure had dominated not only in America, but in the Western world for more than 300 years.

Generally, the typical white, native-born woman had seven or eight pregnancies during her childbearing years. Nationally about 11 percent of all women aged 20 to 24 were pregnant at any one time, and in the North Central region of the country, where data is available, they seem to have given birth to their first child at age 20. Most women were, therefore, exposed to the rigors of almost continuous pregnancy, interrupted only by a painful and dangerous labor, and months of nursing. So frequent were these bouts with nature that many women, conceiving again before fully recovering from a previous pregnancy, gave birth to underweight or physically weakened children who were prime candidates for an early death. Even in a society where large families were the norm and were valued and wanted, at least some women must have dreaded the prospect. Childlessness, according to the data, was so low as to be implausible, and the positioning of non-nuclear adopted children or stepchildren as actual offspring of a mother may be a reflection of a bias in the sampling techniques toward nuclear families.[14] Total fertility and birth rates started the 19th century very high and declined as the century progressed. These were followed by a lagging and uncertain decline in the infant mortality rate and total life expectancy—both of which reversed more than once between 1850 and 1890.

White, immigrant women generally had higher fertility rates than their native-born counterparts, and second-generation immigrants usually evinced an intermediate level of fertility between that of their parents and that of the native population. This may have been due to an Americanization effect, yet many contemporary researches tended to write of "the Irish" or "the Italians" as if they were homogeneous subgroups lacking variations among themselves. This was certainly not the case, and further study has found significant variations among identical ethnic groups living in different parts of the same city.

Recent research suggests that the decline in white reproduction may have been affected by the growing feminist movement with women taking greater control over their reproductive lives—a luxury not afforded to black women of childbearing years who were either enslaved or newly freed during much of the period. Some researchers have also suggested that declining birth rates may be related to land availability, increasing industrialization, the education of women, or the pressure of elderly dependents in the home.[15] It may also be assumed that birth rates everywhere were somewhat depressed by the interposition of the Civil War, as they most surely were in New England between 1861 and 1865.[16]

The data also suggest that white working women were more likely to limit their family size than those who were not gainfully employed outside the home. However, it cannot be determined with any precision whether women with fewer children were more likely to enter the work-force, or if those who were working were more likely to curtail their family size. Both factors may have been in operation. These findings are also confounded by the tendency of unwed mothers to quietly place their children in the homes of relatives while living and working elsewhere, possibly as domestics or as boarders with manufacturing jobs.[17] Further analysis suggests that "the opportunity to work outside the home . . . was more likely to influence the curtailment of fertility through the postponement of marriage than through direct family limitation." In any case working seems to have had a minimal effect on the absolute fertility of individual women, and the overall decline in family size took place in both urban and rural environments.[18]

Nowhere was the role of the rural population more important than in its effect on fertility and birth rates. The level of American fertility in the 18th century was one of the highest in human history, a fact used to entice immigration from Europe, which had a lower rate during the same period. However, in the early part of the 19th century there was an unmistakable downturn in American fertility driven largely by the effect of the rural population. By the end of the century (1900), the fertility of the white rural population was fully 60 percent of that a century earlier. The decline was nationwide, occurred in all of the geographic sections of the country, and cannot presently be explained in terms of ethnicity. Researchers are also at a loss to convincingly explain the downtown other than to note that farm wives in the Eastern and older-settled regions deliberately started their families later and terminated their childbearing earlier than those in the West. At this time "the methods of deliberate fertility control cannot be determined."[19]

Among both farm and non-farm families there was an unmistakable difference in the child-woman ratio when the level of settlement was taken as a factor. The child-woman ratio is a measure of the number of children under 5 years of age per woman of reproductive age usually calculated from published state data. A high ratio might suggest that women were somewhat tied to the household by child-care considerations and consequently unavailable for income-producing labor. The data suggest that in 1860 the child-woman ration in the older and more settled states was perhaps 25 percent lower than that in the newer and less settled ones. This measure of fertility rose "consistently" as one moved "from older to newer settlements." There was one exception to this in the "frontier townships." While the numbers were higher on the leading edges of settlement than in the oldest areas, they were 5 to 10 percent lower than in the areas "slightly behind the frontier." This was where 20 to 40 percent of the land was "improved." Confounding the situation somewhat is the probability that among families on the spearhead of settlement at least some of the children were born elsewhere, possibly in the older settlements.[20] These data may also reflect minor differences in the proportion of married persons in the population and the age distribution of its reproductive females.

Average white life expectancy at birth in 1850 sat at a remarkably low 39 years, and white infant mortality rates for 1850 at 217 per 1000 were significantly higher than those of 1920 with a rate of 82 per 1000. There is no reliable data for infant mortality or life expectancy for blacks until the early 20th century, and most of the analysis of black birth rates in the previous century was focused on the question of deliberate slave breeding by white plantation owners rather than on the intentions of the black slave women who bore the children. Among slaves there were seemingly no income restraints to impinge upon a woman becoming pregnant as "the costs of care and maintenance" as well as "health care and food" for the family were generally "assumed by the slaveowners." Nonetheless, most black slaves nursed for three years in order to naturally limit their fertility during the period of lactation. White women generally nursed for only two years. The end of slavery shifted the decision-making process concerning additional pregnancies to the black family, along with all "the economic, social, and legal arrangements under which children were conceived and raised." The absolute changes in black birth rates are hard to determine as it is commonly agreed among researchers that blacks were undercounted in the 1870 and 1880 censuses. Yet, the initial response of former slaves to emancipation after 1865 seems to have been a continuation of the old fertility patterns of the plantation. Only with time did black fertility decrease markedly.[21]

Blacks (from data beginning in 1850) sustained decreasing, but still higher, fertility and birth rates than their white counterparts throughout the period. In fact the data for these parameters among black women in 1890 were almost equal to the white rates in 1800, with the black decreases lagging almost a century behind those of whites demographically. Many early studies of black fertility were handicapped by their focus on determining a cause for the perceived variations in birth rates among native-born whites, foreign-born whites, and blacks. "There was a widespread fear in some circles that the higher birth rates of foreign-born and black women would diminish the numerical and political importance of the native white population in the United States."[22]

A high rate of infant mortality and a low life expectancy in the general population may have reflected exposure to a number of infectious diseases easily spread in an urbanized environment, including tuberculosis, cholera, typhoid, smallpox, and diphtheria. Nineteenth-century cities were particularly unhealthy places, and not until the 1890s did city managers begin to complete major public works sanitation projects such as piped water, sewer systems, water filtration, and trash collection. On the other hand, frontier and farm living were also dangerous. Starvation, exposure, snakebite, farming and hunting accidents, lack of medical attention, bad water, and Indian attack added to the list of common diseases that made continued life tenuous.

Great care was needed when children were about, but even the most vigilant parents sometimes failed to protect the young. Schoolteacher, John Roberts, sadly reported, "Yesterday one of my smallest pupils was severely hurt by falling from a teeter or plank put across the fence, on which two of them were riding seesaw fashion. I must put a stop to this sport as it is dangerous."[23] Accidents and common childhood diseases claimed nearly half of all children before the age of five. In Henniker, New Hampshire, seven children were scalded to death between 1790 and 1830 and two others died after falling into a fireplace. In 1826 neighbor children of Ruth Bascom, aged two and three and a half, were "sadly scalded . . . by the falling of a kettle of boiling soap from the crane!" Both children died the next day and were buried in the same coffin.[24] A diarist noted, "Mr. Souden's little boy died last night after an illness of a few hours. He has lost two this week. Scarlet fever is said to be the cause. . . . Johnny is the only child left. They have buried four or five small children. It seems impossible for some to raise a child. Mrs. Johns lost a twin boy last night. He was a week old."[25]

At the beginning of May 1850 a "very fine" two-year-old girl plummeted to her death from the third-story window of a house on Greenwich Avenue. The *New York Herald* editorialized, "We hope this notice will prove a caution to parents, who carelessly allow their children to swing themselves at a window without protection." The newspaper noted that a mother, who was "subject to fits of derangement," slit the throats of three of her children, then her own throat. "The father, on his return from labor to his house, found his family in this deplorable condition."

Ten days later the weekly report of deaths in Brooklyn were recorded as two drowned, six dead from consumption, one from "abortion," and 32 others, including 22 children.[26]

For women childbirth remained the greatest danger to their lives; yet, barring complications, the second leading cause of death among women remained death from fire. Open flames and hot stovetops were everywhere, and long skirts made of flammable materials, and children's clothing of cotton or linen, were easy targets for accidental injury and death. Many more people lost their lives to fire than to Indian attacks on the frontier. Moreover, with buildings made largely of wood, towns fires were almost inevitable. Fire destroyed dozens of buildings annually even in small towns, and a single devastating incident could destroy whole communities. Virtually the entire town of Tombstone, Arizona, burned three times in as many decades. The most famous fire of the period was the Chicago City Fire, which consumed 1,700 acres of the city in 1871. This was followed in 1872 by a huge conflagration in Boston that caused city fathers to rethink this aspect of urban and town safety. New building codes and stricter enforcement, architectural designs that included fire exits and escapes, and the development of professional firefighting forces and equipment began to lessen this danger in the final quarter of the century.

Improvements in diet, clothing, and shelter over the two decades beginning in 1870 also contributed to a declining death rate and an increased life expectancy. The advance of life expectancy from the turn of the century onward was remarkable. Ironically, much of this was due to the experience gained by doctors in the battlefield surgeries and convalescent hospitals of the Civil War. In 1890 the newborn grandchild of a Civil War veteran could expect only 46 years of life, yet most lived longer than the statistics predicted. In 1920 the newborn child's own children could expect 57 years of life; and 50 years later, in 1940, the average life expectancy of the original child's own grandchildren had risen to an amazing 65 years, while they themselves had lived two decades longer than originally predicted. These children, born in the wake of another war (World War II) are just now at the threshold of Social Security retirement with a statistical life expectancy of 75+ years.[27]

With all of these statistical and health considerations taken into account, it seems safe to conclude from the remaining data that the average white family in 1850 had between 4 and 5 children more than 1 year of age from a common mother, while black families had between 5 and 6 offspring from a common mother. Data concerning the age of the mother at first marriage from the 18th and 19th centuries shows that young women were delaying marriage from a mean age of 20.7 years in 1739 to a mean age of 24.4 in 1839. Also the mother's age at the birth of her last child suggests a modal shift from between 40–44 in the 18th century to between 35–39 during the 19th century. This indicator suggests that deliberate family limitation was an ongoing process that increased in scope and magnitude through the early 19th century.[28]

The estimates of the total number of births per dwelling in a single year are extraordinary, nonetheless. For states and territories with data available (approximately half of them) in 1850 between 13 percent (South Carolina) and 21 percent (Missouri) of all dwelling places experienced a birth annually. For many of the most populous states with large immigrant communities (where anecdotal evidence suggests that high rates of birth were common) like New York, Massachusetts, and Pennsylvania, complete data in this regard are simply not available.[29]

Nuclear families were also the basic social element in the frontier states of the Great Lake Region. Households in Indiana from 1820 to 1830 featured about 2.2 births per family during the decade. The median range of the number of children more than 1 year old was between 4 and 5 per household. As the frontier moved through and beyond the state boundaries to the west in the next 10 years, the 10-year number of births fell to 1.8 per family. Pennsylvania and Ohio experienced similar rates and changes during the same phase of their development.[30] A sample of family size and birth data taken in central New York in 1865 showed completed families of 4 to 5 children among rural farming households. These data were isolated for 4,300 white women who had been married only once, and omitting any plural marriages or stepchildren for either spouse. Family size and birth rate, in the New York study, were lowest in densely populated areas. In fact, population density was found to be the most important single factor in predicting the birth rate and family size for this sample population. The highest birth rates were found among the isolated but well-established families in "mountainous and hilly sections" of New York. With a high death rate among women of childbearing years and a great deal of speedy remarriage by widowers, it has been estimated that white families there hovered around 5 children per household.[31]

Brothers and Sisters

Siblings in most households were treated in a hierarchical manner with all the male offspring being given a superior position over their sisters—a circumstance sometimes supported by state law. Nonetheless, sisters might exert great influence over their brothers, and a fluid and cooperative interaction between the children formed an important element of a happy household. A boisterous or selfish boy might try to dominate a weaker or more dependent girl, but "generally the latter exerted a softening, sweetening charm. The brother animated and heartened, the sister mollified, tamed, refined." Sisters were like the polished cornerstones of a temple, brothers the rough-hewn foundation stones.[32]

It was noted that many men "passed unharmed through the temptations of youth, [owing] their escape from many dangers to the intimate companionship of affectionate and pure-minded sisters." A true gentlemen's character was formed to a great extent by the ladies with whom he associated before entering the adult world of business and society. Young men were more likely to refrain from mixing with the corrupting influences of unrefined friends and low society when they had sisters at home. "They could not bring home thoughts and feelings which they could not share with those trusting and loving friends [their sisters]; they put aside their wine-cups, and abstained from stronger potations, because they would not profane with their fumes the holy kiss, with which they were accustomed to bid their sisters good-night."[33]

The inferior position of sisters among siblings implied an obligation that was placed upon brothers to defend their honor. This obligation was often extended to brotherless female cousins. Because young women were often thought of as "silly, senseless, thoughtless, giddy, vain, proud, frivolous, selfish, low and mean" and apt to make "an exhibition of [themselves]," a brother could intervene in the affairs of his sisters and their circle of friends with or without their permission.[34] At times these brothers could take on a very combative stance, especially when dealing with a sister's reputation, and her outbreaks of passion and his unbridled impetuosity sometimes made their companionship uncongenial and drove them apart. Yet it was believed that the compensating power of a true friendship would ultimately draw them back together. Thus a balance among brothers and sisters might be struck with "self-control and control over outward circumstances [becoming] alike a duty and a birthright."[35]

The keeping of good company, be they friends and associates of a brother or a sister, was thought to be very important. Appropriate acquaintances were intelligent and well-bred persons, whose language was chaste and whose sentiments were both pure and edifying. Proper deportment was expected among any circle of friends, and their conduct was to be directed by the highest of religious precepts. Young women were particularly enjoined to "hold a steady moral sway" over the male associates of their brothers, "so strong as to prevent them from becoming . . . lawless rowdies."[36]

Yet the necessity of selecting proper female associates for sisters was not considered "a point of so great interest." It was thought that young women of good breeding, under the protection and control of their parents, might not be "thrown into such promiscuous associations" as their more independently minded brothers. Nevertheless, both men and women needed to take great care in avoiding pernicious influences in the selection of their company, and each needed to develop a degree of elegance and manner that would be pleasing in any social circle, whether at home or abroad.[37] Sarah Bennett, editor of the *Advocate and Family Guardian*, a New York publication of the American Female Guardian Society, warned, "If yon beautiful belle of eighteen has no reverence for the Sabbath, no love for the house or worship of God, but only as connected with her own personal display; then is her loveliness perfect deformity, more loathsome than the decay of the carnal house. . . . Remember that piety is a greater beautifier than cosmetics."[38]

As young women were not permitted to interact with men who were not blood relations, many women had little knowledge of men until after their marriage. Although she might pen a formal letter to a gentlemen to whom she had been properly introduced, a brother and his friends were often a young woman's only exposure to the ways of men. After marriage her social relationships with males were further limited to the friends and acquaintances of her husband. Great importance was attached to the prudent selection of these associates, and it was important for a young wife to direct her husband's associations as well as she could.

Courtship and Marriage

The continuation of the family name and fortune through marriage was of great importance, and the rules, customs, and traditions that surrounded courtship and marriage were well established. The obvious objectives of marriage were to provide an acceptable outlet for sexual activity, to recognize the legitimate children of a union, and to assure the continuity of the family fortune through the instrument of inheritance. Since colonial times the instrument of inheritance—usually limited to the handing down of farmland—had been very important. In the 19th century the bestowing of the family fortune, home, business, and social standing on one's children overtook the need to pass on or partition farmland. Moreover, in a period when family name and influence were very important, illegitimate children were often denied access to certain professions, schools, and possible marriage partners. It was very difficult for such persons to go through life expecting to be ashamed of something over which they had no control and could not change. Illegitimate children took great pains to hide their "infirmity," and the legitimate children of some men often went to great lengths to undo those parts of their father's will favorable to their illegitimate siblings. The courts rarely upheld a will favorable to children from the wrong side of the blanket in the face of a concerted effort by their rightful relations, especially if they were the elder sons.

Marriage within one's class was the cement of the social structure. Yet a man could not hope to prosecute a courtship successfully before he had established himself in a profession or come into his inheritance. Courtship could be protracted if the suitor's financial expectations took some period to come to fruition. This fact tended to drive up the age of eligible suitors or increase the disparity in years between a well-established husband and young wife still in her childbearing years. In the North the difference in age between man and wife during the antebellum period averaged a mere two years, while Southern couples were separated by an average of six. All young, respectable women were expected to begin seeking out a marriage partner appropriate to their social position as soon as they left adolescence. "It is of vital interest to every young female, how careful she should be in taking to her bosom for life a companion [husband] of dissolute habits and morals. Such an act might destroy all the domestic felicity she might have hoped to enjoy."[39]

For daughters of the planter class, romance was not to be found among the requirements for a marriage partner. This is ironic in a period known for its romantic trappings. Romantic entanglements were greatly feared by parents because even the hint of inappropriate behavior could create a sexual scandal that would leave a daughter unmarriageable. Wealth was the primary factor in arranging a marriage or choosing a husband, and maintenance of one's social position was a close second. Intermarriage between cousins, far enough removed to dispel charges of consanguinity, was common among the planter aristocracy but almost unheard of in the North. Women in the South married at a younger age—almost four years younger on average—than their Northern counterparts. This may be because many Southern parents expected their daughters to begin the formal courtship process as soon as they entered puberty. Northern parents, more open to the idea that their daughters might become working women for some time before entering a marriage, did not press them as vigorously.

The oppressive control of parents in this regard would not be tolerated by most women today, nor would the absolute domination of fathers or husbands be sustained in a modern household. Yet in actual practice middle-class American women were better treated than their European sisters. In 1876 it was noted that "the Englishman respects his lady; the Frenchman esteems his companion; the Italian adores his mistress; [but] the American loves his wife."[40] American women generally enjoyed higher social status, greater responsibility, and greater freedom at a younger age. By comparison to their British counterparts, young American women were thought to enjoy great liberty till they married, after which "they buried themselves in their families and appeared to live only for them." As wives they were generally faithful and thrifty and, although their social lives were often "joyless and monotonous," they exhibited few of the vices commonly associated with their Victorian era husbands.[41] As the 19th century proceeded, a major cultural change took place as women gradually gained a modicum of control over themselves and the property that they brought to a marriage. These generally paralleled similar developments in Britain.[42]

Women who remained unmarried often lived with other relatives where they hoped to be "regarded and guarded as a daughter."[43] They often relied on these relatives during financial emergencies. Many young women looked especially to their maternal aunts and uncles in this regard for support, guidance, and companionship. In the absence of a father or uncle, a young woman might depend on her own brother for a roof over her head. Few men could shirk their responsibilities to a female relative without a loss of reputation and community standing. This was especially true in the South where the role of benefactor was an essential characteristic of the plantation aristocracy. Nonetheless, an unmarried adult woman was often awkwardly placed in the kinship scheme of a nuclear family, and many found little consolation while living in the household of another woman. For this reason they were often found in the home of a widowed father or brother where they could still be mistress of the household. Often they took on a position as a domestic, a private teacher, or a governess with an unrelated family where their place in the household was a contractual one and their interactions those of an employee with an employer.

Only for a brief period—usually between puberty and marriage—did women have any real control over their fate. Yet this control was very limited, residing solely in the woman's ability to choose a husband from among a set of suitors acceptable to her family. "Women," according to one contemporary observer, "were beautiful until they were twenty-five years old, when their forms changed, and by the time they were thirty their charms had disappeared."[44] A particularly attractive or well-heeled woman might have groups of suitors vying for her attentions. Such groups, calling together upon a young woman at her home, were not discouraged by her parents as the practice prevented unwanted gossip. Under such circumstances young men had little opportunity for measuring the woman's attitude toward their individual suit. Most gentlemen resorted, therefore, to a go-between in the early stages of any serious courting in order to gauge whether their more formal attentions would be rebuffed. The woman's brothers or male cousins often served in this capacity. All but the most eligible men met with a series of mild rebuffs as young women were discouraged by their parents from taking too many prospective fiancés into their social circle before selecting one from a small group of two or three as a husband.

Unmarried couples—even those who were formally engaged—might easily offend the community if their behavior was perceived to be sexual in any context. The betrothed might never have touched, and certainly should never have shared a romantic kiss. A contemporary self-help advisor warned young persons, "During the period that intervenes between forming an engagement and consummating the connection, let your deportment toward the individual to whom you have given your affections be marked by modesty and dignity, respect and kindness."[45]

Courting couples were never left alone, and chaperones (sometimes in the form of an elderly aunt or a trusted slave) were always present when young couples met. This protection was sometimes omitted when the courting pair was composed of older persons or those previously widowed. Nonetheless, anxious parents frequently married off their daughters at 15 or 16, fearing that they might become involved in some sexual impropriety if they waited. Overt sexuality at any stage in a woman's life before marriage would certainly meet with social ostracism and might actually result in criminal indictment for fornication in some jurisdictions.

Upon their marriage young women passed from the domination of their fathers to the equally powerful authority of their husbands. In many Northern homes, the focus of the family increasingly came to rest on the wife and children as fathers spent most of their waking hours away from home at work. Increasingly the whole machinery of the day-to-day operation of the household, "domestic economy and rule, all authority and discipline and influence, devolve[d] upon the wife, who in her own appointed sphere [had] quite enough to do." In response to the increased importance of female domesticity, there evolved a growing formalism and rigid authoritarianism that husbands demanded of their families and households when they were present. Many contemporary observers decried the "neglect" of home that some 19th-century men excused as "the inexorable will of business." These observers questioned what business was so important that it had the right to contravene the traditional organization of the home with the father as the head of household. Self-help advisor John Ware asked, "What right has [business] to so absorb [a man] that he has no time, no heart, for his home duties, [and takes] no pleasure in them?" The natural patriarchal order of the family was thought to have been decided by God. "Who gave man leave to delegate his authority and bind himself to another service?"[46]

On Southern plantations, an older, more traditional male-dominated formalism—highly characteristic of the 18th century—continued to hold sway. Although these factors were most strongly entrenched among the Southern aristocracy, they established a general trend in marital custom throughout all levels of Southern society. A husband and wife were considered one person in law, and the very existence of the woman was often incorporated and consolidated into that of her husband. Until late in the period, women had little or no legal standing in the courts, could not sign enforceable contracts, and held no tangible assets in their own name in most states. The property brought to a marriage by the wife legally became that of her husband. Many widows disdained remarriage, having in their bereavement finally found relief from the overbearing power of even the best of husbands and fathers. Nonetheless, in some states, widows might lose their property rights to their adult sons, if not otherwise provided for by the will of their spouse. A widower with young children was expected to remarry for the sake of his motherless offspring if no appropriate female relation, such as an unmarried sister or aunt, was available to care for them.

Bridal Pregnancy

Although almost all cultures prescribe that sexual intercourse take place within marriage, behavior has not always conformed to this moral norm. The American premarital intercourse record, as measured by the number of seven- and eight-month first babies after the nuptials, is particularly cyclical, showing patterns of high and low incidence since colonial times. The incidence of prenuptial pregnancy in the 19th century was much lower than in the time periods before or after it. High points, or peaks in premarital pregnancies, are found in the second half of the 18th century and the present time (both between 25 and 30 percent of first births). Low points, or troughs, are found in 17th-century colonial America and the middle of the 19th century (both about 10 percent). The proportion of bridal pregnancies follows a similar cyclical pattern found in western European data.[47]

Researchers have not been able to explain this distinct cycle in simple terms. Effective and available means of contraception and abortion since the end of World War II, about the 1950s, has done little to change the high levels of illegitimacy and prenuptial birth in modern times. It has come to be a statistical feature of poor, minority populations where up to 85 percent of children are being conceived or born out of wedlock in some poverty-stricken communities. This suggests a strong association with a number of modern socioeconomic factors. Historic demography, however, suggests that the level of premarital intercourse in the past may be directly related to the extent of social estrangement perceived by young folks in that part of their life cycle between family-dependent adolescence and self-dependent adulthood.[48]

The most persuasive explanation of the premarital pregnancy cycle seems to involve the way morality and moral tenets were viewed by families. The transition period between early colonial times and the 19th century, which included the unsettled social and economic environments of the American Revolution and the early years of the Republic, seems to have lacked both effective external and internal controls on sexual activity. The Puritans of the 17th and early 18th centuries valued external controls on moral behavior, dealing with fornication and prenuptial pregnancy as crimes and responding to their occurrence with physical punishments and fines levied by magistrates and town fathers. The revolutionaries of the 18th century believed in political liberty, but they were not the vanguard of a sexually liberated America. The acceptance of certain sexual practices both evolves and retrenches over time. Victorian Americans, unlike the bawdy and boisterous forbearers of 1776, had an exaggerated aversion to sexual contact of any kind before marriage, but they tended toward internal controls and self-restraint based on socialization strategies rather than on the deterrent qualities of fines and punishment threatened by their Puritan ancestors. This change from reliance on external controls toward internal ones seems to have reflected a retreat from a moral behavior based on the Calvinist pre-determinism of colonial times and toward a wider acceptance of the free-will doctrines related to 19th-century religious revival. Although revivalist denominations differed in social base and religious style, the regulation of individual morality remained their central concern, and sexual restraint through religion rested on the centrality of autonomy and individual choice.

Researchers have noted that "the reappearance of premarital sexual restraint in the nineteenth century [seems to be] based on the autonomy of the young adult and the incorporation of the groups tending toward premarital pregnancy into a new social order." Among the applicable changes in the social position of young people were the economic shift from forced apprenticeship to wage labor, the transition from informal to formal education, the substitution of boarding or lodging for traditional familial living arrangements for independent young adults, the extension of political rights and enfranchisement to a greater number of young men, and the more active part given to young women in 19th-century churches and reform movements. An acceptance of a *place* in the social order for young persons of sexually active age seems to have bolstered their closer adherence to the community's moral norms because they felt themselves a part of it.[49]

The community of respectable matrons was the ultimate source of intergenerational attitudes toward premarital pregnancy—determining what was considered acceptable moral behavior before marriage and passing it from mother to daughter and grandmother to granddaughter. Historical demographers often use the level of official church member-ship to determine the level of adherence to religious principles among such a population, and they have made the following observations in this regard. Church membership among young women tripled during the antebellum period. "With younger conversion, religion could have an effective impact on premarital sexual choices. The concomitant splintering of American Protestantism meant that each stratum [of the social order] had one or more denominations tailored to its particular conditions and needs." Although females did not dominate these religions, the new sects and churches generally incorporated them into their organization to a far greater extent than previously. Their newfound role provided "an important outlet for a wide range of female needs, and young women absorbed the message of sexual restraint more completely."[50]

Victorian-style morality was more than a functional system for preventing unwanted or inconvenient pregnancies. Any type of activity with sexual overtones was prohibited. Such a strict morality was also relevant to the immediate needs of both young men and women as they entered adult life. People were made independent of their parents at a younger age than ever before in the 19th century. A young man was expected to prepared for marriage by accumulating capital and by entering into a stable career. These were the prerequisites for a proper marriage and a successful business life, and few young men would risk an early marriage precipitated by an unfortunate pregnancy that might impede their chances at success. Nor would a young woman risk her social position and eligibility as a marriage partner for a tryst with an uncommitted consort. Alexis de Tocqueville emphasized the importance of appearing chaste among the different classes of American women, "No girl . . . believes that she cannot become the wife of a man who loves her, and this renders all breaches of morality before marriage very uncommon." Commonly held views condemning immorality of any sort before marriage, even between engaged couples, "raised the price of [premarital] sex and thus substantially increased the bargaining power of both single and married women" with respect to the course of any sexual relationship and the promise of matrimony.[51]

This may help to explain the decrease during the middle of the century in the number of short-term, eight-and-one-half-month first births after marriage (17.7 to 9.6 percent) and the six-month shotgun-wedding births (10.3 to 5.8 percent), the latter being the stronger indicator of premarital intercourse when compared to the so-called nine-month weddingnight conceptions (23.7 to 12.6 percent). From 1801 to 1880 all three categories decreased, but the strongest decline was among the last and most committed couples (more than an 11 percent decrease in nine-month births). This may have indicated the strength of opinion that it was simply wrong for people to have sex before marriage regardless of the proximity of the wedding date. By way of comparison between 1880 and 1910 the number of wedding-night conceptions returned to their former high level, and the other categories rebounded beyond their former number to some of the highest rates in more than two centuries.[52]

It should be noted that throughout the course of American history fully two-thirds of all women were not pregnant at the time of their marriage. This suggests a continuity in the efficacy of control with respect to sexual mores. Yet the magnitude of the fluctuations from one historical period to another is compelling. Today premarital intercourse and pregnancy is considered "a mild form of deviancy," but it seems to some researchers to have been "a manifestation of a collision between an unchanging and increasingly antiquated family structure and a pattern of individual behavior which is more a part of the past than a harbinger of the future." Neither the old institutional pattern of control nor the rebellion against it could predict "the subsequent sexual behavior of the young."[53]

Kinship

The overwhelming pervasiveness of nuclear families in America did not mean that they were isolated. Kinship ties persisted outside the nuclear household, and they were of prime importance in determining a family strategy for its interactions with, and within, the institutions of the larger community. The carryover of kinship ties from the rural and agrarian settings of the 18th century to the urban and industrialized settings of large American communities in the 19th century served most families well. Kin acted as immigration agents, labor recruiters, and social supports for working-class persons moving from Europe to America, from the farm to industry, or from one industrial town to another. They offered the members of their group basic protections and economic support while on the move to the frontier or while establishing themselves in a new factory, a new business, or a new home.

Family was the most inviolable of upper-class institutions. Many of the best American families had resided in the same section of the country for hundreds of years. By the time of the Civil War, there was hardly a family of note that did not occupy at least the same social position that it had at the time of the founding of the colonies. Periodically, the family would gather, and cousins, aunts, and grandparents would trace the family tree from long before the Revolution. In order to maintain their high social position and authority, it was important for socially elite families to have a strong sense of obligation to their blood relatives.

In this regard maternal uncles and aunts played an essential role of great trust. "A mother's trust that her [own] brothers and sisters would take care of the children in case of her death gave special significance to the role of the uncle and aunt." While uncles and aunts could be relied upon for monetary assistance, guidance, or support, their nieces or nephews need not be orphaned to call upon them. The extension of business and social influence to nephews was particularly evident at this time, but extenuating circumstances of many kinds could and did bring the influence of these relatives into play in terms of a tightly knit kinship network.[54]

Intermarriage between second and third cousins was common in the South because it perpetuated the family name, fortune, and bloodline. As women were not permitted to freely interact with men except in the most formal of circumstances, it was possible for a susceptible young woman to trade the benevolence of a strict father for the exploitive control and abuse of a less forgiving husband. For this reason many women favored cousin marriages where they were at least familiar with the personality of their prospective partner. However, the practice, though more common in Britain, was almost unheard of among Northern families. In a historical study of Southern and Northern families numbering 100 each, 12 percent of Southern marriages were between cousins while not a single case was found in the Northern sample. While such findings could be laid at the door of Southern clannishness, it should be remembered that many more Northern young people lived in cities and towns where they had opportunities to meet prospective mates unrelated to them by blood. Southern youth were largely isolated on widely scattered plantations.[55]

With kinship came advantage and obligation. Birth into one of America's leading families was essential to making a political career almost everywhere. Social prominence, business and political influence, and the presumption of ability—whether it was present or not in an individual—were inherited from one's father or grandfather in much the same way that businesses, land, or slaves were inherited. Fathers expected their first-born male heirs to follow in their footsteps, and they were protective of their daughters, providing their sons-in-law with influence, if not money. Granddaughters in similar circumstances were treated in much the same way, especially in the absence of a living father. Men were similarly solicitous of their nieces, daughters-in-law, and all their children. So pervasive was the assumption that kinship ruled that men were given positions as sheriffs, justices of the peace, militia captains, or county lieutenants by influential relatives without the slightest charge of favoritism being made by anyone in the system.

Notes

1. From the *Instructions for Taking the Census of the State of New York* (Albany, 1865), quoted in Wendell H. Bash, "Differential Fertility in Madison County New York, 1865," in Maris A. Vinovskis, ed., *Studies in American Historical Demography* (New York: Academic Press, 1979), 435.

2. Fortunately, the library at the University of Virginia in Charlottesville has made all these data searchable through its Historical Census Browser. This also allows ordered lists and proportions to be created with just a few keystrokes. See http://fisher.lib.virginia.edu/collections/stats/histcensus/php/state.php (accessed January 2006).

3. Rudyard Kipling, *American Notes* (1891), http://www.chicagohs.org/fire/queen/pic0521.html (assessed January 2006)

4. Tamara K. Hareven and Maris A. Vinovskis, ed, *Family and Population in Nineteenth Century America* (Princeton, N.J.: Princeton University Press, 1978), 11.

5. For further information on this topic, see Steven Ruggles and Russell R. Menard, *Public Use Microdata Sample of the 1850 United States Census of Population: User's Guide and Technical Documentation* (Minneapolis: Social History Research Laboratory, 1995).

6. Lawrence Glasco, "Migration and Adjustment in the Nineteenth-Century City: Occupation, Property, and Household Structure of Native-Born Whites, Buffalo, New York, 1855," in Hareven and Vinovskis, *Family and Population*, 155.

7. Hareven and Vinovskis, *Family and Population*, 38.

8. Ibid., 34.

9. Ibid., 17.

10. Ibid., 15.

11. Howard P. Chudacoff, "Newlyweds and Family Extension," in Hareven and Vinovskis, *Family and Population*, 204–205.

12. Glasco, "Migration and Adjustment," 178.

13. Ibid., 165–166.

14. Hareven and Vinovskis, *Family and Population*, 38.

15. See Richard A. Easterlin, George Alter, and Gretchen A. Condran, "Farms and Farm Families in Old and New Areas: The Northern States in 1860," in Hareven and Vinovskis, *Family and Population*, 65–73.

16. Bash, "Differential Fertility," 439.

17. Hareven and Vinovskis, *Family and Population*, 91.

18. Ibid., 125.

19. Easterlin et al., "Farms and Farm Families," 65.

20. Ibid., 60–61.

21. Stanley L. Engerman, "Changes in Black Fertility, 1880–1940," in Hareven and Vinovskis, *Family and Population*, 129–130.

22. Hareven and Vinovskis, *Family and Population*, 12.

23. J. Merton England, ed., *Buckeye Schoolmaster: A Chronicle of Midwestern Rural Life 1852–1865* (Bowling Green, Ohio: Bowling Green State University Popular Press, 1996), 174.

24. Jane C. Nylander, *Our Own Snug Fireside: Images of the New England Home, 1760–1860* (New Haven, Conn.: Yale University Press, 1993), 90.

25. Philip P. Mason, ed., *Copper Country Journal: The Diary of Schoolmaster Henry Hobart, 1863–1864* (Detroit: Wayne State University Press, 1991), 263.

26. *New York Herald*, May 15, 1850.

27. See U.S. Bureau of the Census, *Historical Statistics of the United States* (Washington, D.C.: U.S. Government Printing Office, 1975).

28. Nancy Osterud and John Fulton, "Family Limitation and Age at Marriage," in Vinovshkis, *Studies in American Historical Demography*, 408–409.

29. See http://fisher.lib.virginia.edu/collections/stats/histcensus/php/state.php (accessed January 2006).

30. John Modell, "Family and Fertility on the Indiana Frontier, 1820," in Vinovshkis, *Studies in American Historical Demography*, 420.

31. Bash, "Differential Fertility," 438–439. The precise numbers were 4.3 to 4.7.

32. T. L. Haines and Levi W. Yaggy, *The Royal Path of Life; or, Aims and Aids to Success and Happiness* (Chicago: Western Publishing House, 1876), 91.

33. Ibid., 70.

34. Ibid., 83.

35. Ibid., 78.

36. Ibid.

37. Ibid., 111.

38. Sarah Bennett, ed., "Words to a Woman," *Advocate and Family Guardian* 31, no. 3 (February 1, 1865): 27.

39. Haines and Yaggy, *Royal Path of Life*, 111.

40. Ibid., 25.

41. Gaillard Hunt, *As We Were: Life in America, 1814* (1914; repr., Stockbridge, Mass.: Berkshire House Publishing, 1993), 31.

42. Russel B. Nye, *The Cultural Life of the New Nation, 1776–1830* (New York: Harper & Row, 1960), 143.

43. Unidentified author, "The Needs of Working Women: Homes for Working-Girls," *Arthur's Lady's Home Magazine* 37, no. 1 (January 1871): 53–54.

44. Hunt, *As We Were*, 31.

45. Haines and Yaggy, *Royal Path of Life*, 443.

46. John F. W. Ware, *Home Life: What It Is, and What It Needs* (Boston: William V. Spencer, 1864), 38.

47. Daniel Scott Smith and Michael S. Hindus, "Premarital Pregnancy in America," in Vinovshkis, *Studies in American Historical Demography*, 124–125.

48. Ibid.

49. Ibid., 126–127.

50. Ibid., 127.

51. Ibid., 128.

52. Ibid., 137.

53. Ibid., 129.

54. Catherine Clinton, *The Plantation Mistress: Woman's World in the Old South* (New York: Pantheon Books, 1982), 52–53.

55. Ibid., 57–58, 233.

3

Father as a Family Man

The homes of the American revolution made the men of the revolution. Their influence reaches yet far into the inmost frame and constitution of our glorious republic. It controls the fountains of [its] power, forms the character of [its] citizens and statesmen, and shapes our destiny as a people.

—T. L. Haines and Levi W. Yaggy, 1876

Persons of Quality

Men were the unequivocal masters of their households, but family men of the 19th century were expected to exhibit several personal qualities that would lead to a happy and well-ordered home. Among these were *competency, character, identity,* and *industry.* Although they shared with women and children the task of producing the necessities of life, 19th-century men meant much the same by *competency* as their forbearers—an income or degree of wealth sufficient to keep his family in a fashion equivalent to that of his neighbors during his life and off the public dole in the case of his demise. By *character* the 19th-century man meant his good reputation in terms of meeting his family, social, and business obligations. A man's character, measured largely by his integrity, was thought to command the respect of all who knew him, or knew of him. While lesser men might succumb to evil appetites, men of character would triumph over difficulties and sail through perils. Personal and public *identity* were an important part of 19th-century life. A man's identity—who he was in his own mind and the place that he occupied in the ultimate scheme of the world around him—was composed partly from his social position, partly from his religious affiliation, and partly from his chosen vocation. Finally, men were expected to possess the quality of *industry*, the mental and physical energy needed to meet the difficulties of a busy life and overcome them. This was often measured by his perseverance. Such industry gave men the impulse to accomplish every action or effort. A man possessing these qualities in the proper proportions was considered meritorious and worthy of the respect and esteem of his family and community.[1]

Competency

When a man took a wife he was expected to provide for her (and their children) during the rest of his life in a manner similar to that in which he found her in her family home. Moreover, a man's economic endeavors, whether they be in the form of wages, investments, or business enterprises had to be adequate enough to provide some "ease and affluence" in his old age or for his widow, if the occasion arose. Men looked for work that would provide their families with a "comfortable subsistence" and a "maintenance" of their social standing. Beyond this minimum level was "an income" that was often termed "a certain competency of means" that allowed for comfort and security if not wealth. Although material wealth motivated many men to work hard, the pursuit of money purely for its own sake had been viewed with some suspicion since colonial times.[2]

However, reaching this simple standard of competency was often not enough for many men according to the perception of 19th-century observers. "Acquisitiveness," if not greed or avarice, seemingly took a hold on the minds of many men, and they became focused on being more than merely comfortable. They seemed in a great haste to become conspicuously wealthy. Wild ambition, however, was thought to tarnish true success, and it mingled the feelings of admiration and abhorrence of those who observed it. Haines and Yaggy noted, "The road ambition travels is too narrow for friendship, too crooked for love, too rugged for honesty, too dark for science, and too hilly for happiness." No amount of glory or fame could be enduring, according to these advisors, unless it was based on "virtue, wisdom, and justice."[3]

In addition, it became fashionable among the upper classes, especially among the women, to lead generally "idle lives" at home caring for the domestic needs of the household through the management of a score of servants. The "leisure" that this suggested for the female householder was probably overstated by the generally conservatively minded advisors of the day, and it was little different from that of persons of similar social standing and financial circumstances in previous times that required aptitude, organization, and luck. Yet the rising middle class often aspired to an idyllic life filled with pastimes, diversions, and attempts at personal improvement without recognizing these underlying fundamentals. Philo Tower, a preacher and writer from the period, noted that this added to the struggle to reach the state of competency. "No young man" could make such "a fortune to support the extravagant style of housekeeping, and gratify the expensive tastes of young women, as fashion is now educating them." Many marriages were deferred to allow young suitors time to amass a fortune, and many others were avoided or discouraged by parents as young women chose older and more successful men as spouses.[4]

Character

Circumstances like these tended to raise questions among more sober minds about the character and integrity of their fellows. The more philosophical among contemporary observers recoiled at such unfettered ambition and superficial rewards. "The men of our time seek too much for immediate results. They are too impatient for applause, honor and wealth. . . . They seek advancement through letters of recommendation and the influence of friends." Men of real merit and dignity, those who had a good heart and who loved virtuous action because it was right, were considered to have developed "the highest excellence" of character and integrity. Richard Henry Dana considered such a man a virtual paragon, "pure-minded, elevated, intellectual, religious, literary, accomplished in manners, just, humane, kind, polite, with a high degree of pride and reserves, yet truly modest."[5]

In the 19th century the qualities of Dana's "Christian Gentleman" were thought to be "a gift of God."[6] Yet character could be "acquired by effort . . . cultivated by diligence, nurtured by religion, and inspired by truth and heroic example." This idea fed particularly into the beliefs of New Englanders, for whom even as late as 1876 the word *puritan* was still considered by some "one of the greatest words in history."[7] Heroic strength of character—like that of George Washington and others among the Founding Fathers—consisted of willpower tempered by self-restraint, while integrity was largely measured by the standard of honesty. Hence political sobriquets like Honest Abe were used to counterbalance the greed and dishonesty associated with political machines like Tammany Hall. Whether inborn or acquired, character and integrity of this type was considered to be an essential ingredient of success—the blending of many elements, the composite outgrowth of principled actions, and the final result of a lifetime's adherence to truth.[8]

"Deportment, honesty, caution, and a desire to do right" were the truth of human character. "The truest criterion of a man's character and conduct" was to be found in the "opinion of his nearest relations" who had daily and hourly opportunities to form a judgment of him within the privacy of the home.[9] Haines and Yaggy advised that "young men, as they start in life, regard character as a capital, unaffected by panics and failures, fruitful when all other investments lie dormant, having as certain promise in the present life as in that which is to come." Truthfulness, integrity, and goodness formed the foundations of a true "manly" character. For Haines and Yaggy character was closely associated with masculinity and gender identification. They considered business, law, and government—the "higher walks of life"—treacherous, dangerous, and filled with obstacles. Overcoming these "trying and perilous circumstances" required that an "upright man" be brave and filled with confidence.[10] Ransom noted, "As men act in the home, so they will act in society, so will they act in the capacity of citizens."[11]

With respect to the character of the nation, Philip Hone, an upper-class New York businessman and politician, wrote a tongue-in-cheek defense of America in 1843 that viewed the nation as a large dysfunctional family. "The English papers do abuse us shamefully for swindling, repudiation, cheating, and other trifling departures from rectitude, which abuse is all the harder to be borne from the difficulty we have in many cases of contradicting the truth of the charges. . . . and such of us as are honest, besides defending our own characters, are bound by a sort of family pride to the much more difficult task, that of palliating the rascality of our brethren. . . . It is much as we in New York and here-abouts can do to keep on our legs, without having the burden to carry the disgrace of the dishonest part of the family."[12]

A cynical Timothy Titcomb, writing in 1861, believed that absolute integrity was a rarity among 19th-century Americans. "There are men in all communities who are believed to be honest, yet whose word is never taken as authority upon any subject." There was some "flaw or warp" in the perceptions of such men, "which prevents them from receiving truthful impressions. Everything comes to them distorted. . . . [T]he moment their personality, or their personal interest, is involved, the fact[s] assume false proportions and false colors."[13]

All truth for Titcomb was tainted by the medium through which it passed, and that medium in the 19th century was self-interest, the personal vices of greed and alcoholism, and the scourges of sectionalism, slavery, and partisan politics.

It is possible for no man who owns a slave and finds profit in such ownership, to receive the truth touching the right of man to himself, and the moral wrong of slavery. . . . Now when it is sought to be made a permanent institution, because it seems to be the only source of wealth of a section [of the country], it has become right; and even the slave-trade logically falls into the category of laudable and legitimate commerce. It is impossible for a people who have allowed pecuniary interest to deprave their moral sense to this extent, to perceive and receive any sound political truth, or to apprehend the spirit and temper of those who are opposed to them. The same may be said of the liquor traffic. The act of selling liquor is looked upon with horror by those who stand outside . . . but the seller deems it legitimate, and looks upon any interference with his sales as an infringement of his rights. Our selfish interest in any business, or in any scheme of profit, distorts all truth. . . . Of all conscious and criminal lying, I know of none that exceeds in malignity and magnitude that of a political campaign. . . . What, in honesty, can be said of the leading speakers and leading presses which sustain a party in a contest for power, but that they misrepresent their opponents, misstate their own motives, give currency to false accusations, suppress the truth . . . and lie outright when it is deemed necessary. . . . The social lying of the world has found multitudinous satirists, and furnished the staple of a whole school of writers . . . whom in our hearts we despise. . . . Business lying is, after all, the most universal of any. . . . When two selfish persons meet on opposite sides of the counter, there arises between them a sort of antagonism. . . . There is a great deal of business lying that by long habit becomes unconscious. . . . [Yet] in politics, society, and business, the conscious and intentional lie abounds.[14]

Titcomb felt truth to be at the bottom of the 19th-century well, but even an observer as contemptuous of human frailties as he understood that there was hope for improvement. "Men can cultivate the power to apprehend and express truth . . . and no one doubts that the world would be greatly improved by honest efforts directed to these ends."[15]

Nowhere was a man's character more important or more sorely tested than on the emigrant trails to the west. Good judgment, integrity of purpose, and practical application thereof were indispensable to the harmony of the wagon train and the successful completion of the journey. Captain Randolph B. Marcy, a popular advisor to prairie travelers, advised in 1859, "On long and arduous expeditions men are apt to become irritable and ill-natured, and oftentimes fancy they have more labor imposed upon them than their comrades. . . . That man who exercises the greatest forbearance under such circumstances, who is cheerful, slow to take up quarrels, and endeavors to reconcile difficulties among his companions, is deserving of all praise, and will, no doubt, contribute largely to the success and comfort of an expedition."[16]

Identity

Eighteenth-century social structure was based mostly on wealth and ancestry, an accident of birth and bloodline that put a man in his place. Antebellum Northerners openly attacked this stratified order as antiquated and immoral, especially in the South where social life was similarly based, but they substituted a new and equally unsound social order of their own upon the community—that of work. In the mist of the increasing urbanization, industrialization, and capitalism of the 19th century, it was a man's work, in particular, that gave him his place and identity. A man was seen as a banker, a doctor, a teacher, or a tradesman before much else was known of his family background, character, or aspirations. His place in society was as firmly set by his vocation as it had been formerly by his bloodline. Profession or vocation, thereby, defined to a large degree one's public identity. Those men who followed one of the "three black graces"—Law, Medicine, or Ministry—were always thought to be honorable, trustworthy, and respectable.

Ransom believed that one's natural attributes fitted him for his profession and for his place in society. He wrote, "We do not believe that all men, or any considerable number of men, could enter upon . . . totally different lines of action and succeed in all." A man who followed his vocation for a lifetime "with utter faithfulness" and "mastered the duties around him" could expect no surprises as he arrived at eminence and social respectability. "It is entirely natural that he should be there, and he is as much at home there and as little elated as when he was working patiently at the foot of the stairs. There are heights above him, and he remains humble and simple." A man who lost his place at business, or failed in his profession also lost part of his identity.[17]

Most people believed that certain personality traits were attached to a man via his vocation and vice versa. A bookish youth might find teaching or law an appropriate profession; a dull child—manual labor or storekeeping; a clever lad—a trade or craft; an ingenious one—a career in engineering; an aggressive boy—a commission in the army or navy. Haines and Yaggy warned, "Be what nature intended you for, and you will succeed. . . . The young man who leaves the farm-field for a merchant's desk, thinking to dignify or ennoble his toil, makes a sad mistake. . . . He barters a natural for an artificial pursuit. . . . The more artificial a man's pursuit, the more debasing it is, morally and physically. . . . Thousands who might have been happy at the plow, or opulent behind the counter; thousands dispirited and hopeless, . . . disgusted with their vocations, [are] getting their living by their weakness instead of by [the] strength of their natural character."[18]

It was well for young men to have a defined objective in the choice of their vocations. According to Haine and Yaggy the decision to follow a particular vocation "once taken is taken forever, and a mistake at this point is a vital mistake from which it is impossible to recover. . . . To spend years at college, at the work-bench, or in the store, and then find the calling the wrong one, is disheartening to all but men of the toughest fiber." Once in the busy life that surrounded a chosen vocation, a man studied it with zeal and mastered it. Great men were thought to have a mission in this regard, which they followed through peril and difficulty to its full realization. This concept of an internal battle or quest fed upon the perception of the masculine gender role, and many men were thought to have led a life of failure solely due to the lack of a sufficiently noble professional objective.[19]

A man was supposed to be masculine in his manner, his clothing, his interests, and his sentiments. Such traits were part of his identity. Contemporary advisors produced a long list of personal attributes that were thought to be appropriate for the middle classes, but as the century wore on respectable persons increasingly valued those qualities that separated them further from the working classes. Among these were gender-neutral qualities such as obedience, virtue, thrift, or loyalty. However, some traits were thought to have a specific masculine or feminine quality: patience, kindness, affection, or sentimentality for women; honesty, industry, courage, and dedication to duty for men. As the business world expanded its sphere of influence, thrift, punctuality, attention to detail, cleverness, and a reserved manner became highly regarded as workplace attributes.

Industry

The 19th-century environment was a "a laborious world," one filled with work of all types. There was no place in a properly ordered society of this type for men who were indolent or lacking in energy. Haines and Yaggy wrote, "It is not study, not instruction, not careful moral training, not good

A period illustration by Currier and Ives of the successful and honored man in the bosom of his family.

parents, not good society that make men. . . . It is employment. . . . No man feels himself a man who is not doing a man's business. A man without employment is not a man. He cannot act a man's part. . . . Hence [the world] sets its boys to work; gives them trades, callings, professions; puts the instruments of man-making into their hands and tells then to work out their manhood."[20] If a man needed to work for a living, if he needed to pursue a vocation and hoped to attain a "high station" or anything that resembled success, he needed to invest either his "brow-sweat or brain-sweat" until he accomplished it. Haines and Yaggy proclaimed, "Working men walk worthy of your vocation!"[21]

A man could successfully grapple with resistance by applying mental as well as physical force, if he possessed the quality of industry. Possession of this quality enabled him to work his way through "irksome drudgery and dry detail." Haines and Yaggy observed, "What can be more beautiful than to see a man combating suffering with patience, triumphing in his integrity . . . and . . . pressing on with unconquerable zeal to the end?"[22] Honest success, based on merit and gained through the application of perseverance and industry, "should neither be despised or idolized." Moreover, it was thought that success "extends its bright and prophetic vision through . . . the distant time and bequeaths to remote generations the vindication of its honor and fame, and the clear comprehension of its truths."[23]

Family Income

Family income was the measure by which sociologists and social reformers in both Britain and the United States differentiated between the "poor" and the "very poor." In the 19th century it was clear that there was a difference between the "poor," who had small incomes, and those known as "paupers," who were on the public dole. Acting out of concern for an understanding of the working-class unrest that gripped Europe in 1848, statisticians and sociologists began about 1850 to take data and to conduct studies of family income and expenditures in order to shed light on any differences. One of the major figures in this field was Ernst Engle (not Friedrich Engle, the colleague of Karl Marx). Ernst Engle formulated the idea of poverty studies in which family income was compared to family expenditure as a measure of a *standard of living*. Two English sociologists, Charles Booth and B. Seebohm Rowntree, were the first to show that poverty was not simply a matter of low income. Booth and Rowntree, separately, devised the concepts of *primary poverty* and *secondary poverty*—those with barely enough means for independent living, and those whose income was insufficient to meet their daily needs, respectively.

In order to facilitate his research, Rowntree developed the idea of a family *budget* composed of three factors: Food, Rent, and Household

Sundries (clothing, lighting, fuel, etc). The components of his factors were detailed but not exhaustive. The other factors in Rowntree's budget included transportation costs, newspapers, postage and writing materials, church contributions, savings, toys and sweets for the children, and medical care. He calculated different minimum incomes for families of various sizes that defined a *poverty line*. For a family of four (two parents and two children) this amounted to $238(USD) annually, or just under £49(pounds sterling) and for a family of five $274 or about £56.

The 1850 census suggested that the average annual income for male workers was $300, or about £62, which was just above the poverty line. The *New York Times* reported in 1853 that an average family of four living in the city with a minimum of medical expenses required $600, or about £124, per annum. When corrected for inflation this figure was 28 percent higher than the minimum needed by a rural family of five in the previous decade, which puts its accuracy in question. Yet it seems certain that city families required more than an average single income simply to survive. A clear sign of this was the fact from the 1850 census that one-third of the manufacturing workforce in the city was composed of women. The demand market for female labor set the residents of New York City apart somewhat from the experience of the rest of the America.

A prominent American figure in the area of family income and budget was Carroll D. Wright, chief sociologist for the Massachusetts Bureau of Statistics of Labor from 1873 to 1888 and head of the U.S. Bureau of Labor from 1888 to 1905. Wright published one of the earliest studies of American family spending in 1875 in an attempt to understand the growing problems of labor unrest, poverty, and slums in Massachusetts. Wright's study included a sample of 397 working-class families and made it possible to calculate the annual surplus or deficit from income and to gauge the details of family expenditures using categories much like those developed by Rowntree. Wright found that "if a man is earning only $2 or less a day, as is the case with thousands of men . . . with families, he must be very near the condition of poverty or want. . . . If he have no loss by sickness and permit himself no vacation $526 can be taken as a reasonable annual estimate for their poverty line."[24]

The work of Wright and Engle came to the attention of James Cook, a Congregationalist minister and proponent of the social gospel then prevalent among some American Protestant reformers. In a series of talks given in 1877 and 1878 known as the "Boston Monday Lectures," Cook proposed a distinction between *starvation wages* and *natural wages* (just wages). He concluded that a five-person middle-class family in which neither the wife nor the children worked for wages needed an annual income of about $850 (1874) if it was not to "inevitably graduate members unfit to become part of [the] popular sovereignty." He also concluded that a working-class family would need a minimum of between $520 and $624 a year "to live according to the standard of the workingmen of America."

This agreed well with Wright's idea of a poverty line. In another lecture he made a distinction between *family wages* and *bachelor wages* that was very near to the tenets of Marxism, noting that a married man might work for $1.50 per day at the same task as a bachelor who got $0.80 a day with equal justice because the single man had fewer personal needs and family responsibilities.[25]

The cost of food in the family budget was largely based on the work of an American sociologist and nutritional scientist, Wilbur Atwater, who proposed a minimum caloric diet that contained no fresh meat, although boiled bacon was included three times a week. Atwater also used his expertise to develop a series of ideas concerning poverty and family income. He argued that American workers were extravagant in their food-buying habits. The average annual expenditure for food for a workingman's family was calculated to be $422. Atwater said that if workers would use this amount to buy their food more efficiently, they would meet their dietary needs at a cost noticeably less than their current wasteful food expenditures. He held that the purchase of fresh fruits and vegetables and fresh meats was among the most wasteful and extravagant means for working families that needed more calories and protein. He recommended the use of grains, cereals, beans, and preserved meats such as bacon in their place. Of course, the vitamin value of fresh food items was not yet known, but Atwater should have realized the need of fresh foods in preventing diseases such as scurvy and pellagra even if he did not recognize the mechanism by which they were prevented.[26]

Atwater's argument that the poor were poor because they made wasteful and extravagant expenditures appealed to factory and business owners who were under siege by workers demanding higher wages. Likewise his "scientific" theories gave cultural backing to the growing middle-class attitude that poverty among the lower classes was somehow self-inflicted. Social reform movements fueled by true altruism had begun early in the century, but over time as the programs of reform failed to alleviate the problems of society, many persons decided that the poor and unemployed were at fault for their own condition. Nationwide studies done in the early 20th century, however, showed that the idea that lower-class families spent their incomes inefficiently or wastefully was incorrect. Research has shown that 19th-century families repeatedly received more nutrients and a better balance of diet per dollar than higher-income families. The problem was that the dollars were too few to provide for appropriate nutrition.[27]

Finally, in 1890 James R. Sovereign, the Iowa State Commissioner of Labor Statistics, detailed a 33-item standard budget for the "average family." This was a bare-bones survival budget that "contained no carpets, no window curtains, no provisions for social amusements, no street car fares, no feasts for holidays, no contributions for Sunday school and churches, no medicine or medical assistance during illness, no mineral springs or other places of resort to recuperate the minds and bodies of over-worked laborers, and no mementos of love with which to express their affections of the members of the family circle." The total amount of Sovereign's spartan budget was $549. Oddly, at the time 88 percent of Iowa's mechanics and laborers made less than this amount annually. Nonetheless, the agreement among so many observers that the family poverty line resided at approximate $550 during the latter part of the 19th century is remarkable.[28]

By the 1880s many immigrant families had managed to reach parity with native-born households in terms of family income. However, as immigrant family incomes approached that of other Americans, researchers have found that the discrepancy was made up more and more by resorting to the paid labor of members of the immigrant family rather than the increased annual wages of its head. Ironically, due to the needs of child care supplied by the mother, most supplementary income came from child labor. Among Irish working-class families (for whom there is data), it was just about twice as likely for at least one child to be gainfully employed than it was for children in native-born families. "The Irish, kept in a tight position by the lower earning capacity of fathers, found children's earnings essential to consume in an American way."[29]

The incidence of child labor seems to have been largely gender-neutral. Native-born and immigrant families, at all levels of father's income, seemed to have sent just about the same ratio of girls to boys into the labor force. When the age of the youngest child sent to work is considered, however, Americans rather than the immigrants seem more likely to have sent their children to work at a younger age. Data from industrialized areas in New England show American children at work in large numbers as early as age 11. The immigrant samples taken from the same communities showed no appreciable number of children working before age 13. Nonetheless, American families were more reluctant to send out any children to work than immigrants, but when they did, they often sent them out young. Irish families were prone to send out most of their eligible children, but when the Irish father's income rose to American standards (approximately $750), the family generally sent no children into the workforce. Both types of families seem to have terminated schooling at about the same age (13 years), but immigrant families preferred formal schools to on-the-job training, sending several children out to work so that one might stay in school. Conversely, as both groups reached American-style incomes, they tended to send their children to school rather than to work. Nonetheless, because immigrant families tended to be larger than American ones, and because immigrant head-of-household incomes tended to be smaller, the proportion of immigrant children in the workforce was far greater than that of native-born children. In some cases 9 of 10 immigrant children spent time as part of the non–family farm workforce.[30]

Family Expenditures

Although many family budgets were less than precisely detailed documents, those that survive were done with sufficient care to allow researchers to outline the structure of average family expenditures with some confidence. Basic subsistence needs like food, shelter, and fuel were common to all families, and these items were addressed in the poverty line studies of men like Cook, Atwater, Rowntree, or Sovereign.

While the levels of spending on certain budgetary items might be less than accurate in many surviving documents, the absence or presence of certain categories of consumption or expense can be very useful. Among the significant expenditures for New England working families in the 1880s, for instance, are included repeated references to the cost of life insurance, dues to labor unions, and payments to other business organizations (known as *prudent expenditures*). These were among a series of *discretionary expenditures* made after the basic budgetary necessities were covered. Discretionary items included *indulgent expenditures* like alcohol, tobacco, books, newspapers, or private schooling; and *expressive expenditures* like amusements and vacations, charity donations and church contributions, and more-than-purely-functional clothing (such as fancy dresses or business clothing). That charity and religion should be included in the latter group is suggestive of the power that the reform movements and religious revivals of mid-century had on many families.[31]

For both native-born and immigrant families most expenditures increased as the father's income increased, but American families were less likely than their immigrant counterparts to increase their expenditures based solely on increased income from supplemental sources. Americans seem to have been reluctant to spend the income of wives and children on frivolities. They chose instead to put additional cash into their savings. Overall, larger native-born working-class families tended to purchase fewer indulgent items than did small American families, but the opposite seems to have been true among immigrant families living in the same community. "In contrast to the Americans, larger immigrant families were more likely to allocate their resources on almost all expenditure items than were small families."[32]

Researchers have found that by the 1880s foreign-born households (particularly the Irish) and native-born households had assumed essentially the same spending patterns, although the Irish father was still bringing home an income 85 percent that of the native-born head of household. Rent (housing cost) and food were always the largest portions of any family budget, but among the fastest-growing consumer categories were the demands made by labor organizations and expenditures for amusements, vacations, and alcohol. As head-of-household income rose to similar dollar levels, both native and immigrant spending became nearly parallel in all categories other than that of alcohol.

It has been suggested that the emphasis placed on alcoholic consumption by immigrants was "a non-rationalized" response to the demands and pressures of an industrialized and urbanized environment. It is much more likely, however, that it served as a verification of the continued cultural use of alcoholic beverages among Western European groups since colonial times. In the 1770s, for example, Anglo-Americans from New England alone had consumed more than 2 million gallons of rum annually, and anyone over the age of 12 could purchase beer in a tavern. Both the Irish and the Germans maintained positive attitudes toward the consumption of beer and other alcoholic beverages, and each became the target of temperance reformers because of their continued dedication to the use of wine and spirits as part of their daily lives.

On the other hand, expenditures for amusements, theaters, and vacations by many foreign-born persons have been regarded as "non-communal forms of meaningful adaptation to industrial life." This view helps to explain the increased expenditures in these areas by all segments of society, not just foreign-born ones.[33] Many Southern cities saw a dynamic growth in professional theaters, and most Northern urban areas supported theater groups. In most communities acting in the legitimate theater was a respectable profession, and the American stage was filled with excellent actors and actresses. Yet, when a group of players tried to open a theater in Lowell, Massachusetts, in 1833, they were arrested and put in jail for not "pursuing an honorable and lawful profession."[34]

During this period several of James Fenimore Cooper's novels were adapted for the Northern stage, and thereafter a number of distinctive American characters appeared such as the rural Yankee, the noble savage, or the tough-fisted, tenement-dwelling "Bowery Bhoy". However, some critics found the theater vulgar, coarse, and in bad taste. Clearly many stock performances were routine, tedious, or slipshod. Walt Whitman wrote in 1847 that they were becoming "beyond all toleration."[35] Washington Irving noted, however, that "the Theater . . . is the polite lounge, where the idle and curious resort, to pick up the news of the fashionable world, to meet their acquaintances, and to show themselves off to advantage."[36]

The Cost of Modern Living

As people learned to live in a mass society, they progressively spent more for goods and services that they had previously not needed or were able to meet without monetary expenditure. The enduring effects of industrialization, urbanization, and invention can be gleaned from many working-class family budgets. Streetcar fares, gas or kerosene lighting, and the cost of heating fuel can be taken as examples of the financial stress placed on families by modernization.

In a rural and largely agricultural nation, daily transportation expenses were all but unnecessary as a budgetary item. People walked or rode their own animals from place to place, if they traveled any distance at all. Time was on their side, and they could afford to spend an entire day going to market in the town or visiting friends and relatives. The introduction of the factory system and the work-for-wage economy made time more dear than money, however, and a man gladly spent a few cents each day to be at work on time rather than to jeopardize his employment.

Before the widespread development of steam railways in the Northern and middle states, horse-drawn omnibuses crossed through many major cities. In 1826 a horse-drawn railroad paralleled the "Main Line" from Philadelphia to Columbia on the Susquehanna River. In 1828, Quincy, Massachusetts, had the first horse-drawn line of the Old Colony System, and Rochester, New York, established a two-mile-long line that ran to Lake Ontario from the Erie Canal in 1831. New York City opened a horse-drawn service in 1832 from Prince Street to 14th Street, and it was still adding to the extent of track with a line in East Harlem in 1853. Two of the more extensive systems, the Metropolitan Horse Railroad in Boston (1856) and the Baltimore City Railroad (1859), served their cities with well-appointed, horse-drawn cars and miles of interconnecting track right through the Civil War. Travel on the horse-drawn railroad was often accompanied by a thundering noise caused by the combination of iron wheels on iron rails and street stones that was almost deafening.

Artificial lighting had been provided by candles, grease lamps, or floating tapers since colonial times, and in many rural areas they continued to be popular because of their low cost. Most of these were produced at home from the rendering of waste animal fat into tallow or oils, or by actively gathering bee's wax or bayberries. Whale oil was a significant exception to this rule because it had to be bought at the general store and burned in a peculiar double-wicked lamp. Rural and urban families generally continued to use these means of lighting until mid-century. Slowly new lighting devices made their way onto the American scene, and as with most technological advances, they appeared first in the cities. The most significant new means of lighting was the natural gas light, which by 1855 was appearing on both the main and secondary streets of even moderately sized cities and towns. Manufactured gas, acetylene, had been invented as early as 1816, but it was the natural gas pipelines placed under the streets of American cities that fed into even moderately priced homes that defined the Gaslight era. More significant for most Americans, especially those in rural regions, was the development of kerosene lamps. These came into wide use after the development of the petroleum industry in Titusville, Pennsylvania. In 1859 Col. Edwin Drake brought in his first oil well with the specific intent of using the oily kerosene liquid as a lighting fuel. Although its adoption was initially hampered by the Civil War, the kerosene lamp became a ubiquitous device in most homes immediately thereafter. Even with the invention of the electric light in 1879 and its application to street lighting, kerosene remained the main source of artificial lighting in many farming and frontier communities into the 20th century. In 1900 only 8 percent of the homes nationwide were wired for electricity, and most of these were upper-class dwellings, which had their gas fixtures converted to electric lights. Plug-in lamps, while available, were not common before the turn of the century.

In the same vein, farmers and frontiersmen commonly took their fuel for heating and cooking from their own woodlots, from mesquite bushes, corn cobs, or dried manure (buffalo chips). These were provided by the application of one's own time, labor, and sweat rather than by the expenditure of cash. Despite the availability of many kinds of patented iron woodstoves, most Americans experienced cold mornings and chilly nights from November to April. The use of kerosene stoves (or heaters) in many homes became popular after the Civil War, and several kerosene-fueled devices were patented for warming irons for pressing clothes. Yet they, like the lamps and stoves that used the same volatile liquid fuel, were particularly dangerous if upset while lit. Many cities banned the use of kerosene heaters in multi-family dwellings as fire hazards. For many city dwellers, firewood, charcoal, or hard coal needed to be purchased with cash from dealers who carted these items into the city centers. By the latter half of the 19th century, hard coal had become the fuel of choice in city tenements for heating when used in fireplace gratings, cast iron stoves, or tenement furnaces, but charcoal or firewood remained the choice for cooking purposes until they were replaced by gas. In 1870 more than 15 million tons of hard coal were mined in the United States; by the end of the period, this had increased five-fold.

Wealth

The Federal censuses of 1850, 1860, and 1870 gathered information regarding income and property ownership. The 1850 census collected data only on real property, while the subsequent censuses sampled both real and personal property. The data can be disaggregated by race, residence, occupation, place of birth, and age and can be used to provide a look at the economic health of the family during the late 19th century. The 1870 census sampled more than 7.5 million families with an average wealth of almost $3,000, much of the total held by a small minority of very wealthy families. Sixty-nine percent of American families had property valued at more than $100. This included real property (land and houses) and personal property (cash or items of value). Given that the $100 threshold for inclusion masks some details regarding the poorest third of the population, it is still clear that wealth among the majority of families in this mid-19th century sample lacked any equality in how it was distributed.

No one should be surprised that the inequality was greater among blacks than among whites, especially in the South where wealth was most unequally distributed across all subgroups. Researchers using random samples from the censuses taken in these periods, however, found "that property was nearly as unequally distributed in some parts of the Northeast, and in the Pacific and Mountain regions." Moreover, property inequality was also higher in urban than rural areas, higher in industrial than agricultural areas (the plantation South excepted), and higher among sales occupations than among wage earners. Difference in skilled versus unskilled pay rates, a proxy for income inequality, were greatest in areas in the earliest stages of industrialization. Wealth was more equally distributed among farmers, professionals, and clerical or office workers. What is remarkable is that by 1870, at least, there was little inequality based on ethnicity in terms of being native- or foreign-born. Inequalities also varied with age. Not surprisingly, young adults had the smallest portion of income. Older persons within every category of occupation or residence were much closer to one another than the young in terms of wealth distribution.[37]

The average wealth of households headed by older, foreign-born, white males was higher than that of the general population if they were employed in manufacturing. Among these, regional and urban-rural distributions were quite similar as a whole. About 11 percent of all households were headed by native-born, rural females, made heads of households largely because they were widowed. Two-thirds of these female heads of households were black. With their limited economic prospects and an average age five years older than their male counterparts, it is not surprising that black women reported less property or no property more often than other group of persons.

State and regional differences in wealth were pronounced, ranging from an average high of almost $5,000 per family in the Pacific region to an average low of just under $1,000 in the Mountain states. Wealth in the Northern states was two to three times greater than in the South, but in the border states of Maryland, West Virginia, and Kentucky, it was higher than in the Deep South of Georgia, Mississippi, or Alabama. Among the Northern states, the New England manufacturing centers of Connecticut, Rhode Island, and Massachusetts had much higher levels than the more rural states of Vermont, New Hampshire, and Maine. In New England the value of real property (57 percent) accounted for a smaller portion of wealth than elsewhere (70 percent). Property ownership also varied across the region with the North Central states (80 percent) leading, and the Northeast (70) and the Southern states (50 percent) lagging behind.[38]

In terms of wealth nationwide, 27 percent of real property and 38 percent of personal property was owned by the top 1 percent of the population. Wealth was most concentrated among a few families in South Carolina, Louisiana, California, and the New England manufacturing states. The recently settled Western states reported little wealth of any kind, and the agricultural states of New York, Pennsylvania, and the North Central region had a generally equitable distribution of wealth in terms of farm land. Real property inequity was greatest in the South, and personal property inequity greatest in New England and the Mid-Atlantic states. Black families were about 30 percent less likely to report owning any property, and those that did have property valued it at little more than half that of comparable white families. There was no significant difference between native-born and foreign-born real property owners, but immigrants reported about 20 percent less personal property. Literacy and advancing age increased the likelihood of property ownership, but wealth peaked at age 55 to 60. Women, as a subgroup, were less likely to own any reportable property and had less of it than men of the same class when they did. Modest city dwellers were less likely to own property of any kind and the odds of ownership fell with the increasing size of the city. This may have been due to a great number of renters. Those urban families with wealth, however, were generally better off if they lived in a large city than a small one.[39]

There were marked differences in wealth distribution across occupational groups. General laborers and domestics, as expected, were the least likely to own property of any kind, but farmers, because of their land, were the most likely to report real property ownership. In terms of wealth, professionals and managers were among the wealthiest occupations, but farmers also placed very high along the wealth spectrum. Craftsmen and machine operators came next, with salesmen and clerks being last in wealth among persons with specific occupations.[40]

Notes

1. T. L. Haines and Levi W. Yaggy, *The Royal Path of Life; or, Aims and Aids to Success and Happiness* (Chicago: Western Publishing House, 1876), 65–66.

2. Lisa Wilson, *Ye Heart of a Man: The Domestic Life of Men in Colonial New England* (New Haven, Conn.: Yale University Press, 1999), 23.

3. Haines and Yaggy, *Royal Path of Life*, 269–270.

4. Page Smith, *The Nation Comes of Age*, vol. 4 (New York: McGraw-Hill Book Co., 1981), 755.

5. Ibid., 783.

6. Ibid.

7. Haines and Yaggy, *Royal Path of Life*, 186.

8. Ibid., 191–192.

9. Ibid., 115.

10. Ibid., 112–113.

11. J. Clinton Ransom, *The Successful Man in His Manifold Relations with Life* (New York: J. A. Hill & Co., 1889), 315.

12. Allan Nevins, ed., *The Diary of Phillip Hone, 1828–1851*, vols. 1 and 2 (New York: Dodd, Mead & Co., 1927), I 646.

13. Timothy Titcomb, *Lessons in Life: A Series of Familiar Essays* (New York: Charles Scribner & Co., 1861), 73–74.

14. Ibid., 81–82.

15. Ibid., 79.

16. Randolph B. Marcy, *The Prairie Traveler: A Hand-book for Overland Expeditions* (1859; repr., Bedford, Mass.: Applewood Books, 1993), 24.

17. Ransom, *Successful Man*, 435.

18. Haines and Yaggy, *Royal Path of Life*, 131.

19. Ibid.

20. Ibid., 131–132.

21. Ibid., 187.

22. Ibid., 254–255.

23. Ibid., 269–270.

24. Gordon M. Fisher, "From Hunter to Orshansky: An Overview of Unofficial Poverty Lines in the United States from 1904–1965" (paper presented at the Fifteenth Annual Research Conference of the Association for Public Policy Analysis and Management, Washington, D.C., October 28, 1993), 3–4. Available from the U.S. Department of Health and Human Services.

25. Ibid., 5.

26. Ibid., 5–6.

27. Ibid., 6.

28. Ibid., 7.

29. John Modell, "Family and Fertility on the Indiana Frontier, 1820," in Maris A. Vinovshkis, ed., *Studies in American Historical Demography* (New York: Academic Press, 1979), 221.

30. Ibid., 235–236.

31. Ibid., 215–216.

32. Ibid., 224.

33. Ibid., 214.

34. Vincent de Paul Lupiano and Ken W. Sayers, *It Was a Very Good Year: A Cultural History of the United States from 1776 to the Present* (Holbrook, Mass.: Bob Adams, 1994), 67.

35. Whitman is quoted in the Brooklyn *Eagle*, February 8, 1847, in Barnard Hewitt, *Theater USA, 1668 to 1957* (New York: McGraw-Hill Book Co., 1959), 144.

36. Hewitt, *Theater USA*, 65.

37. Joshua L. Robenbloom and Gregory W. Stutes, *Reexamining the Distribution of Wealth in 1870* (Cambridge, Mass.: National Bureau of Economic Research, 2005), 4–5.

38. Ibid., 8.

39. Ibid., 13.

40. Ibid., 28.

4

Father as a Success

What opportunities lie before the ambitious workers of today! What
chances for willing hands and stout hearts and cultured brains! Into
what a heritage has every young man entered! He lives in a veritable
atmosphere of gigantic possibilities, and a life of failure must necessarily
be a history of lost opportunities and squandered possibilities.

—J. Clinton Ransom, 1889[1]

The Solid Citizen

Self-help author and advisor J. Clinton Ransom wrote in 1889, "In every
community there is always some one whom his neighbors call a successful
man. He commands the esteem of the whole circle of his acquaintance. He
is alert and active in business; he is absorbed in the duties of a busy life;
but he has time to be friendly with all and to endear himself to all with
whom he comes in contact. He is spoken of as a clever companion, an
honorable businessman, a prosperous citizen, a man of solid integrity.
This personage is our successful man." Ransom noted that in his opinion
an individual's employment, situation, and station in life did not matter
in determining his success. It was by varying standards of judgment that
a man was pronounced successful by his fellows.[2]

Among these standards the issue of work seems to have been central
to a man's identity, authority, and place in the social order. Only physical
disability (or immense fortune) allowed a man to remove himself from
the world of work to the pleasures of a contemplative retirement. Diligent

labor and financial success had been venerated in America before 1800, and colonial attitudes toward work have been described in sociological terms as an adherence to the *Protestant Work Ethic*, first expounded by William Perkins as the *Doctrine of Work* in 1603. Perkins connected heavenly salvation less to financial success than to diligent labor at some honest trade or vocation. "Somewhere in the battle of life, God gives every man a chance to wear the victor's crown and stand among heroes." Yet many American colonials, especially those dedicated to the Calvinist tradition, fully equated financial success with the earthly symbol of God's approbation.[3]

Antebellum Protestants were also deeply concerned with the work ethic, yet the 19th-century path to success lay not in the workshop or on the farm, but in the emerging industries and enterprises of consumer capitalism. Nineteenth-century men looked less to the quality of a man's labor as an indicator of his respectability and more to the non-religious implications of his financial success. They made work an end in itself and the acquisition of wealth the shining trophy at the end of life. "Money, not work, became the proof of a moral life [and] as Americans came to measure worth by money, they measured lack of worth by lack of money."[4]

Between 1820 and 1840 wealth made a remarkable statistical redistribution to the top of the social ladder, largely due to the crushing effects of overwhelming numbers of poor rural immigrants pouring into the country at the same time that its commercial economy was undergoing a phenomenal rate of expansion. Historian Galliard Hunt noted that "an unbridled love of money was the spring of the Republic." Writing of America for the centennial of the War of 1812, Hunt also noted that in the previous century "there was no country in the world where there was less generosity of sentiment, less charm of life. Everything was sacrificed to [financial] interest. All disinterested acts, all talents purely agreeable, were looked upon with contempt."[5] The burning desire to be a millionaire, a shipping magnet, a railroad king, a war leader, or something beyond their real powers and abilities was thought to make men restless and discontented in their pursuit of success.

Under such circumstances money in sufficient quantities was considered the ticket to social prominence. "Everything favored a vile cupidity."[6] Nonetheless, being born of a prominent family was no simple indicator of success. Even great wealth, if newly found, "needed aging" and a generation of family philanthropy was needed to guarantee a place in the carefully guarded social circles of the uppermost classes. A man's personal manner, dress, voice, style, and bearing were all part of the standards by which success was measured. Moreover, these qualities could not be artificial, affected, or insincere. Richard Henry Dana of New York, who was something of a social snob, noted that "inferiority of caste is noticeable as soon as you get out of the aristocracy and upper gentry with hereditary estates and old names."[7]

In 19th-century America, life was seemingly filled with opportunity, and the successful man was expected to aspire to a level of achievement commensurate with his class and abilities. Anthony Trollope, an English novelist visiting New York, noted of the merchants and businessmen, "The ascendancy of dollars are the words written on every paving stone along Fifth Avenue, down Broadway and up Wall Street. Every man can vote, and values the privilege. Every man can read, and uses the privilege. Every man worships the dollar, and is down before his shrine from morning till night."[8] Only death or physical incapacity relieved a man of his obligation to pursue success. From lowly farmers to captains of industry, successful men were expected to bend their wills to every opportunity that presented itself. "The world is clamoring for men to fill its high positions and shoulder its grave responsibilities." Should a man miss his opportunity through carelessness "the line of his irretrievable failure [would be] marked out . . . with the suddenness of a thunder peal."[9]

The frontispiece from J. Clinton Ransom, *The Successful Man in His Manifold Relations with Life* (1889), showing the two alternate paths of life—one leading from idleness to corruption and the other from industry to honored old age.

This attitude had serious consequences for dealing with the poor, insuring in some quarters that they would never receive generous attention or compassionate treatment. Well-meaning social reformers feared that financial relief might encourage destitution by rewarding the pauper for his lethargy, and few Americans seemed willing to criticize a social system that blamed the poor for their own condition or to denounce a government that allowed people to suffer without relief. Yet "true nastiness" in terms of social care for the poor did not arrive in America until the 1840s when waves of Irish immigrants fleeing the potato famine arrived in American cities. Records indicate that almost 2 million Irish departed for America in the decades surrounding mid-century. Yet as early as the 1840s the problem of Irish beggars in the streets—including women and children—had reached such proportions that the editor of the *New York Tribune* demanded, "Cannot this be stopped?"[10]

Presumably American reformers took their cues for dealing with the poverty stricken from their British counterparts who had discovered the work asylum and the poorhouse as stopgap remedies for impoverishment. These establishments, both in Britain and America, were generally ruled by a disaffected staff of hardened overseers who brought little in the way of humanitarian understanding to their task. The first workhouses had been established in England in the 1720s. The aged, insane, blind, and diseased were put to work at menial tasks, the proceeds of which went to the functioning of the institution. Under such a system the inmates were left with neither a nest egg nor a new skill upon which to build. Rarely in civilized history were the poor and needy treated less kindly or with so little compassion as they were in the middle decades of the 19th century.[11]

Many women abandoned the workhouse to take up prostitution at the lowest echelon of the profession, earning so little that they required neither a pimp nor a madam. They often shared accommodations with other prostitutes or with families of desperately limited means who would tolerate their profession for a small share of the proceeds in the form of room rent. Oddly these arrangements often provided a basic support network for the single parent and a practical form of child care as the women looked out for one another or took turns minding the children. Nonetheless, reform movements spawned a number of institutions to assist "wayward women." These were generally financed through private funds. Albeit that these homes for women were generally clean and safe, they were also austere and constrictive. Inmates were dressed in uniformly drab attire, and the heads of both women and children inmates were often shaved supposedly for health purposes. The inmates labored at domestic chores, and those who did not run away generally entered into domestic service after a period of satisfactory training.[12]

Before continuing, it should be noted that a number of Irish immigrant families with the humblest of beginnings were able to emerge from poverty to gain social, political, and economic prominence within a generation. Although they were victims of severe ethnic prejudice, they came to America with certain advantages over other immigrant groups. They spoke English; they were white and virtually indistinguishable from persons of English extraction; and they had political experience founded in their long struggles with English landlords. Many of these Irish came to be part of the First Families of Boston and New York. The McDonnells, Ryans, Buckleys, Floods, Fairs, Mackays, O'Briens, and Stewarts were all part of this so-called Irishocracy. They began in the penniless slums of America's cities, but they used their ambition, determination, and political savvy to become some of the most powerful families in America.

Many second- and third-generation Irish immigrants were remarkably successful. Robert J. Cuddihy, for example, was behind one of the great successes in the field of publishing—the rise of the *Literary Digest* in the first decades of the 20th century. Thomas E. Murray, though little schooled, was an ingenious electrical engineer who by the end of his career held a number of patents second only to those of Thomas A. Edison. By establishing America's first food-store chain for the carriage trade, Patrick J. O'Connor and James Butler established their own vast family fortunes. As a final example, take Edward Doheny, who made $31 million selling crude oil from southern California and Mexico. He was later a key figure in the Teapot Dome scandal of the 1920s and was reliably reported at one point to have had more money than John D. Rockefeller.[13]

Learn to Earn

Nineteenth-century men considered good work habits and a sound education to be vital to success. The two pressing needs of young men, in particular, were to acquire an adequate preparation for the duties of life that might confront them and to develop a sense for carefully weighing any opportunity before plunging into a task that was beyond their talents to carry out to completion. Instinct and inherent genius were considered laudable characteristics, but without the discipline of the work ethic and the tools provided by an appropriate education, effort alone might prove to be misdirected or meaningless. Moreover, men were expected to have the strength of character to reshape an unlooked-for opportunity into a destiny-changing moment, and to have the integrity and depth of soul to withstand the shock of success. Churches and temperance groups sponsored organizations for young boys and teens that promoted Christian manliness. In the 1870s and 1880s Boys' Brigades and chivalric societies modeled on King Arthur's court sponsored competitive sports, physical education, and encouraged wholesome living.

There was, moreover, a sense of something ennobling in the act of pursuing success at a high level of personal or financial risk—a process of purification and a necessary step in the development of character. This concept had the natural effect of glorifying the accomplishment of seemingly unattainable goals or the ambition to surpass the usual achievements of other men. In line with widely held concepts of duty and obligation, it was as important to finish a job as it was to undertake it. Men did not quit or leave their positions even under the most trying of circumstances, and initial failure required a redoubling of effort. This ideal can be seen in the efforts to put a telegraph cable across the Atlantic, to build a transcontinental railroad, to develop a great machine-powered manufactory, to cross the Great American Desert, or to carve a farmstead out of the wilderness.

Although some of these efforts were monumental in scope, the possibility of failure was not an option to be taken lightly. Haines and Yaggy warned that if "a man is brought into a sphere of his ambition for which he has not the requisite powers, and where he is goaded on every side in the discharge of his duties, his temptation is at once to make up by fraud and appearance that which he lacks in ability."[14] Of 100 men embarking on the same type of business ventures, only a handful attained anything like "distinguished success." This same train of thought tended to trivialize the common affairs of life, leaving some men thinking that they were a failure at everyday living because they were "too ambitious of doing something more than that."[15]

For some men success seemed to come more easily than for others; but if a man lacked genius, he might remedy it through training. Fortunately 19th-century work was being done more and more by men with educations such as engineers, financiers, and scientists. These things could be learned in the universities through the assiduous application of study. If, however, they lacked character in the presence of other vices, which they could not or would not resist, then even the most dedicated of students or workers deserved to fail. The price of success was often great in terms of capital, effort, and time, but some men failed to appreciate the difficulty with which it was won—the "busy days lengthening out into years . . . a long life of closest devotion to single pursuits . . . [and] the hard toil in the face of difficulties."[16]

Mediocrity in any task was considered unacceptable. Yet even men of humble social station were taught that doing good and useful work was noble as long as they enlisted their full powers in the enterprise. "It is not our fault," wrote Ransom, "that we do not possess talents of the highest order. We cannot with reason question that inscrutable wisdom which made some of us prophets and teachers, some of us vine-dressers and husbandmen, some of us money kings and merchant-princes, some of us great and some small, and all servitors in His Kingdom of universal service."[17]

Patriarchy

In some men the drive toward wealth could become excessive or even destructive. The disposition of land through inheritance was a major prop of parental authority and discipline. Yet in the 19th century it was declining as a source of patriarchal power in the family. The sharing of a man's income, in the form of money or wages, among his children or with his spouse quickly formed a more significant source of men's authority than in former times. Unwarranted economy and a tight purse often eroded important ties between fathers and their older children. Even if a man wanted to fulfill his role as financial manager and dispenser of funds, the need to be at work in order to earn a wage often came into conflict with his childrearing role in the household.

Middle-class men who had grown up in the first decades of the 19th century could remember a childhood spent living in a family working environment, either on the farm, in a cottage at the mill, or in a room behind the family shop. But as the century progressed, men's work increasingly took place in the special atmosphere of a business premises like the factory or office. Fathers commonly left the home to work for 10 to 14 hours a day, and their children rarely saw them during daylight hours. A father's work and workplace became foreign to his children in a way unknown to former generations.[18]

Contemporary observers were concerned that children interacted with their father only during the worst hours of the day, "his tired hours." In former times "when business was a thing of comparative leisure," fathers watched over their children, "rewarded and punished, rebuked and encouraged" them on the instant. Children could trace back much of what was best in them to this steady parental interaction. John Ware advised, "Let this generation once feel, as it must feel, that this neglect of home is no necessity, but a sin; let it rest red and hot upon men's consciences that God has given them this charge which they have deserted . . . and you will find business as easy to control as you now imagine it to be difficult."[19]

Notes

1. J. Clinton Ransom, *The Successful Man in His Manifold Relations with Life* (New York: J. A. Hill & Co., 1889), 22.

2. Ibid., 15.

3. Ibid., 17.

4. Annette Atkins, *Harvest of Grief: Grasshopper Plagues and Public Assistance in Minnesota, 1873–1878* (St. Paul: Minnesota Historical Society Press, 1984), 11.

5. Gaillard Hunt, *As We Were: Life in America, 1814* (1914; repr., Stockbridge, Mass.: Berkshire House Publishing, 1993), 31.

6. Ransom, *Successful Man*, 27.

7. Page Smith, *The Nation Comes of Age*, vol. 4 (New York: McGraw-Hill Book Co., 1981), 783–784.

8. Trollope quoted in Roy Meredith, *Mathew Brady's Portrait of an Era* (New York: W. W. Norton & Co., 1982), 35.

9. Ransom, *Successful Man*, 20.

10. Stephen Birmingham, *Real Lace: America's Irish Rich* (New York: Harper & Row, 1973), 19.

11. Atkins, *Harvest of Grief*, 11.

12. See Dorothy Denneen Volo and James M. Volo, *Daily Life in the Age of Sail* (Westport, Conn.: Greenwood Press, 2002), 25–26.

13. Birmingham, *Real Lace*, 105.

14. T. L. Haines and Levi W. Yaggy, *The Royal Path of Life; or, Aims and Aids to Success and Happiness* (Chicago: Western Publishing House, 1876), 12–13.

15. Ransom, *Successful Man*, 28.

16. Ibid., 33.

17. Ibid., 27.

18. John Tosh, "New Men? The Bourgeois Cult of Home," *History Today* (December 1996): 9–15.

19. John F. W. Ware, *Home Life: What It Is, and What It Needs* (Boston: William V. Spencer, 1864), 38.

5

Father as Worker

All labor that tends to supply man's wants, to increase man's happiness, to elevate man's nature—in a word, all labor that is honest—is honorable.

—T. L. Haines and Levi W. Yaggy, 1876

The Nature of Work

In the 19th century every man worked for his living, but not all men worked in the same way. Almost everyone below the uppermost classes of society needed to make a living through the application of their own physical labor. Workers at this time could be divided into several categories, among them laborers, farmers, clerks, craftsmen, machine operators, shopkeepers, and mariners. There were also those who dealt in the extraction trades like mining, timbering, or fishing. Before the Civil War clerks and machine operators represented a numerous, but decided, minority of city workers. In some urban areas unskilled laborers made up to 40 percent of all workers. Craftsmen and shopkeepers have often been considered a privileged class somewhat akin to small businessmen, but many of the persons involved in crafts or shopkeeping were actually women, not the middle-class employers of apprentices and journeymen, but petty proprietors with just enough income and business acumen to rest on the lower rung of middle-class status.

Employment opportunities were not equally available to all classes and levels of society. Young men of the upper class preparing for life in a profession—physician, engineer, or lawyer—expected to be able to maintain a standard of living and social status commensurate with their services to the community. Churchmen and teachers, always resentful of the parsimony of the community, expected a salary that reflected their educational qualifications and a respectful place in the scheme of social hierarchy. Those born to wealth might lead an indulgent life or work as managers of the family business or plantation without regard to the willingness of their neighbors to provide them an income. They formed the highest rungs of the economic ladder because of their birth or family connection. Industrialization brought a new category of worker into the mix. This was the factory manager, or overseer, who directed the labor of others in the mills and manufactories.

The Extent of Industry

Although the 19th century is often thought of as a period of industrial growth, the vast majority of the nation still made its living in agriculture. New York, the most populous state in 1850 with a population of just over 3 million residents, had only 6.5 percent of its workers involved in manufacturing. This data suggests that the state was still remarkably rural in character, as was the entire nation—a fact that is often misrepresented in history textbooks. Massachusetts, Rhode Island, and Connecticut were the most industrialized states in the Union, each with double-digit percentages of persons employed in manufacturing, but none of these even closely approached a majority. Massachusetts, with a population of 986,000, was the most industrialized state in the nation with 17 percent manufacturing workers. Rhode Island (15%) and Connecticut (13%) ranked second and third nationally. Of the six New England states only Vermont (2.7%) had a manufacturing base smaller than 5 percent in terms of employment. By way of contrast, Pennsylvania and Ohio, among the top three states in population with more than 2.2 million and 2.0 million respectively, had 6.5 percent and 3.0 percent working in manufacturing in 1850. Virginia with near a million residents had a mere 3.0 percent involved in industry, and fifth-place Illinois, with 800,000 people, was still remarkably rural with only 1.4 percent of its population working in factories or mills. Only 10 states had greater than 5 percent of their population involved in manufactures in 1850. Of these only Maryland and Delaware bestrode the Mason-Dixon Line, and none of them would enter the Southern Confederacy.[1]

For this reason it is commonly thought that the economy of the American South was deficient when compared to that of the North in many critical areas of industry, including manufacturing, transportation, and communications. Certainly the North, all the states that fought the Civil War treated as a separate nation, was one of the giants of industrial production on the world stage, ranking just behind Great Britain in the value of its manufacturing output. However, the Southern Confederacy, also taken as an independent nation, would have ranked fourth richest among all the economies of the world in 1860, having more wealth than many industrial countries such as France, Germany, or Denmark. Admittedly, Southern economic strength lay largely in its agricultural production, but its manufacturing base was better developed than many other nations at the time that were considered to have entered the industrial age.

Much of the South's fortune and capital continued to be tied up in land and in slaves leaving little for investment. With increasing wealth in the North built upon shipbuilding, whaling, shopkeeping, and textile production, there was no similar lack of uncommitted capital. The growth of the factory-owning middle class in the North during the first decades of the antebellum period was rapid and remarkable. New factories and machinery absorbed more than $50 million of Northern investment capital in the decades of the 1820s and 1830s alone. Some Northern money went to fund canals and other long-term projects. In the 1840s and 1850s capital was diverted toward the construction of railroads, but only a small portion of Northern wealth found its way into Southern industrial development.

Oddly, reliable statistics concerning Southern industry, transportation, and manufacturing are rare and difficult to assess from the distance of more than a century. Some historians have noted that the generally accepted view of the industrial capacity of the South in the antebellum period may need revision, and some limits may need to be put to the present generalizations made by the economic historians of the past. One lynchpin of this novel thinking is the idea that by the very act of secession, the industrial capability of the Southern states "was brought to a pinnacle of development" only to perish in the holocaust of the war that followed. The demands of a wartime economy and the destruction wrought upon it may have blurred a true measure of the extent of the South's pre-war industrial system, while immediate postwar analyses by Northern observers may have been prejudiced against any positive findings.[2]

Southern apologists and other contemporary spokespersons pointed out the strength of the Southern economy before the war intervened. Although some of their positive comments concerning Southern industrial capacity can be classed as propaganda, much of the data they cited could not be denied. Senator Andrew Johnson of Tennessee, later vice president and president of the United States, noted in 1860 that the copper mines of his state kept seven smelting furnaces in constant operation annually and that the number of residents engaged in manufacturing was virtually the same as that in Illinois. Moreover, Tennessee produced more woolen textiles, more corn, more wheat, and 150 times more pig iron than New Hampshire, and it was building 1,100 miles of railway annually while New Hampshire was laying down only 200 miles.

Representative Alexander Stephens of Georgia, later vice president of the Confederacy, made similar, if less accurate, statistical comparisons between his state and Ohio, then one of the most prosperous states in the Union. Stephens noted that with half the population, Georgia produced more agricultural products than Ohio (even if cotton were excluded), as well as more beef, pork, and wool. Georgia had 38 state-of-the-art cotton and woolen mills, 1,000 more miles of railroad than Ohio, and twice the annual capital investment in new manufacturing ventures. Some of Stephens's remarks were disingenuous and did not take into account the fact that much of the investment in Ohio predated that in Georgia, leaving Ohio's present annual rate of investment lower although the absolute dollar amount was higher.

Thomas J. Kettell, contemporary author, economist, and Southern apologist, made a number of interesting comparisons between the Southern states and the nations of Europe. He pointed out that the South as a whole in 1860 had approximately 9,000 miles of railway as compared to 6,000 in England and Wales, 4,000 in France, and a little more than 2,000 in Prussia. There were 31 major Southern canals, 2 of the 10 largest ocean harbors in the world (both serving New Orleans), and two major inland ports (Louisville, Ky. and St. Louis, Mo.). One-third of all the telegraph lines in the United States (15,000 miles of it) were in the Southern states, more than in all of continental Europe at the time.

Joseph Kennedy, superintendent of the Federal Census in 1860, noted the South's 52 paper mills producing 12 million pounds of paper annually; its 1,300 leather shops and tanneries; its three major iron works capable of making locomotives and steam engines; its more than 100 smaller iron furnaces, foundries, and rolling mills; and its 115 precision machine shops. Southern shoemakers produced 65,000 pairs of work boots annually, and Southern workers provided the entire nation, North and South, with most of the hides and most of the tree bark needed for tanning them into leather. Kennedy also noted the establishment in the South of 250 cotton mills, 153 woolen mills, and almost 500 carding and fullering mills. The textile mills alone represented almost 70 percent of the U.S. total, but they were located largely in the border states and northern Virginia. There were 45 woolen mills and 63 carding mills in Virginia alone that produced more than 1 million yards of fabric annually, enough to make 200,000 suits of clothing. Moreover, the Southern textile mills, more recently built and based on a superior technology, were four times more efficient than those in the North and eight times better than those in Great Britain. Based on findings like these, modern researchers have begun to reevaluate historic judgments about the extent of the technological inferiority of the Southern states before the war and to reshape the picture of Southern industry commonly advanced during the century thereafter.[3]

Panics and Depressions

There were several notable economic depressions and panics during the century that affected Americans' ability to work or find a job. In both 1794 and 1819 deep downturns hit the young nation's economy. A wheat failure in 1835 required that Americans import grain from abroad for the first time. Panics caused many European exporters and American businessmen to curtail the extension of credit to all sectors of the economy. This scenario would be played out again and again during the century (especially from 1873 to 1877), placing a heavy burden on the perennially cash-starved Southern plantations and Midwest farms, the under-funded canal and railway projects, and the under-capitalized financial institutions of the country.

The economic paralysis that followed the Panic of 1837, for example, resulted in the worst economic downturn of the period. Prices soared during the Civil War years (more in the South than in the North), and under the influence of a war economy, the value of Southern farmland fell to its lowest point in decades when compared to other sections of the country. The bulk of newly freed black laborers experienced a severe wage depression during the early Reconstruction period as white workers returning from the Civil War displaced them from many jobs. Although prices steadily declined after the war (especially in the North), they rose again during the major Panic of 1873, which was made worse by a five-year plague of locusts that ruined the Midwest wheat crop and spoiled the newfound prosperity of many farmers.[4]

Industrial Frailty

Much of the industrial expansion in the North, and the capital that it represented, was swept away by the economic Panic of 1837. Royal B. Stratton, a clergymen-author from the period, noted, "The banks chartered about the year 1832 ... issued [paper] bills beyond their charters, presuming upon the continued rapid growth of the country to keep themselves above disaster. But business, especially in times of speculation, like material substance, is of a gravitating tendency, and without a basis soon fails. . . . Prices of produce fell to a low figure. . . . Debts of long standing became due, and the demand for their payment became more imperative, as the inability of the creditors became more and more apparent and appalling." Merchants found their shops empty and, dispossessed of goods and cash, were thrown into the panic, and "business of all kinds came to a standstill." This was an unfamiliar circumstance in a rural America that had formerly relied on individual business concerns and small shops to employ the small percentage of non-agricultural workers in the labor force.[5]

Nine-tenths of the factories in the Northeast closed in 1838, and at least 33,000 commercial and industrial failures were reported. By 1839 even the surplus of cash in state coffers had disappeared. Many states had counted on these funds to complete projects creating new roads and canals. Northern factory workers lost their jobs as manufacturers closed their businesses for lack of credit. Tens of thousands of factory workers were suddenly unemployed. Angry crowds of unemployed factory workers, unable or unwilling to return to farming, mobbed the streets of major cities demanding lower prices for food, rent, and fuel, while factory owners appealed to the Federal government for financial help and to the state government for a protecting force of militia. Many canal projects were put on hold for the duration of the crisis only to be redirected to the railroad building mania of the 1840s. The whaling industry declined in this period and virtually collapsed in the 1850s. The glory of the American wooden clipper ship was fading, and Great Britain's steamships threatened to take up much of the global oceanic trade. Slowly the nation recovered, regaining much of its prosperity in the 1840s, and expanding in the 1850s under the influence of the giant gold strike in California. However, overall American shipping went into a decline before the war that lasted into the 1890s.

The Northern industrial economy was again threatened by the financial Panic of August 1857, brought on by the failure of the Ohio Life Insurance Company (a major investor in the Ohio and Mississippi Railroad). This failure caused a week-long stock market crash with issues loosing 8 to 10 percent a day as a whole series of overextended companies failed. Runs on the banks and outright bank failures were the order of the day. Many of these were involved in railroad construction. The editor of the *New York Herald* (October 9, 1857) was revolted by the number of business suspensions, failures, and bankruptcies. Yet the young nation was fortunate in its discoveries of gold and silver during the middle decades of the century. These buoyed the economy somewhat and fueled invention and expansion.

A Nation of Mechanics

In the 19th century, theoretical science and philosophical thinking were the vogue in Europe, and Europeans deemed America a nation of mechanics and tinkers because Americans favored practical inventions over abstract theories. The 19th century sense of the term *mechanics* included artisans, craftsmen, and other persons who worked with their hands. Today we would classify them as technicians rather than research scientists. There was dignity in toil—both that of the hand of the mechanic and that of the head of the scholar. America was certainly a nation of mechanics during the antebellum period, and it continued to be so throughout the remainder of the century. A man's position in 19th-century American society was based on the useful work that he accomplished. "He is a man for what he does, not for what his father or his friends have done. If they have done well, and given him a position, the deeper the shame, if he sink down to a meaner level through self-indulgence and indolence."[6]

While European scientists delved into the nature of matter, heat, light, or electricity, Americans were producing practical applications of these scientific principles in the form of inventions that generally helped to improve life. American inventors made the United States a warehouse of wonders for the world. These inventions demonstrated great mechanical ingenuity, and important advances were made in many fields, including the development of a practical telegraph, the evolution of the mechanical reaper, the use of ether as anesthesia, and the harnessing of steam power for waterborne commerce. Other the other hand, the invention of safety matches, the development of a lace-making machine, and the patenting of the attached rubber pencil eraser all seem frivolous. Yet all of these advances affected the daily lives of those in the antebellum period.

Laborers

The greatest changes in employment and manufacturing prior to the Civil War were in the transitions from hand labor to increased mechanization in almost every task. Household manufacturing, which was still widespread in the 1820s, declined in importance during the next four decades, giving way to industrialization and mass production. Many of the items consumers once made for themselves, including basic things such as tools, textiles, and clothing, now came from factories. The craftsman, who previously made goods to the specifications of individual customers whom they knew, now enlarged his shop or took a place in a factory to turn out ready-made products in standard sizes for the general public. This transition also negatively affected the traditional practice of apprenticeship, allowing formal schooling to displace it as a preferred method of training for many forms of work.

The financial capital needed for increasing mechanization caused certain geographic areas blessed with inexpensive water power, raw materials, or access to interstate transportation to become centers for the manufacture of specific items. Danbury, Connecticut, with its hat factories, Lowell and Lynn, Massachusetts, with their textile mills, and Pittsburgh, Pennsylvania, with its iron foundries and deposits of coal may serve as examples. Domestic manufactures remained strong in many rural areas of the country and in many industries where it was not immediately possible to apply power and machine technology to the required task.

Shoemaking can serve as an example in this regard. At a time when power machinery had not yet been developed for making shoes, the process was ruled by apprentice-trained specialists who made hand-cut and hand-sewn shoes. The invention of a machine to produce small wooden pegs to attach the leather soles to the upper part of the shoe

In New England the shoemaker's shop was a small building where skilled workers joined the machine-sewn tops to the hand-wrought soles. Each man was an independent worker with his own "cobbler's" bench and materials.

initially changed the way shoemakers assembled their wares. The quiet stitching of sole to upper was replaced by the dull sound of the cobbler's hammer driving pegs into hard leather. At the same time, sewing-machine technology was successfully applied to the stitching of leather, resulting in the establishment of factories in which women sewed the uppers together and the men attached them to the lower structure of the shoe, fitting the finished product with soles and heels by hand. By 1858, Lyman Blake had patented a leather sewing machine that attached the soles to the uppers mechanically, greatly facilitating the shoemaking process. This made the price of shoes, especially work shoes, much more affordable. Sizes and widths were first introduced to shoe production at this time. Not only could the general public now buy shoes in sizes, but slaveowners and military quartermasters could provide cheaply made shoes to slaves and soldiers by the barrel in small, medium, and large sizes.

The conversion to machine operations brought many more women into the manufacturing trades. For example, although harness and saddle making remained male-dominated crafts, the extension of power stitching to the entire shoemaking process introduced a larger number of women into the process and left the traditional shoemaker with little beyond specialty work and a small repair business. As a result of this mechanization, more people became involved in shoemaking than in any other industry in the nation save agriculture.

Organized Labor

During the 18th century machines had been adapted to producing cloth, stockings, and socks in both wool and cotton. The immediate effect of this mechanization was to place an entire category of traditional weavers and stocking makers out of work. This had resulted in local uprisings in England and France by workers in this area of clothing production. Stocking frames, machinery, and the slotted wooden cards that controlled the complex operation of the power loom were attacked in both England and France. English weavers were jailed for having combined against their employers, while French workers, who had wedged their wooden shoes, or *sabot*, into the mechanisms to disrupt production, were vilified as *saboteurs*.

Mass production also engendered mass employment in America for the first time, and it wrought changes in the relationship between labor and management that reverberate even today. The right to strike was first established in America by the Massachusetts State Court in 1842 when a group of mill girls in Lowell refused to return to work at their looms because of long working hours. Eight hundred female workers from the shoemaking factory in Lynn, Massachusetts, went on strike for higher wages in 1860. They took to the streets dressed in their best hoop-skirts and carrying parasols in a March snowstorm. The strike lasted more than two weeks, and the results were somewhat ambiguous with the shop manager being thrown into a pond. Nonetheless, as the Civil War began, many Northern women were hired to make pistol holsters, riding boots, infantry shoes, cartridge boxes, and other leather items, and other women wove the cloth and sewed the uniforms for hundreds of thousands of Federal soldiers on water-powered mechanical looms and sewing machines. These ladies generally filled the civilian positions of men drafted away from their trades and into the Federal armies.

In 1877 workers brought the strike to the railroads. Embittered workers on the B & O Railroad began rioting in Martinsburg, West Virginia. State militia was sent in but failed to end the violence. The strike spread to Baltimore, Pittsburgh, and other cities. The 6th Maryland Regiment actually fired into strikers in Baltimore. Strikers burned the Pennsylvania Railroad Yards at Pittsburgh, and Federal troops were finally called up to end the strike. The violence of the railroad strike resulted in a wave of legislation and a number of judicial decisions detrimental to organized labor for the remainder of the century.

Farm Families

In the pitched battles that raged between Agrarianism and Industrialism throughout the 19th century, farming became a symbol of all that remained

Labor organizations were just coming into being at mid-century. Here the unionist and the non-union workers argue on a construction site.

good in America. Farmers were the chosen people of the United States, and after the Civil War the vast farmlands of the Great Plains were the Promised Land. While city dwellers and manufacturers changed the face of the nation with their factories and belching steam engines, farm families maintained their commitment to the traditional Protestant work ethic. Farmers—fathers, mothers, and children—were thought to work in harmony with nature as a cooperative and contented team. The industrious person was considered to be a good person, a moral person. Good work brought both religious and economic rewards. Moreover, with thousands of migrants and immigrants moving west, the universality of the farming culture among them was thought to uphold the family and guarantee the stability, continuity, and order of the frontier community.

The vast majority of Americans were small farmers and planned their lives around rural activities and seasonal chores such as barn raisings, quilting bees, planting, haying, and harvesting. *The Farmers' Almanac* played an important role in keeping track of astronomical, seasonal, and religious events. Family members usually cooperated in completing chores. This togetherness was thought to foster feelings of kinship and traditional family values. Their concept of time was based on sunrise, noon, spring, or summer, and they set their appointments or ended the workday by this standard. Free white laborers, tradesmen, and craftsmen were paid by the completion of a task, and rarely by the clock or calendar. The system provided continuity in the work relationship between employer and employee, and it was not unusual for one family to be employed by another in the same capacity for several generations.

In a study of farm families in 1860 combining 16 Northern states and excluding highly industrialized Massachusetts and Rhode Island, 56 percent of the population of 20,000 lived on farms. Of these, 70 percent owned their own place. Of the farmers without farms—the non-owning workers who reported themselves as farmers—very few identified themselves as tenant farmers. Less than 5 percent of those living on farms reported non-agricultural occupations, and less than 10 percent of the total rural population self-identified as simple laborers. Some of these may also have done farm-related work such as hauling, millwork, or livestock management. The remainder of the population identified itself as living in non-farm residences such as rural villages, but they still may have been part of the overall agricultural economy.[7]

More than 80 percent of the farm families were husband-wife households with both spouses present. In cases where the wife was in her 20s, family size averaged 2.5 children; for wives in their 30s and 40s, the number of children was between 4.0 and 5.5, respectively. There were very few farm households headed by females (7 percent), and these women were

Even with the increased effects of industrialization and urbanization around them, most American families remained farming families. Here in "Preparing for Market," Currier and Ives captured the essence of the agricultural economy.

described as "conspicuously middle-aged," suggesting that this class may formerly have been husband-wife households in which the male spouse died.[8] A third (or fourth) adult residing in the household was most likely to be a non-nuclear male, probably a hired man. This finding dovetails well with the available residence and occupation data.[9]

Of course in 1860 not all of the land that was fit for agriculture was as yet cleared and under cultivation. Older regions and newer ones had different characteristics. For instance, the newest regions to be put under cultivation also showed the highest rate of property ownership, suggesting that a disproportionate number of people were acquiring land with a view to establishing their own farms. Moreover, farm labor wages were highest on the frontier, and most farm families seem to have worked their own places using available family members as laborers. Since there was a variety of tasks on farms that could be done by women and children, their involvement in the agricultural economy was all but inevitable. Nonetheless, very few women were identified as farm workers in the census returns. Children over age 15 were sometimes classified as laborers, but those under 15 were assigned no occupation.

Data suggest that the farm labor of women, ages 15 to 54, was roughly equivalent in all regions regardless of the level of agricultural development found there. The regional variations were also very close for children under 15. There was a regional pattern within these variations, however, with more developed regions having incrementally smaller family sizes than the newest regions. "In general one may say that newer regions have somewhat more child labor available per farm, but somewhat less adult female labor per farm (allowing for the fact that childbearing and raising are more time consuming in the newer regions). In the newest region, there is somewhat less child labor available."[10] Generally, "farm households in the older areas were on the average better off since not only was farm income higher but the number dependent on it was lower."[11]

Agriculture was also the beneficiary of new processes, simplified methods, and the genuine mechanical insight that characterized the period of invention. In 1834 Cyrus McCormick patented the mechanical reaper that increased agricultural efficiency and the volume of food production enormously. Almost 1,000 of the 6,600 patents issued in 1857 and 1858 alone were for agricultural and farm machinery—many of which were variations on McCormick's patent. Theories abound that labor-saving farm machines would have eradicated race-based slavery within the century, but such inventions tended to benefit Northern farm workers more than slaves on Southern plantations where free manual labor remained more economical than costly machines.

Notwithstanding the economy of slave labor, as early as 1794 Eli Whitney saw the need to mechanize the time-consuming removal of cotton seeds from the desirable long staple raw cotton. His invention of the cotton gin made cotton fiber a more thoroughly marketable material and stimulated the growth of cotton agriculture in the South. The widespread adoption of the cotton gin during the antebellum period allowed a slave, who could process 100 pounds of cotton per day without the machine, to produce 1,000 pounds of fiber in the same time with it. Unfortunately, it also breathed new life into the institution of slavery by making cotton production more profitable, providing a financial bulwark for the retention of slavery in the Deep South. By mid-century cotton accounted for two-thirds of the dollar exports of the United States. The profitability of cotton increased both the number and the value of slaves as plantation owners put more and more acreage under cultivation and attempted to spread the practice of slavery to new territories. Estimates show that by 1860 there were more than 3.6 million black slaves in the states that were to form the Confederacy. Without the cotton gin, the archaic plantation system might well have faded into obscurity.

During the financial panics that struck the nation, the South suffered from a resulting crash in demand for cotton as mills and factories, especially those in England, were unable to collect on American debts and themselves went into bankruptcy. Many Southern slaves found that they faced the auction block for the first time as even the most humane slaveowners were forced to raise cash in order to pay the bills they had accumulated in expectation of the sale of their crops. Nonetheless, the agricultural abundance of the South made it one of the more resilient sectors of the national economy, providing abundant food for itself at least in the short term. Unlike the Northern and Midwestern farmlands where wheat was the main crop, corn was the major crop grown in the South. This was used locally as food for man and feed for livestock and poultry. Rice, tobacco, sugar, leather, lumber, turpentine, and cotton accounted for three-fourths of Southern export trade in 1860.

In terms of dollars, however, the antebellum period witnessed cotton becoming "King" in the South. In 1790 annual cotton production amounted to only 3,000 bales, but it rose to 178,000 bales in just 20 years. This increase is generally attributed to the introduction of the cotton gin. The Sea Islands of South Carolina and Georgia were noted for the production of luxury cotton with its long, delicate, and silky fibers that could not be grown profitably anywhere else in the world. Even so, continuous experimentation to improve the quality of luxury cotton produced a superfine fiber that the world eagerly sought for making laces and fine fabrics. Even in the face of widely fluctuating prices, this cotton provided the Southern gentry with a relatively stable market and a virtually inexhaustible wealth. By mid-century the introduction of a superior cotton boll from Mexico, which could be more easily picked, increased production again. Expanded agricultural investment in the new western lands of the South coupled with the widespread utilization of the cotton gin boosted cotton production to almost 4 million bales per annum by the decade of the Civil War. So pervasive was the cotton economy in the Southern states that the

Confederacy thought it could support itself and its war effort on funds drawn from Europe and guaranteed with cotton bonds.

As long as American industrialists prospered, American farmers generally prospered also; during panics and depressions agricultural prices fell, and everyone was hurt. Yet agriculture often faced nearly crushing difficulties even during good times. These included floods, droughts, tornadoes, and other natural catastrophes, some of which were unpredictable.

In 1848 Brigham Young and the followers of Joseph Smith, founder of Mormonism, had turned west to the great American desert to escape the prejudice and open violence that challenged the Church of Jesus Christ of Latter Day Saints almost everywhere. Here in the formative years of the Great Salt Lake settlement, the saints had been unexpectedly attacked by a plague of crop-destroying grasshoppers (Rocky Mountain locusts) that threatened to end the movement through starvation. One farmer described the onset of the plague, "A person could see a little dark whirlwind here and there which after a while turned into dark clouds [of locusts]. . . The air grew so thick that the sun could not be seen." The Mormons responded by attempting to beat the pests to death with brooms, blankets, and wet grain bags. The inefficiency of this method was quickly made clear. Miraculously a swarm of seagulls followed closely on the heels of the arrival of the grasshoppers, eating them faster than they could eat the crops and saving the food supply. For this reason the seagull is used as a symbol of God's approbation by Mormons to this day.[12]

In the middle of the 1870s, just as the Panic of 1873 hit, the Upper Midwest farming region was also plagued by grasshoppers, but no seabirds came to their rescue. Several states were grievously affected, including Iowa, Nebraska, Kansas, Missouri, and particularly Minnesota. The Dakota Territory and the Canadian province of Manitoba were also hard hit. The magnitude of the plague was catastrophic. Seemingly overnight Minnesota alone lost 16 percent of its wheat crop, 18 percent of its oats, and 15 percent of its corn. The grasshoppers returned annually from 1873 until 1877 to these same regions, and they also appeared sporadically during these years in other areas such as Texas, Arkansas, Idaho, Montana, Utah, New Mexico, Nevada, Washington, Oregon, Oklahoma, and in additional parts of the Canada plains. The total loss to the agricultural economy of the United States in this period of devastation may have exceeded $200 million annually.

Historians have studied the five consecutive years of grasshopper plagues in the hardest hit region, and they have determined that the plagues had a profound impact on the community of farmers nationwide. Although grasshopper plagues had appeared before, the consistent reappearance of these pests at a time of economic distress may have changed how Americans viewed the frontier environment as a possible stage for financial success. Moreover, the plagues and the government's response to them may have reshaped the politics of the West and Midwest in the later 19th century.[13]

When threatened by the swarming masses from the sky, farmers set smoky smudge-pots in their orchards, in their vineyards, and in their wheat fields in an attempt to drive them off, but the pests—carried from place to place on the winds and leaving their eggs behind for each subsequent year—could not be scared away, writhing on the ground like a wind-blown shallow sea. Whole families could be seen in the fields shoveling the insects from the earth and into bonfires set for the purpose. A grasshopper killing machine, called the hopperdozer, was invented to deal more efficiently with the problem. It required a piece of metal, shaped into a shallow pan and coated with tar or any sticky substance, that was dragged through the fields behind a team of draft animals. The forward motion of the team forced the grasshoppers into the pan, which, when full, was emptied into the fire. In one county in Minnesota more than 600 hopperdozers were built or bought in a single year, but the grasshoppers usually did their damage faster than the efforts of the farmers could kill them. Nonetheless, in some places these efforts may have thinned out the subsequent populations of insect pests by destroying the bugs before their peak period of egg production.[14]

The devastation was felt at different levels by farmers in different areas. Some farmers escaped damage altogether or were hurt only once or twice while their neighbors had their fields stripped during each successive year. There was no clear-cut pattern to the destruction. "Damage varied from crop to crop, from farm to farm, and from year to year." One farmer in 1875 lost 15 acres of wheat, 500 cabbages, all of his cucumbers, beans, onions, carrots, parsnips, and beets, most of his nursery stock, and most of his 4,000 strawberry and raspberry vines. He saved part or all of his oats, corn, potatoes, melons, and apple trees. Instead of a seasonal profit of $300, he made just $22; and he needed to borrow $5,000 in order to undo the damage, replant, and restock. This was financial ruin at its maximum, and there was little prospect for improvement as the pests returned in each successive year.[15]

In response to the threat, some farmers altered their planting patterns. Wheat was thought to be particularly susceptible to attack, and farmers planted corn, peas, beans, and other crops that were thought less vulnerable to replace it. Potatoes, as ground tubers, were hardly touched at all, but they were planted for domestic consumption rather than for the market. In one Minnesota county in 1873, wheat had made up 64 percent of the crop and corn just 8 percent. Five years later the proportions had reversed only to return again to their original ratios when the threat was no longer imminent. Other farmers turned more effort to livestock production rather than to grains. Pigs became a safe harbor because they were hardy and self-reliant, but fewer chickens were raised because eggs laid by chickens that fed on grasshoppers tasted bad. Vines and orchards put out of production by the insects were pruned, or replanted, or abandoned. Many farmers hard pressed for cash just planted less, falling back to subsistence-level farming and abandoning any hope of bringing a crop to market. In some regions the total acreage under production fell by half and did not recover until after 1878 when the grasshopper threat finally lifted up "in a body clouding the sunshine and left for parts unknown never to return."[16]

Meanwhile the effects of the plague continued even after the insects had gone. Many farmers had mortgaged their farms in order the weather the crisis, and some began to pay interest on the interest incurred as the plagues continued and money was needed to provide the necessities of life. It must be remembered that taking loans against real property was not as common as it is today. Acquiring debt of this sort was considered by many to be an admission of failure, and putting up the farm as collateral was a drastic step. Some farmers used their savings, gave up their newspaper and other luxuries, sold their prized livestock, let go their hired help, or hitched up the farm wagon, loaded their remaining possessions and moved on "east or west, it did not matter so long as there were no grasshoppers." Real estate values in the ravaged region plummeted. Many hard-hit counties underwent a decline in population, "a nearly unheard-of occurrence in a frontier area." Yet it was not the outpouring of residents but the diminished flow of new migrants into the region to replace them that was most dramatic.[17]

"Some people, finding human remedies futile, turned to spiritual assistance. They prayed." If God had sent this plague of Biblical proportions, then only God could lift it. They asked for the forgiveness of their sins; pledged themselves to lead more moral lives; and promised to build chapels and churches if the scourge were lifted. Some asked their neighbors for Christian charity, and vowed to show themselves worthy of God's mercy as they had when they joined together to wage God's war against slavery. When the pests returned year after year an entire values system was threatened, and the frontier was no longer viewed as a promised land.[18]

In a few communities farmers joined together to weather the storm, forming committees and relief efforts among themselves. Others turned to the state government for help; many asked, others begged, and some demanded a part of America's untouched abundance. Many farmers, however, were critical of governmental help, drawing a clear line between those worthy of aid because they were victims of events beyond their control such as tornadoes, floods, droughts, or grasshoppers, and those who were paupers—a permanent under-class whose poverty was considered self-inflicted because of a weakness in their moral fiber. A contemporary observer noted, "There were many families who are heroically enduring this loss. . . . Taking every pain to conceal their real condition they will not consent to receive any assistance till they approach the verge of starvation

[and] then disgrace themselves, and the community in which they live, by applying for relief, and appearing before the world as mendicants . . . hundreds are ashamed to beg or acknowledge their destitution [because of] their repugnance to the reception of charity."[19]

In March 1877 President Rutherford B. Hayes established the U.S. Entomological Commission to identify the most practical methods of preventing any further recurrences of the plague. By 1880 the commission had collected, analyzed, and published its findings, but the grasshoppers were already gone. Although the government responded to the grasshopper crisis with aid, relief, and even generosity, it did not generally display the massive reaction to agricultural devastation that was later seen in the New Deal policies of the 1930s. If the farmers of the 1870s valued the help of the government, and there is some evidence that many did not, then they were equally disappointed by government policies in the late 1880s and 1890s when government agencies, and the American people, were even less sympathetic in responding to drought and agricultural depressions.

Being on Time

While many Northerners were still farmers, a growing segment of the population was becoming tied to the cities and factories. Middle-class men who had grown up in the first half of the century could remember a childhood spent living in a family working environment, either on the farm, in a cottage at the mill, or in a room behind the family shop. But as the century progressed men's work increasingly took place in the special atmosphere of a business premises like the factory or office. Many fathers left the home to work for 10 to 14 hours, and their children rarely saw them during daylight hours. A father's work and workplace became foreign to his children. This tendency to "go to work," rather than to "work at home," led to the virtual removal of men from the urban home environment, leaving it the sole province of the female.

The American Watch Company of Waltham, Massachusetts, developed the first mass-produced, precision pocket watch in the 1850s. These were produced with internal movements that could be made with interchangeable, machine-made parts by semi-skilled laborers. The first such watches were delivered in 1852. Other less notable companies soon followed suit. This made the pocket watch affordable. With the general availability of the pocket watch, working men increasingly lived their lives by the clock. Even those workers without watches were expected to labor in shifts dictated by the public clocks that came to be prominently displayed on towers, in the streets, in the railroad stations, and on the factory walls. The idea of being "on time" represented a significant change in the lifestyle of most city dwellers; and since the North was the most urbanized section of the country, being "on time" became characteristic of Northern life.[20]

Conversely, rural agricultural workers had no need to work by the mechanical clock. They worked a traditional solar day, and were often viewed as shiftless and lazy by those imbued with a love of industrialization. Southern laborers feared the development of the unprecedented "work for wage" economy of the cities, and they saw Northern wage earners as degraded and enslaved persons. The city wage-worker sold himself into economic bondage for a period of time no matter how short, and the expansion of a similar "work for wage" system was dreaded by Southerners almost as much as abolitionists dreaded the expansion of slavery. Southern whites were clearly anxious to maintain their status as freemen, and many in the laboring class believed that the North was determined to enslave them to the factory system or counting house. The modern egalitarian society of the North was viewed with disdain and seen as degenerate and immoral. Rising crime rates in the cities, flagrant and open prostitution, and the squalid conditions of the urban lower classes, were proffered as proof of Northern inferiority.

With rail traffic increasing in the 1850s, the railroads of the New England region had agreed to set their clocks and watches to a single standard time and to calibrate them through the use of the telegraph. Railroad time admitted of no delay. "In this, at the onset," wrote a newspaper editor in 1852, "the engineer has established the rule, firm as the laws of Medes and Persians, that the cars must depart punctually at the time, and make their time. The observance of this rule is a guaranty against collisions." On August 12, 1853, there was a head-on collision between two trains that were approaching on correctly timed schedules because the conductors' watches were not properly synchronized. Fourteen people were killed. This brought about an immediate outcry for more reliable schedules and stricter rules for running on time.[21]

It was not until 1883 that the American Railway Association adopted a five-zone system proposed by William F. Allen, and the public began to accept "railroad time" as part of their daily life. In the interim many towns and cities devised their own time systems. This caused a great deal of confusion in a society that was moving from place to place rapidly for the first time. There were even court cases where the definition of a "midnight" deadline in a contract was argued by the opposing parties. Adherence to standard time, as we know it, was completely voluntary until it was made the law in 1918.

Inventions

During the antebellum period it was not unusual for a person to choose a career as an inventor. Inventiveness seemed to be an American trait, and it was widely believed that any mechanical problem could be solved if one applied enough hard work and creativity to it. As early as 1820, German political economist Georg Friedrich List wrote, "There is no clinging to old ways; the moment an American hears the word invention he pricks up his ears."[22]

Unfortunately, as more inventors worked on a particular problem their solutions tended to converge around the naturally correct one. This is a repetitive characteristic of the practice of engineering known as *convergent technology.* In 1838 Congress created a new patent law to deal with competing claims to inventions. Up to that time anyone who claimed a patent received one, even if competing claims for the same invention were made. The new law established, for the first time, the principles of formal research, requiring the patent office to withhold a patent until all other prior patents had been scrutinized for the inclusion of important original ideas.

Ironically the pace of invention accelerated under the new law. Before 1838 no more than 500 patents had been granted. In the next decade alone, more than 10,000 were issued. Unscrupulous advertisers used this circumstance to advance themselves in the newspapers as agents of the Patent Office, who for a fee, would act as "preparers of Caveats, Specifications, Assignments, and all the necessary Papers and Drawings" so that inventors might be "saved the time and cost of a journey to Washington, and the delay there, as well as [being saved] all the personal trouble in obtaining their patents."[23]

Clothing Production

The development of a practical sewing machine contributed not only to the domestic production of clothing but also to the growth of the ready-made clothing industry. The first American sewing machine was invented by John A. Doge and John Knowles in 1818, but their machine failed to join any useful amount of fabric before malfunctioning. The first functional sewing machine was produced in France by Barthelemy Thimonnier in 1830. This hand-cranked model sewed well, but produced only a chain stitch, like that used in embroidery. If the loose ends of the thread were pulled, the entire stitch might unravel. In 1834 Walter Hunt, an American, produced a hand-cranked machine that could sew in a straight line with remarkable speed, but it was Elias Howe who patented the lockstitch mechanism in 1846. This used thread from two different sources, one following the needle and the other on a reciprocating shuttle, that locked each stitch in place by passing one thread through a loop created in the other.

Howe's lockstitch method was effective, and it was adopted by other inventors in this area. Principal among these was Isaac Singer who put his machines into mass production around 1850. Singer's machine had several improvements over that of Howe. The needle moved up and down rather than side to side, allowing the operator to more readily make turns and curves when joining fabric. Moreover, many of his models were powered by a foot treadle, leaving both hands free to guide the fabric. Singer also incorporated into his mechanism Allen Wilson's invention of a rotary shuttle hook. In 1854, Howe sued Singer for infringement of the lockstitch patent and won patent royalties from him. Howe realized more than $2 million from these royalties during the next 10 years. During the Civil War he donated a large portion of this money to the Union Army, equipping an entire infantry regiment for the field at his own expense.

By 1860 the continuous stitch sewing machine, first used with cloth, had quickly been modified to make lacework. An English patent for a lacework machine had been granted to John Fisher in 1844, but the patent had been lost in the Royal Patent Office, opening this area of manufacture to a wide variety of imitators. However, intricate hand-made lacework remained more fashionable with consumers than the machine-made product throughout the period.

Mass Production

One of the outgrowths of industrialization was the development of the concept of mass production. Among other innovations, Eli Whitney's application of the concept of interchangeable parts in the mass production of all types of mechanical items stands out among his accomplishments. This was particularly true with regard to the manufacture of firearms. Formerly, a musket or rifle was built by a single craftsperson or small group of gunsmiths who fitted the weapon together piece by interconnecting piece—lock, stock, and barrel. Every screw and fastener was hand-made and hand-fitted. The lock, a complicated mechanism that began the firing sequence, might contain a dozen tiny parts, each fitted precisely to its neighbors by hand. However, the parts from one lock might not fit with the parts from another even if they were made by the same gunsmith. Because each weapon produced in this manner was different, the process slowed the manufacturer of large quantities of weapons and made even simple repairs difficult and time-consuming. In a two-year period, using traditional methods, the national armories of the United States produced a total only 1,000 muskets.

By utilizing precision machine tools, Whitney hoped to standardize the precision with which parts were manufactured and ensure that those from one weapon could be interchanged with those of another with little fuss. Moreover, ammunition could be distributed and shared among the troops of the same army, and spare parts could be kept on hand for quick repairs in the field. In a demonstration before President Thomas Jefferson in late 1801, Whitney assembled a number of complete, operable muskets from piles of parts picked at random by generally skeptical government officials. In 1804 Whitney signed a contract with the Federal government for the manufacture of 10,000 muskets in just two years; however, he constantly had to plead for extra time to complete the contract as he ran into unforeseen obstacles.

Nonetheless, by 1818 he had installed an advanced machine milling tool at the Federal arsenal at Springfield, Massachusetts. Thereafter, the ideas of mass production and parts interchangeability that Whitney pioneered remained the basis for the machine manufacture of all types of precision devices. Whitney died in 1825, but his son, Eli Whitney, Jr., continued to operate his father's arms manufactory in Hamden, Connecticut.[24]

In 1835 Samuel Colt invented the first practical revolving pistol. Colt's firearm, with its many imitators, became the standard for all cap and ball revolvers of the Civil War. Colt sold millions of his revolvers in both the military and civilian markets. Exhausted cylinders from one Colt pistol could be quickly interchanged for a new one in a few seconds. In 1854 Horace Smith and Daniel Wesson invented the first practical brass cartridge revolver that could be quickly loaded with a self-contained load of powder and bullet. Smith and Wesson revolvers were generally of too small a caliber to be adopted by the military, but thousands were brought to war by soldiers as "lifesavers." Only with the precision of machines could the cartridges be turned out in vast number. In 1858 Christian Sharps produced an efficient breech-loading rifle for military use based on his own 1848 patent that eliminated the need to ram home a charge from the muzzle end of the weapon. The early forms of the Sharps carbine saw a great deal of action in the bloody conflict between proslavery and abolitionist forces in Missouri and Kansas, and it was one of the weapons supplied to anti-slavery zealots by supporters of John Brown in 1850. Nonetheless, breechloaders were generally issued only to cavalry or other specialty troops by the army, and muzzle-loading long arms remained the premier weapon of most Civil War infantry.

In 1855 the Federal government adopted the highly efficient conical "Minie" ball as a standard bullet for its infantry firearms. This lethal bullet of approximately .58 caliber, developed by Captain Claude Minie, could be loaded into rifles more easily than round balls of the same weight. When fired the soft lead at the base of the Minie ball expanded to grip the spiral rifling in the barrel, thereby increasing, in a single invention, both the accuracy and the rate of fire of a military musket. The adoption of the Minie ball by both sides in the Civil War, and by many foreign powers, is a leading factor in explaining the increased causality rates among soldiers in battle as compared to prior conflicts. Although a few weapons were fitted with new telescopic sights, most military muskets of the period had open sights that could be adjusted to hit targets at 800 yards or more. It has been estimated that more than 3 million Minie balls and other small arms rounds were fired during the three days of battle at Gettysburg (1863) alone.

Metallurgy

By 1840 wood charcoal had been replaced as a fuel in blast furnaces producing pig iron by a more efficient byproduct of coal called *coke*.

The consequent decrease in the price of ferric materials spurred a spate of technological advancement in the areas of architecture, engineering, power, and transportation. In 1840 the first piano fortes were produced using a cast iron frame that would not be crushed under the tremendous tension of the dozens of wire piano strings. This led to a major revolution in concert music. In 1848, cast iron was used for the first time to build multi-storied buildings, and the height of these tall structures, some reaching more than five floors, moved Elisha Otis to invent the safety elevator for passengers in 1853. Higher-quality iron and steel, taken together with a theoretical revolution in steam technology, allowed George Corliss to patent a more efficient four-valve steam engine in 1849, which, in turn, spurred the introduction of horse-drawn steam fire engines. More than 350 patents for improved steam engines, boilers, and railroad or steamboat equipment were issued by the U.S. Patent Office in the decade of the 1850s alone.

Telegraphy

A fundamental revolution in communications was begun in 1844 when Samuel F. B. Morse sent the first telegraph message from Baltimore to Washington. The essential technological advance that allowed Morse to create telegraphy was the ability to draw out copper wire at an economical price developed by the British metallurgical industry a decade earlier. Up to that point, electric communication over long distances was simply not feasible, even if the technological challenges of the telegraph itself had been surmounted earlier. Morse's ability to send a message by electric current over wires many miles apart was done over a decade of research and was built upon the development of the wet cell battery by Italian Alessandro Volta in 1800 and the electromagnetic studies of the American scientist Joseph Henry at Princeton in 1836.

Alessandro Volta had used the natural characteristic of two different metals and an acid to build a "voltaic cell" or battery. The battery, composed of zinc and copper discs placed alternately on top of one another and interleaved with cardboard moistened with a dilute acid, produced a steady electric current as long as there was metal left to be consumed. By the time of the Civil War a practical battery made from two different compounds of lead and sulfuric acid was available. A series of these batteries allowed the U.S. Military Telegraph, a branch of the Federal Army, to send a message over 10 miles of wire from a single wagon fitted with telegraphic equipment.

Joseph Henry increased the size and power of the battery and invented the first electromagnet, the first electric motor, and the first electromagnetic telegraph—sending a faint signal through a mile of wire arrayed around his laboratory. While neither his motor nor his telegraph were more than laboratory toys, Henry had also devised a system of relays by which a current, made faint by traveling through a long length of wire, might be increased and exactly repeated. This was a pivotal discovery that Henry shared with Morse in 1835. Morse utilized the repeaters to make long-distance transmission possible. Henry also suggested in 1843 that Morse's wire could be insulated by stringing it high above the ground from glass knobs fixed to wooden poles. In the same year Morse ran an underwater wire, insulated in a natural material similar to rubber known as gutta percha, 13 miles from Martha's Vineyard to Nantucket.

Alfred Vail, a partner of Morse, designed the telegraph key used to send the sets of dots and dashes. It was a simple strip of spring steel that could be pressed against a metal contact to send letters and numerals via a predetermined code. Later models of the transmitting key and the signal receiver were developed about a pivoting lever action that allowed the gap to be more easily adjusted. Also significant were Morse's consultations with another partner, Leonard Gale, a professor of chemistry at New York University, regarding electrochemistry. Armed with the discoveries of Volta, Henry, Vail, and Gale, and his own innovations, Morse produced a telegraph that was an immediate success. The 1844 patent applications for the telegraph also included a method for recording the dots and dashes on paper. This and the code itself were the only parts of the invention solely attributable to Morse.

Within 10 years of the first telegraphic message, more than 23,000 miles of telegraph wire crisscrossed the country. Newspapers quickly began using the "wires" to collect news, and the Associated Press and other news agencies set up their own wire services. By 1848 even small communities were reading telegraphic dispatches from the Mexican War. However, there was no traffic control system for the various independent telegraph companies or even for individual operators within the same company. Several operators might obliterate any meaning among the hundreds of dots and dashes by trying to use the same line at the same time. In 1856, Hiram Sibley founded Western Union, which eventually bought up all the patents from competing telegraphy systems and combined the best features of each into one dependable system.

In 1858, after two failed attempts, Cyrus W. Field was able to lay a continuous transatlantic telegraphic cable from Newfoundland to Ireland. It worked for some time, and the public reacted with jubilation. However, mishandling of the insulation during the cable's deployment caused the underwater line to fail. Nonetheless, the cause of fault was known and could be addressed, but not before the war intervened.

On the eve of the Civil War, telegraph wires connected most Eastern cities, a transcontinental telegraph connected New York to California, and a transatlantic telegraphic cable—although presently silent—stretched from Canada to Europe. The telegraph profoundly affected Americans. It helped develop the American West, made railroad travel safer, allowed businesses to communicate more efficiently, and spread political speeches and ideas across the country in a single day. The Confederate Army utilized the existing civilian telegraphic system of the South to issue orders between commanders and to communicate with the government in Richmond, and Abraham Lincoln was known to spend long hours contemplating the war reports in the Western Union office in Washington. However, telegraphy also brought the horrors of battle and long lists of casualties from the front lines of the war almost instantaneously to the parlors of America.

Morse was plagued by lawsuits regarding his telegraphic patents. This was a common circumstance among inventors during the period as they sought to claim sole credit for complex inventions. Although Henry consistently backed Morse and frequently appeared in his defense in court, Morse became embittered toward him. This may have been due to the scientific community's recognition of Henry as the first builder of an electromagnetic telegraph. They understood, better than Morse, the complexity and difficulty of his accomplishment, especially the role played by the Henry relay. In 1855 Morse attacked Henry in the press. He wrote, "I shall show that I am not indebted to him for any discoveries in science bearing upon the telegraph." Henry refused to take up the argument himself. Instead he applied to the Board of Regents of the Smithsonian Institution to look into the matter. In 1857 they found Morse's arguments "a disingenuous piece of sophisticated argument [that] perverted the truth." This generally ended the controversy, and Henry went forward to help found the National Academy of Sciences and the American Association for the Advancement of Science. During the Civil War, Henry served as a science advisor to President Lincoln.[25]

Telephone

In 1876 Alexander Graham Bell invented the telephone by combining a series of simple theoretical concepts into a complex but effective mechanism. Within six months he had arranged a public demonstration of his device before a select group of "scientific men" gathered at Lyceum Hall in Salem, Massachusetts. Although the transmission wiring was makeshift, on March 15, 1877, Bell spoke into his instrument and received an answer from far-away Boston. By 1878 the Bell Telephone Company had set up thousands of miles of wires and a series of giant switching boards capable of connecting Americans by voice in many cities. The terms for "leasing two telephones for social purposes connecting a dwelling-house with any other building" were set at $20 a year, and "for business purposes" at $40 a year.[26]

Gardiner G. Hubbard, active director of the company, noted the advantages of a telephone "set in a quiet place" where noise would not interrupt ordinary conversation. "The advantages of the Telephone over the Telegraph . . . are that no skilled operator is required, but direct communication may be had by speech without the intervention of a third person; that the communication is much more rapid [100 words a minute versus 20]; and it needs no battery and has no complicated machinery." Moreover, Hubbard suggested that the telephone lines could be erected by the business owner or "any good mechanic" with the total cost of poles, stringing, and sundries being $10 per mile. "Parties leasing the Telephones, however, incur no expense beyond the annual rental and repair of the line wire."[27]

Science

In Europe during the 1820s and 1830s, an entire generation of science students was being exposed to research laboratories, observatories, medical schools, hospitals, and scientific institutes. Many Americans went to England, Germany, France, Italy, Switzerland, or Sweden to learn the theoretical principles of science, and they returned to America to share the practical aspects of the science they had learned. However, they were faced with an American public that did not see the need for theoretical science of this sort and could not imagine how the marriage of science and technology could be of any use in developing the economy or settling the political questions that faced the nation. Inventions seemed to spew forth from ingenious and creative sources rather than formally trained researchers. Only after the economic and industrial development in America had created a foothold did the need for formal technical education become apparent.

The 1840s was the first period in American history to have an extensive group of professional scientists and researchers on hand, but Americans did not seem to know what to do with them, valuing novel gadgets and innovative machines over high-sounding theories. Nonetheless, in the physical sciences, Joseph Henry in Albany was keeping pace with the electrical discoveries of Michael Faraday in Britain. Charles Goodyear was vulcanizing rubber for which he received a French patent in 1844. George Henry Corliss was busy in Providence, Rhode Island, improving the steam engine. Cotton mills in Massachusetts began producing cloth with water-powered machinery as early as 1823. Uriah Boyden invented a more efficient turbine waterwheel in 1844, and installed it at the company-owned mills at Holyoke, Massachusetts, located at the falls in the Connecticut River. By 1851 steam power had been harnessed to many commercial looms.

In the field of earth science, Matthew F. Maury was charting the prevailing winds and ocean currents of the sea-lanes of the world by consulting the logs of the whaling vessels, taking anecdotal evidence, and compiling the results. He shared his findings with the skippers of the clipper ships that set speed records around Cape Horn by using them. In 1842 James P. Epsy was appointed the country's first national meteorologist, and Charles Wilkes was leading an expedition of discovery along the Arctic coast. In 1854 Benjamin Silliman, Jr., was analyzing crude oil samples from the Titusville, Pennsylvania, oil field of Colonel Edwin Drake, an important development in petroleum exploration in America.

In the field of biological sciences, Asa Gray was on his way to becoming America's leading botanist. At the same time, a 31-year-old dentist named Dr. Horace Wells had discovered the numbing effect of nitrous oxide gas. He convinced Dr. Crawford Long to use the gas in his surgery in 1842 while removing a tumor. The operation was performed with no evidence of additional suffering on the part of the patient. Another dentist, Dr. William Morton, discovered the properties of sulfuric ether as an anesthetic. In 1846 as he applied the ether, Dr. J. C. Warren, a renowned surgeon at Massachusetts General Hospital, performed the removal of a tumor from the face of a patient. At the conclusion of the surgery Warren exclaimed to all present, "Gentlemen, this is no humbug!" The first use of ether as an anesthetic created a great sensation in the medical world and a good deal of controversy over the patenting of the method. Oliver Wendell Holmes, the doctor-poet of the antebellum period, wrote, "Everybody wants to have a hand in [this] great discovery."[28]

Jefferies Wyman, a professor of anatomy at the Lawrence Scientific School (at Harvard) accumulated a vast stock of anatomical data on apes and gorillas that contributed to Charles Darwin's theory of evolution. His careful investigations of the anatomy of the "Negro" and "Caucasian" races in 1850 had great technical merit, but his findings were used in an unfortunate manner by slavemasters to uphold the concept of a natural order of society based on racial slavery. Many of the thousands of patented inventions and technical breakthroughs made during the period have contributed to the modern form of American society.

Strangely, the Civil War would produce an entire cadre of surgeons whose skills were honed in the battlefield surgical tents that characterized the war. Surgeons were pushed to the limits of their skills by battlefield wounds and were forced by circumstances to experiment with new medical procedures and protocols. This experience accelerated the acquisition of medical knowledge and may have saved many civilian lives in the decades after the war as well.

The Extraction Trades

Miners   Mining was one of the extraction trades. Although gold and silver stole the spotlight, the majority of miners worked digging coal, iron, and other base metals from the ground. Composed mostly of men of Irish and Welsh ancestry, who brought a history of mining techniques from Europe and dominated the Eastern industry, the mine workforce of the second half of the century became increasingly populated with foreign-speaking immigrants. The newcomers to the Eastern mines were Poles, Italians, Ukrainians, Hungarians, and Lithuanians who found it difficult to work in cooperation with the established miners. The Irish Catholics, in particular, attempted to maintain the ethnic and religious integrity of the mining communities. They built churches, established community parishes, and demanded priests from the diocese. Second only to the Irish in their cohesion were the Welsh Cornishmen. This helped them to create a remarkable unity, and late in the century they used it to form unions and fight the mining companies for wages, safety standards, and working and living conditions.

Described as a "500-square mile triangle of low mountains, deep valleys, and sharp outcroppings of rock," northeastern Pennsylvanian boasted nearly all the hard coal (anthracite) that heated the homes and offices or ran the factories and engines along the Atlantic seacoast. Places like Scranton, Wilkes-Barre, Shamokin, Mount Carmel, and Shenandoah were made prosperous by the extraction of hard coal. Soft coal mining (bituminous) was actually more widespread. While 10,000 miners worked the hard coal, tens of thousands, possibly 150,000, worked the soft coal deposits of western Pennsylvania, Ohio, Illinois, Indiana, Virginia, North Carolina, and elsewhere. These mines were tightly controlled by a few coal-carrying railway lines that shipped the fuel to Eastern cities and iron foundries. Ironically, while early locomotives all burned wood, only Northern railways had changed over to coal before the Civil War.

The men and boys who worked these mines were generally considered hard rock miners because they pried the valuable substances from the surrounding igneous and metamorphic rock layers. Much of what they removed from surface seams and underground galleries was useless silica rock, shale, or slate. For this reason a miner's ton—the basis on which many miners were paid—was set at 3,360 pounds per ton, and sometimes higher. This was thought to render a standard ton (2,000 pounds) of useful or valuable product. The iron and steel company towns, and the coal fields and iron mines that fed the furnaces, were the domain of industrial giants like the Mellons and the Carnegies. The grip of these companies was tight, and they squeezed hard. If the price of coal fell at market the mine might close, and many miners worked as few as 200 days a year, leaving them with continuing bills that they could not pay. As an example, after an entire month's work, one miner—a boy of 14, the eldest child in his family—brought home only a demand for money due to the company of $396, the current balance on the family's rented two-room house unpaid since the death of his father.[29]

Mining contracts usually restricted the workers' ability to purchase items outside the community if they were available at the company store. An average miner made $8, $10, or $12a week, but he realized a profit of only about $300 per year. In the copper mining town of Clifton, Michigan, in 1863, the local school teacher, Henry Hobart, noted in his diary, "A good assortment of goods, but they are very dear. A common suit of clothes cost $33.00 . . . an everyday coat . . . $26.00. If this is the way things are selling, men must receive more wages. Miners have to pay $13.00 for board now. Everything is going up except wages and I think that they will go up soon. Some miners are making $50.00 per month."[30]

Most boys from mining families followed their fathers into the mines in easy stages, beginning usually at the breakers where slate and rock was picked out from among the coal by boys as young as 8 or 10. The little boys might make 35 cents a day. If all went well, and he did not die from an accident or the inhalation of dust, an adolescent might work his way through a series of jobs in the mines. At 12 he might become a trapper boy, opening and closing the underground mine-shaft doors to let the mule-drawn mine trucks go by, or he might run buckets back and forth between the work-face and the cars. Ultimately he would become a contract miner, or he might specialize as a powder monkey, a blaster, or a blaster's devil (assistant), working with long chisels, fuses, and black powder to blow out the seams from the work-face.

The work was grueling and dangerous; but, as one observer noted, "The miner is constantly exposed to danger; still . . . they do accustom themselves to the work that they would never work on the surface."[31] Another journalist described the tasks facing the hard-rock miner, "It was up to the miner to fire the shots, to use the most delicately exact skill in placing the (supporting) timber. The work required an alert mind and great physical strength . . . Sometimes erect, sometimes on his knees, sometimes on his side or back, the miner worked in an endless night, a soft black velvet darkness, with only the light of his miners lamp to see by." Injury and death threatened from many directions: a quick death from a sudden rock fall or a premature explosion; a slow death from carbon monoxide or methane; a hacking and coughing death while spitting up bloody coal dust from one's lungs. Deep mining made for poor ventilation, damp conditions from seep water, and, in deep mines, high underground temperatures.[32]

Schoolmaster Hobart noted how even simple tasks could prove deadly, "There was a sad accident in the mine today. A man coming up from the 120-fathom level [720 feet] in a shaft he was helping to sink; when he arrived at the 110-fathom level on the top of the ladder his hand missed the top round and he fell backwards to the bottom, a distance of seventy-five feet striking his head on the solid rocks. His skull was broke in pieces and he was brought up senseless and is still living though very little hopes are had for his recovery." The man died within three hours with his wife and three small children in attendance.[33] An old cemetery stone in coal country reads:

> Forty years I worked with pick and drill,
> Down in the mines against my will.

> The Coal King's slave but now it's passed,
> Thanks to God I am free at last.[34]

Safety was always a concern in the mines, but safety measures were few. The descending ladders were usually wet and sometimes frozen. Steam engines were harnessed to pump water from the mines and power-bellows were added for ventilation. "The pump extends down the shaft on one side for drawing the water out of the mine. It is a foot in diameter and goes to the bottom. On the other side of the shaft separated from the Pump and Main Ladder by a partition is the place where the Bucket draws up the copper and rock."[35] Hobart, who was fond of recording disasters both small and large, noted, "Mr. Phillips, driving the pumping engine, had his little finger taken off by putting it in a hole in the feed pump to remove some dirt when the plunger came down and took it off. It was a very careless trick, and he has lost his finger by doing so." Hobart also noted, "Two miners got into a quarrel about a hammer underground and one struck the other a heavy blow on the head with the hammer breaking his hat cap [a hard hat] and a piece of it cut his head severely. The other is now in jail. A hat cap will stand a heavy blow before it will injure the head and I suppose he struck as if he was striking a drill. They are to have a law suit about the affair." Not all the dangers that Hobart recorded were underground. "All of the buildings at the Amygdaloid Mine except the store were burnt the other day. It was very windy and the fire caught from the bush and all the men in the mine could not control it. The place was all in ashes in less than three hours."[36]

One of the greatest feats of mine engineering during the period was that of Adolf Sutro, who began a tunnel 3.8 miles long to drain water by gravity from the Savage Mine in California. The project, originally resisted by banking and railroad forces, was spurred forward by the disastrous Yellow Jack Mine fire of 1869 that killed scores of miners. Sutro argued successfully that given the money and permission to build the tunnel, not only could he drain water from the mine, but also ventilate it and provided an emergency exit. The tunnel, completed in 1878, was found to be higher than the work-face (which had been dug lower during nearly 10 years of construction), but it did provide a smaller lift through which to pump the 150+ degree water.

When a mining community formed, one of the necessities of life became sufficient drinking water for the population. Rich ore deposits and pure drinking water were not always available together, and mine water with its dissolved heavy metals was unhealthy or even poisonous. Hermann Schussler, formerly Chief Hydraulic Engineer for the growing city of San Francisco, formulated a method of moving clear mountain water from Marlette Lake high in the Sierra Nevadas to Virginia City. The pipe, which Schussler envisioned as early as 1864 and others rejected as impractical, had to handle a perpendicular drop of 1,720 feet from the mountains with an end-point pressure of more than 800 pounds per square inch. This required a thick-walled rolled iron pipe ($^5/_{16}$ inch of metal) to withstand bursting under the pressure. On the east-west run of the pipe, Schussler progressively decreased the thickness of metal down to $^1/_{16}$ inch, thereby increasing the capacity and rate of flow of the pipe while decreasing the internal pressure. When completed in 1873 the pipe could deliver more than 2 million gallons of pure mountain water every day. Two more pipes were installed in 1875 and 1887, respectively. Virginia City still uses drinking water from these pipes.[37]

Breaking mineral wealth from the working face of Nature's outcrops or from the seams underground was tiring and difficult. Accomplished by the application of miner's picks, chisels, sledge hammers, and explosions, there was, nonetheless, little room for a full-fledged swing and tons of waste rock needed to be moved to create working space. The introduction of pneumatic drills that could work at almost any angle was initially viewed as a great labor-saving device that promised to increase the miners' productivity and wages. However, the dry dust produced by the drill quickly filled the air and accumulated in the lungs, causing a serious medical crisis among the workers called silicosis. The introduction of a wet-driller that took waste dust from the drill-hole in a stream of water relieved the problem somewhat.

Sudden failure of a rock wall or ceiling was a dreaded threat, and a new type of timber framing was conceived in the mines of Nevada to replace the inevitably weak post-and-beam bracing then used to prevent collapse. Philip Deidesheimer, a German mining engineer working in America, devised a bracing method that utilized square sets of timbers arranged in cubes. The cubes of four, five, or six feet per side provided shoring in all directions, not just from above, and they could be stacked vertically or added to horizontally to follow the mineral seams. Miners could walk to the work-face and ore could be tracked back through the cubes. The open sides allowed for lateral tunnels and elevators. The system increased safety many-fold, but it required a remarkable amount of timber to complete. Whole mountainsides were denuded to provide the bracing for a single local mine. For the good of all miners, Deidesheimer refused to patent his innovation.

Gold Gold and silver mining were the king and queen of the extraction trades, and the series of precious metal strikes between 1848 and 1880 underwrote the nation during the many economic panics of mid-century. They also brought the first permanent settlers to much of the Far West; provided a rationale for the Pony Express and the extension of the telegraph; and made financial support for the transcontinental railways possible. "Each new discovery was followed by an inevitable rush—into Nevada and Arizona; over the Inland Empire of Washington, Idaho, Montana; to the Pike's Peak country and out over the sprawling Rocky Mountains;

and into the Black Hills of South Dakota." Moreover, wherever the miners went, the shopkeepers, traders, lawyers, ministers, saloon operators, gamblers, prostitutes, and all the other appurtenances of civilization followed. The infusion of precious metals into a cash-starved economy helped to lift it out of depression by spurring consumerism and propping up under-capitalized financial institutions.[38]

Under the influence of the gold coming from California in 1849 and 1850, for instance, the economy regained much of the prosperity lost in the prolonged depression following 1837. The economy again experienced minor downturns in 1854 and 1858, but silver and gold discovered in the Washoe area of the Sierra Nevadas in 1859 (known as the Comstock Lode or Nevada Bonanza) relieved the distress somewhat. Development and exploitation of existing mines was particularly important during the Civil War years as both North and South tried to fill their war chests by mining precious metals. Most post-war strikes were in silver instead of gold, and copper and lead mining came into prominence to answer the needs of the military for bullets and brass cartridge casings. Thereafter the region from the eastern Rockies to the Pacific remained an ever-promising but elusive attraction for prospectors seeking additional discoveries. The discovery of gold in the Black Hills in 1874, sparked in part by the assurances of George Armstrong Custer, began a rush of miners to the Dakotas; provoked an Indian war on the Great Plains; and promised to relieve the effects of the Panic of 1873. Overall the discovery of precious metals—California gold in '49, Colorado gold and Nevada silver in '59, and Dakota gold in '74—all tended to shake the economy out of its periodic malaise. Gold was also discovered in the Klondike in 1896, but it was very low grade requiring massive amounts of ore to make it profitable to mine.[39]

The flow of precious metals to the financial and banking centers of the East stimulated the business of the entire country. Gateway ports and towns were overwhelmed by word of a nearby precious metals strike. "There were not enough wagons or mules to keep the stampede moving. The hills above town [Virginia City] were piled high with boxes of merchandise while their owners vainly offered fantastic freight fees for hauling them. . . . Stagecoaches and mule trains were booked up days in advance, streets and hotels, saloons and restaurants, were thronged with a noisy crowd of expectant millionaires."[40]

Yet no gold strike was as effective in sparking the economy as the first rush in 1849. Since the big strike at Sutter's Mill in California, prospectors had focused on looking almost solely for gold, which might turn a profit of $1,000 per ton of ore. The breathless spirit of the California mines marched from golden strike to golden strike, and those who hiked or rode along the rutted trails to the mining camps were often forced to jump out of the way to avoid being run down by freight wagons or mule trains. Many of the young miners of the 1874 rush, as yet unborn or in diapers in 1849, proclaimed that it was "Forty-Nine all over again." Some miners were so mesmerized by the yellow metal that they unknowingly discarded waste materials containing other valuable but less obvious metals like silver, platinum, copper, chromium, lead, and zinc. These sometimes assayed out at up to three times the value of the gold that had been extracted.[41]

In the gold fields a fortunate man could lay up in a month more from even a modest claim than he could accumulate in an entire year elsewhere. During the "rush" years California alone may have produced upward of $200 million worth of gold. In 1852 alone $81 million was taken from the ground and rivers. This was to be the greatest year of the American mining frontier during the 19th century. There were few men that made significant fortunes, and many were fated to return home penniless. Others continued the quest moving from rush to rush and strike to strike.[42]

The people who participated in the rushes—miners, businessmen, traders, and gamblers—were generally below middle age both because the venture appealed to younger men and because the arduous life of the gold fields could be endured by no others. The labor was physically hard, the weather and environment unremitting, and the diet unbalanced or even unhealthy. The mining camps were notorious for outbreaks of dysentery, diarrhea, scurvy, typhoid, and fevers. Violence was the primary outcome of most disagreements. Other than prostitutes, there were very few women in the camps. In their freedom from the remonstrance of mothers, wives, sisters, and sweethearts, the miners let their appearance deteriorate into a stereotypical form that has come to describe all miners in the period. "An unkempt beard and long hair, weather beaten face, flannel shirts, shapeless pants, high boots, an old hat, perhaps an old coat that had seen its last service . . . in the Mexican War." A pair of blankets, a firearm, knife, mining tools, and cooking utensils usually filled out their kit.[43]

Gold strikes often proved more beneficial to industrial miners than to the individual dust-panners and nugget-pickers who stampeded after every golden find. Benjamin W. Ryan, age 38, left Illinois and his wife and family in 1864 for the gold fields in Montana. He kept a detailed journal of his trip and the man-days and profits from working a claim with his partners. In one case, eight men ran the sluices all day for only $11. On another day they took out $66. The following Sunday Ryan received 100 for a whole week's work. On their best day seven men took out $178, but the small pay-offs outnumbered the large ones. Ryan could have made at least $5 a day working in a factory, and after a year in the goldfields he admitted that he "had not noticeably improved his condition by daring the perils of the wilderness and fighting Indians."[44]

Ryan's experience was not atypical of most men who entered the goldfields with shovel in hand. Certainly some men became millionaires overnight, and others made their money by selling liquor, food, entertainment,

Gold rushers were an uncouth lot armed with shovels, picks, and cradle-like rocker sluices for separating the gold from the gravel and dirt.

and mining supplies at exorbitant prices. The Montana strike of 1864, like many other finds, never produced the level of wealth of the strike in California in 1849. A favorite song of "Banjo Dick" Brown, a popular entertainer in the mining towns of the West summed up the national fascination with gold:

> For my heart is filled with grief and woe,
> And oft I do repine,
> For the days of old,
> The days of gold,
> The days of Forty-Nine.[45]

Gold Mining   Placer mining is an open form of mining that requires no tunneling. It can be used to extract many metals, but it is most closely associated with gold mining. Excavation is usually accomplished by the application of water to mineral-rich gravel and sand-bank alluvial deposits that represent old or ancient stream beds. The name derives from the Spanish word, *placer,* meaning sand bank. The deposits were usually too loose to safely tunnel into, and the metal, having been deposited by moving water over centuries, was usually some distance from the parent vein and in very small quantities.

The simplest form of placer mining was nugget picking. Active streambeds often uncover nuggets, grains, flakes, or ribbons of pure metal (native metal) that can be picked up with the fingers or scooped up in a shovel. The initial discovery of gold in California in 1848 by James Marshall was accomplished in this manner when a nugget of gold was discovered in a mill-race at Coloma. Nonetheless, large pieces of pure copper and iron pyrite (fool's gold) could also be collected in this way. Other metals rarely formed in pure native deposits. American Indians had used this method to collect metal for use in decorations and jewelry for generations.

Panning was a slightly more sophisticated form of placer mining. Some of the sediment was placed in a large pan with water and agitated so that the silica and debris overflowed the side. The heavier metal, usually flakes or a fine dust of gold, remained in the bottom of the pan. Although the California Gold Rush of 1849 came to be most closely associated with panning, the same principle was more commonly employed using a sluice box made with barriers along the bottom to slow the movement of metal particles. Impelled by running water, the grains and flakes of metal were captured along the perpendicular edges of the barriers while the sand, mud, and other debris wash over them. The idea was not new. Ancient Greek miners were thought to have placed sheepskins in fast flowing steams where gold particles attached to the strands of wool in a similar manner, hence the stories of the Golden Fleece may have had a basis in fact.

Geological theory at the time suggested that metal concentrations should increase in density as the depth of the alluvial deposit increased. Miners often processed gravels from 50 to 100 feet below the waterline of nearby streams in order to recover a few ounces of gold. Working on this concept in 1853, Edward E. Mattson invented a hydraulic water cannon that used the power of pressurized water to power-wash gold bearing deposits of sand and gravel into giant sluices where the metal could be recovered. The water cannon required a rudimentary penstock (reservoir) of water with sufficient head to provide the pressure, and fabric hoses (much like fire hoses) were used to connect the two. Mattson used the cannon with great success to reclaim gold at Gold Run and the Malakoff Diggings in California. Unfortunately the process resulted in massive amounts of river siltation, and the dam caused extensive, if temporary, land flooding. In 1884, these water cannon were outlawed in California in one of the nation's first acts of environmental protection.

The romantic images that dominated 19th-century mining were almost always associated with the California Gold Rush of 1849–1852. Yet most of those men following the "rush" were dust panners, nugget pickers, or placer miners, not underground workers. In the incomplete census of 1850 two-thirds of the 30,000 who described themselves as miners in the California gold fields were Americans; but the Irish, French Canadian, Spanish American, and Chinese were all part of the gold rush workforce. Because of the nature of the mining claims, an almost universal antagonism and hostility were often the first things that greeted newcomers. Soon, however, those of like nationality or like ethnicity joined together to better work their claims, and they generally directed their antipathy toward other groups. Mexicans, Indians, and blacks were all popular targets of prejudice in the mining camps. When the Chinese began to arrive on the California coast in 1851 and 1852, the Irish Catholics, themselves targets of Nativist prejudice on the Atlantic seaboard, often sided against the Orientals and with the Nativist Americans, who would not have given them the time of day had they been in the East.[46]

A great number of the rush miners were "Westerners," those who had lived a majority of their lives on the lands drained by the Missouri, the Mississippi, or the Ohio Rivers. A surprisingly large number were from New England, New York, or Pennsylvania, some of the latter experienced hard-rock miners that had abandoned the coal works. A remarkably small number in proportion were self-identified as Southerners. Many "rushers" were former city dwellers, clerks, farm boys, and soldiers discharged after the Mexican War. So great was the allure of the goldfields that many sailors jumped ship after reaching California, leaving the harbor at San Francisco a forest of masts as the useless and undermanned clipper ships piled up in the bay.

Lumbering Early loggers and sawmill owners cut down forests with little thought for sustained timber production or for the future of the environment. Consequently, the over-harvesting of prime stands of trees caused the industry to move from region to region with a remarkable regularity during the century. First from New England to the Lake States Midwest, and then from the Midwest to the South. Though the Federal government sold land for as little as $1.25 an acre, and state and private lands sold for little more, many lumbermen simply stole the timber from the land, neither asking nor receiving permission to strip the forests of their produce. As time passed, however, the value of timber increased and the land owners and government agents became more vigilant. This made trespass relatively infrequent thereafter, and the buying and selling of timber rights became more common. The South sought to revitalize its industrial base somewhat after the Civil War through lumbering, but it allowed much of its forest land to come into the control of just a few individuals. Under legislation passed in the 1870s and 1880s more than 46 million acres of existing timber was controlled by less than 1,000 individuals. The South reached its peak of timber production in the 1920s, at which time the industry leadership moved to the Pacific Northwest.

Lumbering had flourished in the forests of New England since colonial times with fuel, building materials, flooring, planking, and ship's masts being the major commercial products. A large number of men found their living in the lumbering trades. These included axe men, sawyers, river drivers, teamsters, rafters, and sawmill operators. The census data from 1840, however, suggest that lumbering operations were very small, with mills seemingly operated by a single person or on a part-time basis by local farmers. There were 31,000 sawmills in the United States in 1840, but only 22,000 workers identified themselves as sawmill employees. This leaves historians with the impression that lumbering remained a facet of agriculture rather than a separate industry until the 1850s when data show a vast increase in the number of sawmills with 20 to 100 workers. A sideline of the timber trade was the production of oak staves and headings for watertight barrels for the beer and liquor industry. Spruce and hemlock were used to make cheap "dry-freight" barrels for shipping items like flour, China dishes, salt, shoes, nails, and fertilizer. Pitch and turpentine were also byproducts of the lumbering trade.

Both Maine and New Hampshire were particularly noted for their production of timber products during the colonial period. Maine supplanted its neighbor around 1810. New York took the lead in 1840, but the New England states as a group were still responsible for about 63 percent of all forest products produced in the United States up to mid-century when the timber stands of upper Midwest states like Wisconsin and Michigan began to come into production. J. M. Holley, writing a history of lumbering for the *La Crosse Wisconsin Chronicle* (1906), noted that in the 1830s no mention had yet been made of the great pine forests of the Midwestern Lake States. Holley concluded that it seemed "quite probable that at that time they had not attracted special attention."[47]

About 1800 some Southern states showed an ability to produce forest products. Georgia, the Carolinas, and later Alabama supplied excellent building materials such as cedar, yellow pine, and live oak, which grew in abundance. Yellow pine was particularly valuable as a flooring material. At the time Virginia and Maryland had more facilities for the production of naval stores than any combination of two Northern states that normally prided themselves on their production. Turpentine and pitch were manufactured in large quantities as a sideline to lumbering, especially in North Carolina where an entire industry flourished well into the 20th century.

Maine was particularly noted for the quantity of the hardwoods it possessed. Hardwoods such as elm and oak were particularly prized as shipbuilding materials. Yellow and white birch, beech, white and red oak, ash, and several types of maple were found in the forests of Maine. One observer noted that in 1854 between 50 and 100 loads of hardwoods passed through his village toward the Kennebeck River every week during the spring and summer.

Nonetheless, it was pine that was the prince of the forests and the most valuable commercial timber during the period of the Civil War. White, red (Norway), pitch, and Jack pines could grow in almost any soil, and because the evergreen trees cut off most of the light that reached the ground, they grew in huge groves of pure straight pine timbers. Tamarack pine was highly prized by shipbuilders for use as ship's knees and other structural parts because it was coarse and durable. The pine lumber industry initially produced mostly masts and spars for shipbuilding. Pine trees six to seven feet in diameter and 250 feet tall were reported to have grown in Maine. Huge masts 36 yards long and 36 inches in diameter were commonly floated down the rivers of Maine for both domestic use and for export to other maritime nations. Both Portland and Falmouth were noted for the production of masts. The advent of steam-powered navigation caused the masting industry to decline somewhat in the middle decades of the century. Yet in 1850 a single giant mast containing 6,500 board feet was hauled by 14 oxen into the town of Belfast where the remarkable specimen sold for $250.

Shifts in the availability of forest resources combined with changes in technology continually changed the face of the timber industry. Lack of conservation affected local industry. As pine production in the East declined, for instance, spruce and hemlock took its place as a commercial product. In 1850 spruce had supplanted pine in terms of the volume of logs removed from the forests of Maine for the first time. Hemlock, meanwhile, had gained a reputation for its use in the leather tanning industry, and from 1830 to 1840 the Washington County-Franklin County region of Maine became a center for the leather tanning industry. By 1880 only 20 percent of the lumber coming from Maine was pine.

After 1850 a pine lumber industry flourished in the north woods of the Great Lakes region. The Panic of 1857 caused a severe depression in the lumber trades, but their revival was a speedy one mainly because of the war. By 1870 the Lake States were in full timber production. A vast number of logs were removed from the north woods of Wisconsin through Chippewa Falls, Eau Claire, La Crosse, Black River Falls, and St. Croix. The industry that centered around Eau Claire, Wisconsin (for which there are good records), can serve as an example of the development of lumbering in general during the middle decades of the century.

Although a steam-powered chainsaw had been invented by P. P. Quimby in 1826, most trees were felled by ax and made into manageable lengths with cross-cut saws during the late fall and early winter. They were dragged over the snow by draft horses to the banks of local rivers and streams where they were stacked on roll-a-ways parallel to the flow. The logging roads to the riverbanks could be five or six miles long, and it was not uncommon for loggers to build long water-carrying flumes that moved the logs while bypassing the logging roads. By the 1880s small logging railroads had begun to appear with their small but powerful "donkey" steam engines.

Upon the arrival of the spring flood, the supporting stakes on the roll-a-ways were undermined, releasing the logs into the water. Using poles and pikes the lumbermen (known as drivers), riding in boats or on the logs themselves, would attempt to keep the timbers aligned and moving freely in midstream. In 1858 Joseph Peavey, a Maine blacksmith, patented an improved long-handled pike for controlling logs (known even today as a Peavey). Log jams often developed, however, and some of them were several miles long. The drivers attempted in these cases to find the "key" logs that had caused the jam and remove them. This was dangerous work that sometimes required the drivers to stand in waist-deep water where, if they were hit by a moving log, they could be killed or drowned. Occasionally explosives were used to free the jam.

The logs were usually made into dimensional lumber at local sawmills. Wate-powered single-blade reciprocal saws (up and down motion) had been in use since colonial times. These had largely been replaced by rotary circular saws in the 1850s, and by more efficient band saws thereafter. Band saws created much less sawdust and friction than other types. Gang-saws with more than one blade acting at the same time allowed one log to be cut into many boards in a single pass. The first steam-powered sawmill was open in the shipbuilding town of Bath, Maine, in 1821. This began a shift to power mill-work of many kinds. In 1826 Oliver Goddard introduced a shingle-making machine, and in the same year, Job White invented a machine for cutting a continuous veneer from a single tree (like paper on a roll). By 1860 there were more than 50 such establishments for power sawing and wood-milling in Maine alone.

From the sawmills the rough-cut green lumber was made up into rafts approximately 16 by 32 feet, with a depth of about 18 inches. These could be fastened together and floated or towed down river. Using oars for steering the rafters helped to guide the rafts in the channel. A bow boat, a small boat placed across the bow of the raft at right angles to the current, allowed the raft to be pushed to starboard or port as the steamer might require to make turns in the river. The rafters cooked and ate on the rafts using a small cook stove and tent erected for the purpose. In 1839 Henry Merrill was the first to successfully raft lumber from Portage, Wisconsin, to St. Louis. At one time "upwards of 100 men and boys were employed" in this work on the Upper Missouri River. By the 1870s, however, most lumber was shipped directly from the sawmills to market by railroad.[48]

Much of the lumber harvested in the United States was used domestically, but there was a significant export business. Maine was responsible for three-quarters of this trade. Lumber was shipping from Northern American ports to the South as part of the coastwise trade, and also to the West Indies where it was exchanged for gold, molasses, and rum. Cuba alone imported 40 million board feet of lumber annually in mid-century, an amount approximately equal to all the lumber used in the city of Boston.

Wood as Fuel   Hardwoods were preferred for fuel because they burned hotter, produced less creosote, and could be made more easily into charcoal for use by founders and blacksmiths than resinous woods. River steamers everywhere favored wood as a source of fuel, and they could be seen periodically nosing up to great piles of firewood left on the riverbank by local landowners to take on fuel. The landowners would also sign contracts to supply fuel along the railroad right-of-way. Without exception every Southern locomotive burned wood as a fuel in the antebellum period. Northern railroads were much more likely to switch to coal. Invariably, behind the engine came the tender, which held as much as 1,000 gallons of fresh water and had space for firewood. The large smokestacks on period engines were needed to divert wood smoke and produce a draft large enough to maintain a satisfactory head of steam. Cordwood was stacked at intervals along every line, and the best and cleanest-burning firewood was reserved for passenger traffic. A cord of wood was a stack 4 feet by 4 feet by 8 feet. Depending on the engine, load, and topography an engine averaged between 50 and 60 miles per cord of wood, requiring long delays every few hours to reload the tender.

Summary

Since colonial times the work ethic had commanded the communities of America. Work was worship, and labor was holy. In the culture war between the North and the South of the first half of the 19th century, the traditions of the South had been set aside. In the culture war between the industrialists and the farmers in the second half-century, the farmers and their beliefs had seemingly also been set aside. Farmers could never produce enough wealth to match industrialists, railroad magnates, or white-collar workers, but they rarely asked for assistance as did other groups among the city dwellers.

Southerners generally feared the development of the unprecedented "work for wage" economy of the cities and factories, and they saw Northern wage earners as degraded and enslaved persons. The city worker sold himself into economic bondage for a wage, and the expansion of a similar "work for wage" system was dreaded by Southerners almost as much as abolitionists dreaded the expansion of slavery. Southern whites were clearly anxious to maintain their status as freemen, and many in the laboring class believed that the North was determined to enslave them to the factory system or counting house. For this reason among others many lower- and middle-class Southerners, who owned no slaves and desired to own none, made common bond with the slaveowning aristocracy during the culture war of the antebellum period and on the battlefield of civil conflict.

By the 1890s the big businessmen and manufacturers had overthrown the farmers from their position of esteem in the national culture. The business of America seemed to be business, and the farmers were forced to view the world in terms of cash and to deal in it in terms of money instead of barter. They too ultimately accepted the money ethic, but it never really fit in with a rural setting. When one looks at the breakdown of "red" and "blue" states in recent national elections, one might conclude that maybe it still doesn't.

Notes

1. The 10 states with more than 5 percent manufacturing workers in 1850 were Massachusetts, Rhode Island, Connecticut, New York, Pennsylvania, New Jersey, New Hampshire, Maine, Delaware, and Maryland.

2. Harold S. Wilson, *Confederate Industry, Manufactures and Quartermasters in the Civil War* (Jackson: University Press of Mississippi, 2002), ix.

3. See James M. Volo and Dorothy Denneen Volo *The Antebellum Period* (Westport, CT: Greenwood Publishing Group, 2004), 58–59.

4. Daniel E. Sutherland, *The Expansion of Everyday Life, 1860–1876* (Fayetteville: University of Arkansas Press, 2000), 149.

5. Royal B. Stratton, *Captivity of the Oatman Girls* (New York: Carlton & Porter, 1857), 27–28.

6. J. Clinton Ransom, *The Successful Man in His Manifold Relations with Life* (New York: J. A. Hill & Co., 1889), 315.

7. Richard A. Easterlin, George Alter, and Gretchen A. Condran, "Farms and Farm Families in Old and New Areas: The Northern States in 1860," in Tamara K. Hareven and Maris A. Vinovskis, ed., *Family and Population in Nineteenth Century America* (Princeton, N.J.: Princeton University Press, 1978), 24–25. The states sampled included New Hampshire, Vermont, Connecticut, New York, New Jersey, Pennsylvania, Maryland, Ohio, Indiana, Illinois, Michigan, Wisconsin, Minnesota, Iowa, Missouri, and Kansas. The New England states of Rhode Island, Massachusetts, and Maine were not part of the sample.

8. Ibid., 28.

9. Ibid., 30–31.

10. Ibid., 58.

11. Ibid., 59.

12. Annette Atkins, *Harvest of Grief: Grasshopper Plagues and Public Assistance in Minnesota, 1873–1878* (St. Paul: Minnesota Historical Society Press, 1984), 26.

13. Ibid., 4.

14. Ibid., 30–31.

15. Ibid.

16. Ibid., 38–39.

17. Ibid., 33–34.

18. Ibid., 39.

19. Ibid., 41–42.

20. John Tosh, "New Men? The Bourgeois Cult of Home," *History Today* (December 1996): 9–15.

21. Unsigned article attributed to the editor, "The Pacific Railroad," *The Republican*, December 10, 1852, 2.

22. Carroll C. Calkins, ed., *The Story of America* (Pleasantville, N.Y.: Reader's Digest Association, 1975), 280.

23. Ibid.

24. One of the first targets of the Confederate army in 1861 was the federal arsenal at Harper's Ferry, Virginia, with its inventory of arms and its two

complete sets of precision rifle-making machinery, which were captured and removed to Richmond.

25. Michael Blow, "Professor Henry and His Philosophical Toys," *American Heritage* 15, no. 1 (December 1963): 104–105.

26. James Truslow Adams, ed., *Album of American History,* vol. 3 (New York: Charles Scribner's Sons, 1946), 307.

27. Ibid.

28. Mitchell Wilson, *American Science and Invention: A Pictorial History* (New York: Simon & Schuster, 1954), 106.

29. Robert L. Reynolds, "The Coal Kings Come to Judgment," *American Heritage* 11, no. 3 (April 1960): 58.

30. Philip P. Mason, ed., *Copper Country Journal: The Diary of Schoolmaster Henry Hobart, 1863–1864* (Detroit: Wayne State University Press, 1991), 146.

31. Ibid.,171.

32. Reynolds, "Coal Kings," 57.

33. Mason, *Copper Country Journal,* 171.

34. Reynolds, "Coal Kings," 56.

35. Mason, *Copper Country Journal,* 82.

36. Ibid., 163.

37. See Douglas McDonald, *Virginia City and the Silver Region of the Comstock Lode* (Carson City: Nevada Publications, 1982).

38. Rodman Wilson Paul, *Mining Frontiers of the Far West, 1848–1880* (Albuquerque: University of New Mexico Press, 1963), viii.

39. Sutherland, *Expansion of Everyday Life,* 149.

40. Remi Nadeau, "Go It, Washoe!," *American Heritage* 10, no. 3 (April 1959): 37.

41. Ibid.

42. Paul, *Mining Frontiers,* 26–27.

43. Ibid., 26.

44. Dorothy M. Johnson, *The Bloody Bozeman* (New York: McGraw-Hill Book Co., 1971), 133–134.

45. Paul, *Mining Frontiers,* 179.

46. Ibid., 25.

47. J. M. Holley, "History of the Lumber Industry," *La Crosse Wisconsin Chronicle,* October 21, 1906, 52.

48. Ibid., 55.

6

Faith of Thy Fathers

About three thousand people appeared on the ground, and the rejoicing of old saints, the shouts of the young converts, and the cries of the distressed for mercy, caused the meeting to continue all night.
—Lorenzo Dow, circuit-riding preacher

Father's Role in Religion

During the 19th century religious intolerance often colored the functioning of government as well as the social, economic, and cultural order of America. During the colonial period religious hostilities had dominated much of the thinking and politics of Americans. Much of the emotionalism of the religious and theological controversies raised by the Protestant Reformation had been transplanted to America, and many Protestants retained antipathetic feelings toward other sects and toward Catholics of all nationalities. In the 19th century Americans were still overwhelmingly Protestant, but the majority of these Protestants belonged to the many evangelical denominations that served different segments of the American population.[1]

Irish-Catholic immigrants, in particular, experienced severe prejudice at the hands of the Protestant majority, but as the century progressed beyond the Civil War, the Irish gained some standing in the community. Nonetheless, Roman Catholicism remained "an evil fiercely to be hated, deeply to be feared, and unremittingly to be fought."[2] Incredibly poor, the Irish were the first truly urban population in American history. They were largely confined to the poorest areas of the cities, and lived in slums and tenements without any reasonable expectations of gainful employment or advancement. Yet the Irish were not the sole target of religious intolerance.

Although numbering a mere fraction of the Irish, the adherents of the Church of Jesus Christ of Latter Day Saints, better know as the Mormons, may have been the most persecuted religious sect in 19th-century America. The Mormon sect had its roots firmly planted in American Protestantism, yet its adherents were chased from state to state and territory to territory, burned out, shot down, arrested, and hanged. The hatred was ostensibly based on the Mormon adherence to polygamy, but there is good evidence that the economic and political power of the Mormons was greatly feared. The Mormons finally set down roots in Salt Lake, from which base they ruled the region known as Utah with an iron hand until the end of the century.

Religious Revival

The United States has been a predominantly religious country from its inception, and the antebellum period was one of great religious revival fueled largely by a Protestant crusade in the East, camp revivals in the settlements and on the frontiers, and a political backlash brought about by an immense influx of Irish Catholics into the cities of America. The religious character of the country was essentially rooted in the Protestantism of England, Scotland, and Wales, but many new sects had joined the list of traditional Christian religions popular before the Revolution. Europe was swept by great religious wars and moral awakenings during the colonial period that resulted in waves of religious zealots and exiles crossing the Atlantic. Spanish and French Catholics, Protestant Walloons and Huguenots, Dutch Calvinists, English Puritans, Quakers, Scotch-Irish Presbyterians, German Lutherans, Baptists, Anabaptists, and Moravians were all moved by much the same religious spirit. Yet religious bigotry influenced many largely well-meaning clergymen, both Catholic and Protestant, and encouraged intolerance among those who chose to do God's work.[3]

The First Great Awakening, a complex movement among a number of interrelated religious groups, swept through colonial America in the 18th century. Begun in the 1720s by Reverend Theodore J. Frelinghuysen, a Dutch Reform minister from New Jersey, this movement spread into New England to reach its peak in the 1740s under men like Jonathan Edwards. It continued through the American Revolution in several distinct phases led respectively by Presbyterians, Baptists, and Methodists. Everywhere the First Great Awakening stressed personal religion and effectively multiplied the number and variety of churches and congregations in America. An estimate of the number of religious congregations in the English colonies at the close of the colonial period has been made and gives a total of more than 3,100. While this number was almost equally divided among the three regions of New England, the Middle States, and the Carolinas, there was an unequal distribution among the different denominations, giving each region a distinct religious character.[4]

The Protestantism of New England had been essentially related to the Puritanism of the Congregational churches, while that from the South was generally Church of England (Anglican). Quakers, considered dissenters since colonial times, congregated mainly in Pennsylvania, while pockets of Catholicism could still be found in Maryland. The Scotch-Irish immigrants added an element of Presbyterianism to American religious life, and later the Baptist church became popular among the Welsh and Germans. The frontier digested a wide variety of these immigrants, and most were assimilated with little fuss into the American social fabric.

Yet not all of the religious sects of antebellum America were considered legitimate by society in general because many sects espoused doctrines that were obviously on the fringe of traditional Christian beliefs. Some Christian evangelical revivals, particularly those headed by incendiaries such as Rev. Charles G. Finney of western New York and Rev. Lyman Beecher of Boston, provoked less thoughtful followers of mainstream American Protestantism to take up the rhetoric of the anti-immigrant and anti-Catholic. They created and published salacious rumors and anecdotes that distorted the beliefs and activities of many of these minority religions. A number of these minority religions can be considered Pietist in nature because they generally abandoned a strict church structure and hierarchy. Shakers, Quakers, Moravians, Fourierists, Mennonites, Anabaptists, and other Pietist sects generally placed their emphasis upon inner spiritual life and a personal path to salvation, while denying the need for a more formal ecclesiastical organization.

Although Quakerism had been a major component of American religious life since colonial times, it was essentially a pacifist religion and its adherents were viewed with suspicion by many Americans. Moreover, the English-speaking Quakers, Shakers, and Fourierists were largely distinct from the Mennonites, Amish Anabaptists, and Moravians that had their origins in Germany, Switzerland, and other parts of central Europe. The Germans penetrated into the far northwestern portion of New Jersey and west into the region of Reading and Harrisburg, Pennsylvania. They tended to separate themselves from other groups, a process aided by their lack of the English language. Joshua Gilpin traveling through this region noted, "I never knew before the total want of a language for in this respect we might as well have been in the middle of Germany." Isolated in this manner, the Germans achieved a far greater social solidarity than any other group on the frontier.[5]

A Second Awakening

It was the Christian revival at the beginning of the 19th century, generally viewed as the Second Great Awakening, that most affected the religious life of American society before the Civil War. Many writers from the period have recorded an intense devotion to the spiritual part of their lives, and though they might sin with vigor, they repented and atoned with great enthusiasm. This religious revival drew its vitality from the Southern and Western frontiers rather than from New England. Beginning near the Gaspar River Church in Kentucky in July 1800, the spark of faith was ignited at camp meetings in the Midwest and was proclaimed throughout the nascent frontier settlements by an army of traveling evangelists and self-ordained preachers. Some ministers, having been brought up on "rigid Calvinism" and having been taught to preach "the doctrine of particular election and reprobation" in earlier years, revolted; and having no correct books on the new theology, "plunged into the opposite extreme, namely, universal redemption." This sort of evangelism, with its strong emotional appeal, spirit of optimism, and promise of unconditional salvation to all of mankind, was particularly influential among 19th-century Americans.[6]

Peter Cartwright, a contemporary observer of the process, noted, "Ministers of different denominations came in, and preached through the country: but Methodist preachers were the pioneer messengers of salvation in these ends of the earth. . . . A Methodist preacher in those days, when he felt that God had called him to preach, instead of hunting up a college or Biblical institute, hunted up a hardy pony, or a horse, and some traveling apparatus, and with his library always at hand, namely the Bible, Hymn Book, and Discipline, he started, and with a text that never wore out or grew stale, he cried, 'Behold the Lamb of God, that taketh away the sin of the world!' In this way he went through storms of wind, hail, snow and rain; climbed hills and mountains; traversed valleys; plunged through swamps; swam swollen streams; lay out all night, or tied to a limb slept with his saddle blanket for a bed, his saddle or saddle bags for his pillow, and his old big coat or blanket, if he had any, for covering."[7]

During the day nothing appeared unusual in the sprawling and smoke-filled revival camps with their scattering of white tents, knots of canvas-covered wagons, and bands of scurrying children and barking dogs. The occupants followed the same slow-paced routines of cooking, cleaning, and caring for the livestock found in other camps on the emigrant trails. However, nighttime drew the faithful together and transformed them into an army of God. With campfires blazing, a thunderous din of singing, and preachers beseeching the gathering to repent so that they might be saved from the fires of hell, the crowds reached a peak of religious frenzy. A circuit-riding preacher, Lorenzo Dow, described a typical camp meeting in his journal, "About three thousand people appeared on the ground, and the rejoicing of old saints, the shouts of the young converts, and the cries of the distressed for mercy, caused the meeting to continue all night." Many shook, jerked, and rolled on the ground until they fell away in a faint.[8]

Methodists and Baptists reaped a rich harvest of souls at this time. By the 1830s Methodism had become one of the two largest religions in the country, and the Baptists, in particular, had made great inroads into the black population, both free and slave. Under the influence of an evangelical spirit, most American Protestants came to believe that the path to salvation lay in placing themselves in a position to receive God's grace if they were worthy. This belief was to have a profound effect on Civil War soldiers, who strove to be worthy of God's protection by exhibiting courage and steadiness under fire.

The Second Great Awakening spread new religious sects like a wildfire. Campbellites, Shakers, Rappites, Fourierists, and other minor religions popular in the North espoused theories of associative communism and utopian socialism by making provisions for the correction of inequalities of temporal possessions among their members. Many members gave up all their wealth or placed it at the disposal of the congregation. Unitarians (the followers of which were largely devoted abolitionists), Universalists, and Disciples of Christ splintered away from established churches, while Mormons and Adventists sprang from the soil of America itself. Non-revivalist churches, especially in the more traditional South, trailed behind. Of 891 Unitarian and Universalist churches known to exist in 1850, only 23 existed below the Mason-Dixon Line.

Quakers

Quakerism, or the Society of Friends, was begun in 17th-century England by George Fox and Margaret Fell. The first adherents to the new sect—many of whom were of Welsh ancestry—were drawn largely from farmers who lived on the fringe of the cultural, economic, and social mainstream. Quakerism was a radical religion that attracted these generally independent people by preaching the virtues of the family as the basic disciplining and spiritualizing authority in society as opposed to that of magistrates and church prelates. Thanks, in part, to their devotion to the decentralization of authority, many Quakers devoted themselves to their religious duties by creating nearly autonomous personal households.[9] Everything in the Quaker household—wives, children, and business— was subjected to a familial order rooted in morality. The burden of producing, sustaining, and incorporating morality, civility, and economy into the household was taken on by the entire family and supported by the community at large. Outside authorities such as an intolerant established priesthood, an authoritarian upper class, or even a pedantic university system were considered "not only unnecessary but even pernicious."[10]

Although sparsely settled throughout much of the country, Quakers maintained a political influence in Pennsylvania that well outweighed their number. Their neat, well-tended farms, and social solidarity were among the characteristics that made the state one of the most prosperous in America. In applying their principles Quakers relied heavily upon a religious and spiritual form of human relations. They radically reorganized their church from one that required the performance of a series of external disciplines and the reception of a well-prepared sermon, as among many Protestant sects, into one in which the silent meeting and a personal conversion took precedence.[11]

The Quaker community also gave unprecedented moral authority within the household and within the congregation to women. They thereby radically changed the structure of the traditional household, especially in the areas of authority over child-rearing, courtship, and marriage. Women were encouraged to discuss and legislate on "women's matters" in specially designed women's meetings set up for the primary purpose of controlling courtship and marriage within the community.[12]

The basic unit of Quaker settlement was the family farm of about 250 to 300 acres—an initial size to which much was added with time. Family holdings were often widely dispersed, and Quaker farmers were accustomed to moving about on horseback or in wagons over the undulating and often flat countryside of southeastern Pennsylvania. Quaker fathers devoted a great deal of their energy to the accumulation of land that would be devolved onto their sons, or would otherwise benefit their daughters when they found husbands. The overwhelming majority of Quaker children married locally and tended to stay within the meeting house discipline. They thereby quickly found themselves related to one another in their local communities, not only by religion, but also by shared genetics. This web of kinship was partly responsible for the strong ties exhibited by a community of people who were otherwise defiantly anti-institutional.[13]

Moravians

The Moravians were among the least fanatical of the sects that came to America. With roots in the teachings of John Huss and John Wycliffe, the Moravians had become one of the most important Protestants groups in central Europe at the beginning of the 17th century. Nonetheless, they suffered decades of persecution in the Thirty Years' War (1618–1648), being hounded from their homes until only a few faithful families were left in the sect by the end of the century. Most of these took refuge in Saxony. From there they began to spread their faith to the West Indies, Africa, Asia, and America—particularly to the native populations of southeastern Pennsylvania, Delaware, and the backcountry of the colonial South. They dealt fairly with the Indians in terms of buying land and scrupulously adhered to their agreements. Moravian preachers and settlers thereby provided an important positive link between the early immigrants to America and the native population on the frontier.

The Moravians professed a common unity among all Christians, a goal that proved too high minded for most Americans who were dedicated to a more narrow field of Protestant doctrine. Although Moravian influences were more important in colonial times than in the antebellum period, their religious beliefs strongly influenced John Wesley, a leader in the evangelical movement and the founder of Methodism, one of the fastest-growing of 19th-century religions. Nonetheless, because Moravians refused to take oaths or to bear arms in times of war, they were viewed with a good deal of suspicion by the majority of other Protestants. Only their very small numbers and general isolation from other communities kept them from being the targets of prejudice and repression.[14]

Shakers

Founded in 1758 by Ann Lee, who styled herself as the Mother of the community, Shakerism was a celibate religious movement rooted in Protestantism. The religion is most noted for being founded by a woman, and there was a strand of early feminism that punctuated its doctrine and organization. Actually named the United Society of Believers in Christ's Second Coming, the religion took on the name of Shakerism because of the dancing and shaking that characterized some of its rituals. Shakerism was brought to America by Mother Ann Lee in 1774 and was most widely followed in New England. In the antebellum period it made great gains in membership in Ohio and Kentucky, as the Eastern congregations sent out colonies to the Midwest. Like many other groups that followed a sort of social Christian doctrine, the Shakers believed in communal living, productive labor, and a closed self-sustaining economy. "Without Money, Without Price" was one of their mottos. Shakers came to be known for a distinctive craftsmanship and folk art characterized by its utter simplicity and lack of ornamentation. They also printed, published, and widely distributed their own writings.

The religious doctrines of the Shaker community included a belief in the direct communication of some of its members with other celestial realms inhabited by Most High God, Holy Mother Wisdom, Lord Jesus Christ, Mother Ann, and a cast of Angels, Patriarchs, Prophets, Apostles, and Saints drawn from the Bible. Shakers practiced absolute celibacy, and suffered from the need to attract new adherents to their communities as there was no natural increase due to birth. By the 1850s this aspect of the religion caused a good deal of concern, as the number of young men entering the fold diminished to the point that many communities were almost solely composed of women and had to hire non-adherent male workers to perform heavy tasks such as plowing.

Fourierists

The followers of social architect Charles Fourier would be relatively unimportant except that they included a group of literary giants from

New England known as Transcendentalists, who practiced a form of Christian humanitarianism at Brook Farm in Massachusetts. These included Ralph Waldo Emerson, who wrote of the group's adherents, "in obedience to [their] most private being, [they] find [themselves], though against all sensuous probability, acting in strict concert with all others who follow their private life." As can be seen, Fourier's views were somewhat convoluted and difficult to grasp. The basic tenet of Fourierism was a crusade for social harmony. Fourier believed that the basic force that ruled all the aspects of social order, including passion, was attraction. Social harmony could be attained only by balancing all the possible attractions.

The religious aspects of Fourierism were essentially organized around the shared Protestant beliefs of its adherents, while the social aspects of the movement were dedicated to balancing individualism and ego with group membership and shared responsibility. Communal production was segregated into specific working groups with more than 40 discrete craft specializations that were ultimately assembled into larger series. The final products were meant to sustain a small, self-contained community. The New England group at Brook Farm sought to propagate the movement by buying a weekly column in Horace Greeley's *Daily Tribune* and by publishing their own work in *The Dial*. Nonetheless, the movement was largely unsuccessful in sustaining itself, falling heavily in debt because of the lack of expertise exhibited by its adherents, who were much better at crafting essays and poems than furniture and textiles.[15]

Mormons

Those who chose to follow the Mormon religion (Church of Jesus Christ of Latter Day Saints) may have been among the persons most vigorously persecuted for their religion in the antebellum period. Probably the most important fringe religion of the period, Mormonism was the great catch-all of the evangelical movements. Patriarchs, angels, and demons seemed to punctuate the semi-Biblical rituals of Mormon metaphysics. At one time or another every Protestant heresy in America was championed by one or the other of the spokesmen for the Latter Day Saints. Yet Mormons were generally courageous, dedicated, and hard-working people unfairly targeted by the more established religions.

The Mormon religion was founded in 1823 by Joseph Smith, who saw himself as a present-day biblical prophet. Smith based the religion on the Book of Mormon, a new scripture translated from golden plates originally written by a person named Mormon who had made his way to the North American Continent with others from Jerusalem. Here Mormon organized certain records that he and his fellows had brought with them from Israel and inscribed them on the plates before his death. The Latter Day Saints believed that Mormon's son, Moroni, hid the plates in the hills of Cumorah near Palmyra, Missouri, hundreds of years before the discovery of America. The Lord purportedly spoke directly to Joseph Smith revealing their contents. The resulting *Book of Mormon* restored all the ancient orders of the Bible—elders, teachers, apostles, enforcers, and deacons—and all the ancient rights, including baptism by immersion, and the sacraments. Other doctrines were added from modern-day revelation; but a return to polygamy (taking more than one wife at the same time) was the cause for which the Mormons were most often persecuted.

Brigham Young is more closely associated than Smith with the church leadership in the antebellum period. Young was a convert to Mormonism in 1832. Within months of his conversion, his first wife died, leaving him with two small daughters, and he quickly remarried for the sake of the children (he ultimately took 17 wives). Originally from New York state, he traveled the country trying to make converts, and he turned much of his energy to the work of his new religion. He moved to Kirtland, Ohio, at the urging of Joseph Smith who advised that all the "Saints" do so. Young brought a little knot of converts with him from New York and found that dozens of such groups were pouring into Kirtland. Here, in a form of religious socialism, a good part of the possessions of each newcomer was turned over to the church treasury for its support.

In 1834, Brigham Young was selected as one of the Twelve Apostles who stood next in line to the three-man presidency of the church headed by Smith. This group decided to move the church to Missouri in order to support their brethren who were suffering from burnings and beatings at the hands of the general population. Once in Missouri, Smith and some of his companions were arrested by the territorial governor, who officially warned the growing horde of Mormons to leave the state or face the ire of the territorial militia. Young, who had quite accidentally missed being apprehended, suddenly found himself the only major leader of the group with freedom of movement; but he was now solely responsible for almost 12,000 homeless and frightened people. He made arrangements to purchase land on the banks of the Mississippi River in Illinois in the name of the church, and he moved his charges there.

Meanwhile, Joseph Smith and his companions managed to escape jail in December 1839. Shortly thereafter they joined the Saints in Illinois. Here Smith unfolded his plan for Nauvoo, the "beautiful" city of the Saints, and began an impressive building project. However, many of the non-Mormon residents in Illinois became fearful of the large, well-equipped military force that the Mormons maintained for their own protection. They began to view Joseph Smith as a danger both economically and politically. In 1844 the Mormons decided to run Smith for the U.S. presidency. This decision led almost immediately to Joseph Smith's assassination at the hands of a mob in Carthage, Illinois; the abandonment of Nauvoo; and the removal of the Saints to Iowa. Brigham Young, braving the storm of internal church politics, reassumed the leadership of the Twelve Apostles and became church president in 1847. This series of events put practical control of the Mormon religion in his hands for the next three decades.

In 1848, having decided to leave the United States to escape further persecution, Young turned west to the great American desert. Having been persecuted in Ohio, Missouri, and Illinois, advanced parties of Mormons hurried into the Great Salt Lake Valley of Utah, leaving more than 13,000 refugees waiting in Iowa and Nebraska for the signal to move west. By 1849 Young's vision of a Mormon Empire in the West had taken root. Exactly two years after they had entered the valley, the Mormons had built a city with an irrigation system, established themselves across the Great Basin, and entered into treaties of peace with the local native population. Brigham Young successfully helped the Mormons to maintain their influence in the West until his death in 1877.

Slave Religion

The Africans, who were first brought to the Americas as slaves, came from diverse cultural and religious backgrounds. Upon arrival at a plantation, they found themselves intermingled with other blacks who held a wide range of beliefs and practiced a multiciplicity of religious rites. The desire to hold true to ancestral customs was a strong one, and some slaves would periodically steal away to neighboring farms to join with others from the same ethnic group. This diversity, however, produced an openness that transcended cultural differences with a common mystical relationship to the divine and the supernatural. African religious practices were marked by a communication with the natural world and a joyful expression of overt sexuality that shocked the generally prudish Protestant plantation owners. Lacking an understanding of the African culture and having no desire to cultivate one, slaveholders did their best to strip slaves of their native religious cultures. Effectively, however, these practices were merely driven underground to be practiced in secret.

By the close of the 18th century and as an outgrowth of the Great Awakening, many whites felt it was their duty to bring Christianity to the slaves. Protestantism leveled all men as sinners before God, regardless of wealth or color, and an intense commitment by evangelists and revivalists to black conversion was focused largely on the slave communities. The success of the undertaking was facilitated by a number of factors. Generally, the slave community was open to this religious movement. Second-, third-, and even fourth-generation slaves had fewer cultural and linguistic barriers to Christian instruction than their forbearers. The emotionalism, congregational response, and plain doctrine of revivalist preaching proved favorable to welldisposed African Americans, and it resonated somewhat with their religious heritage. Remnants of African dance and song found a home in the spirituals of evangelical Protestantism. Finally, black freemen generally abandoned their former religious practices in favor of Christianity in order to be less conspicuous within the white community.

The egalitarian perspective of this religious movement opened the way for black converts to participate actively in churches as preachers and even as founders of their own congregations. Slaves had the freedom to attend church with their owners (although discretely seated in the rear or among the rafters), but in some instances, they were allowed to worship at independent black churches. Even so, the majority of slaves who had the opportunity to become church members in the first decades of the 19th century were household servants, artisans, and urban residents rather than field hands.

By the 1830s evangelical churchmen had become increasingly committed to the idea of an aggressive program of plantation missions in order to bring Christianity to rural slaves. Planters were generally amenable to the concept of slave conversion in a theological sense, although two slave revolts led by black preachers Denmark Vesey and Nat Turner found validation for their cause in scripture. These uprisings produced huge setbacks in any latitude afforded slaves regarding their religion. Planters were expected to join missionary societies and to support local churches with money for the plantation missionaries. Proponents of the cause adopted the techniques of Northern bible and temperance societies to raise Southern consciousness by printing sermons and essays, adopting resolutions, and devoting entire conferences to the topic. However, the distance between plantations made ordinary pastoral care almost impossible.

Southerner slaveowners began to see that scripture could be used to sanction a kind of Christian social order based on mutual duty of slave to master and master to slave as found in Ephesians 6:5–9. The ideal of a Christian master-slave relationship fed the Southern myth of the benevolent planter-patriarch who oversaw the simple, helpless black. As the decades advanced, growing uneasiness toward Northern abolitionists created an ambivalence in Southerners regarding the instruction of slaves in Christianity. However, the criticism of Northern churchmen made Southerners more sensitive to their duty, and the supporters of plantation missions continued to remind slaveholders of their religious duties toward their blacks. Plantation mistresses in particular were urged to take an active role in slave instruction by reading sermons to them, including them in family prayers, and conducting Sabbath schools. Some household slaves were led in prayer each morning by the mistress.

By the eve of the Civil War it was not unusual for slaves to outnumber whites at racially mixed churches. This manifestation of the plantation missionaries' success was misleading, however, because it represented only one component of the slaves' religious experience. In the secrecy of their cabins and amid brush or "hush arbors," slaves met free from the owner's gaze and practiced a religion that addressed many issues other than a slave's Biblical subservience to his master. Absolute freedom was often the subject of their prayer. Through prayer, song, and "feeling the spirit," slaves gained renewed strength through hope. These informal prayer meetings were filled with spirituals that perpetuated a continuity with African music and performance. The drums, which had once been a vital part of African spiritual expression, were replaced by rhythmic hand clapping and foot-stomping known as "shouting." Rather than truly adopting Christianity, the slaves had adapted it to themselves.

Generally, slaves faced severe punishment if they were found attending non-sanctioned prayer meetings. Gathering in deep woods, gullies, and other secluded places, they created makeshift rooms of quilts and blankets that had been wetted down to inhibit the transmission of voices. A common practice was to place an iron pot or kettle turned upside down in the middle of the floor to catch the sound. The roots or symbolism of this belief have been lost. On occasion, rags would be stuffed into the mouth of an overzealous worshiper. Slave narratives repeatedly speak to the uplifting nature of these meetings.

An underground culture of voodoo, magic, and conjuring were practiced in areas where there were large numbers of slaves from the islands of the Caribbean or where African snake cults—which handled serpents as part of their ritual—had been imported and adapted. It would be a mistake to believe that the majority of slaves followed voodoo. That was more characteristic of those from Haiti and other West Indian Islands. However, many slaves exhibited a respectful attitude toward occult practices in general. Newly imported slaves from Africa brought with them a periodic infusion of non-Christian religious practices and mystical beliefs that kept the echoes of an older naturalistic religion alive. Nonetheless, the power of the voodoo priests and other conjurers never reached the level it had enjoyed in the islands or in Africa.

The Quaker religion openly welcomed black and Native American worshipers. While the Catholics had minority representation in their churches in the North, they were able to maintain their position in the South only by making concessions to the etiquette of white supremacy. Separate black congregations also grew in number among many Protestant sects because the white congregations of their several denominations did not welcome them. A growing army of black ministers was, thereby, able to found parishes among the freemen and slaves of the South. The African Methodist Episcopal (A.M.E.) churches had some of the most prominent black ministers of the period.

Judaism

Jews made up only a small proportion of the American population before the late 19th century. However, Sephardic Jews, those whose ancestry lay in the Iberian Peninsula, had significant communities in both New York and Louisiana. The practice of Judaism in New York was almost as old as the colony itself, and at least one Jewish congregation was active in New Amsterdam under Dutch rule during the 17th century. In 1845, an economic depression caused many European Jews, especially those of German descent, to immigrate to America. They brought an early form of Reform Judaism with them. In their synagogues, they innovated the ritual, used German, English, and Hebrew in their services, and allowed men and women to be seated together. Nonetheless, most still observed the traditional laws in their homes, and read and spoke the Torah in Hebrew only. The lack of intermarriage between the German- and Russian-speaking newcomers to America and the more established Sephardic Jews tended to keep the communities apart. There were about three dozen recognized synagogues in the United States in 1850. In the next decade this number more than doubled as new congregations formed mainly in California or in growing urban areas. Apparently because of their small number, Jews experienced little overt anti-Semitism in the antebellum period, and a significant number of individuals played important roles in the coming war as military commanders or as government officials.

Catholics

Added to the confusion caused by a myriad of immigrants entering America's cities was the fact that many of the poorest and least educated were Catholic. In the 1830s the Roman Catholic Church was possibly the only religion in America not divided over doctrine. The Roman Church was intolerant of criticism, unapologetically authoritarian, resolute, and unalterable in its structure. It was the oldest and best-organized religion in the Western world, and it demanded the unquestioned obedience of its members to the will of the Pope. A "Protestant Crusade" to stem the growing influence of the Catholics began in the 1820s and increased in proportion to Catholic immigration, which grew most precipitously in the 1840s and 1850s with the flood of Irish immigration. The Nativist movement, truly reactionary and discriminatory in its nature, was rooted in a traditional abhorrence of authoritarian Roman papism, and it focused largely on the mass of Irish Catholic immigrants who were filling the Northern cities.

Among the texts circulating through the bookstores and publishing houses of America were a number of anti-Catholic works, including "escaped nun" publications. The ostensible theme of this genre was the immorality of the Catholic Church and its institutions. While in the guise of being uplifting and informative, these stories actually served as a sort of pornographic literature. The most successful of the so-called escaped-nun stories was Maria Monk's *Awful Discourses of the Hotel Dieu Nunnery of Montreal* that was first published in 1834. Herein Maria detailed her stay in the Ursuline convent and charged that she saw holy sisters killed for failing to surrender their bodies to the lusts of the priests. Having been ravished in this manner herself, she claimed to be pregnant. Maria also detailed the hiding places of the bodies of the babies born to the inmates of the convent and killed to keep the awful secret of Catholic lust and degeneration. The book, conveniently interspersed with the intimate details of this sexual activity, claimed that the Roman Church actively promoted the "prostitution of female virtue and liberty under the garb of holy religion."[16]

Maria Monk's tale was as false as the author herself. She was almost immediately unmasked as a prostitute of long standing who had never seen the inside of a convent. Unscrupulous publicists and radical crusaders continued to use the work with reckless abandon, however. A mob of about 50 workmen, incensed in part by the book, took it upon themselves to burn the Mount Benedict Ursuline Convent-School in Charlestown near Boston in 1834. Irish Catholic homes were burned, and a number of Irish men were attacked in the streets. In 1844 a similar incident took place in Philadelphia where two Catholic churches and 30 homes were burned. Protestant crusaders clashed with Irish Catholic bands, leaving more than a dozen dead and scores injured. Maria's book, more popular than most slave narratives and anti-slavery tracts, sold more than 300,000 copies before the Civil War, a volume of sales rivaled at the time only by Harriet Beecher Stowe's *Uncle Tom's Cabin*. It was trotted out again by anti-Catholic forces in 1928 when Alfred E. Smith, a Catholic, ran for president of the United States.[17]

The Catholic archbishop of New York, John Hughes, took an unquestionably militant stand in defense of his church. He rallied the largely Irish Catholic population of the city in defense of Catholic institutions, and surrounded churches, convents, and schools with armed guards after his house was attacked by anti-Catholic, anti-Irish rioters. Hughes also fought to have anti-Catholic books and the King James version of the Bible banned from the public schools. Catholic radicals burned a great number of Protestant Bibles that came into their possession. Hughes undertook a series of lectures in which he predicted the inevitable victory of Catholicism over the Protestant heresy. Ironically, this very early separation of church and state crusade, led by a priest, clearly sharpened the dispute and helped to swell the ranks of the Nativist, or Know Nothing, political party in the 1840s and 1850s, which used anti-Catholicism and the evils of Popery as foundation stones of their all-American rhetoric.

A number of parochial schools were operated under Catholic auspices in the 17th and 18th centuries, but large-scale development took place in the 19th century. In both 1829 and 1854 the ecclesiastical council of Baltimore promulgated the establishment of a system of Catholic schools. These began as parish elementary schools and developed into a system of high schools. The leading figure in Catholic education was Bishop John L. Spaulding, who emphasized the Americanization of Catholic educational thought and also recommended a denominational public school system.

Religious revival led to the establishment of Sunday Schools as a means of teaching the rudimentary principles of education to working children during their free time on the Sabbath. The idea is generally attributed to an Englishman, Robert Raikes, and it was promoted by Methodists and other religious groups. A Sunday School Society was organized in Philadelphia in 1791, and Sunday Schools were opened in most of the larger cities for the benefit of poor children. The Sunday School Society was prominent as a supporter of the public education movement in its earliest stages.

The First Amendment to the Federal Constitution generally removed the possibility of an alliance between religious groups and the state or Federal governments with regard to education. Gradually, sectarian control over education in Virginia, Maryland, and Massachusetts (in operation from colonial times) declined. However, the development of free public schools under state control caused a continuing controversy over questions of state aid for religious programs that were a common feature of 19th-century education. In October 1841, Hughes made an "inflammatory speech" supporting the alteration of school funding, and attempting "to mix up religion with politics—an unpalatable dish." Philip Hone was in New York in 1841 when Governor William Seward authorized the use of state money "for the establishment of separate schools for the children of foreigners, and their instruction by teachers of their own faith and language." The public outcry that followed was as immediate as it was massive. Seward was faced with the partisan charge of trying to curry favor with the Irish Catholics, and it was alleged that he was in a conspiracy with Hughes. The final result of the New York controversy was the elimination of all Bibles and Bible reading from the tax-supported schools. Hone observed, "Bishop Hughes . . . deserves a cardinal's hat at least for what he has done in placing Irish Catholics upon the necks of native New Yorkers."[18] This struggle was important because it was the denomination college or university that was the focus of cultural advancement in much of America at the time. Although many were short-lived, more than 500 denominational colleges were founded in the 19th century, evidencing the continued importance of religion in American life. (See Table 6.1 for the growth of religious denominations in America.)[19]

Table 6.1 Religious Denominations in America, 1650–1850

Affiliation	1650	1750	1820	1850
Congregational	62	668	1,096	1,706
Episcopal	31	289	600	1,459
Quaker	1	250	350	726
Presbyterian	6	233	1,411	4,824
Lutheran	4	138	800	16,403
Baptist	2	132	2,885	9,375
Dutch Reformed	0	90	389	2,754
Catholic	6	30	124	1,221
Methodist	0	0	2,700	13,280
Disciples of Christ	0	0	618	1,898
Unitarian/Universalist	0	0	0	891

Notes

1. Daniel E. Sutherland, *The Expansion of Everyday Life, 1860–1876* (Fayetteville: University of Arkansas Press, 2000), 17.

2. Russel B. Nye, *The Cultural Life of the New Nation, 1776–1830* (New York: Harper & Row, 1960), 198.

3. Paul A. W. Wallace, *Conrad Weiser, Friend of Colonist and Mohawk: 1696–1760* (Lewisburg, Penn.: Wennawoods Publishing, 1996), 51.

4. The Congregationalists had 658 mostly in New England. The Presbyterians were strongest in the Middle States with 543. Scattered throughout the early Republic were Baptists with 498, Anglicans with 480, Quakers with 295, German and Dutch Reformed with 251, and Lutheran with 151. The Methodists with 37 were largely found in Maryland and Virginia. The Catholic churches were mostly confined to Maryland and numbered about 50; while a very small undetermined number of Jewish synagogues—composed of Sephardic Jews whose ancestry lay in the Iberian Peninsula—were found mostly in New York City See North Callahan, *Royal Raiders: The Tories of the American Revolution* (New York: Bobbs-Merrill, 1963), 125–126.

5. Peter O. Wacker, *Musconetcong Valley of New Jersey. A Historical Geography* (New Brunswick, NJ: Rutgers University Press, 1968) 50–51; Joshua Gilpin, "Journey to Bethlehem," *The Pennsylvania Magazine of History and Biography* 46 (1922): 25.

6. Henry Beston, ed., *American Memory* (New York: Farrar & Rhinehart, 1937), 299.

7. Ibid., 299–300.

8. Gilbert Chase, *America's Music: From the Pilgrims to the Present* (New York: McGraw-Hill Book Co., 1966), 211.

9. Ralph Bennett, ed., *Settlements in the Americas: Cross-Cultural Perspectives* (Newark: University of Delaware Press, 1993), 146.

10. Ibid., 149.

11. Ibid., 152, 157.

12. Ibid., 169.

13. Ibid., 152–153.

14. Wallace, *Conrad Weiser*, 56.

15. Ralph Waldo Emerson, "Uncollected Prose," *The Dial* (1840).

16. Harvey Wish, *Society and Thought in Early America: A Social and Intellectual History of the American People through 1865* (New York: Longmans, Green & Co., 1950), 319.

17. Ibid.

18. Allan Nevins, ed., *The Diary of Phillip Hone, 1828–1851,* vols. 1 and 2 (New York: Dodd, Mead & Co., 1927), 570.

19. Francesco Cordasco, *A Brief History of Education* (Totowa, N.J.: Littlefield, Adams & Co., 1970), 131.

7

Man of Honor and Good Counsel

There is no moral object so beautiful to me as a conscientious young man.
I watch him as I do a star in the heavens; clouds may be before him, but
we know that his light is behind them and will beam again; the blaze of
others' popularity may outshine him, but we know that, though unseen,
he illuminates his own true sphere.
                                        —T. L. Haines and Levi W. Yaggy, 1876

Good and Seasonable Counsel

A family man was expected to know his children, to interact with them, and
to help form their character. Like fathers today, 19th-century fathers were
deeply concerned for their children's future; and although they loved their
daughters and their sons equally well, they expended a great deal more
effort in terms of argument and persuasion to guide the choices made by
their sons with regard to their educations and careers. Sons needed to settle
into permanent, honest, and reliable careers. Daughters were expected to
learn proper housekeeping and fine needlework and to find husbands to
care for them. Fathers hoped that their girls would find honest and well-
heeled husbands, and they often devolved money or land upon them to
sweeten their eligibility. Most fathers were quick to take corrective steps
when they observed those flaws developing in their own children that were
normally attributed to persons of lesser character.

Self-help author John Ware considered the comment that fathers
of his time (1864) did not know or understand their own children "a

most unwarrantable impertinence . . . an absurdity." Nonetheless, he attests to the existence of a problem in family management. He wrote, "observation and experience both assure us that it is very common . . . how little those who stand at the head [of a family] understand those placed in their charge."[1] Ransom noted of upper-class homes, "The man comes home to eat and sleep after work by day and [goes to] his club by night. . . . The children are turned out to hired nurses, and the home which was intended as a school of virtue is turned into a hotbed of vice through the chill of neglect." The upbringing of the children was left to "brainless servants" and "paid nurses." Thereby, according to Ransom, "they grow up in a willful childhood, indolent and frivolous youth, into selfish manhood and useless womanhood." Thus the homes of the rich became "mere fashionable boarding-houses for an idle, wasteful family."[2]

Children, even siblings, were thought to have individual characters of "every conceivable range and gradation." This dissimilarity was considered one of the most perplexing characteristics of family management, requiring patience, care, and impartiality on the part of the parents. Dealing with children, "always a difficult matter," could not be left to the caprice or impulse of the father. He must seek out the knowledge of how to bring up his children and attempt to understand the "charm" of the family unit in order to bring "harmony" to the household through a "superintending wisdom."[3]

Ware doubted that many men sought such knowledge of the hearts and minds of their children, this being better suited to the temper of the mother with her more confiding ways and more genial sympathies. "How much real conversation goes on in our homes? How much questioning of what is learned at school, from books, from others? How much of what each one learns from himself?" Ware advised fathers, "[The child] turns to us, who are its natural teachers, whom it looks up to with the same love and reverence it looks on all things. What do we do? . . . [D]o we rebuff, and send the opening spirit shuddering back within itself, and teach it in its earliest hours to keep close-locked all its inner wants?"[4]

Fathers were enjoined to provide their children with a strong sense of morality, a proper gender identity, and an appropriate amount of secular knowledge so that they could succeed in a newly industrialized economy and attain a future commensurate with their social status and place in the community. Men often took the role of part-time caretaker or even playmate during the first year or so of a child's "innocent" life, but thereafter a marked change usually took place in the father-child relationship. A particularly impetuous or injudicious child could expect to experience the stern authority of even a benevolent father. Fathers had a duty to train their children and command their obedience lest "the roots of rebellion" find a "permanent hold in the child's character." They had a fundamental duty to subdue their child's willfulness, and often took a firm hand during early episodes of cherubic assertiveness. Many men took a rod to their children at the first opportunity, thinking that it was the responsibility of a loving caregiver to do so. Others resorted to spankings, withheld food, or inflicted other corporal punishments even on toddlers.[5]

The accepted Christian principle was that humans were innately sinful. If their wills were not properly shaped, they would tend to run free and blunder into evils as adults even greater than the brief and passing moment of pain or discomfort the rod might impart when they were children. Nonetheless, Elihu Burritt, author, peace advocate, and Consul to Great Britain in 1861, seemed adverse to corporal punishment. He advised, "Be ever gentle with the children God has given you; watch over them constantly; reprove them earnestly, but not in anger."[6]

The memory of corporal punishment in young children often discouraged inappropriate behaviors, but fear of the father stayed with the children until they were older and had become habituated to obedience and proper behavior. Nonetheless, older children often resented their father's continued attempts to dominate them physically. The frequency of physical punishment in the pre-adolescent and adolescent years is difficult to ascertain as most men did not rush to their diaries to record the spanking of their 10-year-olds. Moreover, the common perception that such brutal tactics were in common use in 19th-century families is not borne out by the available sources. Although the powerful position given men in society buttressed their absolute authority in the home, the army of self-help authors generally advised against physical abuse. "The child shuns [such a] father, makes the mother confidante, learns to persuade her, and gets her to persuade the father, and each time [the child] gains his end the separation is more complete."[7]

Ware warned, "Fatal is the mistake that father makes who in these years separates himself more and more from his children, and fearful shall it be visited upon him . . . in the days of his [own] decrepitude and need . . . turned out [by his grown children] to the cold charities of almshouses; sometimes, pitiful complaints of children's ingratitude."[8] The governance of the family was not the government of the "old Roman stamp . . . the exercise and control of mere will—but the government which results from a wise, considerate, intelligent, and impartial love."[9] A contemporary father made the following notable, if inelegant, thought, "I talk to them very much, but do not like to beat my children. The world will beat them."[10] The father was also warned against becoming a "bugbear" who was constantly unapproachable, disturbed, or disagreeable. Men who ran such an uncongenial household may also have done little to make them better. "The men who complain of homes are mostly those of whom the homes complain."[11] The ideal was a home where children and parents grew together, sharing in each other's confidence and partaking of each other's sorrow and joy.

Older children especially required discipline and governance (not physical punishment) if chaos was not to reign. "If we let things take their own course," voiced Ware, "we have no guiding or controlling law, and then wonder that our homes are the unsatisfactory, chaotic things they are."[12] A child's future happiness and its future usefulness in life depended almost entirely upon the manner in which its father met this solemn duty. Many fathers utilized their economic power to withhold their purse from older children, others extended it in approbation of good behavior—a series of petty bribes and rewards usually in the form of treats, favors, or finery. Moreover, children were made to understand clearly that their future happiness was under the control of a father, who would and could limit their opportunities by withdrawing funds for their education or by augmenting their prospects through the liberal use of personal, family, or financial influence.[13]

Fathers hoped that all their adult children would enjoy the prospect of home ownership and freedom from want that came with an adequate income. As children became adults, got married, and evidenced their own commitment to appropriate family values, tensions between them and their father tended to ease, and the interactions between parent and child thereafter took on a tone of equality and mutual respect. Nonetheless, many adult children continued to seek out the advice and guidance of parents and receive permission before making life-changing decisions into their mature years.[14] Ransom noted, however, that this was not always the case, especially if the parent had been particularly ungenerous, petty, or reluctant to part with funds during the child's upbringing. When "the long bank account of the parsimonious father [was] left behind . . . the children leave home, and the old folks are left to pass a discontented and unhappy old age. Oh, the temples of pollution that are reared in the name of the American home!"[15]

Parents often tailored their child-rearing practices so that the proper set of characteristics might be impressed upon their children. The inculcation of proper gender identity in all of his children was the ultimate responsibility of the father, but men were sometimes clumsy and ill-suited to giving their daughters gender-specific instruction or advice. It is not surprising, therefore, that men took the lead in training their sons in the masculine gender role, while mothers tended to encourage and shape their daughters' character. Thus the entire household was tied to the process of gender identification. Haines and Yaggy advised, "Our habits . . . are formed under the molding power of home. The tender twig is there bent, the spirit shaped, principles implanted, and the whole character is formed. . . . The home influence is either a blessing or a curse, either for good or for evil. It cannot be neutral."[16] Ransom noted, "Home [is] the school of character. . . . [and] those higher elements of true manhood are never nurtured in the barren regions of a vagabond life . . . [but] in the home."

It was the Divine plan that made "domestic life preparatory to social and political life [and] the great responsibilities of citizenship."[17]

Yet it would be an oversimplification to think that men were given only a store of masculine values. "The measure of [a child's] usefulness in manhood is decided by the kind of treatment he receives in the early years of childhood."[18] Rather, there was an emphasis on stressing those things considered manly. Kindness, affection, and helpfulness were taught to both genders. However the "manly arts" like riding, shooting, or hunting, and those diversions that developed leadership, strength, and vigorous health were highly valued in boys, while the domestic and decorative arts and the qualities of amiability, chastity, good sense, refinement, and a lack of affection were most highly valued in girls. "The woman who is rude, coarse and vulgar at home [will] mortify [herself] just when she wants most to hide them in her heart. . . . [and] her home coarseness will appear most when she is in refined circles. . . . Every young woman should feel that just what she is at home she will appear abroad."[19]

This dichotomy may have led fathers to support a certain level of male aggressiveness in their sons (but not in their daughters) that mirrored the boys' natural inclination to quarrel, fight, and generally assert themselves physically in the presence of others. Many fathers made an unambiguous connection between a masculine manner and courage. In the 19th century behaving like a boy had not yet been raised to the level of a pathology that it has in more recent times. Clumsiness, crying, cringing, and timidity, even in very young boys, was unacceptable. Thomas Kirby Smith advised his sons, "Bear [yourself] upright, always tell the truth, look everybody square in the eye and never take an insult from any boy."[20]

Moreover, as the crisis of civil war loomed larger, the prospect of military service, the declaration of war, and actual combat had the effect of increasing men's concerns about their son's honor and manliness. Many parents—while fearing that their sons might have to go off to fight—were equally hopeful that once brought to the battlefield, their sons would be willing to serve and possibly die honorably. Thereby the acceptability of fisticuffs between bad-tempered boys in the alleyway turned into bitter and bloody encounters on the battlefield both in the Mexican War and the War between the States.

At the same time, it should be noted that there were few things of which 19th-century men were more proud than their daughters. The young father cherished his girl, and "she [was] his morning sunlight and his evening star." When grown, she became "the pride and ornament of his hospitality, and the gentle nurse of his sickness, and the constant agent in those nameless, numberless acts of kindness which one chiefly cares to have rendered because they are unpretending, but all expressive proofs of love." The aged father leaned on his daughter as the crutch in his declining years, and "when he pats the cheeks of the little grandchildren, it is chiefly because the bond which unites him to them passes through the heart of his darling . . . daughter still."[21]

Duty and Honor

Although the qualities of duty and honor were not mutually exclusive, there is a difference. Duty was an external force requiring that a man act appropriately in sacrificing his own interest to some other matter, while honor was an internal facet of one's personality. There is some truth in viewing the South as a society with a profound sense of honor, primarily a masculine concept that dealt with one's public image and reputation; while the North as a whole seemed driven more by duty, a communal conscience analogous to a compact made with God. Acknowledging duty was to prepare oneself to do God's work in the world. Americans of the early 19th century were strongly influenced by such sentiments. The consciousness of duty resonated particularly well with the parallel development of social reform in the North. To shirk duty was to violate the collective conscience, and offend morality by omission. Devotion to one's duty was viewed as a personal responsibility rather than as a collective obligation. "We all of us have a duty to perform in this life," wrote one journalist. It was not enough to support the norms of society from a distance. In the crisis-charged atmosphere of mid-century, duty required that a man place his life on the line. Northerners and Southerners cited both duty and honor in their writings and speeches, but Southerners were much more likely to speak of honor.[22]

The contemporary view of Northerners seemed to link moral virtue with duty, while Southerners tended to link martial valor with honor. Yet both of these connections seem perversions caused by the polarization of sectionalism. There was ample evidence of an association between the romantic theme of moral virtue and the classical concept of honor, and these appeared repeatedly in the popular literature of the period and among the letters, diaries, and journals of the more literate upper classes.[23] "True honor, as defined by Cicero, is the concurrent approbation of good men; those only being fit to give true praise who are themselves praiseworthy," wrote Haines and Laggy. "[T]he Romans worshipped virtue and honor as gods; they built two temples, which were so [situated] that none could enter the temple of honor without passing through the temple of virtue."[24]

Although the views of some contemporary writers suggest a different conclusion, many Southerners believed that Northern sentiments toward honor had changed with the surest path toward its acquisition being increasingly associated with the accumulation of wealth. Honor, thereby, became an article of base commercial trafficking, and respectability became a measure of the thickness of one's wallet. Nonetheless, Southerners also viewed honor in a contemporary light, and the continued popularity of dueling attests to the vitality of the sentiment in the Southern psyche. There was no true glory, no true greatness "when gold could purchase with ease the honors that patriotism and valor could once secure only with difficulty."[25] They often wrote of being dishonored in the eyes of their "revolutionary ancestors" should they fail to defend their families or the Southern cause and lifestyle.

Northerners retaliated by pointing out the tendency of Southern aristocracy to build great mansions and populate them with scores of servants and black slaves. "[F]ine palaces make us despise the poor and poverty; [and] a great number of domestics flatter human pride, which uses them like slaves; valor oftentimes turns brutal and unjust; and a high pedigree makes a man take up with the virtues of his ancestors, without endeavoring to acquire any himself."[26]

Dueling

In the decades before the Civil War, the specter of dueling shadowed every successful or prominent man. Dueling, in defense of honor, was a curse that might appear at any fashionable social function, the theater, the opera, anywhere, in fact, where there might be the least breach of etiquette, the slightest lapse in politeness, or the smallest hint that a business dealing was unethical, even if it was. A word and a challenge were the purest form of the dueling code. A 19th-century commentator, Maj. Ben C. Truman, noted in 1884 that the purpose of the duel was to resolve the point of honor, not simply to kill an enemy. Opponents who lost sight of this might be looked upon as murderers by dueling purists, who saw the entire process as an exercise in character.

The possibility of being involved in a duel was a social reality for all those who considered themselves gentlemen or who dealt in politics. Even in the midst of polite conversation, gentlemen were always on guard to protect their integrity. As Southern society also favored a relaxed cordiality, the two notions often required a delicate touch. Dueling among military and naval officers was forbidden, however, during times of war or on active service in the face of the enemy, but men of equal rank might defend their personal honor by stripping their uniforms and resorting to bare knuckles as long as they otherwise acted within the bounds of the code of military justice or articles of war.

Quarrels among citizens of the upper class never ended in simple fisticuffs, and it was social suicide to strike a blow in anger. At all levels of Southern society, individual liberty, manliness, and respect for social position were held in such high esteem that one put his life and personal honor on the line to protect them. Iron-clad rules and traditions governed every stage of such encounters from the moment of the "insult" up to the hours immediately after the combatants had met on the field of honor. Defending one's honor reached such heights of absurdity that a moment of awkwardness might result in a challenge that could not, with honor, be ignored.

Dueling had a long history in America. The dancing masters of the 18th century, who had taught the finer points of swordsmanship to their well-heeled pupils, abandoned the dance in the 19th century to open fencing schools and academies of dueling openly dedicated to teaching the requisite skills of both sword and pistol. Well-known duelists occupied much the same position in antebellum society as sports figures do in modern times. They were followed through the streets, fawned upon by waiters in restaurants, and had their mannerisms and dueling styles copied by young men.

Although formal in its procedures and socially acceptable at the highest levels of society—Vice President Aaron Burr and Secretary of the Treasury Alexander Hamilton fought a tragic duel in New Jersey—dueling quickly lost favor in the North, and in mid-century the practice came to be regarded as characteristically Southern. This view has been reinforced in modern times by numerous films, romantic novels, and television shows. It is certain that nowhere in America, and possibly nowhere in the Western world, was dueling so universally practiced as in the antebellum South.

The golden age of dueling lasted from 1830 to 1860. It was in New Orleans that the practice of dueling reached its zenith. In some circles the *Code Duello,* supported by an incredibly strict adherence to a sense of Southern honor, was regarded with the same reverence as a religion. Truth might be an admirable defense against libel or slander in a court of law, but it had no standing in affairs of honor. Initially, only swords were used in dueling and, consequently, there were few fatalities. However, with the advent of the more lethal percussion cap pistol and its reliable ignition system, fatalities increased. No attempt has been made to determine the absolute number of duels that were fought in the South, as the task is both daunting and the records of duels were somewhat concealed by the need to evade the laws that tried unsuccessfully to prevent them. Certainly, the number of duels fought in this period figures in the thousands, and the fatalities in the hundreds.

In the decades before the Civil War, there was hardly a man in public life in Louisiana who had not faced a duel, and many had fought several. Ten duels were fought on a single day at the Oaks, a favorite field of honor. Many of these affairs grew out of political party wrangling, which was, unfortunately, lacking in restraint and sophistication in this period. Duels sometimes ran through a political party or social grouping in a series involving one individual after another, one encounter producing the next. Only the violence of the Civil War was able to overshadow this apparent lust for individual combat.

An ardent states' rights advocate and governor of South Carolina, James Hamilton, was a noted duelist and was much sought after as an assistant in Southern dueling circles. President Andrew Jackson was not unfamiliar with dueling. As early as 1788, he had called out a lawyer who found himself facing a young Jackson after a momentary slip of verbal discretion in court. The details of the confrontation were arranged, but conciliation won the day with the two men firing their pistols in the air to satisfy their honor and then shaking hands. However, not all of Jackson's affairs of honor ended as affably. Prior to his election as president, Jackson fought a duel and killed a man in defense of his wife's honor. This affair dogged all of his future political campaigns.

Dueling began losing favor in the South prior to the Civil War mostly because it degenerated either into bloody contests with shotguns, axes, and clubs or into barroom brawls between groups of lower-class men using fighting knives and repeating pistols. In the post-war era, it was replaced by the frontier gunfight, which was loosely justified as an act of physical self-defense rather than an affair of honor. The main streets of Western towns like Dodge City, Deadwood, and Tombstone hosted innumerable gunfights in the pages of the dime novels, yet the rate of death due to gunfights in these lawless, gun-toting towns was actually many times smaller than that in many crime-ridden metropolises.

Notes

1. John F. W. Ware, *Home Life: What It Is, and What It Needs* (Boston: William V. Spencer, 1864), 51.

2. J. Clinton Ransom, *The Successful Man in His Manifold Relations with Life* (New York: J. A. Hill & Co., 1889), 308–309.

3. Ware, *Home Life*, 53–54.

4. Ibid.

5. Shawn Johansen, *Family Man: Middle-Class Fatherhood in Early Industrializing America* (New York: Routledge, 2001), 96–97.

6. Elihu Burritt, *A Walk from London to John O'Groat's.* Available at http://www.gutenburg.org/author/Elihu+Burritt/ (accessed April 2006).

7. Ware, *Home Life*, 56.

8. Ibid., 57.

9. Ibid., 67.

10. Burritt, *Walk from London.*

11. Ware, *Home Life*, 64.

12. Ibid., 65.

13. Johansen, *Family Man*, 102–103.

14. Ibid., 141.

15. Ransom, *Successful Man*, 311–312.

16. T. L. Haines and Levi W. Yaggy, *The Royal Path of Life; or, Aims and Aids to Success and Happiness* (Chicago: Western Publishing House, 1876), 64–65.

17. Ransom, *Successful Man*, 306–307.

18. Ibid., 312.

19. Haines and Yaggy, *Royal Path of Life*, 67.

20. Smith quoted in Johansen, *Family Man*, 126.

21. Haines and Yaggy, *Royal Path of Life*, 89.

22. James M. McPherson, *For Cause and Comrades: Why Men Fought in the Civil War* (New York: Oxford University Press, 1997), 24.

23. Ibid.

24. Haines and Yaggy, *Royal Path of Life*, 490.

25. Ibid., 491.

26. Ibid., 492.

8

Father Protector

He is the shield of woman, destined by nature to guard and protect
her. Her inferior strength and sedentary habits confine her within the
domestic circle; she is kept aloof from the bustle and storm of active life;
she is not familiarized to the out of door dangers and hardships of a cold
and scuffling world; timidity and modesty are her attributes.
—Thomas R. Dew, 1835, "Dissertation on the Characteristic
Differences, between the Sexes, and on the Position, and
Influence of Women in Society"[1]

Militarism

Militarism rather than diplomacy was to prove the most efficient tool
for achieving the nation's manifest destiny. In 1790 the entire Army of
the United States numbered just 80 men. By the time of the Civil War
there would be more than 2 million men under arms. Statesmen of that
latter day seemed willing to accept the scourge of war in order to shape
American society. Moreover, the American public from New York to
New Orleans and from Charleston to Chicago generally supported these
military efforts and followed their development—and the war news in
particular—with rapt attention. The shifting tides of battle were often
viewed like a sporting event.[2]

Although the American Civil War stands out as the major conflict
during this period—some say the formative experience in the history of
the nation—from 1785 to 1898 the country was involved in several other

conflicts that helped to formulate its character. About once a decade during this period, fathers, sons, and brothers were called forth in defense of their homes and country. The military system of mid-century had become so specialized that it needed to be described on a series of schematic diagrams, yet the old tradition of cavalier gallantry—drinking, carousing, and fighting—remained alive, permeating the ranks of both the army and the navy. A contemporary observer expressed the absolute faith that 19th-century Americans had in their military, "It is our army that unites the chasm between the culture of civilization in the aspect of science, art, and social refinement, and the powerful simplicity of nature."[3]

Military Schools

As early as the first decade of the 19th century an interest in military education had been clearly manifest in the South, and by the 1850s the movement toward military education and the establishment of schools dedicated specifically to the martial arts had gained marked momentum. The extension of settlements into the newly acquired territories populated by fierce and independent Indian tribes, in particular, had made specific military training important. "The life of the wilderness is an art as well as that of the city or court, and every art subjects its votaries to discipline in preparing them for a successful career in its pursuit. The Military Art, as enlarged to meet all the requirements of border service. . . embraces many other special arts which have hitherto been almost ignored."[4]

Although less popular in the North, a military career became increasingly acceptable for the sons of the plantation aristocracy. Henry Belcher, a British observer of the process, noted that many thoughtful parents "pitch forked" a younger son or a dullard into the army as a convenient avenue to his social betterment. The success of Southern warriors during the Revolution and the Mexican War of 1846 also greatly enhanced the prestige of a military life. Moreover, a wider usefulness was recognized in having a cadre of military personnel that could quickly respond to slave rebellions and Indian uprisings. In 1854, a Charlestonian noted that the very nature of domestic slavery required that the South cherish a military spirit and a military science so that its young men might defy the world in arms.[5]

In order to insure that the army remain an organization dedicated to democratic, rather than elitist, principles, in 1802 President Thomas Jefferson approved the establishment of the United States Military Academy at West Point, New York. Yet the Academy did not gain its reputation for discipline and academics until taken in hand by Colonel Sylvanus Thayer, who served as superintendent from 1817 to 1833. So highly prized was a military preparation at West Point that more than one-third of the student body had Southern roots, although public sentiment increasingly frowned upon education at a Northern institution.

Schools in the Carolinas, Mississippi, and Alabama showed great interest in military education by the second quarter of the century. Yet military schools required financial support, and most simply added to the ordinary branches of academics the study of infantry tactics, fencing, and cavalry evolutions as a regular part of their course of study—a modification that was found agreeable to most youths of spirit and good health.

Nowhere did Americans better understand this than in Virginia and South Carolina. In 1836, Virginians decided to substitute a military school for the company of state guards by diverting the financial resources of the state from the Lexington Arsenal to the Virginia Military Institute in its stead. Virginians pointed to the development of VMI as thoroughly and exclusively Virginian and pointed with pride to the state patriotism engendered therein. South Carolinians attempted to combine a military character with the acquisition of a scholastic education by converting the Arsenal, at Columbia, and the Citadel and Magazine, at Charleston, into military schools. A third major military school, the Georgia Military Institute, was opened in 1851.

The remainder of the antebellum period saw various activities, including riding, military drill and tactics, incorporated into the academic curriculum of many schools in the Southern states. Companies of uniformed cadets were established in many places. Most prospered only briefly to be abandoned when the novelty wore off. State support was generally limited to providing the school with tax exemptions and as many arms as could be spared from the state magazines for the purposes of drill.

As the war approached, town after town in the South boasted new military academies that enjoyed excellent public relations, engaging in activities designed to excite the interest of the populace. Cadets made frequent off-campus visits to communities to display their skills at drill and their attractive, if rather gaudy, uniforms by parading in the town square or on the county fairgrounds. An unbridled martial spirit was abroad by the 1850s, and most Southerners regarded their military schools as among their most valuable regional assets. Some of these institutions received increasing public support as the sectional disputes tearing at the nation proceeded toward war.

The War of 1812

The American entry into the war in 1812 is somewhat of an enigma, and the study of the decision has filled numerous volumes. Although no American troops served in the European theater, the free-trade Federalists of New England were vociferously opposed to it. At the time of America's entry to the war, Napoleon was seemingly the master of the European continent. He had installed his family members as kings and queens in more than a half-dozen European states and made his infant son King of Rome. He had successfully invaded Russia—getting back out was going to be the trick, and the Peninsula War in Spain, having dragged on for years, had not yet become an abject failure. Madison and the War Hawks had no way of knowing that these initiatives would blow up in Napoleon's face.

The political influence of about two dozen outspoken proponents of war with Britain in the Congress convinced President Madison to declare war in June 1812. These "War Hawks" expected the war to be short, and they were convinced that the United States could gain part or all of Canada while the British were expending most of their energy fighting the French. However, Britain retained control of the seas, had bases in nearby Canada, and enjoyed the allegiance of many tribes of Native Americans. Moreover, Spain still controlled much of the southern border of the United States with troops and fortifications in parts of present-day Alabama, Florida, California, and Texas. To enter the war was to invite attack from almost every quarter.

The British policy of inciting Indian raids on the American frontiers as they had in the Revolution made a new frontier war against the Indians likely. The British warship *Orpheus* commanded by Captain Hugh Pigot actually ascended the Apalachicola River to arm 3,000 warriors recruited from 10 local tribes of Creek and Seminole. Constant trouble with the Indians on the frontiers and the threat of a British attack at almost any point on the Atlantic seacoast or on the border with British Canada kept the Americans in the field throughout the war years.[6]

With the declaration of war, Madison called up all the state militias, with each state satisfying a particular quota. Except for a few hundred regulars, the United States had no standing army at the time, and it relied on the citizen soldiers of the local militias and state-sponsored regiments for defense. In America independent riflemen and rangers patrolled the backwoods areas, but a well-regulated and trained militia was thought to provide the most practical solution to the defense needs of most frontier settlements. There remained, as a relic of Revolutionary tradition, the cherished and romantic concept of the militia as a mythical army of self-trained and self-armed warriors springing from the native soil in times of trouble. This picture hardly aligns with the known facts of the War for Independence. The colonial militia system had been a carefully constituted organization of Provincial regiments, well established in all the colonies by the middle of the 18th century, and tested in the French and Indian Wars.[7]

For most colonial Americans the most noxious tool of impending tyranny was a standing army, whereas a militia for defense was considered a sign of a healthy and vigorous society in which citizens took on the responsibilities by actively safeguarding "property, liberty, and life itself."[8] The local militia companies—composed largely of father, sons, grandfathers, nephews, cousins, neighbors, and friends—were merely a stop-gap, a quick response force for dealing with Indian raids and local emergencies, not the foundation of a standing army. While less than adequate to substitute for a national military, the militia was, nonetheless, able to defend the settlements, drive back the Indian raiders, and hold open the newly abandoned Native American lands for white acquisition. The reality of continuing to rely on the militia for national defense or for the prosecution of foreign wars quickly proved a disastrous illusion.[9]

It would be unfair, incorrect, and naïve to assume that the army of 1812 suddenly sprang from the soil of America composed of farmers, shopkeepers, or mechanics and commanded by a cadre of inexperienced lawyers, plantation owners, and merchants. Although almost all Americans were military amateurs, most had served under arms in some capacity. Those men between the ages of 16 and 60 were formed into local units for training, but state militias were pragmatically composed of adult males in the prime of life rather than of old men and young boys. Studies suggest that the average age of men serving in the army was just under 26, with 80 percent under 35 and less than 2 percent, many of them officers, over age 55 who had served as privates in the Revolution. Almost all of these men were true volunteers, unlike the soldiers of European armies who may have been impressed or conscripted. The United States also lacked a European-style professional officer corps, but many of the older men now serving as officers and NCOs had seen service in the Revolution or with their state militias on the frontiers.[10]

Despite the proclamations of the governors of the various states describing distinctive uniforms and standardized weapons, many men went to war in the everyday clothing in which they had enlisted. Others attempted some degree of regimentation by adopting distinct emblems, hats, or pieces of clothing. Captain Henry Brush of Virginia left a precise description of the newly enlisted men who turned out to fight in 1812. The soldiers were outfitted for service with unbleached, coarse linen hunting shirts and trousers almost identical to those used in the Revolution four decades earlier. In many cases their clothing was that of the backwoodsman, failing entirely to approach anything military in style. Yet it was well fitted to the vicissitudes of the weather and the physical exertion that would be expected of soldiers on campaign. Each man wore a characteristic hunting frock, or shirt, of heavy unbleached linen that had a shoulder cape and lines of fringe of the same material. The loose frock, reaching halfway down the thigh, with large sleeves, was open in front and so wide as to lap over a foot or more when belted. Each unit, in the absence of formal military attire, was ordered to dye their linen hunting frocks a uniform dark color, but no particular hue was designated. The order was widely ignored, leaving many frocks an unbleached white, but others were dyed brown, blue, green, gray, and even purple with both matching and contrasting fringes. The men generally wore square-crowned, short-brimmed hats with a ribbon cockade on the left side.

Each man had a leather belt around his waist on which he fastened items such as a knife, a bayonet, or a tomahawk depending on the sophistication of his gear. A cartridge box filled with up to 60 rounds of ammunition, carried either on the belt or on a diagonal shoulder strap, was essential. On his back was a linen or leather knapsack with a blanket rolled on its top. Both could be covered with an oilcloth to protect them from wet weather. This could also be used as a ground cloth when sleeping. Soldiers had a one-quart canteen or water bottle with them as an essential part of their kit. Orders to the contrary, little notice was taken of where the soldiers filled their canteens, but the many fast-running streams, brooks, and private wells that dotted the American countryside usually provided sufficiently potable water.[11]

Almost all military firearms were based upon the same standard smooth-bore, flintlock technology that had served in the American Revolution and continued to characterize the Napoleonic Wars in Europe. Most firearms, including pistols, fired a generally large lead ball between .63 and .75 caliber weighing almost an ounce, but other calibers were used. The effective range of muskets remained under 100 yards, while the visually intimidating pistols were actually useful only at very close quarters. Rifle fire, provided by the technology that gave America the Kentucky and Pennsylvania long rifles, was particularly accurate even at long ranges of 300 to 400 yards. Although the rifle was slow to load and fired a smaller ball (generally .36 to .58 caliber), the spin imparted to the projectile by the spiral grooves in the barrel (rifling) made it a deadly and precise weapon.

The effectiveness of the rifle had been proven in the American Revolution, and most European armies had adopted at least some rifle companies. Although riflemen could reach out hundreds of yards over open ground to kill or wound an enemy, in dense woods they were less effective due to the shortened line of sight through the brush and trees. Moreover, when the rifle was empty, it took a long time to reload. This characteristic of rifle fire insured the continued use of muskets for most military organizations until the Civil War. Regiments of soldiers continued to use the quicker-loading muskets to provide a volume of fire on the open battlefield. From the slow rate of rifle fire came a woodland tactic called the *Indian rush*—a false attack by one individual that drew fire followed by a headlong sprint by others to close with the shooter before he could reload. Intelligent riflemen worked in pairs or in concert with a musket man or two, who provided close-in support.

The Americans entered the naval war in 1812 with 6 frigates, 5 sloops of war, 2 brigs, and 62 gunboats ready for sea. Nine new vessels were building in various harbors, including two new 74s, but these would not be ready until 1814. Only one American vessel was patrolling Lake Ontario, although several other warships were building or refitting for service on the Great Lakes. It seems obvious, therefore, that the American plan for its naval defense was somewhat optimistic. A navy 20 times the number would have been needed to stand eyeball to eyeball with any of the fleets of Europe. The British Royal Navy had more than 100 warships larger than 64 guns, while the frigates deployed by the Americans had no hope of standing up to a lone 50-gun warship.

The naval strategies of the War Hawks were quickly shown to be faulty as the British immediately set almost 100 warships on the station solely directed against the American coastline. To counter the British presence, the Americans had six large frigates designed to carry 44 guns and several smaller vessels of the *Essex* class. Nonetheless, the double-banked American frigates proved vastly superior to any other warships in their class. Naval authority and author C. S. Forester has pointed out that they were not "extra powerful frigates" but rather "not-too-small two-decked ships of the line."[12] Like many American merchant vessels of the day, these frigates were particularly fast and could run from any vessel they could not match in size. Nonetheless, their superiority over other warships in their class was largely due to the attention to detail of their designer Joshua Humphreys and to the talent of their officers and crew.[13]

Of the six vessels—*Constitution, President, United States, Chesapeake, Constellation,* and *Congress*—the best-known was *Constitution* with its many single-ship actions, including the defeat of the British frigates *Guerriere* and *Java.* The strength of *Constitution's* sides in these battles was so great that many of the enemy's shot bounced off into the sea. This observation led to the frigate's nickname, "Old Ironsides." The *United States* served to bring Captain Stephen Decatur to renewed prominence when he trounced the 38-gun *Macedonian* and brought her into the American Navy. Yet not all went well for the U.S. Navy. The 38-gun *Chesapeake* was lost in an ill-considered ship-to-ship duel with *Shannon* (36) within sight of Boston. Late in the war, *President,* the fastest of the six Humphreys frigates, was pounded into submission by a small squadron of British ships, including the 44-gun *Endymion,* a British large frigate. The remaining frigates captured a few merchant vessels in the Atlantic but generally failed to distinguish themselves otherwise.

The Federalists, especially those in New England, opposed Madison's war with Britain, but strong support for the war came from Southerners and those in frontier communities. As the Federalists feared, the Northern border was the first to feel Britain's wrath. A red-coat army of 14,000 veterans attacked south from Canada through New York, but a remarkable American naval victory on Lake Champlain turned back the invasion. Nonetheless, the general American war strategy along the Canadian border was mismanaged; the gunboat navy proved useless; Chesapeake Bay was blockaded, Norfolk attacked, and Hampton Roads sacked. Fort McHenry in Baltimore withstood a determined British attack in 1814, and its defense provided inspiration for Francis Scott Key's "Star-Spangled Banner." Yet the capital at Washington, D.C., was captured and the Executive Mansion (the White House) burned. Madison's enemies in his own party thwarted any attempt to seize Florida, and after two years of war, there was little enthusiasm left among Southerners for creating more anti-slavery Northern states from Canadian territory. Federalists threatened Madison with the secession of the New England states in the final months of the conflict if he did not sue for peace. Ironically, the Federalists would not survive this confrontation with the president as a viable political party.

With the armistice in December 1814, Madison found that not a single American war aim had been attained. Notwithstanding these setbacks, history has dismissed the dismal failure of American arms in "Mr. Madison's War" for the less-bitter illusions of success offered by the victories of the U.S. Frigate *Constitution;* the successful defense of Fort McHenry; and the minimal successes on Lake Erie, Lake Champlain, and at Fort Erie. None of these had proved decisive. The only truly decisive engagement of the war was the defeat of the British regulars at the Battle of New Orleans—significant in that it was to catapult Andrew Jackson to national prominence. The American riflemen at the Battle of New Orleans were particularly effective because they were stationed behind giant cotton bales arranged as temporary fortifications while the British, armed with smooth-bore muskets, marched in a line formation restricted to the width of the open levees.

With the war at an end in 1815 and with Napoleon removed from the stage of European politics, the world entered an era during which many nations turned their focus inward. For most of the next 50 years, European countries struggled with the internal social upheavals that culminated in widespread national revolutions from 1848 to 1860. The Sicilians and Neapolitans revolted in Italy under Garibaldi; the Piedmontese struggled with Austria; and the Sepoys mutinied against the British in India. In 1854 the world focused on the Crimea, as the French and British allied against Turkey and Russia in what some historians consider the first modern war. Meanwhile, the United States passed through a long period of internecine brawling over Indian removal, nullification, states' rights, and slavery, which ultimately led to the Civil War.

The Early Indian Wars

The great heartland of America was occupied by tens of thousands of Indians at the birth of the nation. Estimates as high as 3 million have been made for the total native population of the North American Continent. The Indian nations residing east of the Mississippi River were generally considered as just two groups: those of the Northwest Territory and those of the Southeast. Although the dividing line was generally drawn along the Tennessee and Ohio River valleys by white Americans, no single set of material or physical characteristics was used to differentiate the diverse nations that made up these populations. In the 1830s ethnologists settled on a commonality of language as a gauge to determine lineal relationships among the tribes, and such simplifications seemingly satisfied period anthropologists and ethnologists. There were several linguistic stocks of native peoples—the Iroquoian, Algonquian, Muskhogean, Timucan, Siouan, and Caddo among them—but tribes related by language could be found on either side of any arbitrary geographical divide. Colonials of the 18th century found that simply because certain tribes spoke the same language did not mean that they were allied in a political or economic sense. Algonquian, for instance, was one of the most widespread linguistic stockscomprised of 50 or more distinct tribal languages.[14]

The resulting fragmented pattern of Indian villages exposed each to dissension with its warlike neighbors and left pockets of conflicting ethnicities throughout the region. The whites used this to undermine Indian solidarity by setting one group against the other. At the end of the Revolutionary War, America's Indian allies formed treaty relations with the United States while the Loyalist tribes generally passed to the west of the Appalachians or removed to Canada to take advantage of British protection. Other nations, which had attempted an uneasy neutrality during the Revolution, viewed the new republic with cautious curiosity. American diplomats sent to the tribes attempted to resurrect the old ceremonial vocabulary of the "Great Father" and his "Indian Children" formerly utilized by the British in forming treaties with the president taking the place of the king. However, in the first decades of the 19th century, the British retained control of Canada and much of the Great Lakes region, and they willingly incited the Indians to cause trouble on the American frontier.

The Mohawk war leader and British supporter, Joseph Brant, worked with native tribes throughout the Ohio country and the lakes region of Canada to create a Western Confederacy to coordinate a resistance to the Americans and set the Ohio River as the border between Indian lands and the new republic. Brant's confederacy thoroughly defeated two armies sent to occupy the newly created Northwest Territory in 1790 and 1791, respectively. The force of 1,400 militiamen and volunteers led by Arthur St. Clair lost more than 600 killed and 300 wounded, making the defeat one of the worst proportionately ever visited on Americans in any war. In response, a punitive force under Gen. "Mad" Anthony Wayne won a battle against the tribes at Fallen Timbers, after which the British abandoned the survivors. This changed a minor American victory into a huge diplomatic success, with the Indians yielding most of the Ohio country to white settlement.[15]

Throughout the crisis the British had feigned neutrality, but their agents assured the Indians of their support in terms of arms and ammunition. In 1794 the Jay Treaty required that the British abandon their western posts, but British pretensions to the Old Northwest were not truly eased until 1815, leaving the Indians to make the best deal with America that they could. The tribes thereafter utilized the border with Canada as an invisible, but effective barrier (a Medicine, or magic, Line) to American pursuit. The Oregon treaty line with Canada was not permanently settled at the 49th parallel until 1846, and it was used in a similar manner during the Plains Indian Wars of the second half of the century.

Among the major objectives of the Lewis and Clark Expedition (1803–1805) were efforts to make a show of American sovereignty over the Louisiana Territory and to establish relations with the Western tribes then resident in the region who had formerly owed allegiance to the British, French, or Spanish. Yet from the inception of the United States, treaties and alliances between the Federal government and the Indian nations were conveniently broken whenever coveting white settlers became numerous or aggressive enough to work their collective wills upon the politicians. The efforts of the Indian population to thwart white incursions into their lands often brought the government to intervene, usually on the side of the settlers and with devastating military force. Nonetheless, in 1809 Federal troops forcibly removed 1,700 white squatters from Indian lands, but they were so quickly replaced by other intruders that without a constant military presence the policy of protecting treaty lands seemed doomed to failure.

Indian policy at the Federal level was initially crafted by Secretary of War Henry Knox, and it was carried out by most of the administrations that followed. Knox envisioned a policy of "civilization" and "Christianization" for the tribes. He sought to teach the Indians to abandon their traditional gender-based communal economy of male hunting and warfare, and female agriculture and child-rearing for a Euro-American lifestyle of male-oriented farming and female domesticity that would allow the tribes to prosper on a much smaller land base. This, it was hoped, would open former Indian lands to white settlement without eradicating the Indians. Federal agents relentlessly pushed this civilization program, or a near facsimile, throughout the 19th century.[16]

The lands of the southeast quadrant of the present United States promised to be among the most productive in America. The dark, rich soils of Georgia, Alabama, and Mississippi initially attracted a scattering of pioneer farmers, many of them Scotch-Irish immigrants who passed through the established colonial settlements to carve out farmsteads on the frontier. The settlers thereby placed themselves in position to directly confront some of these fiercest warriors among the Indian tribes. Among them were the Muscogee, the Cherokee, Chowtaw, Chickasaw, and Seminole who resided in the heart of what would become cotton country in a few generations. The land was "perfectly suited to growing cotton, plenty of land for raising cattle, forests of elms and red oaks, peach trees, and magnolias." From 1810 to 1820 the region was flooded with white invaders, many of whom would create the great plantations of antebellum society. They bought land for as little as $1.25 to $2.00 an acre.[17]

During Andrew Jackson's two terms as president, almost 100 Indian treaties were signed. Some of them were legitimate, and the tribes agreed to various amounts of compensation to give up their lands and move west. Other agreements were questionable with agents misrepresenting the intent or meaning of the treaties or with tribes selling rights to lands that they did not possess. Some tribes went peacefully to the lands west of the Mississippi, but others dared to fight against the invaders. Chief among these in the minds of the American public were the Creek, the Shawnee, and the Seminole.

There were a number of reasons why Indian resistance to white intrusion was doomed to failure. Foremost among these was the characteristic nature of Indian strategy, which preferred minor engagements and limited attacks on isolated farmsteads and emigrant wagons to major confrontations. Yet their tactics were simple and effective in producing a great deal of terror. They generally struck without a formal declaration of war, using the basic offensive tactic of surprise. They commonly attacked at dawn or mid-day, often assaulting solitary farmers, women, or children working in their fields. More than once an abandoned cart or a column of smoke was the first sign of a larger problem. Most attacks, however, took the form of ambushes made in forested regions. These were especially effective against non-military targets such as small parties of settlers or fur traders.

The Indians evolved their tactics with time and with contact with whites. They shifted from traditional weapons to firearms as quickly as they became available, but it has been pointed out that the Indians "never really mastered the white man's weapon."[18] The Indians were usually armed with gunpowder weapons of inferior quality, and they often failed to measure out the gunpowder charges in proper quantities, possibly in an attempt to stretch out their limited stock. The heavy wool coats of many whites were actually known to have deflected some of these low-velocity bullets, changing lethal shots into glancing blows. This was not the case during the Custer battle of 1876. At Little Bighorn, evidence suggests that the Sioux and Cheyenne with repeating weapons were better armed than many of the soldiers with their single-shot carbines. Nonetheless, the native war practices in terms of tactics, prisoners, and personal behavior on the field of battle changed little, even with the introduction of firearms.[19]

Tribal resistance to invasion of white emigrants led to the rise of the "Indian fighter"—American cultural heroes noted for their hand-to-hand conflicts with the natives. Among these were several real men like Daniel Boone, Davy Crockett, Sam Dale, William Cody, Kit Carson, and George Custer, and fictional characters like James Fenimore Cooper's Natty

Bumpo, better known as Hawkeye or the Deerslayer, who figured as the main character in five popular novels.

For a time antebellum voters became fond of Indian fighters, and military men in general, as political candidates; and a good Indian fight on one's record could catapult an otherwise unspectacular local politician to national status. This fascination, which replaced an earlier but similarly inspired enchantment with the long-gone military heroes of the Revolution, began in earnest in the 19th century with the election of Andrew Jackson, 7th president of the United States (1829–1837), who fought the Creek at Horseshoe Bend in 1813, virtually wiping out the Upper Creek nation, which was forced to relinquish 23 million acres of tribal homeland to white settlement. The remnants of the tribe moved west to Arkansas and ultimately to Oklahoma. Jackson thereby set the protocol for dealing with recalcitrant Indians.

The fascination with Indian fighters continued with William Henry Harrison, 9th president (1841), who fought the Shawnee under Tecumseh at Tippecanoe in 1812, and with Zachary Taylor, 12th president (1849–1850), Seminole Indian fighter in 1837 and hero of the Mexican War of 1846.

So persuasive was this sentiment that Abraham Lincoln, 16th president (1861–1865), relied on his service in the militia during the Black Hawk War, a minor Indian uprising in 1832, to qualify himself as executive timber. Lincoln, who had been elected captain of his local militia unit, helped to chase Black Hawk and his Indians back into the Wisconsin wilderness. This was to be Lincoln's only military experience, yet as president during the Civil War, he consistently interfered with his generals in the field, second-guessing their strategies, and sending preemptory orders by way of the U.S. Military Telegraph. Ulysses S. Grant, 18th president (1869–1876) rose to office based solely on his Civil War performance.[20]

Indian Removal

During his operations in the Creek War and First Seminole War, Andrew Jackson, like William Henry Harrison, came to believe that there was no real distinction between friendly and hostile Indians. In 1828 Jackson won the presidency. Ultimately, like his predecessors, John Adams and James Monroe, President Jackson came to believe that the government should institute policies known as forced relocation, or removal, that would displace the remaining tribes of the Old Northwest to an area of the Great Plains west of the Mississippi River now known as Oklahoma. Congressional debate between Whigs and Democrats questioned what was best for the Indians, but neither side suggested that the Indians retain their homelands or reestablish their former aboriginal lifestyle elsewhere. Realistically, the inter-tribal raids and free-roaming hunting associated with their traditional existence could no longer be accommodated within the boundaries of the developed states without conflict between Indians and whites.

The issue of removal was complicated by two additional facts. First, the "Civilized Nations" of the South—the Choctaw, Chickasaw, Creek, Cherokee, and Seminole—were settled in villages in the region of white encroachment and were using agricultural techniques that made them greatly more advanced than the western tribes of the Great Plains. The Cherokee and the Creek mounted a particularly strong opposition to removal for this reason. Secondly, there had been intermarriage between the native peoples and both whites and blacks, producing many persons of mixed race. This was particularly true among the Seminole. The lifestyle adopted by these mixed-race persons very closely resembled that of neighboring white farmers: dressing in the same style, following Christianity, and even owning slaves. Full-blooded natives, however, tended to retain their tribal dress and customs.

In 1846 Francis Parkman recorded a description of a "civilized" Shawnee village on the Arkansas River. "It was a beautiful alternation of fertile plains and groves, whose foliage was just tinged with the hues of autumn, while close beneath them rested neat log-houses of the Indian farmers. Every field and meadow bespoke the exuberant fertility of the soil. The maize [corn] stood rustling in the wind, matured and dry, its shining yellow ears thrust out between gaping husks. Squashes and enormous yellow pumpkins lay basking in the sun in the midst of their brown and shriveled leaves. Robins and bluebirds flew about the fences: and everything in short betokened our near approach to home and civilization."[21]

Congressman Wilson Lumpkin of Georgia was determined, nonetheless, to give the president of the United States the legal authority and the budget to clear out the Indians from the most desirable lands in America, especially the Cherokee of his own state of Georgia. Lumpkin worked hard to develop support for the Indian Removal Bill in Congress. In both the Senate and the House the bill was highly divisive, generating hot and bitter debate. "The whole country was watching what was going on in Washington. Newspapers and magazines had long articles about the Indian question. Preachers preached sermons about it. Letters from clergymen in the North and farmers in Pennsylvania poured in on Congressmen. Men and women in sleepy little New England villages held meetings and passed resolutions and wrote protests and petitions to Congress. . . . Rescue these intelligent, civilized, Christian people." The *Cherokee Phoenix*, an Indian-language newspaper made possible by the alphabet created by the Cherokee scholar Sequoyah, printed letters of protest from Indians and whites alike that reminded the government of the debt it owed to the Cherokee for having fought against the "Red Sticks." It was obvious that the Indians had white supporters from all over the country.[22]

People had waited nervously for word of the act's fate in Congress. In 1830, the Indian Removal Act was signed into law, and many were shocked when they learned that it had passed. The whole American people had seemed to be against it, yet for the next 100 years, removal to reservations in the West remained a basic Indian policy of the Federal government. The Removal Act empowered the states, if they so chose, to expel any of the native residents of a region by a forced exchange of land in the East for land in the West. The land that was being taken from the tribes was worth 100 times that allotted to them. Alabama and Mississippi followed Georgia in passing laws requiring the Indians to comply. With the discovery of gold in Georgia on Cherokee land, further laws were passed that forbade any meeting of the Cherokee tribal council, but the Indians remained steadfast in their opposition to relocation. In 1838, after the Cherokee had withstood court challenges, threats, bribes, confiscation of property, severed supplies, and other harassments to remain on their tribal lands, an escort of armed troops under the supervision of Winfield Scott forced a great column of displaced Indian families westward. More than a quarter of these Indians died on this journey, which came to be known among the Cherokee as the "Trail of Tears."

The Creek in Alabama had a multitude of legitimate grievances against the state when they met with the Secretary of War, Lewis Cass, in 1838. More than 10,000 whites were already moving into Creek lands in anticipation of their removal, burning native homes, and confiscating their livestock. It was reported that many whites were willing to lynch Federal soldiers if they attempted to protect the natives. Indian pleas to the government fell on deaf ears, and the Creek were gathered together and marched off, many in manacles, to the western lands. As a result of the treatment of the Cherokee and Creek, many other tribes simply relinquished their resistance and moved west.

Only in Florida, among the Seminoles, did the native, black, and mixed-race populations form an effective alliance against the white troops sent to remove them. Fought almost constantly during the first half of the 19th century, the war with the Seminoles is often considered the longest lasting struggle between Indians and whites waged in America.[23] In 1823 the government reneged on its previous agreements with the Indian leaders and an estimated 4,000 Seminoles were ordered to leave Florida and remove to Oklahoma. Many refused when they discovered that any of them who had black blood would not be allowed to leave and might be sold into slavery. One of the reasons for the almost continuous prosecution of a five-decade long war against the Seminoles was the refuge they afforded to runaway black slaves and their acceptance of blacks into their families and among their leadership. This fueled support for the war among the plantation owners and white yeomen farmers who lived in constant fear of slave revolts.

Scattered war parties raided isolated cabins, but no major action took place as the Indians generally stayed in the swamps. Nonetheless, the white population on the Florida frontier was greatly distressed by the rumors of Seminole solidarity. A contemporary observer noted, "Men, women, and children are seen flying in every direction, and leaving everything behind them save a few articles of clothing. Many families that were comfortable. . . are now reduced to want; their houses. . . having been plundered and burned by small bands of Indians."[24]

In 1834 Zachary Taylor was given command of 1,100 men to fight the Seminoles. Taylor had a military career that spanned 40 years, and he saw action in the War of 1812 when he and 50 men defended themselves against 400 Indians in Indiana Territory. In the Seminole Wars he served under a number of generals, but rose to prominence on Christmas Day, 1837, when he fought a pitched battle against 400 to 500 Seminole and African-Seminole warriors at Lake Okeechobee. Taylor emerged from the battle as a martial hero and a national figure. He was made a brigadier after winning the battle but failed during the next three years to eradicate the Seminole problem.

The Everglades region of Florida, called the "River of Grass" by the Indians, was composed of swamps, twisted rivers, and directionless streams that disappeared into the tangled overgrowth or became vast watery marshes without warning. The Seminole had been moving their families into the swamps since the trouble started, taking all they had with them. They could live there for years, perhaps forever, among the hammocks or small hills that dotted the landscape. It was an "impossible country" for military operations. U.S. troops entering the swamps met with repeated defeats and sometimes disaster at the hands of the Seminole. The Second War years were the most intense of the five-decade-long Seminole conflict. Seven generals in as many years tried desperately, in some cases, to bring the Seminole to heel without success.[25]

In the fall of 1837 the government asked representatives of the Cherokee nation to serve as intermediaries with the Seminole leaders, who came in under a flag of truce to talk. However, after an extended period of lagging discussions, the Seminole leaders were seized. The outraged Cherokee led by chief John Ross, a mixed-race member of the Cherokee Council, protested "the unprecedented violation of that scared rule which has ever been recognized by every nation." Nonetheless, the military continued to seize Seminole under false pretenses throughout the war. Osceola, one of the most important Seminole leaders, was encouraged to come to a peace conference in 1837, but was assaulted and bundled off to jail in Charleston, where he died in 1838 and was buried on the grounds of Fort Moultrie.[26]

After 1842, the government abandoned its focus on exterminating the Seminole; and some of the tribal leaders agreed to removal to Oklahoma. The government declared the Seminole conflict over in May 1858. Moves to end the war by negotiation were met by cries of shame from Floridians on the frontier; but, among other Americans, Congressman Henry Wise complained that the "fatal, disastrous, disgraceful Seminole campaign" was being continued "without inquiry, and without discussion." Wise asked, "Would any corporation or company take 30 millions of dollars to pay the expenditures of this disgraceful Indian war?"[27] About 120 Seminole remained behind, quietly residing in the swamps throughout the Civil War. In the end, the cost of Indian removal was approximately one white death for every three Indians transported.

A morbid antiquarianism and curiosity surrounding the Indian wars quickly affected the American public. The most compelling fact was the removal of Osceola's head from his corpse before burial by Dr. Frederick Weedon, the attending doctor at his death. Weedon may have anticipated selling the head or saving it for examination—not an uncommon activity among medical men in the first part of the 19th century. Several years later the head, carefully labeled and protected in a glass and mahogany case, was in the possession of Dr. Valentine Mott of New York City as part of his vast anatomical collection. In 1865, Mott willed the head to a New York medical college, but the specimen was lost in a fire at the school.

Less bizarre by modern standards, but highly characteristic of the times, were the series of lectures given by veterans of the Seminole Wars to expectant audiences who paid well to hear them. Ranson Clark, one of only three survivors of the Dade Massacre of 1835, was slow to recuperate from his shoulder wound and was discharged from the army in 1836 with a monthly pension of eight dollars. Considerably disabled, Clark attempted to make a living by giving talks about the battle in which 108 of his fellow soldiers died, with his wounded arm conspicuously supported by a sling. He died about four years after returning to his home in Griegsville, New York, from infectious complications of his wound. Likewise, Benjamin Alvord, only briefly a subaltern officer in Dade's command, was called upon to give a speech before the Dialectic Society of the Corps of Cadets at West Point commemorating the third anniversary of the battle and the nine Academy graduates who at that time (1838) had given their lives fighting the Seminole. He was later a serving general officer in the Mexican War and American Civil War.[28]

Texas and the War with Mexico

Although the War Hawks of 1812 envisioned the quick acquisition of parts of Canada and Spanish Florida among their war aims, the conflict between newly independent Mexico (1823) and the United States was the first major military campaign clearly driven by the concept of Manifest Destiny. The Mexican War (1846–1848) inevitably followed from an earlier crisis between American settlers in the Mexican state of Texas and the government of Gen. Antonio Lopez de Santa Anna in Mexico City.

In 1836 an army of Texans (Texicans) led by the former governor of Tennessee, Sam Houston, wrested all of Texas from the Mexican republic at the Battle of San Jacinto. While this army was being formed, a small group of about 200 audacious Texans under the leadership of William Travis, James Bowie, and David "Davy" Crockett had fortified an adobe mission (known as the Alamo) and its surrounding buildings in San Antonio de Bahare for 13 days against an overwhelming force of 3,000 Mexicans under Santa Anna. On the final day of the siege of the Alamo, Santa Anna's troops overran the defenders, killing all but a handful. The surviving men, including Crockett (a former member of the U.S. House of Representatives), were summarily executed. Three women, two white children, and a black boy were the only survivors.

The defense of the Alamo mission was foolhardy and doomed to failure. Nonetheless, almost 1,600 of Santa Anna's troops were killed during the action, and the defense of the mission served as one of the most glorious events in the short history of the Republic of Texas. The brutality of the siege's climax, taken together with the execution of more than 400 Texans at Goliad shortly thereafter, created popular sympathy for Texas in the United States, but America was busy at the time fighting the Seminole. Southerners (in fact, all Americans) were nonetheless quick to incorporate the defense of the Alamo into their own martial mythology—a circumstance that served as a factor in later disputes between the Southern states and the Federal government. It was altogether fitting that Southerners felt as they did as the majority of the Texans at the mission exulted in their own Southern heritage and ancestry. Nonetheless, as a result of the savage fighting, the American public everywhere developed an unreasonably negative stereotype of the Mexican people and their government.

Partly due to continued friction with Mexico, Texas decided to join the United States when the offer was made by President James K. Polk in 1845. The annexation was accepted by Congress on July 4. Competing claims concerning the boundaries of Texas with the states of Sonora and Chihuahua became a major point of international friction with Mexico, which sent in troops to occupy the contested region between the Nueces and Rio Grande Rivers. On April 25, 1846, an armed clash took place between Mexican and American troops stationed in the region. An American scouting party sent to the north bank of the Rio Grande to tweak the Mexican's diplomatic nose was ambushed without provocation.

Unlike the War of 1812, the Americans serving in the army raised against Mexico were almost entirely regularly enlisted troops. The conflict included the deployment of a combination of traditional European-style arms, including cavalry and naval support, but whereas the artillery was the queen of European battlefields, the combat arm of decision in America remained the infantry. Several of the senior commanders of America's Civil War in the 1860s gained their first command experience in the war with Mexico, among them Generals Winfield Scott, Robert E. Lee, Thomas

"Stonewall" Jackson, William T. Sherman, George Meade, George B. McClellan, Ambrose Burnside, and future presidents Zachary Taylor and Ulysses S. Grant. Also in the group was future U.S. Secretary of War and Confederate President Jefferson Davis.

Francis Parkman, then 23 years old, was on the Upper Arkansas River in the summer of 1846 when for the first time he witnessed the passage of part of the army (Price's Missouri Regiment) headed for Santa Fe. He wrote:

They all belonged to a company raised in St. Louis. There were some ruffian faces among them, and some haggard with debauchery, but on the whole they were good-looking men, superior beyond measure to the ordinary rank and file of the army. Except that they were booted to the knees, they wore their belts and military trappings over the ordinary dress of citizens. Besides their swords and holster pistols, they carried slung from their saddles the excellent Springfield carbines. . . . The Missourians . . . were excellent irregular troops . . . owing to a singular combination of military qualities in the men themselves.[29]

The military spirit of the entire nation was aroused. Eager for the American nation to expand and expecting a quick victory, many young men rushed to the recruiting stations, and a number of regiments had to turn away additional enlistees when their ranks became filled to overflowing.

It should be noted that the armed forces of Mexico and the United States were essentially equal in the 1840s in terms of weapons technology and the manpower they brought to the field. Indeed, the Mexicans had a better-defined military tradition, a battle-practiced artillery, and a field-tested tactical protocol and command structure. They had spent almost two decades putting down insurrections among their own people and among the Indian population, particularly the Apache, Yaqui, and Comanche nations. Although the Americans were often outnumbered by five to one at the critical point of contact with the enemy, they visited humiliating defeats upon the Mexicans at almost every turn through the ardor of their attacks. "No men ever embarked upon a military expedition with a greater love for the work before them."[30]

From the beginning the American military commanders envisioned a three-pronged strategy to seize control of northern Mexico. Two American armies moved south out of Texas while a force under Colonel Stephen Kearney traveled west to Santa Fe (New Mexico) and then to California. Meanwhile the U.S. Navy seized the California ports at Monterey and Los Angles. At Palo Alto and Resaca de Palma, Gen. Taylor defeated the Mexicans and moved south. Taylor then fought a bloody three-day battle at the Mexican city of Monterey; however, the extended desert fighting was taking its toll on his contingent. Under these conditions a successful march to Mexico City seemed unlikely.

To that end Gen. Winfield Scott landed an army of 12,000 men on the beaches of Vera Cruz in March 1847. This combined arms operation with the Navy was the largest amphibious landing of American troops attempted up to that time. During the next eight months, Scott fought a series of difficult battles on his way to entering the Mexican capital in September. These battles included Cerro Gordo, Contreras, Churubusco, Molino del Rey, and Chapultepec. Their names became everyday words among the American public at home. The series of defeats visited on Mexican forces had sparked armed rebellions in both California and New Mexico, which were surrendered to U.S. authorities or their representatives almost without resistance.

On February 20, 1848, the Treaty of Guadeloupe Hidalgo was signed, yielding much of northern Mexico and California to the United States for a payment of $15 million. The war added to the heroic legend surrounding Zachary Taylor and made him a president. Meanwhile it made Winfield Scott the premiere soldier in the American Army, a position he would retain until the Civil War. It also raised the profile of Robert E. Lee, insuring his appointment as Colonel Commandant of the U.S. Military Academy at West Point. Here he helped to train many of the officers who served on both sides in the Civil War. The surge of American patriotism that followed the Mexican War, strengthened by the acquisition of a firm boundary for the Oregon Territory from Britain, added to the national euphoria for completing its manifest destiny.

However, the results of the war were not universally popular with all Americans. The cost of the war itself had topped $100 million and more than 13,000 Americans and at least 25,000 Mexicans had lost their lives, mostly to disease. This represented a combined U.S. casualty rate from all causes of between 30 and 40 percent. Approximately 1,700 Americans were killed in battle. This last figure shocked many Americans in 1848 who, after 1861, would think it low compared to the daily carnage of the Civil War.

The first American peace societies had sprung forth in New York, New England, and Ohio in 1815 in response to the continued war with Britain, and they had coalesced in 1818 under the banner of the American Peace Society. These pacifists were most successful in limiting the funds for armaments and naval building programs. They simply assumed that ships and guns were the most probable causes of any future international involvements. In 1842, the Tyler administration failed to get even as much money as had been appropriated in the previous year. Nonetheless, James K. Polk, an otherwise humorless and unexciting candidate, had captured the Executive Mansion under the slogan concerning the Oregon boundary of "Fifty-four Forty or Fight." With the outgoing Tyler signing the Texas Annexation Act, Polk had seemingly dedicated the nation to a two-front war against Mexico and Britain. Charles Sumner provided the pacifists with a springboard in 1845 when he gave a Fourth of July oration regarding the approaching Texas and Oregon crises. "Can there be in our age any peace that is not honorable, any war that is not dishonorable?"[31]

Among the anti-war voices that could be heard at this time were those of Ralph Waldo Emerson and former president John Quincy Adams, who considered the war with Mexico a blatant form of aggression. The classic anti-government essay of Henry David Thoreau, *On Civil Disobedience,* was written at this time to protest the use of tax money to prosecute what he considered an unjust war. "When a sixth of the population of a nation [the United States] which has taken to be a refuge of liberty are slaves, and a whole country [Mexico] is unjustly overrun and conquered by [our] army and subjected to military law, I think it is not too soon for honest men to rebel and revolutionize." By refusing to pay his poll taxes, Thoreau protested the war and was hauled off to jail. The episode, brief as it was, produced a work of political philosophy so profound that it reached out to the minds of Mahatma Gandhi and Martin Luther King, Jr., more than a century later.[32]

Elihu Burritt was the American founder of the first International Peace Congress held in Brussels in 1848. He was also affected by the Mexican War. Playwright Victor Hugo presided over the second "Peace Congress" in Paris in 1849. Successive meetings from 1850 through 1853 were all held in Europe, and attended mostly by Europeans. In 1854, the Crimean War jolted Burritt into a realization that both his fellow countrymen and the leaders of other nations were unimpressed by his calls for world brotherhood and international arbitration, and he turned his attention to abolition, temperance, and justice for Irish immigrants in America. He was Consul to Great Britain during the Lincoln administration.

The center of this anti-war disaffection was generally to be found among the academic communities of New England, but the bulk of the unrest was largely related to the abolition movement, which feared the expansion of slavery in the Union. One of the strategic errors made by pro-slavery apologists at this point was to allow the abolitionists to turn the slavery argument into a debate over whether the practice would be extended into the vast expanse of unorganized territories that the nation had assembled in meeting its manifest destiny. Although the South vociferously demanded a share in the nation's territorial opportunity, by mid-century the question of slavery in the territories had, in fact, become nothing more than symbolic in itself. Few regions remained into which slavery could be introduced economically. Cotton, rice, and sugar—the labor-intensive crops that seemingly demanded a slave workforce for their cultivation on a commercial scale—could not be grown in most of the bone-dry desert Southwest or in the cold and damp Northwest. Crops like rice and sugar demanded moisture, and cotton needed at least 200 frostless days of growth. These facts limited their practical production to those areas of the South in which it already existed. It seemed equally unlikely that slaves could have been employed economically among the apple orchards of Oregon or the vineyards of California. Nonetheless, Southerners rarely made these arguments, and the question of the extension of slavery persisted. The debate remained a focus of sectionalism and a catalyst for discord throughout the 1850s.

In the period between the Mexican War and the Civil War, military matters moved west of the Mississippi River and away from the cities of the United States. No large number of civilians or great population centers would again be threatened by Native Americans, excepting the city of New Ulm, Minnesota, which was attacked by the Sioux in 1862. The resulting period of peace meant that Indian fighters had, for the moment, less chance of pursuing a political career based on a successful Indian campaign. Yet the generally belligerent military officers of the 19th century would find new fields of sanguinary endeavor to plow.

On the West Coast

The California tribes were among the first to feel the armed threat of white intrusion brought on by the discovery of gold in California. In the 1850s the tribes that had resided in the Sierra Nevadas were driven away from their hunting, fishing, and gathering grounds by the miners and lumberjacks. The native population of California decreased by as much as 70 percent before the Civil War. In 1847 Marcus and Narcissa Whitman, a married couple serving as missionaries to the Indians in Oregon for the American Missionary Board, were killed along with 14 other whites by Cayuse Indians upset by the death of nearly all their children during a measles epidemic. Although the Whitmans administered to all the sick, only half of the infected white children had died. Subsequently, the militia took the field looking for retribution and escalating the incident into a war.

From 1851 to 1856 whites undertook supposedly punitive raids against the Yakima, Walla Walla, and Cayuse nations. In 1855, Yakima attacks on parties of prospectors brought in the U.S. regular army under Col. George Wright, who broke the tribe and forced the Indians onto reservations. Not until the interposition of Gen. William S. Harney did the raiding and counter-raiding end. Harney, promoted to general and transferred to the command of the Oregon Territory in 1858, used his understanding of the Indians to initiate a relatively peaceful settlement out of the ongoing troubles in the Northwest.

On the Plains

The withdrawal of Federal troops to the East to fight the Civil War changed the nature of Indian Wars during 1861–1865. On the Great Plains in the 1850s the army had been very active in mounting an offense against the tribes. In 1854, Harney, then a colonel, had mounted a series of bloody raids on the villages of the Lakota Sioux in Nebraska; in 1857, Col. Edwin V. Sumner attacked a large body of Cheyenne warriors on the Solomon River in Kansas; and finally, Col. Earl Van Dorn fought the Comanche at Rush Spring in Oklahoma and at Crooked Creek in Kansas in 1859 and 1860, respectively.

In 1861 the Federal government was concentrating on winning battles in Virginia and Tennessee, and it more or less ignored the "Indian problem" in the Great Plains, leaving the policing of the tribes to volunteer forces and irregular partisans. What resulted was a series of mistakes, blunders, and massacres throughout the Civil Wars years made by part-time soldiers and amateur officers. As one observer noted, "Every once in a while the soldiers themselves got cleaned out, [and] the Indians. . . massacred everyone in the whole place." Unfortunately, many of these same errors would be repeated by regular troops in the post-war years.[33]

In 1861 an irregular force of Americans attacked a previously peaceful encampment of Chiricahua Apache under the leadership of Cochise. The Apache Wars that followed this incident lasted for a quarter-century. In 1862 a column of California volunteers under Col. James Carleton fought several skirmishes with the Apache in Arizona. Also in 1862, the Santee Sioux of Minnesota opened a series of raids against settlers, traders, missionaries, and lumberjacks, killing nearly 1,000 whites and losing hundreds of their own people. Gen. Henry Sibley, a former fur trader and governor of the territory, met the Santee in battle at Wood Lake and defeated them. Sibley sentenced 303 captured Santee warriors to death by hanging, but President Lincoln commuted the sentences of all but 38 of the Indian leaders. These men were hanged en masse in December 1862 as a lesson to other Plains tribes.

The relatively peaceful Navajo of the Southwest were engaged by militia and frontier forces in 1861. Kit Carson, the frontier scout, made his reputation fighting the Navajo. With the outbreak of Civil War, Carson resigned his post as Indian agent in New Mexico, and organized a volunteer militia. With the rank of colonel of volunteers, he commanded 60 percent of the Union forces in the territory, and he fought the Texas Confederates under Sibley at the Battle of Valverde in 1862. Thereafter, all regular Union forces were called East, and Carson instituted a scorched-earth policy against the Navajo. In this he was aided by the Ute who were long-standing enemies of the Navajo. In 1864 he added to his reputation at the battle at Canyon de Chelly, where dozens of warriors were killed and hundreds captured. In the spring of that year, 8,000 Navajo men, women, and children were forced to march 300 miles to reservations near Fort Sumner.

Finally in 1864, Col. John M. Chivington and the 3rd Colorado Volunteer Cavalry attacked a peaceful Cheyenne/Arapaho village at Sand Creek. The Indians under Black Kettle—men, women, and children—were horribly massacred and many of their bodies desecrated. The horrors of the Sand Creek Massacre set off renewed warfare with the Plains tribes. In 1865 the Arapaho and Lakota tribes sacked Julesburg, Colorado, cut the telegraph, destroyed the supply trains, and drove the cavalry into their forts on the South Platte River and in the Powder River country.

The New Indian Fighters

The military heroes of the antebellum period were often professional career army officers who had used their prominence to secure a political career at the state or territory level. They could usually attain a place in the local legislature or use their service to embarrass a political opponent. After the Civil War, with almost every adult male capable of claiming war service, no political party was forced to emphasize the military career of a candidate in order to win high office. The failure of George B. McClellan, the Federal commanding general from 1861 to 1862 to beat a disliked, handicapped, and weakened incumbent (Lincoln) in 1864 presaged this development, and the inglorious presidency of Ulysses Grant left future military candidates in disfavor. Presidential candidate Rutherford B. Hayes had been wounded five times in the war, yet he failed to carry the popular vote in 1876 and received the electoral victory only after an election committee, voting along strict partisan lines, decided three disputed states in his favor. Not until the era of Teddy Roosevelt would martial prowess again be held in high esteem. The Indian fighters of the last half of the 19th century were the "boy generals" of the Civil War. Chief among these were George Armstrong Custer, Nelson A. Miles, and George A. Crook.

Army officers serving in the West in the 1860s and 1870s were usually Civil War veterans. Many, like Custer who was a brevet (temporary) major general in the war emergency, reverted after 1865 to their formal rank. This was not a demotion, but a return to the officer's actual rank. Custer was a lieutenant colonel, but many of his admirers, including his wife, continued to call him "General," the highest rank he had ever held. Under army regulations at the time, this was perfectly correct. Many high-ranking officers served against the Indians in grades from colonel down to lieutenant. This could cause severe strains among officers serving together whose relative superiority was somehow upended.

Officers, like those serving today, usually brought their families to live with them at the forts and larger posts where there was only a minimal danger from Indian attack. A limited number of NCOs—usually long-term sergeants—were permitted to bring their families on the posts. The wives of officers and those of enlisted men formed two mutually exclusive societies on the post. This was reinforced by a strict military caste system that applied to all persons related to those in the military. However, the presence of civilian women and their offspring created a number of more practical difficulties for army families, especially in terms of their homes, which were often limited to a set of rooms in simple frame buildings similar to the barracks in which the soldiers lived. Some women attempted to set up schools for the young children taught by the better-educated wives and mothers, but anything other than a rudimentary schooling had to be sought elsewhere, usually in the East.

The cavalry and infantry companies that fought the Plains tribes numbered about 75 men. There were 10 companies in an infantry regiment and 12 troops of cavalry in a mounted unit. Recruits, after the Civil War, were hard to find, and many recruiters depended on enlisting immigrants in order to fulfill their quotas. Many ex-Confederate officers served in the ranks, sometimes under assumed names. When posted to their regiment recruits rarely changed establishments. Once assigned, their squads and companies quickly became their home and family. The men ate, slept, and fought together, and they were forced by circumstances to trust each other implicitly.

Enlistees were short on training and long on discipline, which was very harsh. Punishments for even minor infractions could include extra fatigue duty, fines, time in the guardhouse, and physical punishment. William Murphy of Company A, 2nd Battalion, 18th U.S. Infantry, witnessed a man "spread eagled" for drunkenness, "At the guard tent four stakes were driven into the ground and the drunken soldier was stretched at full length and tied to them. . . . The sun was beating down on him when I saw him, and I thought he was dead. Flies were eating him up and were running in and out of his mouth, ears and eyes." Murphy also reported that a man was branded with a hot iron before being drummed out of the army.[34]

Prominent among the men who fought in the Indian Wars were the buffalo soldiers of the 9th and 10th Cavalry, and the 24th and 25th Infantry. These were black soldiers, many of whom had volunteered to remain in the service after the Civil War. Although they were commanded by white officers and had strict segregation practiced against them, they did have their own NCOs and were treated with respect as Indian fighters. Custer had been offered the command of the 9th Cavalry, but demurred because he considered blacks poor soldiers. Instead he accepted the 7th Cavalry, a unit noted for the number of alcoholic Irishmen in its ranks.

Soldiers on campaign were limited to hardtack, bacon, and beans as a daily ration, but when at their homes, the fare varied more widely. Common among the meals prepared by army housewives were variations on meat dishes, including beef, pork, and chicken like hashes or stews. Buffalo meat and fresh game were available. Coffee, sugar, flour, vinegar, and salt were almost always part of the common ration, but the army did not provide dairy products like milk, butter, and cheese, and fresh vegetables, if not grown in a local patch, were difficult to get. Potatoes, onions, and rice could be bought at the sutler's store, as well as canned foods, with oysters, sardines, peaches, and condensed milk being popular. As with other frontier families, army families relied on a diet of dried fruits, preserves, and salted or pickled meats that they prepared themselves when in season.

The Plains Wars

The Plains tribes had first been encountered by the Lewis and Clark Expedition as it crossed the northern plains during their exploration of the Louisiana Purchase (1803–1805). These nations included many inter-related tribes and discrete bands, some of which were bitter enemies. These included Arapaho, Ute, Pawnee, Crow, Nez Percé, Cheyenne, and Sioux. Many recognized bands were actually subdivisions of others. For instance, the Blackfoot were generally considered to be part of the Siouan language family, while others like the Cheyenne and Sioux formed political or defensive alliances. Other nations were traditional enemies.

The most historically colorful of the Plains tribes were the Sioux (Lakota or Dakota), who gave their name to two U.S. states. Their several bands generally followed the migrating herds of buffalo, camping freely in Colorado, Wyoming, Nebraska, western Kansas, southern Montana, the Dakotas, and parts of Canada. The holy ground and cultural anchor of the Sioux was an area of Wyoming known as the Black Hills. When first contacted by Lewis and Clark, the Sioux were found to be so unfriendly as to be labeled hostile, yet they freely traded with French Europeans, the agents of the British Hudson's Bay Company, and the mixed-race métis in the 18th century and early 19th centuries.

In 1849 the Federal government purchased a trading establishment at the confluence of the North Platte and Laramie Rivers and made it into a military post. Rechristened Fort Laramie, the substantial structure was meant to protect and aid travelers along the newly developed Oregon Trail and to establish a central position from which to treat with the Indians. In 1851 a commission headed by David Mitchell, Superintendent of Indian Affairs, extracted a commitment from the local tribes for the safe passage of wagons to Oregon. John Young Nelson, a white who lived on and off among the Sioux from 1845 to 1888, wrote:

The Indians saw their doom by the increased traffic through their country, and protested. A commission was sent out by the Government to negotiate, with a view to guaranteeing the safety of the caravans upon receiving an annual subsidy. This was fixed at some thousands of dollars, and it was agreed that it should be paid in goods, such as blankets, cloth, cotton stuff, powder, muskets, beads, kettles, and in fact whatever articles were required. These were sent to Fort Laramie, the general rendezvous, where the various tribes would come for their share of the tribute. Government agents were appointed, and everything was fixed to the satisfaction of both the contracting parties.[35]

The Civil War stemmed the flow of settlers moving through Indian country on the Oregon Trail, and the only recognized and significant attempt to move through the Powder River country north of Laramie by another route during the war years was made by a group of men led by a trailblazer named John M. Bozeman. Attracted by gold strikes on the Salmon River in Montana, 25-year-old Bozeman left a wife and three small daughters in Georgia in 1862 and went west with 15 companions. His father, William, had left a wife and five children to chase gold in 1849. Neither father or son ever returned home. Because the new trail through the Bighorn and Yellowstone country was outside the treaty area, the Indians drove the Bozeman party back.

At the end of the Civil War, in 1866, the Federal government established three outposts on the trail in order to secure passage through the region. Beginning in June 1866, the Ogallala Sioux, under the leadership of Red Cloud and Crazy Horse, began to raid wagons and forts along the Bozeman Trail. Although the Indians had initially allowed the trail to be cleared and used, war parties under the direction of Red Cloud began attacking isolated groups of woodcutters that left the protective confines of the fort to bring in lumber and firewood. Ultimately these outrages produced their own brand of conflicts and victories.

On December 21, 1866, William J. Fetterman, "an impetuous officer who had contempt for the fighting qualities of the Indians," went out with 80 men to relieve a party of woodcutters ostensibly under attack by a small party of Sioux believed to be led by Crazy Horse. Fetterman decided to carry the fight to the Indians and rode out of sight of the fort in pursuit. The small party proved to be a decoy, and Fetterman and all his men were killed in an ambush.[36]

On August 2, 1867, Red Cloud attacked a party of 14 woodcutters' wagons under the command of Capt. James W. Powell. Once alerted, Powell formed an enclosure of wagon boxes and prepared to repulse the attack of more than 100 mounted warriors. The Indians had learned to attack whites in successive waves, the first to draw their fire and the second to close before the standard muzzleloader could be reloaded, yet on this day the Indians attacked again and again, each time receiving undiminished fire from the wagon-box enclosure. The Indians were repulsed with great loss of life. It seems that Powell's men were armed with breech-loading Springfield rifles, which had been developed at the end of the Civil War. These could be loaded almost as quickly as they were fired, using a new .50 caliber self-contained cartridge.

Notwithstanding the new weapons, the attacks along the Bozeman Trail became so vehement that the government agreed to abandon the forts and remove from the region. The Indians burned both Fort C. F. Smith and Fort Phil Kearny after they were abandoned. This was a great victory for Red Cloud, yet the government used the quiet after the crisis to call for a treaty negotiation at Fort Laramie in 1868. The Fort Laramie

Treaty brought temporary peace to the Plains by closing the Bozeman Trail and promising that no new forts would be built. "We [the government] will protect you against all future inconvenience. We wish to set aside a part of your territory for your nation, where you may live forever, you and your children. . . . [And] so that your children may become as intelligent as the whites, we wish to send to you teachers who will instruct them." Among those who signed the treaty was Red Cloud. Congressional leaders ratified the document but insisted that the government was not perpetually bound by it. This attitude laid the groundwork for conflict in the 1870s.

Gen. William T. Sherman—the man who burned Georgia on his march to the sea—was put in charge of the Indian problem in the American West after the Civil War. His strategy included a continued attack on Indian villages not on reservations, the destruction of the Indian "pony herds," and the unremitting pursuit of those tribes deemed hostile by the government even during the winter months. Sherman envisioned the coordinated advance of several columns of troops (usually three) to converge on the Indians and to prevent their escape.

Yet Sherman did not take the field against the Indians, leaving the tactical command to younger, or more active, men, notably George Armstrong Custer of the 7th Cavalry and Nelson Miles of the 6th Infantry. Considered a rash and impetuous glory hunter, the figure of Custer would dominate the late Indian Wars even though men like Miles would be more effective. Other commanders took the field, but it has been noted that these were the only two who were not seemingly handicapped by senility or a sickbed.[37]

A Civil War hero, some say he saved the day for the Union during the cavalry battle at Gettysburg, Custer began fighting Indians at age 26. He was a flashy and courageous fighter, who had been given the brevet rank of major general of volunteers during the war, but in the post-war years had reverted to his permanent rank of lieutenant colonel of the 7th Cavalry Regiment. In November 1868, Custer and the 7th were called upon to retaliate for Indian raids throughout Kansas and Colorado by a group of warriors from the Fort Larned Reservation. At dawn Custer swept down through the snow-filled morning onto the village of Black Kettle on the Washita River. "Half-naked braves popped out of their tepees, sounding the war whoop. Grabbing their rifles, bows and arrows, they sprang behind frosted trees or bounded over the frozen banks and into the snow-filled gullies. Armstrong and Tom Custer picked them off with their revolvers as they weaved in and out of the trees and pounded around the lodges . . . shouting like buffalo hunters riding down game." At battle's end it was found that 103 warriors had been killed and 20 soldiers, cut off in the fight, had been killed. Seventy-five lodges had been burned and 53 women and children captured. Black Kettle, who died early in the fight, had had little to do with the original depredations. The frontier newspapers acclaimed Custer and the 7th Cavalry, and declared the result proper treatment for all Indians.[38]

In 1873 Custer began a rush to the Black Hills by confirming the discovery of gold there. The Sioux, under the religious leadership of Sitting Bull of the Teton band and the military leadership of Crazy Horse of the Ogallala band, resented the intrusion of white miners on their sacred ground and refused to sell the region to the government. On June 17, Gen. George A. Crook's command, mostly infantry, was fought to a standstill on the Rosebud River by the well-mounted warriors under the overall command of Crazy Horse. Then at the Little Bighorn River on June 25, Custer's 10 troops of cavalry, accompanied by a contingent of Crow Indian scouts, several civilians including newspaper reporters, and several male members of Custer's family (his brothers Tom and Boston, brother-in-law James Calhoun, and nephew Armstrong Reed) were met by unexpectedly overwhelming numbers of warriors. The attack stirred up a hornets' nest of Sioux, Cheyenne, and Arapaho who poured forth in defense of their own families. No white man knows what happened to Custer and his 215 men. The last trooper to see him alive was an Italian-American dispatch rider, Giovanni Martini.[39] The rest of the 7th Cavalry dug in on a ridge and fought off repeated attacks until evening, but they suffered heavy losses. The Custer "massacre" became the greatest defeat visited upon regular American troops by native forces in history. Gen. Phil Sheridan attributed the disaster to "a misapprehension of the situation and a superabundance of courage."[40]

Nonetheless, Lt. James H. Bradley felt that Custer wanted to "get there first and win all the laurels for himself and his regiment." In fact Custer had attacked within hours of his planned rendezvous with columns under Crook and Alfred Terry, who were the first to reach the site of the battle from the north.[41] Nonetheless, Custer, who had just passed the minimum age to be president of the United States in 1876, may have been positioning himself for a run at the Executive Mansion in 1880. Certainly in the months before the Little Bighorn campaign, Custer had purposely embroiled himself in a public debate with President Grant concerning corruption in the Indian Department. He made headlines everywhere.

The year 1876 saw the end of a full century of American independence. Colorado, the Centennial State, was admitted to the Union. America had grown into a modern industrial giant, and many Americans believed that there was no reason to continue to coddle savages in their midst. With the death of George Custer, the minds of the general public became completely closed to the plight of the Indians. The alliances between the tribes dissolved as the individual bands tried to evade detection or made for the Medicine Line in Canada.

Nelson A. Miles now took the reins in the Indian Wars. In 1876, the Modocs of northern California and southern Oregon were forced to flee and fight for their lives at Tule Lake, and in 1877 the Nez Percé were removed from Oregon to reservations in Idaho. The Nez Percé made an attempt to flee to Canada but were stopped by the U.S. Cavalry just a few miles short of the Medicine Line. In January 1877 Crazy Horse and Sitting Bull escaped to Canada during the spring of 1877. By September, Crazy Horse was dead, killed by the bayonet of an Indian guard at Fort Robinson. Word of his death caused 2,000 Indians to flee to Canada.

Part of Miles's strategy was to keep the recalcitrant tribes from their traditional food source—the buffalo. The migrating herds flowed north in summer into the Canadian plains and south in winter into the United States. For generations the Plains Indians depended on the annual buffalo hunt. Government policy encouraged the slaughter of the herds by white buffalo hunters so that the remnant bands, faced with starvation, would be forced onto the reservations where they were promised beef, corn, flour, and blankets. Miles also might have turned his Indian fighting glory into a political career, but he was more interested in commanding the army and had not sufficiently paved his way with a campaign of public relations by the time he was prepared to run for office in 1904.[42]

In 1881 the great shaman Sitting Bull and 176 of his most loyal followers reentered the United States and surrendered at Fort Bufford on the Missouri River. The chief, who would appear as part of Buffalo Bill Cody's Wide West Show before his murder at the Standing Rock Agency in 1890, said at the surrender, "I wish it to be remembered that I was the last man of my people to surrender my rifle." Yet the surrender of Sitting Bull did not close the last chapter of America's disgraceful fight to dispossess the Indians of their birthright.[43]

War in the Desert

Since 1821 the Mexican government had followed an official policy of genocide regarding the Indians of the great Southwest, and the Treaty of Guadalupe Hidalgo that ended the Mexican-American War and the Gadsden Purchase had thrown much of the Southwest and much of the Indian problem into American hands. Initial contacts with the native tribes of the region were peaceful, but these soon became strained as Americans refused to recognize Indian rights and miners and settlers arrived in the territories. In a series of despicable incidents, Americans pretending friendship to the Indians killed or poisoned them, setting off a series of wars that lasted from 1850 until 1886.

The desert tribes of the Southwest, particularly the Comanche, Kiowa-Apache, and Apache, had defied the authority of both the Spanish and American governments and had managed to delay white settlement of much of Texas, Arizona, and New Mexico for more than 100 years.

The Comanche were originally residents of the Yellowstone region of Wyoming and Colorado, where they split away from their Shoshone relatives after acquiring horses. The Kiowa were refugees from Teton Sioux aggression in the Black Hills. Besides these there were five major divisions of the Apache and these were separated into innumerable subtribes. There were two types of grouping: those based on territory and those based on kinship. In the 19th century there were more than 50 named clans with matrilineal-matrilocal bands composed of multiple households organized around a central woman, her husband, her married daughters, and their families. Although most marriages were monogamous, an individual man might be married at the same time to any number of sisters. Since the family lineage was based on the female and marriage was prohibited between closely related clans, kinship ties could be extremely complex. Apache men often sought eligible wives from among distant bands and were forced by the matrilocal family structure to reside away from their own clan.

Local leadership was supplied through the family hierarchy, but tribal or band leaders rose to prominence through the force of their personalities. Led in the second half of the 19th century by Mangas Coloradas, Cochise, Victorio, Geronimo, and others, marauding bands of Apaches attracted few friends, Indian or white. They were tireless and implacable enemies when pursuing a vendetta. When on the prod, they exhibited an uncanny slyness, a bottomless well of physical reserve, and a macabre and sometimes gruesome cruelty.

Up to the time of the Mexican-American War of 1846, the Apache reveled in attacking Spanish settlements and less aggressive tribes like the Pueblo or the Navajo. The Pueblo and Navajo Indians were no complacent people (digger Indians as some whites called them), but their time had passed. Few remained recalcitrant into the 19th century, and most had found life on Federal reservations adequate, if poor.

The Apache began raiding in the United States around 1850 and were soundly defeated by U.S. Army forces in 1856. They resumed their raiding when white forces were ordered east during the Civil War. Many fled their reservation in 1865 and remained hidden from official view until 1870, when, like other nations threatened by starvation or extermination, they accepted peace terms and a place on the reservations. These reservations were highly missionized, first by the Evangelical Lutherans and later by Catholics, Mormons, and Baptists. From their long exposure to the Catholic missionaries of Spain, it is not surprising to find that many Apache were exclusively Christian, while others followed their traditional religion in part or in whole. Many Apache spoke fluent Spanish, which facilitated communication and relieved misunderstandings somewhat. Gradually military posts were established in Apache territory, but they were constantly made smaller in land area, especially under presidential executive orders in 1873, 1876, and 1877. Many Apache bands railed under the poor government treatment, and small groups of warriors regularly left the agencies and raised terror throughout the region.

The Chiricahua Apache led by Cochise had initially made a truce with the Americans while continuing to raid into Mexico. In 1861 Lt. George Bascom falsely imprisoned five of Cochise's family, including his wife and child. Cochise retaliated by taking four whites captive and offering them in exchange. Bascom refused, and Cochise tortured his captives to death in a most humiliating and painful manner. Although Bascom released Cochise's wife and child, he hanged the Chiricahua leader's brother and two nephews. Cochise now sought tribal help in avenging his relatives' deaths, and gained in reputation and status in a series of strikes and counterstrikes against the whites. During an 11-year war with the Americans (1861–1872), he attracted recruits from among all the Western clans, and his position as an overall leader of the Apache nation was cemented when Mangas Coloradas was executed during a parley with U.S. forces. During much of this time Cochise fought both the Mexicans and the Americans, but he began to suffer defeats when the troops on both sides brought mobile prairie howitzers into the field against him. The Apache began to lose many lives as troops under George A. Crook pursued them incessantly. In 1872 a civilian, Thomas Jeffords, arranged a treaty with Gen. Oliver O. Howard, the one-armed veteran of the Civil War who helped to found Howard University. The Chiricahua made peace and maintained the treaty under the leadership of Cochise until he died in 1874.

The entire Southwest was considered to be under Apache threat from 1866 to 1886. Only during 1875 and 1876 were no Indian raids reported along the border with Mexico. The open revolt of the Plains tribes during those years caused the government to respond immediately to any raiding, and many Apache returned to the reservations during that period. In 1879 the Mescalero Apache under the leadership of Victorio raided on both the Mexican and Texan sides of the Rio Grande. Col. George Baylor, late of the Arizona Brigade of the 2nd Cavalry, transferred to the Frontier Battalion of the Texas Rangers and campaigned aggressively against Victorio, but was not able to capture him. Victorio was killed by Mexican forces in 1880, and in 1881 his followers were killed or captured by the Rangers as they returned to Texas, ending the Apache threat in that state.

Col. George Crook had been in charge of the operations that ended the war with Cochise in 1873, and he was made a brigadier. He spent 30 years on the frontier as an Indian fighter, setting the tactical parameters for all future operations against the Apache in Arizona.

Immediately after the death of Cochise, the war chief named Geronimo (*Goyathlay*) was able to recruit a small band of Chiricahua Apache to raid across New Mexico and Arizona. He had a deep belief in the traditional Apache spirits and was seemingly entrusted by the other bands with avenging the many Apache deaths that had taken place over time. Geronimo acquired a recognition among his people as an intrepid and cunning fighter. He seemingly moved in and out of Mexico at will, even though the American Army under Crook and the Mexican Army were constantly trying to intercept him. Crook returned Geronimo to the Turkey Creek Agency in 1884, but within a year the warrior and a small group of followers and their families had fled. It was at this point that Crook was replaced by Nelson A. Miles. When Geronimo finally surrender to Gen. Miles in 1886, he was one of the best-known Indian warriors in America, with stories about his exploits and atrocities filling the Eastern newspapers. He and his people were sent to Florida with almost 500 other Apache, including a number of former Apache scouts and their families. This was a disgraceful reward for those who had provided invaluable assistance to the government. In 1892 the Apache were removed to Oklahoma, where Geronimo sustained his family by ranching, farming, and selling autographed photographs of himself. He appeared at the St. Louis World's Fair and marched in Teddy Roosevelt's inauguration parade. The Apache were released by an act of Congress in 1913.

Meanwhile in 1890, there arose a final attempt by the Plains tribes to overcome the intrusions of the white man. The Plains tribes embraced the "Ghost Dance," a religious ritual that would return the buffalo and cause the whites to disappear. Government officials, seeing the tribes reassemble, grew suspicious and apprehensive. Troops from the 7th Cavalry surrounded a group of some hundreds of Indian men, women, and children at Wounded Knee and opened fire. Almost all the Indians and 29 soldiers were reported killed. The notorious massacre is usually considered the final battle of America's Indian wars.

The destruction of the Native American way of life in the 19th century may have been inevitable. A few tribes, notably those of the Southeastern woodlands like the Cherokee, attempted to interact positively with the whites and were either given reservation lands or were allowed to keep part of their own property. They began to assimilate a new culture that might have evolved had it been given a chance, but ultimately they were driven off or surrounded and fenced in as the whites dissected the public domain that once had been all Indian land.

The imposition of Anglo-European culture on native peoples had profoundly shocked and angered many Indian nations. Yet the fighting tribes did not give in easily, and what followed were wars, uprisings, raids, hunger, and desperation. They fought thinking that the white man was like the other Indian nations with whom they warred incessantly, but they soon found that the whites were a different kind of enemy, armed with powerful weapons, greater in number than their traditional opponents, and cold-blooded in their killing.

Notes

1. Thomas R. Dew, "Dissertation on the Characteristic Differences between the Sexes, and on the Position and Influence of Women in Society (1835),"

quoted in Leonard Pitt, ed., *Documenting America: A Reader in United States History from Colonial Times to 1877* (Dubuque, Iowa: Kendall/Hunt Publishing Co., 1989), 241.

2. Walter Millis, *Arms and Men: A Study of American Military History* (New York: A Mentor Book, 1956), 13.

3. Randolph B. Marcy, *The Prairie Traveler: A Hand-book for Overland Expeditions* (1859; repr., Bedford, Mass.: Aplewood Books, 1993), xi.

4. Ibid., xii.

5. Quoted in Millis, *Arms and Men,* 14.

6. See Harry Fritz, "The War Hawks of 1812," *Capital Studies* 5 (Spring 1977).

7. The discussion of the militia and provincial force that follows is largely taken from the authors' earlier work. See Dorothy Denneen Volo and James M. Volo, *Daily Life on the Old Colonial Frontier* (Westport, Conn.: Greenwood Press, 2002).

8. James Kirby Martin and Mark Edward Lender, *A Respectable Army: The Military Origins of the Republic, 1763–1789* (Arlington Heights, Ill.: Harlan Davidson, 1982), 8–9.

9. See John R. Gavin, *The Minute Men: The First Fight: Myths and Realities of the American Revolution* (Washington, D.C.: Brassey's, 1996).

10. See Fred W. Anderson, *A People's Army: Massachusetts Soldiers and Society in the Seven Years' War* (Chapel Hill: University of North Carolina Press, 1984).

11. David Hackett Fischer, *Albion's Seed: Four British Folkways in America* (New York: Oxford University Press, 1989), 732–733.

12. C. S. Forester, *The Age of Fighting Sail: The Story of the Naval War of 1812* (Sandwich, Mass.: Chapman Billies, 1956), 44–45.

13. Frances D. Robotti and James Vescovi, *The USS* Essex *and the Birth of the American Navy* (Holbrook, Mass.: Adams Media, 1999), 32.

14. The most widely accepted classification of Native American languages for the continental United States is that suggested by Edward Sapir in 1929. These included six groups of unrelated linguistic stocks.

15. Daniel K. Richter, *Facing East from Indian Country: A Native History of Early America* (Cambridge, Mass.: Harvard University Press, 2001), 225.

16. Ibid., 227.

17. Sean Michael O'Brien, *In Bitterness and in Tears: Andrew Jackson's Destruction of the Creeks and Seminoles* (Guilford, Conn.: Lyons Press, 2003), 9.

18. John K. Mahon, "Anglo-American Methods of Indian Warfare, 1676–1794," *The Mississippi Valley Historical Review* 45 (1958): 255.

19. Ian K. Steele, *Warpaths: Invasions of North America* (New York: Oxford University Press, 1994), 222.

20. See Thomas Mitchell, *Indian Fighters Turned American Politicians: From Military Service to Public Office* (Westport, Conn.: Greenwood Press, 2003).

21. Francis Parkman, *The Oregon Trail* (New York: Lancer Books, 1968), 441.

22. Anne Terry White, *The False Treaty: The Removal of the Cherokees from Georgia* (New York: Firebird Books, 1970), 65–66.

23. The Seminole were a loose aggregate of Indian bands that migrated from the river valleys of Georgia and Alabama to Florida. Today the Seminole and Miccosukee peoples are organized into two federally recognized tribes with seven reservations across the state of Florida.

24. John Missall and Mary Lou Missall, *The Seminole Wars: America's Longest Indian Conflict* (Gainesville: University Press of Florida, 2004), 94.

25. Frank Laumer, *Dade's Last Command* (Gainesville, FL: University of Florida Press, 1995), 19.

26. Missall and Missall, *The Seminole Wars*, 141.

27. Ibid., 189.

28. Laumer, *Dade's Last Command*, 229–230.

29. Parkman, *Oregon Trail*, 416.

30. Ibid., 414.

31. Millis, *Arms and Men*, 91.

32. Bernard DeVoto, *The Year of Decision, 1846* (Boston: Little, Brown & Co., 1943), 208–209.

33. Francis Marion Watkins as told to Ralph Leroy Milliken, "The Story of the Crow Emigrant Train of 1865," in a 1935 pamphlet reprinted by *The Livingston Chronicle*, January 1937, 12.

34. Murphy quoted in Dorothy M. Johnson, *The Bloody Bozeman* (New York: McGraw-Hill Book Co., 1971), 205.

35. John Young Nelson as told to Harington O'Reilly, *Fifty Years on the Trail: The Adventures of John Young Nelson* (Norman: University of Oklahoma Press, 1963), 104.

36. Alvin M. Josephy, Jr., *The Patriot Chiefs* (New York: Viking Press, 1962), 283.

37. D. A. Kinsley, *Favor the Bold: Custer, the Indian Fighter* (New York: Holt, Rinehart, & Winston, 1968), 205.

38. Ibid., 88.

39. Martini, the only man of Custer's five companies to survive the battle, became a subway worker in New York City in the 1880s, and was killed in a street accident by a beer truck early in the 20th century.

40. Kinsley, *Favor the Bold*, 232.

41. Ibid., 203.

42. Mitchell, *Indian Fighters*, 207.

43. Alvin M. Josephy, "The Custer Myth," *Life* 71, no. 1 (July 2, 1971): 48.

9

Father and the Civil War

An irrepressible conflict between opposing and enduring forces.

—William H. Seward

The sorrow for the dead is the only sorrow from which we refuse to be divorced. Every other wound we seek to heal, every other affliction to forget; but this wound we consider it a duty to keep open; this affliction we cherish and brood over in solitude.

—Town's Fourth Reader, 1866

Sectionalism

Americans were blessed with abundant rainfall, fertile land, a generally temperate climate, superior seaports and extensive inland waterways, and a remarkably resilient population; but they were also cursed with a growing sense of sectionalism that threatened to break the nation apart. By the middle of the 19th century, Americans had added substantially to the original list of 13 states. The hotly divisive political issue of advancing slavery into these newly acquired regions first came to a head in 1820–1821 when Missouri and Maine were admitted as slave and free states, respectively. Known as the Missouri Compromise, this free-state-for-slave-state protocol dominated the political tinkering of Congress until the Civil War and further polarized the nation. Of the 16 states to join the union by 1853, Louisiana, Mississippi, Arkansas, Missouri, Florida, Texas, Kentucky, and Tennessee were thought to align with the Southern way of thinking, while Maine,

Vermont, Ohio, Indiana, Illinois, Michigan, Iowa, and Wisconsin were formed up on the Northern side of the Mason-Dixon Line politically. While Maine and Vermont remained uniquely representative of New England, the states of the new Midwest tended to act as a separate entity economically, avowing distinct sectional issues of their own but joining the North in the call to limit slavery and to support a strong Federal government.

The deal-breaker for this political realignment was the passage of the Kansas-Nebraska Act in 1854, which seemingly sabotaged the political compromises that had characterized the previous decades of American politics. The passage of the act all but destroyed the already weakened Whig Party. Although the measure was popular among Northern Democrats and the Southern Democrats gave it support, its passage ultimately caused a split in the party. Outraged by the act, moderate Northern voters began to speak of the existence of a "Slave Power Conspiracy." In response, moderates in the South began to harden their position and seriously consider disunion. It was this division and the splintering of the electorate that allowed the newly formed Republican Party and its abolitionist base to gain a political plurality in the national elections of 1860.

This simple dichotomy between Northern principles and Southern sentiments during the run up to the Civil War is the stuff of history textbooks and grammar school recitations, but the reality on the ground was more complex and replete with contradictions. The national capital itself, central symbol of the unity of the republic, lay unfulfilled and unfinished in 1860 even after seven decades of labor. The plans for the city of Washington, like the plans for the republic, were as pretentious as they were visionary, and both were incomplete and open to revision. Meanwhile the city of Alexandria, Virginia, clearly visible across the Potomac River to the south, maintained itself with traditional style and architectural beauty.

Standard histories often focus on dissecting the causes of the war and the consequences that followed it to the exclusion of the people who lived it. No list of individual qualities can be truly representative of every American, nor could it exhaust all the traits represented in millions of individual citizens living in different sections of the country. Yet certain generalizations can be made. Most Americans exhibited traits that were generally representative of their sections, but the people themselves were perceptibly typical of their local communities. Both the war and its causes had serious effects on American families. One hundred years ago a historian of the Federalist period noted, "In the North one found English manners; in the Middle region a thousand shades had colored English manners; in the South the manners were those of the West-Indies." Americans from each section were well aware of their social distinctions and of their own loyalties, often to the point of being aggressively proud of them.[1]

Bleeding Kansas

In 1853, the House of Representatives decided to designate a large portion of the unorganized land in the Midwest into the Territory of Nebraska. The Kansas-Nebraska Act of 1854 revised the division of this territory into two parts, repealing the provisions of the Missouri Compromise regarding the extension of slavery and replacing them with the doctrine of Popular Sovereignty, which allowed the settlers of Nebraska and Kansas, respectively, to decide the question of slavery by majority vote. By 1855, Popular Sovereignty made Kansas a literal battleground of opposing forces. Armed companies of hastily organized militia and small quasi-military gangs intimidated settlers, overturned wagons, scattered stock, and smashed opposition presses. Before long, Missouri "border ruffians" had crossed into Kansas to attack and burn the free-state stronghold of Lawrence. Radical abolitionist John Brown, with his four sons, reacted quickly by killing five pro-slavery men at Pottawatomie Creek. Murder, lawlessness, and violence filled the territory. James Redpath, Brown's first biographer, observed that the anti-slavery men in Kansas trusted alone for victory to their Sharpe's rifles and the god of battles.

The Civil War

The election of Abraham Lincoln in 1860 assured the immediate secession of at least seven Southern states. In the weeks following, four more states left the Union, and several border states were prevented from doing so by the interposition of Federal troops. "If the Confederate experience did nothing else, it gave Southerners, many for the first time, a sense of corporate identity," noted an observer of the process.[2] Even the citizens of Tennessee, who had previously disavowed the idea of secession, overwhelming voted in favor of separation from the Union once Lincoln called for troops to suppress the rebellion. Hundreds of suggestions poured in from all levels and classes of Southern society when a committee of the Confederate Congress asked for designs for a new national flag. Nine out of ten of these were from women. A Southern woman's diary noted in April 1861, "Upon returning to my boarding-house . . . I found the ladies making secession flags. Indeed, the ladies everywhere seem imbued with the spirit of patriotism, and never fail to exert their influence in behalf of southern independence."[3] Women wore secession flags as part of their daily costume in the streets. Southern ladies formed Gunboat Societies that sponsored dances, bake sales, rummage sales, and auctions to raise money for the building of ironclads for the infant Confederate Navy to use in defending the harbors and waterways. Southern women were intensely aware of the need to maintain a Southern tradition and culture that had roots several decades deep, and their diaries and letters are replete with nationalistic themes.[4]

In the spring of 1861 enthusiasm for secession hastened Southern men to join the Confederate Army. The expectation of an eyeball-to-eyeball standoff across the Potomac or an early Southern victory convinced the South that few men would actually be needed. Enlistments of from six months to one year were common in these early days, and the war would surely be over before then. Volunteers swelled the recruiting offices, and the Confederate War Department had to turn away more than 200,000 men because they could not adequately provide supplies for them.

The first battle of the Civil War, Bull Run or First Manassas, dispelled much of the euphoria for war. More than 5,000 casualties littered the field. No such number of Americans had ever before been killed in a single day. The North was horrified by its complete defeat, while the South was buoyed somewhat by its victory. It was suddenly clear to everyone that the contest was going to last much longer than previously thought and that it would test the will of the nation to be brought to an end. While only 5 percent of all Federal soldiers were killed or mortally wounded in combat during the war, almost 12 percent of the Confederates suffered a similar fate. The death rate from all causes, including accidents and sickness, was much higher, however. Almost 630,000 Americans died in the conflict. As many as 25 percent of all Southern soldiers may have died. The North actually suffered more war deaths, almost three men for every two lost by the South. The battle at Gettysburg had the highest number of casualties in the war, but it was one of largest battles in terms of the number of men engaged.

Tilly Pierce, a 15-year-old resident of Gettysburg, Pennsylvania, recorded the sentiments felt by many who witnessed the results of a battle, "Some of the wounded from the battlefield began to arrive where I was staying. They reported hard fighting, many wounded and killed, and were afraid our troops would be defeated and perhaps routed. The first wounded soldier whom I met had his thumbs tied up. This I thought dreadful, and told him so. . . . Soon two officers carrying their arms in slings made their appearance, and I more fully began to realize that something terrible had taken place. Now the wounded began to come in greater numbers. Some limping, some with their heads and arms in bandages, some crawling, other carried on stretchers or brought in ambulances. Suffering, cast down and dejected, it was truly a pitiable gathering."[5]

Conscription

Ultimately, the South was forced to resort to conscription to preserve its forces in the field. The Confederate Conscription Act of 1862 was the first general draft of soldiers in America. Neither the Confederate Congress nor Jeff Davis wanted it, but conscription was seen as an absolute necessity. Its purpose was twofold. The 12-month enlistments, entered into in the spring of 1861, were about to run out. It was feared that these men, now veterans of war and free from many of the romantic notions they had brought to their first muster, would fail to reenlist. The Conscription Act insured that the Confederacy would retain the men it had in the army, and, since the war had already lasted longer than anyone had predicted, it provided for the additional men that would be needed.

The Conscription Act passed through the Confederate Congress by more than a two-to-one vote. The act made all white males from the ages of 18 to 35 eligible for three years of service. The Federal Congress followed with its own conscription act in August of the same year, but Lincoln refused to sign it into law until March 1863. The draft, almost identical in its characteristics both North and South, was universally unpopular, but it was accepted with a certain equanimity, rather than reservation, in the South. In the North, the first drawing of names in July 1863 set off a violent four-day long riot with a mob of more than 50,000 working men swarming through the streets of Manhattan. Federal troops, just back from the grim scene at Gettysburg, were called upon to quell the riots, leaving more than 1,000 rioters dead. Small disturbances also broke out in Boston, Troy, and other towns in the East and in Ohio.

There were a number of ways by which a man could avoid the draft. If he was found to have a physical disability, he would be exempt. Disqualifying disabilities included genuine health problems like blindness, missing limbs, lung disease, venereal disease, or an unsound heart. Other genuine problems were less evident. Urine samples were taken; a man's balance and coordination were tested; and even if he could see, his eyesight needed to be normal or at least correctable with the use of glasses. Those who were epileptic or insane were exempt. Chronic conditions such as coughing, shortness of breath, and back pain were more difficult to prove and harder for the authorities to evaluate. Two very simple physical characteristics also freed a man from conscription. He could not be less than five feet six inches tall, which suggests that people were not really shorter in the 19th century than they are today. Second, as a purely practical matter, he needed at least two opposed teeth because the bullet cartridge needed to be torn open with the teeth in firing the musket.

A man could have an exemption from the draft based on a war-related occupation considered more critical to the cause than his service at the front. Iron founders, machinists, miners, and railroad workers; ferrymen, pilots, and steamboat workers; government officials, clerks, and telegraphers; ministers, professors, teachers of the handicapped, and private teachers with more than 20 pupils; and other occupations exempted men from the draft. There were protests over the exemptions; but the only outcome of a public outcry was an extension of the exemption to physicians, leather workers, blacksmiths, millers, munitions workers, shipyard workers, salt makers, charcoal burners, some stockmen, some printers, and one editor for each paper. Conscientious objectors, belonging to recognized non-violent sects, did not have to serve if they provided a substitute or paid $500 to the government.

One of the more flagrant exemptions under Southern law was that one slaveowner, with more than 20 slaves under his care, would be exempt from each plantation. White overseers were also exempt because of the fear of slave uprisings. Many felt that this exemption led to "a rich man's war and a poor man's fight." Although this attitude was strongly held in many circles, many slaveowners and their sons voluntarily served in the war, very often as officers and leaders of local partisan groups.

Finally, in both the North and the South, a man could buy his way out of the draft by finding a substitute. As much as $400 in gold was offered in 1863 for a draft substitute. There was a tremendous amount of fraud perpetrated in the hiring of substitutes, and this may have been the greatest weakness of the draft system. Physically unsound men were found to replace sound substitutes before they reached the training camps; underage boys and overaged men were used in the same manner; and many paid substitutes simply deserted, often repeating the process over and over again under different names.

The conscription act and the exemptions were modified as the war progressed, and more and more men became eligible for the draft. The Federal act made all men 20 to 45 eligible. The Confederates accepted boys of 17 and men between 46 and 50 as local defense forces or as railroad guards. These men who were too young or too old to fight on the front lines were able to free thousands of soldiers to do so. The draft had the positive effect of retaining veteran soldiers in the ranks. Without these the Southern armies would soon have collapsed. The conscription system was, nonetheless, amazingly inefficient, and filled with abuses; moreover, it provided a rallying point for anti-war sentiment.

Common Soldiers

Applying statistical analysis to the Civil War is difficult at best, and foolhardy at least, yet the war generated a noble body of data that begs to be interpreted. Still, hard and fast conclusions based solely on this data should be avoided. Facts and figures for the men who faced one another in 1861–1862 are largely unreliable when grouped together with those of 1863–1864. The volunteers of the earlier period tended to differ significantly from the troops that included draftees, substitutes, and bounty claimers of the later war. Moreover, it is difficult to ascertain reliable statistics for Southern troops as they are simply not available for all theaters or periods of the conflict. Similar inherent inaccuracies in the data notwithstanding, some simple facts stand out about the men who fought in the Civil War.[6]

The men who opposed one another on the battlefields of the Civil War possessed more similarities than differences. Generally, the soldiers on both sides came from similar backgrounds, spoke the same language (apart from their widely divergent regional accents), had the same political history, cherished the same Constitution, and suffered the same hardships and dangers offered by soldiering. But the differences between Billy Yank and Johnny Reb were, nonetheless, meaningful enough to sustain four years of bloody conflict and may help to explain the relationship between these enemies.[7]

The great difference between Billy Yank and Johnny Reb seems to have been in their style of fighting—a characteristic noted by many observers. "Three points I noted with regard to our opponents," noted Federal Captain John W. De Forest, "They aimed better than our men; they covered themselves (in case of need) more carefully and effectively; they could move in a swarm, without much care for alignment and touching elbows. In short, they fought more like [Indians], or like hunters, than we. The result was that they lost fewer men, though they were far inferior in numbers."[8]

Of all the soldiers who served in the war, it has been estimated that between 30 and 40 percent were Confederates, yet a reliable figure for their absolute number cannot be obtained because of the lack of records for the Western armies. Between 1.0 and 1.5 million men may have served in the rebel army. On the other hand, the records of the government of the United States, which are more complete and reliable, show that Federal forces contained precisely 2.2 million men. Approximately three-quarters of each opposing force was composed of infantry, with cavalry making up 15 percent and artillery about 7 percent. The remaining portion was composed of engineers, medical personnel, teamsters, and other ancillary personnel. About 10 percent of each army served as officers. Only 3 percent of all Federal personnel served in the navy, and less than 1 percent served in the minuscule Confederate States Navy.

It was generally young men who fought the war. Their average age at enlistment in the Federal army was just under 26 years. The Confederates averaged just over 26 years, a remarkable agreement with the Federal figure when the traditional view of the Rebels is of an army composed of old men and young boys. The size and weight of Federal recruits is well documented to have averaged five feet, eight inches and 145 pounds. As 19th-century men were about this size, it can be presumed that Confederates were of a similar height and weight. Of the Federal soldiers, 29 percent were married when they enlisted, while more than 36 percent of their Southern counterparts seem to have been married men. This may reflect a greater mobilization of the available population in the South.

While many men wrote regularly to their families and expressed pitiable longing and loneliness for them, a Federal officer testified about receiving a letter from a destitute wife, anxious for news of her husband's health. The wife had received no word of him in months and only nine dollars since he had enlisted. She and her children had, therefore, been evicted from their home. "Here are four pages of pathos that make me want . . . to kick him for not deserving them," wrote the officer. "Apparently a fairly educated and quite worthy girl has married a good-looking youth of inferior nature and breeding who has not the energy to toil effectively for her, nor the affection to endure privations for her sake."[9]

Billy Yank was generally better educated than Johnny Reb, owing, in part, to the greater number of prestigious colleges and universities located in the North and the greater emphasis placed on basic public education at the lower academic levels. While the South had a number of impressive universities, their number was small in proportion to the total in the country, and Southerners were wary of pubic education. The rate of illiteracy among Civil War soldiers should not be over empha- sized, however. Most of the troops could write their names and read from the Bible. However, the spelling and grammar found in letters, diaries, and journals frequently fell well below schoolroom standards. A typical white regiment on either side of the contest probably had few illiterates and many units had none at all. The highest rate of illiteracy was found among black units. This is to be expected, as many of these black soldiers had been denied an education. Nonetheless, there were many well-educated black freemen in the ranks. Even the totally unlettered soldier could easily impose himself on a literate comrade to read a newspaper out loud or write a letter to home for him.

The vast majority of the men who served were neither professional soldiers nor draftees. The largest percentage were farmers before the war. The Southern soldier was more like to be an agricultural worker of some type than the immigrant recruit from the more highly industrialized North. The available data make no distinction between the plantation owner, the small farm owner or his children, and the paid agricultural worker. The data also ignore all those who were too young to have an occupation when they enlisted such as teenagers and students. Many of these were listed as unskilled workers.

Skilled laborers made up the second-largest group of men to serve in either army. These skilled laborers included carpenters and furniture makers, masons, machinists, wheelwrights and cartwrights, barrel makers and coopers, shoemakers and leather workers, smiths of many kinds, and other skilled tradesmen. The particular trade by which an artisan made his living rarely prepared him for military service. Exceptions to this may have been made for artisans like butchers, blacksmiths, and farriers who were organized within the service to practice their trades for the army.

Professional and white-collar occupations made up the largest portion of those who served as officers. Professional men included lawyers, physicians, clergymen, engineers, professors, and army and navy officers. The white-collar category is somewhat obscured as it is distinguished from the professional class more by degree than any other characteristic, and many men often crossed the line between the two. These included bankers, merchants, manufacturers, journalists, clerks, bookkeepers, and school teachers.

Each man who entered the army came with a set of values that mirrored the occupation, the home, the community he had left behind. The majority of the recruits in the first year of the war were volunteers, and they pledged themselves to serve for three months, expecting that the first major battle would decide the issue of secession. Nonetheless, their commitment to serve, their personal and economic sacrifice, and the distress experienced by their families and loved ones should not be minimized because of this limited initial commitment. The motivation of most volunteers seems to have been rooted in the compelling and deeply personal forces of duty and honor. In 1861 both of these were closely linked with concepts of masculinity, morality, conscience, and romance.[10]

Buried among the more-popular motivations for going to war—such as adventure, excitement, patriotism, and ideology—was the need for Civil War soldiers to prove their masculinity. Southerners tended to be more boastful in this regard than the Yankees. "They were amiable, gentle, and unselfish in disposition, yet were fearless and daring in spirit, and devoted . . . to those bodily exercises that make the strong and vigorous man," noted one observer.[11] Northerners tended to be more circumspect, worrying whether they would pass the test of manhood posed by battle. The psychological importance of passing this test should not be minimized. Particularly among the young volunteers, the experience of battle, "seeing the elephant" in 19th-century terms, was seen as a rite of passage.

A young woman wrote, "It seems very patriotic and grand . . . for one's country to die. . . . A lot of us girls went down to the train and took flowers to the soldiers as they were passing through and they cut buttons from their coats and gave [them] to us as souvenirs."[12] William H. Bayly, a 13-year-old resident of Gettysburg on the day of the battle, wrote, "There was the thunder of guns, a shrieking, whistling, moaning of shells, before they burst, sometimes like rockets in the air. . . . No results of this conflict could be noted; no shifting of scenes or movement of actors in the great struggle could be observed. It was simply noise, flash, and roar. I had the sensation of a lifetime."[13] Yet a young man's performance on the battlefield quite literally separated the men from the boys. Those in uniform quickly repudiated the romance, adventure, and glory of war once they had "seen the elephant" for themselves. "My Dear Papa," wrote Capt. Henry L. Abbott of the 20th Maine Infantry, "When our great victory was just over the exultation was so great that one didn't think of our fearful losses, but now I can't help feeling a great weight at my heart."[14]

Perhaps the many references to sentiment were a reaction to the pressures brought upon the men by the communities and social groups to which they belonged. As volunteers generally served in companies and regiments raised from the eligible men in a local neighborhood, it may have been socially impossible for them to do otherwise. A contemporary commentator noted, "The associations of . . . boyhood and early manhood were with these people . . . [their] dearest and most intimate friends and companions. . . . These men found gratification in a military organization composed of those of their own class."[15]

If the recruits' own motivations for volunteering, as set down in their personal letters and diaries, are not accepted at face value, it is difficult to rationalize how so many individuals could have been willing to die for a cause or how such massive volunteer armies could have been raised. Nonetheless, it remains an extraordinary fact that during the first year of the war, all those who enlisted and fought on one side or the other chose to do so.

While the vast majority of soldiers, both North and South, were native-born Americans, a large number of foreigners were to be found in both armies. It has been estimated that between 20 and 25 percent of the Union army was foreign-born. Millions of Europeans had migrated to North America in the decades before the war, and the majority had settled in the North. Most of these had established themselves in the great urban areas. Close to 4 million aliens were living in the North when the war began. They tended to identify with that section of the country, and joined the Federal forces. As little as 4 or 5 percent of the Confederate army was composed of foreigners. There were fewer than 1 million foreign-born residents in the Confederacy, and, therefore, they made up a smaller proportion of the Southern forces. The crews of the minuscule Confederate States Navy were almost entirely recruited from abroad. As a proportion of the available population, however, foreigners seemed to have supported both the North and South equally.

Almost 8 percent of the Federal generals and 2 percent of the Confederate generals were foreign-born. The largest group of foreigners to serve in Federal ranks, about 200,000, were of German origin. The Irish were next, numbering about 150,000, followed by the Canadians and the English, each totaling about 50,000 men. Scandinavians, Frenchmen, Italians, and other nationalities also served in small numbers. Although the largest foreign group to serve the Confederacy seems to have been the Irish, other nationalities were also present in the Rebel ranks, including Englishmen, Canadians, Frenchmen, Italians, and Mexicans.

The motivation for foreign-born soldiers to participate in an internecine conflict in the absence of obvious personal advantages is difficult to pin down. Some like British officer Sir Percy Wyndham, who had once served with Garibaldi in Italy, were simply soldiers of fortune. Men from the socially unacceptable and impoverished immigrant populations may have served in an attempt to win for themselves and their families a place in post-war American society. In this they were at least partially success-ful, as with the Irish who came to dominate early 20th-century urban politics. Whatever their motivation, the foreign-born soldiers generally gave a good account of themselves. The Irish troops, in particular, provided some of the most momentous and courageous combat of the war. The fighting reputations of the Federal Irish Brigade and the Louisiana Tigers, both composed of working-class Irish immigrants, stand up well beside the reputations of any native-born American unit on either side of the contest. Many units, like these, were solidly foreign or ethnically related in their composition; but others, like the 5th Confederate Regiment, a "foreign legion" serving under General Hood in Tennessee, were composed of men from many nationalities.

Blacks, Jews, and Native Americans were also represented in the service. Throughout the war, blacks were generally made to serve in non-combatant roles at the front that could free white soldiers for the battleline. A Federal officer in occupied New Orleans, where some of the first black regiments, with black and white officers, were raised, expressed the following thought. "The colored troops will probably be kept near here and used to garrison unhealthy positions; they will be called on for fatigue duty such as making roads, building bridges and draining marshes; they will seldom be put into battle." Allotted to white regiments, blacks dug ditches, built fortifications, and served as laborers, wagoners, carpenters, farriers, orderlies, stevedores, track layers, and porters.[16]

Ultimately, the Union had almost 180,000 black soldiers under arms. The acceptance of the "Sable Arm" of the Federal Army was not immediate, however. Although free blacks were enlisted, they were placed in segregated units largely under the command of white officers who felt that such an assignment would "afford small chance for distinction." Based upon prejudicial notions that they could not equal a white soldier in a fight, these units were often given non-combatant duties far from the front. However, it should be noted that the Union Army expected menial services from all its troops, regardless of race—a policy that raised some objections among the insecure Irish who were asked to labor beside the blacks. Ultimately, under severe pressure from Northern abolitionists, black troops were placed in combat roles where their performance proved laudable and, at times, heroic. The best-known black unit was the 54th Massachusetts Colored Infantry, but other black units were raised throughout the occupied South as well as in almost every Northern state. Although the use of black combat troops was not necessary to win the war, blacks came to represent 9 percent of all Union forces—a higher proportion of free blacks in service than were represented by their percentage in Northern society.

Initially, white Federal troops were opposed to this policy. Black men wearing the same uniforms as whites had disturbing implications of equality for men whose own status in a recently restructured Northern society was suspect. Many white soldiers, willing to die in order to free a black man from slavery, were unwilling to fight beside him. Federal soldiers from the border states strongly expressed a reluctance to serve in the same army with men who had been considered menials, servants, and chattels. However, basic logic, which dictated that blacks could stop Confederate bullets just as easily as whites, overcame such bias. This thread of reasoning quickly made many a Northern segregationist into a closet abolitionist.[17]

The immediate reaction of the Southern government to the arming of blacks by Federal forces was to declare that any black found in arms against the South, and any white Federal officer found leading such men, would be executed upon capture. Few individual Confederate soldiers acknowledged killing blacks in their letters and diaries. Nor did they express much racist sentiment. The cases of massive race-based retaliation are reserved for the battles at Fort Pillow, Tennessee; Poison Springs, Arkansas; Plymouth, North Carolina; and the "Crater" at Petersburg, Virginia. In each of these instances, it is quite certain that blacks were purposely killed after they had surrendered to Confederate troops.

Southern forces used blacks almost exclusively as laborers and servants. A Southern woman noted, "We have never made the cowardly Negro fight, and it is strange, passing strange, that the all-powerful Yankee nation with the whole world to back them . . . should at last take the poor Negro to help them out against this little Confederacy." Nonetheless, a vocal minority in the South had called for the arming of blacks from the beginning of the war, and even General Lee called for their enlistment. At the end March 1865, the Confederate Congress, sorely pressed for manpower, approved the enrollment of armed blacks in the Southern forces, offering freedom as a reward. This promise lured many blacks, even in the face of the Emancipation Proclamation, and a number actually came to serve under arms in the Confederate Army. The question of what effect black Confederate soldiers would have had on the white Southerners fighting beside them was made moot by the collapse of the war effort almost immediately thereafter.[18]

Boys in War

The enlistment of minors in the 19th century was based on tradition, and boys had served in armies and aboard vessels for centuries. Minors under 16 were allowed to enlist in the armies and navies of both forces. More than 40,000 minors may have served in the war, and the majority managed to survive. Many boys considerably younger than 14 served. While figures for the Confederacy are unavailable or incomplete, in the Federal Army alone, there were 300 boys aged 13 or under and two dozen who were 10 or under.

Parental consent was needed in both the Federal and Confederate forces for minors to enlist. On this subject Lincoln wrote to the Secretary of the Navy, "The United States don't need the services of boys who disobey their parents." It is hard to imagine under what circumstances parents would send such young children to war. Yet it was not until March 1864 that the Federal Congress prohibited the enlistment of persons under 16 under any circumstances.[19]

Underage youths managed to scheme their way into the ranks of both armies. Hard-pressed enlistment officers often turned a blind eye to the evident youth of willing recruits in order to fill their recruitment quotas. Many boys entered the Confederate state militias as railroad and bridge guards or served in the mounted guerrilla units. They often performed necessary but routine duties that freed older soldiers to fight. They functioned as water carriers, barbers, orderlies, kitchen help, mounted couriers, or hospital attendants. Youngsters served at sea as cabin boys, as galley helpers, and as powder-monkeys bringing shot and powder to the gundecks in battle.

However, most boys served as musicians, drummers, or buglers. These helped to organize the daily routine of the camp by signaling reveille, assembly, officer's call, sick call, and taps; and their music provided a form of entertainment for the troops and a festive flare on formal occasions such as regimental reviews. Yet, the primary purpose of music on the battlefield was to communicate orders over the din of warfare. Precisely blown bulge calls and accurately played drum beats could carry commands more clearly than the human voice at great distances and more quickly than the fleetest runner or mounted courier. Drummers were generally assigned to infantry regiments behind which they marched into battle. Buglers were allocated to the cavalry or horse artillery as the bugle is more convenient to carry and play while mounted and riding across the field than the drum.

However, very young or small boys faced some unique obstacles in these positions. Some cavalry buglers were too short to mount a horse and had to be hoisted into the saddle, and young drummers often had great difficulty in maintaining the regulation 28-inch pace while marching beside the troops carrying a regulation-sized drum. Moreover, small uniforms needed to be secured and replaced periodically. This was usually done at the expense of the officers, who sometimes provided elaborate and impractical outfits. Properly enlisted boys were paid and drew supplies like the soldier, but frequently needed items such as child-sized shoes, socks, and shirts that were often difficult to resupply.

The War on the Home Front

At the commencement of the war, almost all of the South's most fertile land was devoted to agriculture, much of it in cotton. The North, which relied so much on manufacturing for its economic domination, might thereby have been at a disadvantage with regard to food, but the reverse was true because a great portion of the Northern population was composed of wheat and corn farmers. Preconceived notions of a rising wartime demand for food caused Northern farmers to overplant in 1860. Wheat and corn production soared. An additional boon came in the form of good weather, an event not shared by Europe, which experienced crop shortages during this period. The North was able to sell surplus wheat and flour to Europe, thus gaining additional funds that could be invested in the war.

The war actually provided an impetus to the development of farming in the North as underdeveloped land was put into production to support the war effort. Pork production for commercial use in 1865 was twice that of 1860. The Homestead Act was quickly passed in 1862, granting free land to anyone willing to plant it. This virgin soil produced impressive yields, unlike the exhausted soils of the South. Northern industry developed and produced machinery that could additionally improve productivity. In 1861 McCormick's reaper was offered for sale at $150 but required only a $30 down payment. The balance was to be paid in six months if the harvest was good, or longer if it was poor.[20]

Southern communities were never able to organize anything that approached the organization and productivity of the North, and the war brought about many shortages. On Southern plantations in areas controlled by the Federals, the situation was temporarily acute as slaves with their new-won freedom abandoned the fields and streamed north across the Union lines. Plantation families that had lived in an atmosphere of wealth and refinement all their lives were often reduced to abject poverty because of the lack of labor.

As the war progressed and was continually fought on Southern soil, Federal troops destroyed even the modest plantings in the gardens of Southern families. Cornelia Peake McDonald described a visit by the blue-coated soldiers. They "began to pull up the potatoes . . . [and] did not stop after getting enough for dinner, but continued amid roars of laughter and defiant looks at me to pull them till all were lying on the ground . . . to wither in the sun. The [potatoes] were no larger than peas, and the destruction seemed so wanton that I was provoked beyond enduring."[21]

The blockade of Southern ports caused great hardship, and a poor system of transportation prevented the Confederacy's small resources from being effectively distributed throughout the South. Children were often recruited to solicit funds door to door and to collect non-perishable groceries such as jellies or crackers from merchants to be sent to soldiers at the front. In some farming communities, families set aside portions of their land to the production of easily stored crops, such as potatoes, onions, and turnips. Schools held "onion" or "potato days" to collect produce, which was later delivered to the troops.

Blockade Runners

A unifying feature of the Southern nation in its struggle with the North was the continued existence of the blockade runners. Often called the "Lifeline of the Confederacy," the blockade runners were largely foreign-owned vessels that attempted to evade the Federal blockade and bring military and other goods into Southern ports. The inability of the Federal Navy to stop these vessels served as a rallying point for Southern nationalism. The Confederacy's importation of military supplies through the blockade was incredible. More than 400,000 rifles, 3 million pounds of lead, more than 2 million pounds of saltpeter for gunpowder production, as well as food, clothing, shoes, accouterments, medicines, and paper were brought through the blockade. To pay for these, more than 500,000 bales of cotton were shipped out of the South during the war and bonds worth millions of Confederate dollars were issued to creditors.

The price of consumer goods was most directly affected by the blockade. From 1860 to 1863 the monthly cost of feeding a small family was reported to have gone from $6.55 to $68.25.[22] The following specific prices were recorded in the months indicated by a concerned observer. In May 1862: meat—$0.50 per pound; butter—$0.75 per pound; coffee—$1.50; tea—$10.00; boots—$30.00; men's shoes—$18.00; ladies' shoes—$15.00; shirts—$6.00; room and board for one—$30.00 to $40.00 per month; and house rent per year—$1,000.00.[23] In September 1862: firewood—$16.00 per cord; coal—$9.00 per load; blankets—$25.00; sheets—$15.00; and bleached cotton shirting—$1.00 per yard.[24] In March 1863: corn meal—$8.00 per bushel; chickens—$5.00 each; turkeys—$20.00 each; turnip greens—$8.00 per bushel; bacon—$1.50 per pound; bread $0.20 per loaf; and flour—$39.00 per hundredweight barrel.[25]

Blockade runners took tremendous risks and expected tremendous profits. In order to make the risk worthwhile, they tended to carry luxury items for those who could afford to pay, rather than the staples of daily life for everyone. Prices soared in proportion. In November 1862, Judith McGuire wrote, "Coffee is $4 per pound, and good tea from $18 to $20; butter ranges from $1.50 to $2 per pound; lard 50 cents; corn $15 per barrel; and wheat $4.50 per bushel."[26] In an April 1863 message to Southerners, President Jefferson Davis urged people to give priority to food crops over cotton and tobacco and to plant corn, peas, and beans.[27]

With a scarce supply of gold and the value of the Confederate dollar down to $18.50 per Federal greenback by November 1863, the Southern government began impressing items of all kinds, including "horses, wagons, hogs, cattle, grain, potatoes—leaving the farmers only enough for their own subsistence."[28] In March 1863, the Confederate War Department issued a schedule of standardized prices for impressed goods that reflected only half of their market value. Some counties were so alarmed by this development that they threatened to take steps to prohibit the export of foodstuffs from within their boundaries to the rest of the country.

The Bread Riots

The eventual success, or failure, of the Confederacy was largely dependent on the will of the people to support the war by enduring privation and tolerating wartime prices. A severe food shortage seems to have developed in urban areas of the South in the latter part of March 1863. Initially a group of woman in Salisbury, North Carolina, demanded that store owners charge them no more than the fixed price the government would ordinarily pay for foodstuffs and goods. Some of the merchants obliged the ladies by lowering their prices. There were several such episodes in the South at the same time. The most significant took place in the capital city of Richmond where Mrs. Mary Jackson promoted a concerted action by the women of that city to influence the price of goods and foodstuffs.

Beginning at the Belvidere Hill Baptist Church, the women, armed with persuaders such as pistols, knives, and hatchets, and led by Mary Jackson, marched on Capital Square in protest. Here the governor of Virginia, John Letcher, spoke to the crowd and expressed his sympathy, but he offered no concrete solution to their problem. As the crowd disgorged from the square, the gathering of women clearly became a mob and began to loot the stores and take the goods of the merchants. Seemingly no attempt was made to buy articles at any price, including those fixed by the government. A number of merchants simply tried to close their doors, and at least one, Mr. Knott, tried to appease the women by handing out packages of sewing needles—considered a luxury item at the time.

This episode was widely reported in the anti-government papers and the Northern press as a "Bread Riot." Although there is no indication that any bread was taken or asked for, some foodstuffs, including bread, meat, and rice, were distributed by the Young Men's Christian Association to the needy. "Boots are not bread, brooms are not bread, men's hats are not bread, and I have never heard of anybody's eating them," retorted a government clerk to the reports.[29]

The riot was not a particularly large affair; and, from its beginning at the Belvidere Church to its end in the downtown merchant quarter, it lasted little more than two hours. Nonetheless, President Davis had gone so far as to threaten to have the mob fired upon by the Public Guard, which had mobilized in the streets. The *Richmond Examiner* suggested that future rioters be shot on the spot. The city council initiated a formal investigation of the affair and found the riot to be totally unjustified. Several of the instigators of the protest were arrested. Of these 12 women were convicted of misdemeanors, and four men and one woman, Mrs. Jackson, were convicted of felonies.

Southern nationalism, and the traditional "Old South," died as surely in the city streets and farm yards as it did on the battlefields. The Southern landscape was littered with debris. The skeletons of horses and mules left unburied, human remains washed from their shallow graves, broken muskets, and wagon wheels decorated the sides of rutted ditches that once were pleasant lanes through the countryside. Homes had been shelled or dismantled to build fortifications, roads, and bridges. Parts of the South were said to actually stink with the odor of death.

The immediate cause of defeat was a lack of sufficient manpower for the Confederate armies, but the inability of the civilian population to withstand any more war after four years of mourning their loved ones insured that the war would not long endure. For four brief years, Southerners, charged with a spirit of revolution and nationalism, took charge of their own destiny. In the aftermath of the war, the unique Confederate identity would never be the same again. Yet the new South, rising from the ashes of the old, would reassert many of its traditional ideologies from the postwar years to the present.[30]

Disbanding the Armies

For some concerned officials the disbandment of the armies at the end of the war was not an encouraging prospect. The Federal army alone had just over 1 million men under arms at the war's end. Besides the sudden influx into the peacetime economy of almost 2 million soldiers, the close of hostilities also meant the end of a large number of war-related industries in the North. Thousands of men would be thrown out of employment, but for most Northern soldiers, demobilization meant a return to the farms from which they had come. Although there were many fewer Southerners under arms at the end of the war—men had been abandoning the Confederate cause for some months—the South, with its economy all but destroyed, faced massive unemployment. Even agricultural workers had to face the destruction of their farm buildings and livestock. Wells and fields had been fouled; and almost every fence rail in the South had been torn down or burned. The cost of replacing the fences on Southern farms alone proved a substantial economic burden estimated to be in the millions.[31]

In the North "all the anticipations of evil proved groundless." Freed of the sectional controversies of the antebellum period, massive economic growth seemed to take hold after the war. The war destroyed the hold that the anti-industrial South had on Federal policy and paved the way for industrial development by placing factions sympathetic to business in undisputed control of the country. The Federal soldiers who left the army in late 1865 and early 1866 "reentered civilian life with apparent contentment and even with certain advantages." Speaker of the House James G. Blaine noted that veterans "were found to be models of industry and intelligence." The experience of war had "proved an admirable school" and given the soldiers "habits of promptness and punctuality, order and neatness, which added largely to their efficiency in what ever field they were called to labor."[32]

The war had ended and any cogent plan for bringing the South back into the Union had died with Lincoln in April 1865. There was no plan to deal with the seceded states and their people, nor was there any idea of what to do with millions of suddenly freed slaves. Accustomed to being taken care of and told what to do, many freedmen did not know how to proceed. Others interpreted freedom as meaning that they would be fed and housed without having to work. As one historian has noted, the Southern veteran and the black former slave both faced "a ruined home, desolate fields, no money, no laborers—and bitterness."[33]

Notes

1. Gaillard Hunt, *As We Were, Life in America, 1814* (1914; repr., Stockbridge, Mass.: Berkshire House Publishing, 1993), 30.

2. Emory M. Thomas, *The Confederacy as a Revolutionary Experience* (Columbia: University of South Carolina Press, 1991), 114.

3. Quoted in Drew Gilpin Faust, *The Creation of Confederate Nationalism: Ideology and Identity in the Civil War South* (Baton Rouge: Louisiana State University Press, 1988), 8; Also see Earl Schenck Miers, ed., *A Rebel War Clerk's Diary, by John B. Jones, 1861–1865* (New York: Sagamore Press, 1958), 3.

4. James M. McPherson, *For Cause and Comrades: Why Men Fought in the Civil War* (New York: Oxford University Press, 1997), 95. Also see James H. Croushore, ed., *A Volunteer's Adventure, by Captain John W. de Forest* (New Haven, Conn.: Yale University Press, 1949), 30.

5. Editors of Time-Life, *Voices of the Civil War* (New York: Time-Life, 1995), 62.

6. See McPherson, *For Cause and Comrades*, preface.

7. The origins of the terms *Billy Yank* and *Johnny Reb* in reference to Civil War soldiers are not quite apparent. It is evident, however, that the soldiers referred to themselves and their enemies using these terms.

8. Croushore, *A Volunteer's Adventure*, 190. De Forest uses the unfortunate term *redskins* at this point.

9. Ibid., 46.

10. See John Keegan, *The Mask of Command* (New York: Vintage, 1987), 191; McPherson, *For Cause and Comrades*, 94. Keegan may have exaggerated this characteristic of Civil War armies in his study, but there is general truth in the statement.

11. Thomas A. Ashby, *The Life of Turner Ashby* (New York: Neal Publishing, 1914), 29–30.

12. Caroline C. Richards, *Village Life in America, 1852–1972* (Gansevoort, NY: Corner House, 1997), 131.

13. Time-Life, *Voices*, 105.

14. Ibid., 159.

15. Ashby, *Life of Turner Ashby*, 34, 40.

16. Croushore, *A Volunteer's Adventure*, 50–51.

17. McPherson, *For Cause and Comrades*, 126.

18. Dolly Sumner Lunt, *A Woman's Wartime Journal by Mrs. Thomas Lunt Burge* (Atlanta: Cherokee, 1994), 37.

19. David Mallinson, "Armed with Only Their Drums . . . " *America's Civil War* (November 1992): 8.

20. James Trager, *The Food Chronology* (New York: Henry Holt & Co., 1995), 262.

21. Minrose C. Gwin, *A Woman's Civil War* (Madison: University of Wisconsin, 1992), 58.

22. Douglas O. Tice, "Bread or Blood, the Richmond Bread Riot," *Civil War Times Illustrated* (February 1974): 12.

23. Miers, *Rebel War Clerk's Diary,* 79.

24. Ibid., 99.

25. Ibid., 178.

26. Judith McGuire, *Diary of a Southern Refugee by a Lady of Virginia* (Lincoln: University of Nebraska Press, 1995), 173.

27. Trager, *Food Chronology,* 267.

28. Miers, *Rebel War Clerk's Diary,* 310–312.

29. Tice, "Bread or Blood," 14–16.

30. Thomas, *Confederacy,* 127.

31. Virgil Carrington Jones, *Gray Ghosts and Rebel Raiders* (New York: Galahad, 1956), 45.

32. James G. Blaine, "The Disbanding of the Northern Army, 1865," in Francis W. Halsey, ed., *Great Epochs in American History* (New York: Funk & Wagnalls, 1884), 201–204. Blaine was Speaker in 1861–1862, and again beginning in 1869.

33. James Truslow Adams, *Album of American History,* vol. 3 (New York: Charles Scribner's Sons, 1946), 191.

10

Women as Mothers

Children . . . come to us from heaven, with their little souls full of innocence and peace; and, as far as possible, a mother's influence should not interfere with the influence of angels.
—Lydia M. Child, *The Mother's Book*, 1833

Mothers of the Republic

Motherhood was a serious and all-consuming occupation for 19th-century wives, largely replacing the role of helpmate that had been the norm for wives in early America. Frances Trollope observed during her visit to America, "It may be said that the most important feature in a woman's history is her maternity."[1] With the expansion of the industrialization, the daily lives and responsibilities of women and men had begun to diverge away from the ideal of a team and toward discreet tasks and obligations. With men away from the home for the day working, women began to take on greater responsibility for the home and its residents. Early in the century, day-to-day authority over children and their moral upbringing began to shift from a paternal duty to a maternal one. This change was one of the foundation stones of the growing *Cult of Domesticity*. By mid-century, this concept had expanded to the point that mothers were expected to make the home a moral bulwark that would provide children with an idyllic childhood.

As a young woman, Betsey Reynolds contemplated the importance of maternal care and instruction, noting in her diary that "as business obliges the father to be about [town], the care of our infancy devolves upon the

WATCHFUL CARE.

The position of caregiver and nurturer remained that of females throughout the period.

mother, [and] upon the formation of our principles, our happiness in this life depends."[2] The editor of *Godey's Lady's Book* proffered, "Woman has a higher pursuit than the industrial arts afford; a better inheritance than earth can offer is in her keeping—to raise humanity toward the angelic is her office. The most important vocation on earth is that of the Christian mother in her nursery."[3] Henry E. Woodbury wrote, "Of all the impressions made upon the youthful mind, none are so lasting as those received from a mother . . . these become . . . a part of our nature, controlling motives, exerting a powerful influence over us in all the affairs of life. . . . Truly weighty are the obligations devolving on woman in the discharge of her duties in this relation. The formation of character is hers."[4]

Weighty, indeed, was this responsibility, as both religious convictions and social paradigms charged mothers with the formation of the very "soul of the babe." L. H. Sigourney cautioned, "Every trace that we grave upon it [the child], will stand forth at the judgment. . . . Every waste-place, which we leave through neglect, will frown upon us."[5] Sigourney further instructed mothers, "No longer will you now live for self—no longer be noteless and unrecorded, passing away without name or memorial among people. . . . You have gained an increase of power. The influence which is most truly valuable, is that of mind over mind. How entire and perfect is this dominion, over the unformed character of your infant."[6] T. S. Arthur wrote, "How vastly important is it, then, for mothers to have a higher regard for their duties—to feel deeply the immense responsibilities that rest upon them! It is through their ministrations that the world grows worse or better."[7] *The Mother's Book* cautioned, "Every look, every movement, every expression, does something toward forming the character of the little heir to immortal life."[8]

Attitudes such as these became common as they spread through the community of matrons, and they were embraced by both women of childbearing years and society in general. As a mother, Betsey Reynolds Voorhees wrote a letter declaring her stress, "The great anxiety I feel for my children leaves me little all, I fear, too little time for my own concerns. . . . I feel much interest in their moral and intellectual improvements while my children remain the principal object of all my cares and all my hopes."[9] Susan Huntington similarly felt the pressure of this role, "[W]hen I see an increasing family of immortal souls, whom I have been the instrument of bringing in to this wretched world, cast upon my care, when I think, that I am to be a principal instrument in forming their characters, and thus, in fixing their destinies for eternity . . . I tremble."[10]

Pregnancy

While motherhood came to be the penultimate fulfillment of a woman, the pregnancy itself was a socially awkward time. Sex was a very private matter and talk of it was taboo. The presence of a pregnant woman was an unspoken reminder of sexual intercourse. Phrases such as "in a delicate condition" and "confinement" were used to describe the pregnancy and labor. Women were expected to avoid the public view as much as possible. Many women of the leisure class remained indoors for the latter part of their pregnancy rather than display their change of figure. One woman explained how she attended a friend's party while seven months pregnant, "I am allowed a seat where I can creep in and out easily and keep out of harm's way. I am not a pretty figure for company, but I hope to manage so as not to be obnoxious."[11] A period journal advised mothers-to-be, "Breathe the atmosphere of refinement and peace, and in this time of seclusion . . . commune with your own heart and be still."[12]

Most women delivered their babies at home, attended by an assortment of relatives and neighbors. Such a gathering of women provided support and encouragement for the new mother and the extra hands were welcome should the labor be lengthy or an emergency arise. Birth was entirely a woman's domain. This practice had existed for centuries and predominated through the first half of the 19th century. While women's diaries usually used the phrase "brought to bed" to describe delivery, women usually delivered, by a midwife, while supported by a chair, another woman's lap, or on a specialized chair called a "birthing stool."

Early in the 19th century it became fashionable for upper- and upper-middle-class women to be delivered at home by a male physician, particularly in Eastern cities. Physicians warned women that they were in danger if they did not receive proper medical attention during childbirth. Childbirth was always a danger, so, to allay their fears, increasing numbers of women began to choose physicians over midwives. By the latter part of the century physicians became available even to poorer women.

This shift from midwife to physician had a dramatic effect on the birthing process. With midwifery, the women who came together for the birth of a child were completely in control and solidly bonded. Their authority had been powerful and unquestioned. It was the one time when men kept to the shadows awaiting news while the women were in the forefront managing information and activity. Once delivery was in the hands of a physician, it became male-controlled. It also altered the event from one of community and support to one of privacy and isolation. Physicians prohibited the participation of relatives and friends in the birthing process because the presence of these ancillary people was seen as a distraction and it weakened their authority.

Physicians charged more than midwives, and perhaps to justify their expense they utilized procedures that would not have been offered by midwives. Doctors sometimes administered purgatives to the expectant woman at the onset of delivery or bled her until she fainted, thus stopping her from crying out. It was not unusual for physicians to use forceps to speed the delivery of the child, a novel procedure that sometimes resulted in rips in internal organs. One of the more horrible complications was vesico-vaginal fistulae. The result of tears in the walls between the vagina and bladder, this condition was characterized by continual leakage from the bladder. Thousands of women suffered from this complication that often made them lifelong invalids and social outcasts.

By the end of the 19th century, birthing increasingly moved into the institutional environment of the hospital. This was especially true for newly arrived immigrants, unwed mothers, and homeless women—none of whom had strong community supports nor a corps of experienced relations. It was hoped that the controlled environment of the hospital would help to eliminate the great killer of new mothers and their babies known as childbed or puerperal fever. Ironically, the reverse occurred. These lying-in or maternity hospitals were hotbeds of infection. Only women in the most desperate situations would go to a hospital to deliver. The poor women, who turned to them, were often used as subjects of examination and experimentation by doctors and medical students. Childbed fever reached epidemic levels in hospitals during the 19th century as doctors, who failed to wash their hands between internal exams, carried the infection from patient to patient. Women who were attended by midwives occasionally contracted the disease, but because they did fewer internal exams and treated only one patient at a time, midwives rarely spread infection. In 1883 at the Boston Lying-in Hospital, 75 percent of the mothers confined there contracted the infection and 20 percent died from it. While a number of physicians suspected that the infections were being spread by dirty hands, most doctors refused to believe that they were the cause of the problem, and the advocates of sanitation were ridiculed for their claims. It was not until Pasteur and Lister concluded that washing could prevent infection did the practice become accepted, but even then not everyone washed effectively, allowing the infections to claim mothers into the early decades of the 20th century.

Feminine modesty among some women brought about the situation where babies were delivered from beneath layers of sheets or even yards of skirts worn by the mother in order to protect her private parts from the doctor's eyes. Medical students were not permitted to watch actual deliveries and relied on mannequins and textbooks to learn their procedures. The *Obstetrical Catechism* of 1854 urged physicians to be aware of "the sense of delicacy, on the part of the female" and suggested that he obtain permission from the husband or "matronly female" prior to a hands-on examination. The doctor was then advised that "the cloths should be properly raised at their lower edges, by the left hand, and then the right hand . . . passed cautiously up the clothes without uncovering the patient."[13]

Postpartum

The new mother was encouraged to rest after delivery but she was still expected to receive callers. Sarah Goodwin employed a nurse to assist her with "all who called on the fourth and fifth weeks." The nurse slept with the baby, did the laundry, and "also kept the baby and [mother] in elegant toilets and waited on all the company upstairs and to the street door." She also recalled, "Before every confinement a great batch of plum cake was baked in a great brick oven. After being put to bed the Doctor and such friends as were being useful had a great feast of good things downstairs."[14] This custom was a hold-over from earlier centuries. The explosion of temporary residents in the house as labor progressed required that a large number of people be fed. One of the responsibilities of the expectant mother was to provide refreshment for those in attendance during the childbirth. "Groaning cakes," "groaning beer," and other items that would keep without spoiling were made in advance of the expected event. By the time Goodwin delivered her last child in 1844, the doctor forbade the custom of serving cake and wine in the mother's chamber, labeling it "unsanitary."[15]

The length of time that a woman remained "abed" after delivery varied with her constitution, personality, and economic situation. Many obstetric texts suggested that mothers who walked about too soon after giving birth would be struck with blood clots or a prolapsed uterus, and they commonly recommended nine days of complete bed rest. This was particularly true for upper-class women who were thought to be more delicate and more susceptible to postpartum complications. Less-affluent women could not spare this much time away from family duties. Anne Jean Lyman would "the very next day sit up in her large easy chair, with her mending basket and book beside her, making the first one and then the other her pastime for some hours of each day." By the second week she would "resume all the duties of the house and was driving all over the country" with her husband.[16]

Birth Rates

During the 19th century the average native-born white woman gave birth to seven children, not counting those lost to miscarriages and still-births. By 1900 the number was cut in half. As noted earlier the fertility rate remained high, however, among black and immigrant women. Some rural farm areas maintained higher rates as well. To some extent the declining birth rate among native-born whites was a result of the changing economics of the era. In previous centuries, children were valued contributors to the family economy. The more children a family had, the more hands there were to work and improve the family's productivity and wealth. Changes in manufacturing and marketing no longer required artisans to have children to which skills and secrets needed to be passed so that the family would be sustained in the future. In the new market economy, children became an expense. They required substantial investments of time, care, and limited resources unless they could find wage-paying employment outside the home.

Lower birth rates can also be attributed to new cultural attitudes toward the role of women. Concern also rose about women's health. Women generally bore their first child 16 months after they married and continued to have children approximately 15 to 20 months apart. A woman's last child was likely born when she was in her 40s and may have been the same age as her first grandchild. During Julia Patterson's 30 years of marriage, she was pregnant or nursing for 19 years and 3 months. She married when she was 21 and had her first child 9 months later. Her 11th and last child was born when she was 45 years old. Spending most of their adult lives either pregnant or nursing took its toll on the health and vitality of many women, and acceptance of this lifestyle role was becoming less acceptable to many 19th-century women.

The 1830s saw a beginning of advice literature that suggested either abstinence or the use of contraception, and by the 1870s there was an abundance of commercial products that were advertised to assist women in this matter. A mainstay of urban newspapers were ads for birth control pamphlets, medical devices such as diaphragms and syringes, condoms, spermicides, and pills that promised to induce abortions. Ads for these products were often distributed on street corners. If the ad contained the word "French" in the title, it indicated that the item was a contraceptive. If it used the word "Portuguese," as in "The Portuguese Female Pill always gives immediate relief," the product was meant to be an abortive.[17] Sellers frequently made outlandishly false claims about their products, but many were nothing more than alcohol and flavored water. Although not socially acceptable, abortions performed very early in a pregnancy were generally considered to be a form of contraception.

Infant Death

Although children were more likely to reach adulthood in the 19th century than in the past, childhood mortality was still high. The romanticism and sentimentalism of the 19th century viewed death from a different perspective than in earlier times, or even than it is viewed today. Death was a part of daily living. Although the loss of a child was felt most deeply, acceptance of it showed deep faith and religious conviction. Popular literature such as Harriet Beecher Stowe's *Uncle Tom's Cabin* celebrated the passing of young innocents. Early death provided the assurance of being "free from the sin and stain of this low earth."[18] Their brief existence protected them from corruption. Upon the passing of her infant child, Cornelia Peake McDonald recalled her friend's words, "You may live to thank Him for taking your precious little babe from the sorrow and evil to come."[19]

Cemeteries provided separate sections for children, making it easier for a young family, yet unable to secure a family plot, to bury their child. Their young or stillborn children could later be re-interred when the family was more established and could afford a family plot. Children's graves received unprecedented attention. Families that could afford it often created gravestone markers steeped in sentiment and imagery. The most common image was that of the sleeping child. Sleep, as a tie between life and death, was a recurring theme of the period. The image made a connection back to the home where the youth once slept. It brought to mind the comforting picture of a child safely tucked away in his bed. The child with a lamb was another recurring image that reinforced the belief in the closeness of children and nature. Empty furniture was also depicted on memorials. An unfilled chair or bed was commonly used to symbolize the child's unfilled life.

Other items appearing on memorials included rattles, dolls, or favorite playthings incised in stone. The use of toys in such a permanent form reflected the period's recognition of the naturalness of play and a lasting reminder of the separate worlds of children and adults. Sculptural portrayals of children and their belongings insured that they would remain forever one with the goodness of the home. They would be undisturbed and constant, forever innocent in the world. Months after the loss of her own child, Cornelia Peake McDonald recorded an incident wherein she was told that she should be thankful that her babe had been taken. "I thought of that when I looked at old Mrs. Dailey's face when she stood by her son's corpse. Would my darling's forehead ever have looked so dim and weary? Her work was finished, and she went to rest 'while yet 'twas early day.' I would not bring her back if I could to resume the burden her

Savior removed that day when she fled from my arms as the sun was setting."[20]

Period advertisements carried the names of many photographers who specialized in posthumous photographs. Infants were the most common subject of this type of photograph. Perhaps, this was because there had been little opportunity to capture the child's likeness in life. Perhaps, it provided a concrete reminder of a life that had passed too quickly. Sometimes the deceased child would be posed cradled in its mother's arms. Other poses might show the child resting on a pillow. Photographers sometimes borrowed from the imagery of portrait painters and included a cut rose in the picture, symbolizing a bloom cut early.

Care and Feeding

Most women breast fed their babies and, for many, this was the most common form of natural contraception as it had been for centuries. Wet nurses were never popular in the North, although there was greater support for the practice in Southern plantation households. While bottles were available well prior to 1800, bottle feeding did not become popular until the last decades of the century. Many factory-employed mothers, however, had little choice but to have their babies given cow's milk while they worked. The problem was that the cows from which the milk was obtained were often diseased and filthy. They were fed on distillery swill and housed in unsanitary conditions in the crowded cities where these women worked. The milk, which was thin and bluish, was frequently diluted with water and doctored with plaster of Paris, magnesia, or chalk in order to make it look creamy and white. Referred to as "swill milk" or "slopmilk," this "milk" was truly a danger to the infants who were given it and was likely a contributing factor to the astounding infant mortality rates of cities such as Boston's 43 percent in 1830 and New York's 50 percent in 1839. A number of physicians began to study human breast milk in order to determine its beneficial qualities. In the 1850s J. R. Meigs published a recipe for infant formula that combined cow's milk, cream, sugar, and lime water. Commercial infant food soon became popular.[21] As the century drew to a close, Thomas Morgan Rotch developed the "percentage method" to create a perfect infant formula. Popular from 1890 into the first decade of the next century, the method fell out of favor due to its complexity. Other advancements in this field came when Pasteur's germ theory led to the practice of boiling of bottles in order to sterilize them and his pasteurization process that was first applied to milk in Denmark in the 1890s. In 1893 Nathan Straus opened one of the first pure milk stations in the country. It cut the death rate at New York's Orphan Asylum in half.

Mothers took great care to protect their infants. They dressed their babies in long gowns that were often twice the length of the child. Many period photographs show tiny infants enveloped in yards of fabric. Long gowns could not be cast off as loose blankets could. It was felt that the gowns would provide the child with greater warmth. These garments were generally white to withstand the frequent washings that infant clothing required and were of "soft material, entirely free from starch."[22] For the first few weeks after birth, infants wore long narrow strips of fabric known as belly bands. These were several yards long and were designed to protect the navel. In addition to diapers, or napkins as they were called, infants wore a shirt, a pinner that contained their lower limbs, a skirt or skirts, and a dress. As the century progressed, this practice of binding up the baby earned increasing criticism from both the medical profession and popular publications. One book declared that swaddling clothes endangered "the breadth and vigor of whole generations."[23] More enlightened women freed their children from such encumbrance but, for many, the custom persisted. Babies also wore caps both indoors and out. Women's magazines frequently carried patterns for these accessories. As the child grew older clothing adjustments were made. Mothers were advised, "keep socks on after the child is two months old; before this, its pinners will be sufficient protection. . . . When a child shows a disposition to creep, shorten its clothes that it may have free use of its limbs, and protect its feet with stockings and shoes."[24]

Learned at Mother's Knee

After the War of 1812 concerned mothers formed maternal organizations in order to discuss topics such as effective methods of controlling the willfulness of children. At about this same time, there began the first trickle of what would become a deluge of advice literature on the raising of children. The young nation's sense of cultural nationalism desired advice literature that was distinctly American. Ministers, physicians, educators, and social reformers authored a plethora of such material centered around the shaping of the child's character. This literature proffered that children were malleable creatures that needed to be shaped into responsible citizens. Elizabeth Elery Sedgwick, wife of a New York attorney, recording the events of her children's early years, illustrated this new view. Of her young children she wrote, "At this period, which seems at first glance a blank, impressions are received which are the germs of future character."[25] America's success or failure as a republic was seen by many to rest upon the ability of parents to impart a strong moral character into their offspring. Catharine Beecher explained, "The success of democratic institutions . . . depends upon the intellectual and moral character of the mass of the people. If they are intelligent and virtuous, democracy is a blessing, but if they are ignorant and wicked, it is only a curse, and much more dreadful than any form of civil government . . . The formation of the moral and intellectual character of the young is committed mainly to the female hand. The mother forms the character of the future man."[26] Mothers were responsible for the nurturing and development of the nation's future citizens. Devoted motherhood was not only seen as a family and moral obligation but it was also touted as a patriotic duty. Daniel Webster acknowledged the important role that mothers played, "It is by the promulgation of sound morals in the community, and more especially by the training and instruction of the young, that woman performs her part towards the preservation of a free government."[27]

In addition to the moral and social guidance mothers were presumed to develop in their children, they were expected to provide them with an affectionate home that would create an idyllic childhood rich with wonderful experiences that would create fond memories and produce healthy minds and bodies. The Beecher sisters wrote that they knew "families where the mother's presence seemed the sunshine of the circle around her; imparting a cheering and vivifying power."[28] An orphaned boy who resided with the Alcotts for several summers described Mrs. Alcott saying that she "was sunshine herself to her children and to me, whom she looked upon as a son; No matter how weary she might be with the washing, and ironing, the baking and cleaning, it was all hidden from the group of girls from whom she was always ready to enter into fun and frolic, as though she never had a care."[29] *The Mother's Book* advised that "the first rule, and most important of all . . . is that the mother govern her own feelings, and keep her heart and conscience pure."[30]

With lower birth rates and high mortality, surviving children were lavished with attention by their middle-class mothers. Susan Huntington advised mothers, "Always to gratify every reasonable desire when a child is pleasant in his request that your children may see that you love to make them happy."[31] In fact, *The Mother's Book* instructed, "An infant's wants should be attended to without waiting for him to cry."[32] The mother appeared in the role of constant attendant. Sally Phelps noted that, "foolishly I can't yet sit patiently and hear my little darling cry, and though he is a charming good Boy yet he will be in my arms the greatest part of the time."[33] *The Mother's Book* advised that the mother should "take the entire care of her own child . . . the infant should, as much as possible, feel the mother's guidance."[34] Motherhood became extremely child-centered.

The toy chest replaced the child's work basket. Where once mothers gave children tasks to help share the family workload, they were now expected to provide the children with stimulating activities and playthings that would help them to develop intellectually, physically, and morally. "As soon as it is possible to convey instruction by toys, it is well to choose such as will be useful," advised *The Mother's Book*.[35] The growing market economy generated a plethora of commercially produced toys, many of which were of an educational nature. Mothers were expected to be active in their children's learning. "When a child is able to spell a new word, or count a new number, kiss him, and show delight at his improvement."[36]

These suggestions seem obvious to us today, but they were new concepts compared to the child-rearing of previous centuries.

Mary Livermore's mother was a "patient" woman who would beg her children to give her a respite from their noisy play by pleading that they "rest [their] throats." The children thereafter "cut out dresses for our hideous rag dolls, botch[ed] them into shapelessness, and then coax[ed] . . . dear mother to make them 'look like something,' which she did." The children might then turn to quieter play that wholly mirrored adult behaviors. They would "hold pray-meetings, preach sermons, [and] tell stories of our own invention,—what was there that we were not at liberty to undertake in that kitchen, if we would not quarrel or get into mischief! Blessed are the children who are under the care of a wise, loving, patient mother!"[37]

While indulgence with time and attention was advocated, ladies' advice manuals cautioned against spoiling children with playthings, clothing, and permissiveness. Mothers could never lose sight of the fact that they were forming the character of the child. They were exhorted to teach their children order and responsibility by having them care for their clothing and playthings. They were encouraged to instill in their children the value of time by keep them employed in positive pursuits. They were discouraged from promoting vanity and a love of finery in dress by displaying these qualities in their own lives. Mothers were urged to develop in their charges an appreciation of nature and of making things with their own hands.

With fathers away from the home, mothers became the chief administrators of discipline. Rather than physical punishment, mothers turned to subtle manipulations of the child's behavior. *The Mother's Book* advised, "example and silent influence were better than direct rules and commands" and that "firmness united with goodness." Mothers were encouraged to "make the punishment similar to the offenses . . . [the child's] offenses having been anti-social, his punishment should be so likewise. Being deprived of social intercourse will teach him its value."[38]

Even farm mothers grew concerned that extensive farm labors kept them from filling the "sacred office" of motherhood, and they began to concentrate on child nurture. While rural mothers may have lived in greater isolation than their urban counterparts, women's magazines and advice manuals were in wide circulation and farm mothers embraced the new ideology. A woman, identified only as "Annette," agitated for a women's column in the *Genesee Farmer*, explaining that it could help mothers to raise generations of clear-thinking, forward-looking farmers.[39] Farm nurseries moved closer to the dining room, sitting room, or family room and away from the potentially hazardous kitchen. While different from middle-class nurseries that were often found on the second floor, playrooms began to appear in house plans for farmhouses. Children's needs began to take precedence over the order of the home. The 1893 *Agriculturist* reported, "even among [families with no formal nursery] there is one room inhabited by a baby to the exclusion of most others; a room where he is at liberty to crawl about, where he takes his nap and makes the most of his infant existence."[40] In an article describing the rear-ranging of sitting room furniture to make a place for baby, Edna Donnell wrote, "What if the room does look a little cluttered, the baby comes first."[41] An anonymous author of an article in 1888 addressed the same issue, explaining, "The child is monarch of all he surveys."[42]

Surrogate Care

While farm mothers may have been able to make inroads toward embracing the child-centered culture of the middle class, urban working-class mothers had little opportunity. Many children were left in the care of older siblings who were barely old enough to care for themselves. Social reformer Jane Addams was horrified by injuries sustained by small children whose mothers had gone to work. She discovered that in one community "one [child] had fallen out of a third story, another had been burned." Yet a third child, with no one to look after him, "had a curved spine due to the fact that for three years he had been tied all day long to the leg of the kitchen table."[43] Desperate for child care, these women placed their children in nurseries modeled after French crèches. By 1892 there were 90 day nurseries in American cities, many run by religious or charitable organizations. Unfortunately, the level of child care was often very poor. Overcrowded and understaffed, these nurseries gained a dubious reputation and were utilized only by women in the most dire circumstances. In an effort to offer a more viable alternative, Jane Addams opened Hull House in Chicago in 1889 as a place where working-class and immigrant mothers could bring their children. Inspired by a settlement house Addams had seen in East London, Addams along with Ellen Starr originally envisioned the house to be a place where educated middle-class women could share the pleasures of art and literature with the surrounding, mainly immigrant, neighbors. Addams and Starr soon realized that the women had tremendous needs relating to the care of their children. Hull House rapidly expanded to include a day care center, nursery school, kindergarten, well-baby clinic, and a place where mothers could sit and talk. Hull House and other settlement houses that were to follow created a kind of socialized domestic sphere for lower-class mothers in need of support. It provided these women and their children a place of caring, comfort, and succor.

Settlement house workers assisted the urban poor by living among them and providing services directly to them. The first American settlement house was the Neighborhood Guild founded in New York by Stanton Colt in 1886. The Henry Street House, founded by Lillian Wald in 1893, is also very well known. Settlement houses continued to grow into the 20th century, and the volunteers there are considered to have pioneered the modern profession of social work.

With the increasing recognition that childhood was a unique stage of life, the 19th-century mother was charged with a greater responsibility to proceed with care and to follow the latest trends in scientific child-rearing. Middle- and upper-class women were extremely conscious of the stress of conforming to community standards in this regard. Improved methods of child-rearing quickly took hold that required a conscious effort and devotion to effect on the part of the mother. It fell to the mother to shape the child's character and instill habits of self-control while emphasizing lessons in industry, order, and restraint. It was through this maternal nurture that children were to be sheltered from the corruption of the outside world and prepared for the role of future citizen. As with much in the 19th century, the degree to which this took place corresponded directly with the socioeconomic condition of the family.

Notes

1. Frances Trollope, *Domestic Manners of the Americans* (1832; repr., Mineola, N.Y.: Dover Publications, 2003), 173.

2. Mary Antoine de Julio, *What a Rich Reward: Betsey Reynolds Voorhees and the Collection of Her Handiwork* (Fort Johnson, N.Y.: Montgomery County Historical Society, 1986), 9.

3. Sarah Josepha Hale, "Editor's Table," *Godey's Lady's Book,* January 1852.

4. Henry E. Woodbury, "Woman in Her Social Relations," *Godey's Lady's Book,* October 1852.

5. L. H. Sigourney, *Letters to Mothers* (Hartford, Conn.: Hudson & Skinner, 1838), iv.

6. Ibid., 5.

7. T. S. Arthur, *The Mother's Rule; or, The Right Way and the Wrong Way* (Rochester, N.Y.: E. Darrow & Brother, 1856), iii.

8. Lydia M. Child, *The Mother's Book* (Boston: Carter & Hendee, 1831), 9.

9. de Julio, *What a Rich Reward,* 16.

10. Benjamin B. Wisner, ed., *Memoirs of the Late Mrs. Susan Huntington* (Boston: Crocker & Brewster, 1828), 124.

11. Daniel E. Sutherland, *The Expansion of Everyday Life, 1860–1876* (Fayetteville: University of Arkansas Press, 2000), 121.

12. Ibid.

13. Jessica Mitford, *The American Way of Birth* (New York: Dutton, 1992), 37.

14. Jane C. Nylander, *Our Own Snug Fireside: Images of the New England Home, 1760–1860* (New Haven, Conn.: Yale University Press, 1993), 28.

15. Ibid.

16. Ibid., 29.

17. Gail Collins, *America's Women* (New York: Perennial, 2004), 128.

18. Mrs. L. G. Abell, "The Dying Girl," *Christian Parlor Magazine* 9, no. 12 274.

19. Minrose C. Gwin, *A Woman's Civil War* (Madison: University of Wisconsin, 1992), 72.

20. Ibid., 91.

21. The first true artificial formula available in the United States was Nestlé's Infant Food, a product that only needed dilution with water to prepare.

22. E. F. Haskell, *The Housekeeper's Encyclopedia* (New York: D. Appleton & Co., 1861), 384.

23. Marilyn Yalom, *A History of the Wife* (New York: Perennial, 2002), 199.

24. Haskell, *Housekeeper's Encyclopedia*, 385–386.

25. Steven Mintz, *Huck's Raft: A History of American Childhood* (Cambridge, Mass.: Belknap Press/Harvard University Press, 2004), 80.

26. Catharine E. Beecher, *A Treatise on Domestic Economy* (New York: Harper & Brothers, 1856), 12.

27. Daniel Webster, "Influence of Woman," *Godey's Lady's Book*, January 1852.

28. Catharine E. Beecher and Harriet Beecher Stowe, *The American Woman's Home* (New York: J. B. Ford & Co., 1869), 162.

29. Margaret M. Lothrop, *The Wayside: Home of Authors* (New York: American Book Co., 1968), 74.

30. Child, *Mother's Book*, 4.

31. Wisner, *Memoirs*, 125.

32. Child, *Mother's Book*, 23.

33. Nylander, *Our Own Snug Fireside*, 31–32.

34. Child, *Mother's Book*, 4.

35. Ibid., 53.

36. Ibid., 54.

37. Mary Livermore, *The Story of My Life* (Hartford, Conn.: A. D. Worthington & Co., 1899), 46.

38. Child, *Mother's Book*, 24, 50, 30.

39. Sally McMurry, *Families and Farmhouses in Nineteenth Century America* (Knoxville: University of Tennessee Press, 1997), 61–62.

40. Ibid., 195.

41. Ibid., 194.

42. Ibid., 195.

43. Mintz, *Huck's Raft*, 179.

11

Mother as Wife

She rose to his requirement, dropped
The playthings of her life
To make the honorable work
Of woman and of wife.

—Emily Dickinson, "The Wife," c.1863

Of Woman and of Wife

The wave of romanticism that swept the nation in the 19th century left its mark on more than literature and art. It raised love to an important, if not the most important, reason for selecting a mate. Sarah Anderson wrote the following lines in her diary a few days prior to her wedding. "Will Dr. B. be all that I want in a husband? In short will he love me as I desire to be loved? I don't look for perfect bliss, . . . the whole soul of my Husband devoted to love me . . . I would be foolish to expect perfect happiness, but my heart will demand perfect love."[1] Eliza Chaplin spoke for many of her generation when she wrote to a friend in 1820, "Never could I give my hand unaccompanied by my heart."[2] Certainly, some couples entered into marriage primarily for economic considerations or to please their parents, but increasingly, couples were drawn to make the commitment out of love. James Fenimore Cooper observed, "attractions lead to love; and love in this country, nineteen times in twenty, leads to matrimony."[3] Harriet Martineau, during her visit to the United States in 1837, was struck by how different marriages in America were from those in Europe. "If there is any country on earth where the course of true love may be expected to run smooth, it is America. It is a country where all can marry early, where there need be no anxiety about worldly provision, and where the troubles arising from conventional considerations of rank and connection ought to be entirely absent."[4] It had been noted by another European visitor in the 1820s that no American girl believed that she could not become the wife of a loving husband.[5]

American girls had greater liberty in the selection of a mate than their European counterparts. Gustave de Beaumont said of the American woman, "Since she is so early the mistress of herself and her own conduct, she makes her own choice."[6] Certainly, some parents made strong attempts to influence a child's choice but advice manuals warned against it. Counseling mothers "with regard to matrimonial specula- tions" for their daughters, Lydia Marie Child bid them, "Leave the affections to nature and to truth, and all will end well."[7] Young, single women were given far more latitude in their social interactions as well. James Fenimore Cooper stated, "In no other country is the same free- dom of intercourse between the unmarried of two sexes permitted, as in America."[8] European diarists were disconcerted by what they observed. Alexis de Tocqueville wrote, "Imagine the daughters of the first families, from one o'clock in the afternoon on, tripping all over the streets of New York, doing their shopping, riding horseback, without father or mother, uncle or aunt, without even a servant. [If] a young man . . . encounters one of these travelers [and] is already aquatinted, [he] stops . . . [and] chats . . . a quarter of an hour at the corner curb-stone, and at the end of the conversation the young lady . . . indicates the hour at which [he] will find her at home."[9] De Beaumont was similarly surprised to find that "young people . . . reveal their mutual inclination and tender feelings."[10] While young women may have invited whom they wanted into their homes and couples were given privacy in the parlor or on the porch, there was generally someone within earshot.

The "price" of premarital sexual conduct among the upper classes— should it be detected—was just too great in terms of the social conse- quences that it engendered. Couples from the lower classes were less restricted in their romancing, and they were given greater freedom away from watchful eyes and ears. Yet some conservative observers were critical of the fact that it was "customary for them to go out together unaccompanied."[11]

While the chastity of the bride was always presumed, this was less likely to be the actual case outside the socially elite classes. Records often show significant numbers of "early births" and "wedding night conceptions" to couples who were married less than a year. These, of course, were mostly a convenient fiction. One Southern doctor, more frank than his colleagues, professed that, in his locale, illegitimate births among the poorer classes were as common as those born in wedlock.[12]

The proposal of marriage was not taken
lightly, and if accepted, the engagement was
all but binding.

Proposal

Courtship and marriage were undergoing a number of changes during
this time. Women were always expected to wait for the man's profession
of love before she gave voice to her own. Convention prescribed that a
young man first speak to the father of the young woman whom he desired
to make his wife; but the reality, even among the upper classes, was that
most couples had made their plans prior to the future groom's petition.
Jefferson Patterson and Julia Johnson were engaged on January 3, 1833,
but Patterson did not speak to her father until January 21. Two days later,
John Johnson wrote the following to his future son-in-law, "Your family
and connections have long been known to me; your own character from
report and personal knowledge stands very fair. I could not, therefore,
for a moment have any objections to the proposal you make, the consent
of my dear Daughter being previously had."[13] One young woman even
became annoyed at her fiancé when he insisted upon addressing her
father. "I knew that Pa's consent did not make one hair's difference to
you. He knew that we would marry despite his consent, we both knew
it was hypocritical asking & we are neither favorably impressed with
sham courtesies, especially when they involve the observance of an old
barbarous relic & recognize woman as property."[14]

A period advice book for young women addressed this issue counseling, "If a gentlemen addresses you on the subject of marriage . . . it is proper that you make his proposal a subject of immediate and serious consideration . . . it is unnecessary to ask advice of any besides your parents. It is due to the filial respect that they should be consulted . . . [but] you have to decide in order to form your ultimate conclusion, . . . [be sure] you are satisfied with his character, and . . . the degree of affection for him."[15] Sarah Clapp certainly heeded this advice. Writing to her brother, she explained, "You have probably heard that I am not expecting to be married very soon, and that my engagement is broken, there are several reasons for this, but the most important one in my mind is that he is not pious, and that we do not think alike on important subjects."[16]

Once accepted, the marriage proposal was more binding on the man than on the woman. Social and in some cases legal consequences were imposed upon men who repudiated an engagement, yet it was acceptable for a woman to call it off. As a law student, George Cutler ruminated about a bride-to-be in his diary, "I give her the liberty of violating her engagement in lieu of her power of choice . . . because the contract is so much more important in its consequences to females than to males . . . they subject themselves to his authority—they depend more upon their husband than he does upon the wife for their society & for the happiness & enjoyment of their lives,—he is . . . their only hope . . . I will go further & apply the case I would justify any woman in treating me in that way—provided she did it in a delicate manner."[17] Hopefully, any woman who did refuse a proposal heeded the advice of *The Daughter's Own Book*, which urged the woman who declined to "make it known to him in a manner which will least wound his sensibility." She was further cautioned, "let not the secret of his having addressed you ever pass your lips."[18] Continuing his contemplation, Cutler took a stand in support of women in his diary, saying they "ought to have all the advantage in the matrimonial contract & instead of her present oppression ought to be able to make the most of every advantage & opportunity which fortune throws her way."[19]

Weddings

The general trend in matrimonials was toward larger and more elaborate wedding ceremonies with greater focus on the couple than their parents. In the 1830s brides began wearing white gowns and veils made specifically for their wedding day. Prior to this women were usually married in their "best" dress, and many young women continued that practice for decades. Those fortunate enough to be able to afford such a specialized garment tended to wear dresses that might be considered plain by ballroom standards. Expense was more likely to be put into the fabric rather than the trim. Mary Chesnut noted the fabric of one bride's dress in her diary, "The stuff was white and sheer, if a little coarse, but

By the 1860s wedding dresses had become more common than in former times when a best dress sufficed.

we covered it with no end of beautiful lace. It made a beautiful dress."[20] Generally, weddings were held during the day. Wedding dresses were, therefore, day dresses with jewel necklines and long sleeves. Headdresses and veils tended to lie flat on the head. Coronets of real or artificial flowers were arranged so that they framed the face. Chesnut described another bride. "Maggie dressed the bride's hair beautifully, they said, but it was all covered by her veil. Which was blonde lace—and the dress tulle and blond lace."[21]

Wedding ceremonies became more elaborate during this period, particularly in cities and for those who could afford the expense. By the second quarter of the century bridal parties were expanded to include multiple bridesmaids. The typical wedding party had one or two bridesmaids and groomsmen. In 1839, Henry Poor reported, "We have adopted the good Massachusetts faction of having bridesmaids and groomsmen."[22] An account of a Boston wedding detailed the bridal party as it appeared "all ready for the ceremony." The two groomsmen and two bridesmaids stood in the new fashioned way "each gentleman by his lady."[23] During the first decade of the century, weddings were commonly held on Tuesday, Wednesday, or Thursday to accommodate the minister's busy Sabbath schedule. It had also been the custom for weddings to take place in the family parlor, but by the 1860s more couples were choosing to be married in a church that could accommodate a larger number of guests.

Elaborate wedding dinners and dancing usually followed the ceremony. These events were generally held at a hotel or at the bride's parents' house. Dr. Bentley recorded the "fashionable display" of these new wedding customs. "The rooms were furnished elegantly & filled with chairs. Upon entrance after sundown into the brilliantly illuminated apartments four bridesmaids were ready to receive the guests, receive their outer garments & to introduce the Ladies to the Bride. Four young gentlemen had the same offices to the gentlemen They were then seated in their respective rooms & served with the best cake & wine that could be obtained."[24] From the 1830s on, middle-class couples sent out printed invitations to scores of guests, a custom that had been embraced by the upper class during the previous decade. De Tocqueville recorded, "They have a good custom . . . after a young woman is married, she has it announced that she wants to see all her friends and that she will be at home or her parents' . . . That being known, everyone who has any relations with the family comes."[25]

Wedding cake became the featured food item at these celebrations instead of the meats and pies served in previous times. Ruth Henshaw Bascom attended several weddings in 1810. She noted of the first that they had a supper of "roast turkey, beef, pies & etc." followed by cake and wine in the evening. At the second wedding, later that year, they "sent around their tea, cake & etc. as is customary of late."[26] The wedding cakes of the 19th century were usually rich fruit cakes similar to modern holiday cakes of the same name, and for many decades—even into the 20th century— the topmost layer of wedding cake remained a fruit cake so that it could be saved for the couple's first anniversary. Dr. William Bentley recorded that "the cake alone served on the occasion exceeded 130 pounds." When Elizabeth Carter married William Reynolds, her mother, sisters, and cousins made 14 loaves of cake, weighing altogether over 200 pounds. When completed, the cake was "purely white; Paradisiacal grains scattered over its surface, & it was studded with gilded almonds. In the center towered a beautiful collection of artificial flowers and round its body was a wreath of laurel. The groomsmen cut it up, and the bridesmaids assisted by Old Lady Parsons handed it round & oh it was astonishing to see how it vanished from sight." In some places, the served pieces of cake were passing around the company in attendance three times for good luck.[27]

One Midwestern woman recorded her own more down-to-earth wedding day, "All marched solemnly into the kitchen. At a signal the door opened, and stepping in, the ceremony was immediately begun." She added the following comment on the event. "Start not! ye fairy brides. Beneath your veils and orange blossoms, in some home where wealth and fashion congregate, your vows are no truer, your heart no happier, than was this maiden's in the kitchen of a log cabin, in the wilderness of Nebraska."[28]

Other matrimonial traditions changed as well from those of the previous century. Beginning in the 1840s it became fashionable for both the man and the woman to wear engagement rings, and rings specifically designated as wedding rings began to be mentioned at about the same time. An etiquette book from 1846 counseled, "If a ring is to be used, the bridegroom procures a plain gold one previously."[29] The nomenclature related to weddings also began to be refashioned. In the past "betrothals" were announced in church, usually by the minister at some point during the Sabbath service. By the 1860s, however, couples began announcing their "engagement" themselves through letters to friends or in the local newspapers. Nonetheless, several religious groups—particularly the Roman Catholics—continued to post the traditional "bans of marriage" from the pulpit into the 20th century. Newlywed couples no longer traveled with friends and relatives on their "wedding tour," but went instead on a "honeymoon." Honeymoons, thereafter, became a more private period for the couple than was previously the case. An etiquette book of the period advised that following the ceremony, the couple should enjoy "a honeymoon of repose, exempted from the claims of society."[30] Popular honeymoon destinations included New York City, Niagara Falls, the Green Mountains of Vermont, Montmorenci Falls in Canada, and—in the Midwest—the city of Cincinnati (a new metropolis considered worthy of a visit).

Suspended Identity

Marriage was a far more crucial decision for a woman than for a man because the woman often had her own identity legally incorporated into that of her husband. Husbands were increasingly described as providers, and wives (and minor children) were identified as dependents. This dependency—whether real or imagined—had unfortunate consequences. The *Baltimore American and Commercial Daily Adviser* charged wives to "never forget that a wife owes all her importance to that of her husband."[31] Even familial nomenclature changed. Instead of calling the wife "Mistress," a title used to describe the woman's responsibility over servants, apprentices, and journeymen, she was now referred to as "Mrs." with her husband's name fully appended. Her given name was not used in the address. The wife's identity was totally absorbed by the husband. Many women authors even published as "Mrs. ___" without mention of their given names. Newspaper accounts would identify a woman as "Mrs. ___, wife of _____."

Prior to the passage in 1848 of a series of comprehensive married women's property rights acts in New York, upon marriage a woman lost any right to control property that was hers prior to her union. Married women did not have the right to acquire any property solely in their own name during marriage. They could not make contracts, transfer property, or bring a lawsuit. Their legal persona was totally overshadowed by that of their husbands. The 1848 women's property rights acts were a bellwether development in this regard, and they were amended in 1860 to provide even more rights for New York women. Late in the 19th century women's rights to control their property were extended even further, but they did not reach full equality until the second half of the 20th century.

Ironically, women's property rights were often more closely protected in the Southern states where the maintenance of property and wealth within the family was considered of primary importance even in the face of the death or divorce of a spouse. Martineau noted, "In Louisiana, and also in

Missouri, (and probably in other States,) a woman . . . may always be considered as possessed of half [her husband's] gains during his life [and] the husband interferes much less with his wife's property in the south, even though her voluntary relinquishment of it, than is at all usual. [Nonetheless], the cases of woman having property during their marriage are rare."[32]

Lucy Stone and Henry Blackwell protested against coveture laws that deprived married women of their legal rights. At their marriage in 1855, the Rev. Thomas Wentworth Higginson, who performed the ceremony, read a document the couple had signed prior to the wedding. It began with the following statement, "While acknowledging our mutual affection by publicly assuming the relationship of husband and wife, yet in justice to ourselves and a great principle, we deem it a duty to declare that this act on our part implies no sanction of, nor promise of voluntary obedience to such of the present laws of marriage, as refuse to recognize the wife as an independent, rational being, while they confer upon the husband an injurious and unnatural superiority, investing him with legal power which no honorable man would exercise, and which no man should possess." They proceeded to detail six specific points to which they took issue that assured the domination of the husband. According to the couple, these gave husbands "the custody of the wife's person . . . exclusive control and guardianship of their children . . . sole ownership of her personal property and use of her real estate . . . absolute right to the product of her industry . . . inequitable treatment of property for widows and widowers . . . [and] the whole system by which the legal existence of the wife is suspended during marriage." Higginson not only read this declaration, he distributed it to other ministers as a model that he urged other couples to follow.[33]

Domestic Duties

"The event of marriage marks an important era in the life of a young female," warned an advice book, "It devolves upon her a set of cares, and duties, and responsibilities, to which she has hitherto been unaccustomed."[34] Many felt that the carefree and frivolous life that middle class and affluent young women were allowed to enjoy ill-prepared them for the serious duties of being wives and mothers. Lydia Marie Child asserted, "The bride is awakened from her delightful dream, in which carpets, vases, white gloves and pearl earrings, are oddly jumbled up with her lover's looks and promises . . . by the unpleasant conviction that cares devolve upon her."[35] De Beaumont put it succinctly, saying that when a woman marries "she retires from worldly pleasures to live among the austere duties of the domestic hearth."[36]

A wife had three major areas of responsibility. She was expected to obey and satisfy her husband; she was charged with keeping the children physically and morally healthy; and finally, she was accountable for the

A period illustration of what was considered a country home
for a family of moderate income.

maintenance of the household. In an editorial entitled, "Advice to the
Bride," Sarah Josepha Hale enjoined, "Your duty is submission [and] your
husband is by the laws of God and of man, your superior; do not ever give
him cause to remind you of it."[37] Continuing her counsel she wrote, "Let
all your enjoyment center in your home. Let your home occupy the first
place in your thoughts for that is the only source of happiness.[38]

In the 19th century, the home was the center of both family and society;
and while the husband was the head of the household, the wife was the
heart of the home. She was the essence of domesticity, a font of virtue and
the quintessence of nature. *The American Woman's Home* declared, "The
family state is the aptest earthly illustration of the heavenly kingdom, and
in it woman is its chief minister."[39] Newspaperman Wilber Fisk wrote,
"Someone has said that Woman carried civilization in her heart [and] a man
that lives in . . . the privileges of woman's society becomes more refined. "[40]
Women were considered central to good social order. Middle-class ideology
in the 19th century saw the home as an oasis or haven set apart from a corrupting world. De Beaumont wrote, "The domestic hearth is an inviolable
shrine which no breath of impurity must besmirch."[41] A Connecticut
soldier made this assessment of military life during the Civil War in this
way, "There is no society here, [because] there is nothing but men."[42]

This bifurcation of male and female obligations was a major change
from previous centuries when home and work were less distinct. Men
and women in colonial times spent most of their time living and working
side by side. It was common for the wife of a shopkeeper or tradesman
to work with her spouse in the retail establishment. The wife of a weaver
might wind the quills for him. A farmer's wife would help at critical times

such as planting or harvest. The daily routines and tasks of a husband and a wife might have been very distinct, but they worked toward a common goal, the well-being of the family. The wife could cross over into her husband's world without staking claim to it.

In the 19th century this changed drastically. Industrialization increasingly drew husbands away from the home to work in towns and cities. The nature and manner of their work became foreign to their wives, who remained at home isolated from pressures of the business world. In fact, wives were cautioned to "never be curious to pry into [their] husband's concerns."[43] De Beaumont described the middle-class wife, "When she has children, she lives in close contact with them, cares for and loves them. Thus pass her days. In the evening the man comes home full of care, restless, overcome with fatigue . . . his wife knows nothing of the affairs that preoccupy him; in her husband's presence she is still isolated."[44]

This physical separation of the household and workplace helped to bring about a new concept of the family and family roles. Men went to work, and women stayed at home. The midday meal—where the entire family had taken a respite from their duties to gather together in the shop or in the fields—was replaced by an evening meal consumed in increasing formality. Even farm families adopted a more distinct gender division of labor. Jobs that farm wives would have done in prior centuries was now being done by hired hands. Free of many of the time-consuming drudgeries of home production, women began to define their roles in terms of nurturing and child-rearing. The average home no longer housed a productive economic unit and subset of a larger community, which provided the physical needs of its residents. It now served the intellectual and emotional needs of the family, and became a sanctuary and refuge from the community. Such levels of privacy were particularly important to middle-class families whose level of wealth failed to insulate them from the seamier realities of urban life.

The public sphere was thought to be too harsh for a woman. It was full of temptations, violence, and distress. A woman's place was thought to be in the private sphere of the home where she could be protected from the harsh realities of the world. Women's magazines, religious tracts, advice books, and novels all described this new ideal of womanhood and the home. Referred to as the *Cult of Domesticity*, this ideology redefined a woman's duty and prescribed a set of virtues that all proper women should cultivate. Nineteenth-century women were expected to uphold values of stability, morality, and democracy by making the home a safe haven from an immoral world. *Godey's Lady's Book* promulgated the idea that the wife was "the guardian of the home; she can regulate the arrangement of her household: she can form the habits of her children; she does form them."[45]

In that home women were expected to be pure, pious, submissive, and domestic. Feminine purity was highly revered and any mention of female sexuality became taboo. As the period progressed, women's legs were increasingly referred to as "limbs," and the breast meat of chicken, turkeys, and water fowl at dinner came to be known as "white meat" so that no illusion to female anatomy might inadvertently be made. There were those who advocated the covering of the legs of chairs, tables, and pianos so that they would not be suggestive of the female anatomical counterparts.

Religion was seen as a remedy for the potentially restless feminine spirit. It would guide women to accept their role as handmaidens of the Lord who would help to bring the world out of sin. Evangelical leader Horace Bushnell wrote, "Home and religion are kindred words: names both of love and reverence . . . home . . . is the seat of religion."[46] This new role for woman was largely a response to the Second Great Awakening, a religious movement that swept the nation during the early 19th century. The clergy promoted women by praising their moral virtue. Frances Trollope observed that "it was from the clergy only that women of America receive the sort of attention which is so dearly valued by the young female heart throughout the world."[47] Soon the press took up the cry, anointing women as the moral guardians of society. The proliferation of newspapers, magazines, and books that characterized the period abounded with moralistic stories and editorials that reinforced women's role as society's moral compass. Trollope noted, "I never saw, or read, of any country where religion had such a strong hold upon the women."[48]

Acquiescence to a husband was advised by mothers, pastors, and advice books. Prior to her marriage, Julia Johnson received a letter with the following counsel, "Try to learn your husband's feelings and view of things and endeavor to conform to them. Make him your counselor on all occasions and your confidant."[49] An advice book proffered the following on "the true sphere of women," advising "the one quality on which woman's value and influence depend is the renunciation of self."[50] Yet another advice book for young women is more specific, "And this will be the spirit of every wife. Her pleasures will all bend to her husband's business. If duty requires him to leave the crowded city, and go away to some new region she will not deem it a hardship; nor when there, will she sigh for the comforts of her former house. A cottage with her husband will be a better place than a palace without him and if the circumstances so demand, she will with her own hand be willing to prepare her frugal meal, without the dainties of her more favored sisters."[51] Women were counseled to give their husbands what they wanted and to make as few demands as possible upon them. "Command his attention by being always attentive to him," advised one newspaper.[52] A wife was not to burden her husband with the troubles of her day as he already bore the burdens of his business, and if he was "out of temper," the wife was urged to "behave obligingly to him."[53]

William Alcott echoed many of these qualities, listing a dozen "Female Qualifications for Marriage" in his advice book for young men. First, he counseled that a wife should be of "moral excellence," as it was the "highest as well as noblest trait in female character." Next he placed "common sense" because it "implies judgment and discrimination, and proper sense in regard to the common concerns of life." He also advised that a perspective wife possess a "desire for improvement . . . physically, intellectually and morally." A "fondness for children" was essential in a society that loved and indulged its children. He felt strongly that she have a "love of domestic concerns" and that "the lover ought to have it continually in his eye." Alcott warned, "It is cold comfort for a hungry man to tell him how delightfully his wife plays and sings. Lovers may live on a very aerial diet, but husbands stand in need of something more solid." He also valued "sobriety" in a wife—not as regards temperance, but as "steadiness, carefulness [and] scrupulous propriety of conduct." Industry and "early rising" went hand in hand in Alcott's utopian estimation. He elaborated, saying that "the woman . . . who does not resolve to labor moderately as long as she lives, whatever her circumstances, is unfit for life, social or domestic." The ideal of "frugality"—the opposite of extravagance—was also included. Personal neatness and a good temper were also essential. Lastly, Alcott listed "accomplishments [in] those things, which are usually comprehended in what is termed a useful and polite education."[54]

Family developed very differently for the urban working class, and the concept of cooperative family work from prior centuries persisted for them even as that of the social elites evolved. Very few families were able to achieve the middle-class ideal of the husband as sole breadwinner and provider. Older children were expected to remain at home longer and to contribute to the household income. Wives took on additional domestic burdens such as sewing, doing laundry, or taking in boarders in order to earn money. Increasing financial pressures took their toll. Husbands often worked hours that prohibited them from eating at the same time as their children. Mothers were sometimes forced to send the children out to play in the streets so that their fathers could rest in the cramped quarters of their apartment. Some men left home for extended periods of time, working at higher-paying jobs that were far away.

Wifely Deportment

While unmarried women enjoyed a greater freedom of social interaction than their European counterparts, once they entered into marriage, women were subject to strict rules of deportment, manners, and dress. Cooper noted, "[T]here is more restraint imposed upon the . . . married; in this we reverse the usages of all other civilized nations. . . . One rarely sees married women foremost in the gay scenes. They attend, as observant and influencing members of society, but not as the principal actors. . . . The amusements of the world are more appropriate to the young, who are neither burdened nor sobered with matrimonial duties."[55] De Tocqueville described the situation even more severely, "When a woman marries, it's as if she entered a convent, except however that it is not taken ill that she have children, and even many of them . . . no more balls; hardly any more society."[56] Frances Trollope believed that American wives were "too actively employed in the interior of their houses" and remarked that if it was not for church services, they "would be in danger of becoming perfect recluses."[57]

Married women were so totally sheltered from public life that in the beginning of the century they were even absent from holiday festivities such as the Fourth of July, when military musters and all-male parades were the hallmark of the annual communal celebration. "Staid [*sic*] in all day and saw the procession and all there was to be seen from my window," wrote one woman.[58] By mid-century women could be seen on porches, balconies, or on special stands waving and cheering, but they were not included in the parade even though young unmarried women could be seen on the floats. New holidays, that centered around the home, began to become popular. Women's participation in these would not only be possible but central to their prosecution. Sarah Hale spearheaded a movement to get Abraham Lincoln to declare Thanksgiving a national holiday. Christmas evolved from a strictly religious observance to a more secular event. Hannah Rogers affirmed her role in society, writing in her diary that "the sphere of a woman's usefulness ought chiefly to be her family and friends."[59]

One activity outside the home open to women of the upper classes was visiting (calling). In addition to its recreational value, calling was a required social function that was strictly governed by convention. *Martine's Hand-Book of Etiquette* postulated, "Such visits are necessary, in order to maintain good feeling between the members of society; they are required by the custom of the age in which we live, and must be carefully attended to."[60] Visiting not only upheld a woman's social position, it enhanced that of her husband. Ceremonial calls were to be kept brief. "Half an hour amply suffices for a visit of ceremony. If the visitor be a lady, she may remove her victorine, but on no account either the shawl or bonnet, even if politely requested to do so by the mistress of the house. Some trouble is necessarily required in replacing them, and this ought to be avoided."[61] Upon exiting, the caller would leave a card, which would be placed in a cardholder kept in the front hall for that purpose. Elaborate cardholders were made from silver or china. Ladies' magazines contained patterns for crafted ones. "In leaving cards you must thus distribute them: one for the lady of the house and her daughters . . . one for the master of the house, and if there be a grown up son or a near male relation staying in the house, one for him."[62] The distribution of cards allowed a woman "to keep up a ceremonious acquaintance with a circle too large for friendly visiting, as that consumes far more time than could be given to the number of persons you must be acquainted with."[63]

Socially conscious women kept a list of family members and business acquaintances who formed a basic calling circle. It would be expected that persons on this list would be visited at least twice a year. Failure to reciprocate would be considered a grievous slight. Naturally, close friends and family would see each other more frequently. Martine counseled, "Keep a strict account of your ceremonial visits. This is needful, because time passes rapidly; and take note of how soon your calls are returned. You will thus be able, in most cases, to form an opinion whether or not your frequent visits are desired."[64] Brides were kept particularly busy making rounds as they introduced themselves in their new social position. Women were reminded that "it is the custom for a wife to take her husband's cards with her, and to leave one or two with her own."[65]

Another acceptable activity outside the home was philanthropy and social activism. Women, who were financially able to free themselves from household toil through the use of domestic servants, often dedicated time to organizations that helped the old, the poor, or those considered socially distressed. Even less-affluent women visited invalids and tended to the sick. Prior to the Civil War, charitable endeavors were usually limited to neighbors within a community, but in the early 19th century there was a great movement to reach out to those in need.

Women collected clothing and sewed for the urban poor and Western Indians. Some women ventured into urban ghettoes to personally help in the missions. Others, less comfortable outside the home, raised money to hire workers to carry out these good works. Louisa May Alcott worked in such a capacity at a Boston mission, collecting clothing, teaching sewing, distributing food to immigrants, and conducting a school for black children. A group of free black women advertised in 1847, "The Ladies (of color) of the town of Frankfort propose giving a FAIR . . . for benevolent purposes. . . . All the delicacies of the season will be served up in the most palatable style—such as Ice Creams, Cakes, Lemonades, Jellies, Fruits, Nuts &c."[66]

Trollope provided a glimpse into a ladies' missionary society, following one participant as she attended a meeting of the Dorcas Society. "She enters the parlour appropriated for the meeting and finds herself with seven other ladies, very like herself . . . she produces from her basket three ready-made pincushions, four ink-wipers, seven paper-matches, and a paste-board watch-case; these are welcomed with acclamations. . . . She then produces a thimble and asks for work; it is presented to her, and the eight ladies all stitch together for some hours. Their talk is of priests, and missions; of the profits from their last sale, of their hopes from the next . . . of the very ugly bonnet seen at church on Sabbath morning, of the very handsome preacher who performed on Sabbath afternoon and of the very large collection on Sabbath evening."[67]

Some women became involved in social reform movements such as temperance, women's rights, abolition, prison reform, and child protection. Women conducted prayer meetings in front of bordellos. They marched in the streets advocating temperance, even occasionally breaking up saloons. After a young man was killed in a bar in Ohio, "a large number of respectable ladies of the town . . . accompanied by the bereaved mother, proceeded to the saloon and with axes and other weapons knocked in the heads of barrels and casks, and demolished bottles and fixtures."[68]

Mary White's diary of 1838 shows that this mother, grandmother, and wife of a shopkeeper and farmer was active in her church and social reform. Amid entries of "making a black velvet waistcoat for William," and "I finished knitting a pair of mittens for Francis," Mary documented a life that was dedicated to her church and to social reform. She regularly attended "maternal associations and moral reform societies" as well as "religious meeting[s] at the Vestry," sometimes attending two meetings in one day. Obviously a deeply religious woman, she also participated in the "Monthly concert (of prayer.)" She attended a "lecture on political freedom," signed petitions to the "state legislature & one to Congress," attended an "Antislavery meeting" and "work[ed] for the antislavery society." These provided a full plate of acceptable actives for wives outside the home.[69]

The abolition movement received tremendous financial support from money raised by women at antislavery fairs. Women made scarves, doilies, and needlework bags with antislavery messages such as, "May the points of our needles prick the slaveholders' consciences." They sold pen wipers exhorting "Wipe out the blot of slavery." Lydia Child made a cradle quilt embroidered with the words "Think of the Negro mother when her child was torn away."[70]

When the Civil War began, Northern and Southern women had similar responses to the holocaust. They attended meetings to proclaim their allegiance (to the Union or Confederacy), pledged to roll bandages, and made clothing and flags for the soldiers. The Northern women's efforts soon mushroomed into a national organization called the United States Sanitary Commission, which played a major role in providing food and medical supplies to the Federal troops. Alfred Bloor of the Sanitary Commission credited women, saying that all the supplies "were almost universally collected, assorted, and dispatched, and re-collected, re-assorted, and re-dispatched by women, representing with great impartially, every grade of society in the Republic."[71]

Women's groups raised money not only for soldiers but also for their orphans and widows. One method of raising money was the charity cookbook, in which women compiled favorite recipes into books and published them. The first charity cookbooks were published during the Civil War. In one such cookbook, published to benefit Civil War victims, Maria J. Moss wrote, "When I wrote the following pages . . . I did not think it would be of service to my fellow creatures, for our suffering soldiers, the sick, the wounded, and the needy."[72] Bearing such lengthy and intriguing titles as *The Massachusetts Women's Temperance Union Cuisine* and *The Parish Cookery Book of the Ladies Aid Society of Saint Peter's Church,* charity or community cookbooks became very popular fundraisers to support causes that were religious, political, and local.

Involvement in such causes permitted women to have a social standing outside of the home. These activities were socially acceptable because, in essence, they were an extension of a wife's nurturing role. The Beecher sisters explained that a woman's "great mission is self-denial [and] self-sacrificing labors for the ignorant and weak: if not her own children, then the neglected children of her Father in heaven." They urged women to help "the orphan, the sick, the homeless and the sinful, and by motherly devotion train them to follow . . . Christ, in educating his earthly children for true happiness in this life and for his eternal home."[73] A period advice book for young women encouraged such involvement, saying that women "will fulfill their own high and lofty mission; precisely because the manifestation of such a spirit is the one thing needful for the regeneration of society. It is from her being the depository and disseminator of such a spirit, that woman's influence is principally derived. It appears to be for this end that Providence has so lavishly endowed her with moral qualities and, above all, with that love,—the antagonist of selfishness, that the spirit which, as it is vanquished or victorious, bears with it the moral destinies of the world!"[74]

Involvement in social causes strengthened the bond of womanhood among the matrons of the community, served as an example for unwed females, and breached the isolation of the home. These activities gave women the strength to organize and to exert their influence. Ultimately, the church groups, aid societies, charitable leagues, antislavery and temperance organizations laid the foundation for women to make the move into public life and careers in the following century.

Notes

1. Marilyn Yalom, *A History of the Wife* (New York: Perennial, 2002), 207–208.

2. Ibid., 176.

3. James Fenimore Cooper, *Notions of the Americans Picked up by a Traveling Bachelor* (Albany: State University of New York Press, 1991), 115.

4. Harriet Martineau, *Society in America: Observations Made during a Stay in 1837* (London: Saunders & Otley, 1837), 340.

5. Daniel Scott Smith and Michael S. Hindus, "Premarital Pregnancy in America," in Maris A. Vinovshkis, ed., *Studies in American Historical Demography* (New York: Academic Press, 1979), 128.

6. Gustave de Beaumont, "On Marriage in America: Beaumont's Letter to His Family," http://xroads.virginia.edu/~HYPER/DETOC/FEM/beaumont.htm (accessed December 2006).

7. Lydia Marie Child, *The American Frugal Housewife* (Boston: Carter & Hendee, 1832), 92.

8. Cooper, *Notions of the Americans,* 107.

9. Alexis de Tocqueville, "Letter to His Sister, Describing Courtship and Marriage Habits of the Americans," http://xroads.virginia.edu/~HYPER/DETOC/FEM/tocqueville.htm (accessed December 2006).

10. de Beaumont, "On Marriage in America."

11. Ibid.

12. Yalom, *History of the Wife,* 207.

13. "Crossings at the Rubicon, American Rites of Passage 1846–1868," http://www.cola.wright.edu/PublicHistory/rubicon/marriage.html (accessed December 2006).

14. Daniel E. Sutherland, *The Expansion of Everyday Life, 1860–1876* (Fayetteville: University of Arkansas Press, 2000), 117–118.

15. Anonymous, *The Daughter's Own Book* (Boston: Lilly, Walt, Coleman & Holden, 1833), 156–157.

16. Sarah Clapp, "Clapp Family Letters," American Antiquarian Society, http://www.osv.org/education/LessonPlans/Show/Lessons.php?PageID = P&LessonID = 32 (accessed December 2006).

17. George Younglove Cutler, "Journal of George Younglove Cutler," in Emily Noyles Vanderpoel, ed., *Chronicles of a Pioneer School* (Cambridge, Mass.: University Press, 1903), 196–197.

18. *Daughter's Own Book,* 157.

19. Cutler, "Journal of George Younglove Cutler," 196–197.

20. C. Vann Woodward, ed., *Mary Chesnut's Civil War* (New Haven: Yale University Press, 1981), 456.

21. Ibid., 649.

22. Marc McCutcheon, *Everyday Life in the 1800's* (Cincinnati, Ohio: Writer's Digest Books, 1993), 207.

23. Ibid., 208.

24. Jane C. Nylander, *Our Own Snug Fireside: Images of the New England Home, 1760–1860* (New Haven: Yale University Press, 1993), 259.

25. Alexis de Tocqueville, "Diary Account of a Wedding Reception," http://xroads.virginia.edu/~HYPER/DETOC/FEM/tocqueville.htm(accessed December, 2006).

26. Nylander, *Our Own Snug Fireside,* 258.

27. Ibid., 259.

28. Sutherland, *Expansion of Everyday Life,* 120.

29. McCutcheon, *Everyday Life in the 1800's,* 208.

30. Sutherland, *Expansion of Everyday Life,* 120.

31. Susan Burrows Swan, *Plain & Fancy: American Women and Their Needlework, 1650–1850* (Austin, Tex.: Curious Works Press, 1977), 208.

32. Martineau, *Society in America,* 341.

33. R. D. Owen, "Marriage protest—1832: On the Occasion of the Marriage of Robert Dale Owen and Mary Jane Robinson," http://womanshistory.about.com/od/marriage19th/a/owen_robinson.htm (accessed December 2006).

34. "A Father to His Daughter," *Daughter's Own Book,* 144.

35. Child, *American Frugal Housewife,* 97.

36. de Beaumont, "On Marriage in America."

37. Sarah Josepha Hale, "Advice to a Bride," *Godey's Lady's Book,* May 1832, 288.

38. Ibid., 288–289.

39. Catharine E. Beecher and Harriet Beecher Stowe, *The American Woman's Home* (New York: J. B. Ford & Co., 1869), 35.

40. Reid Mitchell, *The Vacant Chair: The Northern Soldier Leaves Home* (New York: Oxford University Press, 1993), 74.

41. de Beaumont, "On Marriage in America."

42. Mitchell, *Vacant Chair*, 73.

43. Swan, *Plain & Fancy*, 207.

44. de Beaumont, "On Marriage in America."

45. Laura Schenone, *A Thousand Years over a Hot Stove* (New York: W. W. Norton & Co., 2003), 113.

46. Horace Bushnell, *Christian Nurture* (New York: Charles Scribner's Sons, 1890), 406.

47. Frances Trollope, *Domestic Manners of the Americans* (1832; repr., Mineola, N.Y.: Dover Publications, 2003), 103.

48. Ibid., 104.

49. "Crossings at the Rubicon."

50. Anonymous, *The Young Lady's Mentor, by a Lady* (Philadelphia: H. C. Peck & Theo Bliss, 1851), 228.

51. Rev. Daniel C. Eddy, *The Young Woman's Friend; or, The Duties, Trials, Lives and Hopes of Woman* (Boston: Wentworth, Hewes & Co., 1859), 191–192.

52. Swan, *Plain & Fancy*, 207.

53. Ibid.

54. William A. Alcott, *The Young Man's Guide* (Boston: Perkins & Marvin, 1839), 263–305.

55. Cooper, *Notions of the Americans*, 112.

56. de Tocqueville, "Letter to His Sister."

57. Trollope, *Domestic Manners*, 43.

58. Gail Collins, *America's Women* (New York: Perennial, 2004), 89.

59. Swan, *Plain & Fancy*, 205.

60. Arthur Martine, *Martine's Hand-Book of Etiquette, and Guide to True Politeness* (New York: Dick & Fitzgerald, 1866), 113.

61. Ibid., 112–113.

62. Ibid., 116.

63. Swan, *Plain & Fancy*, 213.

64. Martine, *Martine's Hand-book,* 116.

65. Ibid.

66. Schenone, *Thousand Years*, 131.

67. Trollope, *Domestic Manners*, 173.

68. Collins, *America's Women*, 96.

69. Mary White, "Diary of Mary White, Boylston, MA, 1836–1844, Vol. I," Old Sturbridge Village Research Library, http://www.osv.org/education/LessonPlans/ShowLessons.php?PageID-P&LessonID=34 (accessed December, 2006).

70. Collins, *America's Women*, 172.

71. Ibid., 192.

72. Schenone, *Thousand Years*, 129.

73. Beecher and Beecher Stowe, *American Woman's Home*, 35.

74. Anonymous, *Young Lady's Mentor*, 231.

12

Mother as Homemaker

Hearty, honest work is a good thing for us all; but how much of it? That is the question. For my part, I think a little rest—a blessed little idleness now and then is good.

—Mrs. E. P. Allerton, "Dairy Factory System—A Blessing to the Farmer's Wife," 1875

Home, Sweet Home

The 19th century was one of tremendous evolution for the homemaker. The century opened much like the previous one, where the home was a self-contained unit and the homemaker was responsible for virtually all the needs of her family. A wife's domain consisted of her home and the yards surrounding it. The specifics varied—as did a family's economic situation and, to some extent, whether the location was rural or urban. Yet, in general, once inside the home, the wife's purview encompassed the kitchen and its appendages, the cellars, the pantries, the brew house, the milk house, the wash house, and the buttery. Outside, it would include the garden, the milk yard, the pigpen, the hen house, the well and, to some extent, the orchard. In season, it would reach into the woods for berry or mushroom gathering.

It was the woman's responsibility to manage and direct the economic productivity of her household. This included caring for the children and overseeing the servants. Certainly the scope and nature of the duties of a plantation mistresses or the lady of a town mansion differed from those of the frontier woman or a poor farmer's wife, but no matter what her social status, the comfort of a family was directly linked to a woman's skill in the ways of homemaking.

As the century progressed, however, the effects of industrialization brought dramatic changes to the ways of home management. The family no longer stayed together during the day. Men left home to go to work and children went to school. The family home and its management increasingly fell to the women. The rhythm of sunrise and sunset was replaced by the order of clocks and calendars. Factories began to produce once domestically produced necessities such as soap and textiles. This shift from homemade to store-bought items started slowly, but by mid-century it had become widespread. Catharine Beecher, Harriet Beecher Stowe, Sarah Josepha Hale, Lydia Marie Child, and other women writers spoke at length about the honor of this new kind of domestic life, urging the wife to "regard her duties as dignified, important, and difficult."[1]

One of the first domains of the housewife to experience change was food production. Prior to industrialization, farm families bartered some portion of their excess food production with tradesmen and others in exchange for services, luxury items, and cash. Samantha Barrett's 1828 diary contains many references to such transactions. After he had helped with haying, "Mr. Hamlin came for his pay for work—let him have four pounds seven of pork, three pounds butter, three of cheese, [and] Levi cut wood for us, paid him in pork and bread." Domestically produced commodities were even being exchanged in stores. "Loda rode to the store— got some pepper and spice, carried some butter to pay for them."[2]

As the 19th century unfolded, however, it became increasingly common for a woman to purchase food commodities rather than make them herself, and a cash economy came to dominant in many places. Husbands left the home to earn money that would allow families to purchase what they would have produced themselves. Urban living and industrialization removed people from their food sources, transforming many of the former food producers into food consumers.

For centuries, most families ate with the main purpose of consuming a sufficient amount of calories to satisfy their hunger. There was often little variety in diet, and in the years before refrigeration menus were largely reflective of the season's bounty. What was available to a family in the winter and spring depended upon a wife's careful preservation of their excess. A woman's expertise in this area was the difference between comfort and starvation through the winter and well into the spring. By mid-century, the market teemed with a surfeit of cookbooks that told women that the food they prepared could be so much more than mere sustenance. Cookbook authors advised women that with proper cooking, they could encourage better health, raise morality, end alcoholism, decrease infant mortality, and help their families become upwardly mobile. Although some of these outcomes were held to be true only by fringe elements among dietary reformers, cooking was indeed becoming a more social act, creating a role of increased importance for women in society. Mrs. Lee, author of the *Cook's Own Book,* declared, "The cook exercises a greater power over the public health and welfare than the physician."[3]

Sarah Josepha Hale, an editor of *Godey's Lady's Book,* proffered, "The intemperance in eating, of luxury in living is more the fault of woman than of man [because] she is the guardian of the home."[4] Women were advised to eliminate alcohol and excessive seasonings from their recipes lest they tempt their families to overindulgence. In her book, *Christianity in the Kitchen,* Mrs. Horace Mann cautioned, "There is no more prolific,—indeed, there is no such prolific cause of bad morals as abuses of diet,—not merely by excessive drinking of injurious beverages, but excessive eating, and by eating unhealthful food." She continued declaring, "Compounds like wedding cake, suet plum puddings, and rich turtle soup, are masses of indigestible material which should never find their way to any Christian table."[5] Dietary reform advocates popularized their advice via a proliferation of magazines and cookbooks designed for socially aware women. Readers were regularly warned to cease preparing fried foods and rich pastry or cakes and to eliminate brandy and wine from sauce recipes.

Catharine Beecher even included a chapter entitled "Temperance Drinks" in her cookbook, which contained recipes for sarsaparilla mead, effervescing fruit and jelly drinks, and ginger beer. She introduced the section with an explanation of the various positions held by temperance supporters that ranged from those who "will not use any kind of alcoholic liquors for any purpose [and] such [who] will not employ it in cooking, nor keep it in their houses." To those like herself who professed a more moderate view on alcoholic consumption, Beecher said that she thought "it proper to use wine and brandy in cooking and occasionally for medical purposes." Beecher further speculated that "the cause of temperance [would] be best promoted by going no further."[6]

In addition to the moral benefits of diet, dietary reform was brought about by the national concern regarding dyspepsia. Lydia Marie Child included a recipe for making dyspepsia bread in *The American Frugal Housewife.* Indigestion and a host of related stomach ailments seem to have plagued the middle and upper classes during this period. In the *Cook's Own Book,* Mrs. Lee proclaimed, "After insanity, the most grievous affliction of Providence, or rather of improvidence and imprudence, is Dyspepsia: a malady that under different names has decimated the inhabitants of civilized countries."[7] Perhaps, it was due to the shift from physical labor to more sedentary jobs without a change from the high-calorie, high-fat diets. It might also have been the new abundance of food that was available as a result of improved transportation and increased wealth. Catharine Beecher preferred a technical explanation, "In many dyspeptics, fat does not become properly chymified. It floats on the stomach in the form of an oily pellicle, becoming odorous, and sometimes highly rancid, and in the rare state excites heartburn, disagreeable nausea, eructations, and sometimes vomiting."[8] Whatever the cause, it was up to the housewife to provide the solution.

By mid-century, cookbooks began to contain charts with food nutrients and lengthy descriptions of the working of the body. The "Healthful Food" chapter in *The American Woman's Home* contained illustrations of the stomach, lungs, skin, spine, and sweat glands. These books often provided misguided information about eating. In *The Good Housekeeper,* Hale informed her readers, "Fish is much less nutritious than flesh."[9] Catharine Beecher explained, "Bathing should never follow a meal as it withdraws the blood and nervous vigor demanded for digestion from the stomach to the skin."[10] She also warned against the use of pepper, mustard, and spices stating, "Persons in perfect health, and especially young children, never receive any benefit from such kinds of food . . . as they quicken the labors of the internal organs. . . . A person who thus keeps the body working under an unnatural excitement, lives faster than Nature designed, and the constitution is worn out just so much sooner."[11] Other admonitions cautioned against drinking ice water, eating warm bread, and giving children too many fluids.

Women certainly would need formal training if they were to understand the complexities of proper meal production and housekeeping. Catharine Beecher's domestic guides addressed the concerns of Northern Christian women who aspired to higher standards of cleanliness and beauty in their well-ordered homes. These women wanted to understand all aspects of the home and its residents. They wanted to understand the plumbing and architecture of the house, the skeletal infrastructure of the body, and the chemical composition of foods. Beecher was a champion for the education of women in what she termed "domestic science" and founded several schools where it was formally taught. She believed that with education and exacting attention, housekeeping could transcend drudgery and rise to the level of a venerated calling on equal footing with the work of men.

These culinary attitudes were mainly centered in the Northeast. Cooking in the South reflected an entirely different paradigm. Southern plantation mistresses were known for their role as hostesses, not as cooks. Cooking was done by slaves or servants. Just as the South had developed a separate culture, it evolved its own particular style of cooking. In all but the poorest households, slaves did the bulk of the cooking until the Civil War. These cooks were familiar with African foods such as bene (sesame) seeds and okra. They were much more accepting of non-English ingredients such as peanuts, eggplants, tomatoes, sweet potatoes, and yams, creating rich and spicy dishes that were distinctively Southern. Even modest households dined on egg-thickened fricassees, savory ragouts, crusty yeast breads, myriad vegetables, and delicate custards. Period letters and journals often describe parties of multi-course meals—which one would imagine would be reserved for holidays or the most special occasions—taking place with regularity. One breakfast description included cornbread, buckwheat cakes, boiled chicken, bacon, eggs, hominy, fish, both fresh and pickled, and beefsteak all being served at a single sitting.

Dinner offerings were likely to be equally as impressive. An 1833 letter detailed a dinner that began with a very rich soup and continued with a saddle of mutton, ham, beef, turkey, duck, eggs with greens, potatoes, beets, and hominy. After the circulation of champagne came dessert, which offered plum pudding and tarts followed by ice cream and preserves and peaches preserved in brandy. Lastly came figs, raisins, almonds, and wine: port, Madeira, and a sweet wine for the ladies. After visiting Virginia, Frances Trollope wrote, "They consume an extraordinary quantity of bacon. Ham and beefsteaks appear morning, noon and night. In eating, they mix things together with the strangest incongruity imaginable. I have seen eggs with oysters."[12]

Pork was the most common kind of meat consumed in the Southern diet. It was a common practice among farmer's and upper-class planter's wives alike to sell their cured hams as well as surplus lard, butter, and eggs in order to make a little extra money. In 1856, the mistress of a Georgia plantation recorded the selling of 170 pounds of ham. Poorer families lived on a "hog and hominy" diet of bacon, turnip greens, corn pone, coffee sweetened with molasses, and little else. Pork might be served three times a day in some households without engendering comment. However, it was not likely to be fresh pork. Salt-pork and smoked pork were the staple varieties during most of the year, except during the harvest season. *Knickerbocker Magazine* reported that the inn in Georgetown, South Carolina, served "hog and hominy, and corn-cake for breakfast; waffles, hog and hominy for dinner; and hog, hominy, and corn-cake for supper."[13] Food in the South was prepared for its taste and satisfaction. There was little interest in making dietary social statements.[14]

Food Preservation

There were many women who could not achieve the middle-class ideals set forth in cookbooks and household advice manuals. Farm wives still raised their own food in small gardens and preserved it for the winter. For these women home food preservation remained an essential household activity. The harvest season came but once annually, and if a family was to live comfortably through the year, careful attention had to be paid to "putting up" harvest surplus until the next growing season. Lyndon Freeman of Sturbridge, Massachusetts, recalled rural dietary habits. "At the setting in of winter every farmer was presumed to have pork and beef of sufficient quantity. The larder was well supplied with butter, cheese, applesauce, pickles, sausages, souse, etc. The dinner commonly consisted of boiled pork or beef, or both, potatoes, cabbage, beets, carrots, etc. A mug of cider was upon the table never forgotten. . . . The meat and sauce left of the dinner were hash-up for breakfast the next morning. The supper was usually brown bread and milk for all."[15] This simple diet seems to have suited many. Elihu Hoyt of Deerfield, Massachusetts, had the occasion to dine in Boston with the governor and a number of members of the Senate. He wrote to his wife, "I had much rather have dined at Deerfield in our common pork and cabbage style."[16]

Farm families generally ate well through most of the winter as the household was still enjoying the abundance of the harvest. While food might have been sufficient, it was generally monotonous and composed largely of tubers and root vegetables. A Muncie housewife described the winter diet as "steak, roasts, macaroni, Irish potatoes, sweet potatoes, turnips, cole slaw, fried apples, and stewed tomatoes, with Indian pudding, rice, cake or pie for dessert." To provide variety, families "swapped around from one combination to another, using pickles and chow-chow to make the familiar starchy food relishing." She concluded, "We never thought of having fresh fruit or green vegetables and could not have got them if we had."[17] Spring, and even early summer, were generally the hardest time. Fresh produce was not yet up and stored foods were often becoming limited. Catharine Beecher cautioned housewives, "One mode of securing a good variety in those months in spring when fruits and vegetables fail is by a wise providence in drying and preserving fruits and vegetables."[18]

Produce was preserved by a number of methods and much of it was stored in crocks and jars. Instructions for sealing these vessels included a number of methods for sealing storage containers: "Soak a split bladder and tie it tight over them [jars]. In drying, it will shrink so as to be perfectly air tight."[19] "Cover each tumbler with two rounds of white tissue paper, cut to fit exactly the inside of the glass."[20] "Secure [jars and crocks] with paper dipped in brandy and a leather outer cover."[21] Finally, "cement on the covers [of stone jars] with composition of bees-wax and rosin melted together, and thickened with powdered brick dust."[22]

Hundreds of men and women obtained patents for jars that would ease these time-consuming processes. Perhaps the most famous of these was John Mason who patented his Mason Jar in 1858. These threaded glass jars had zinc lids with threaded ring sealers. Newspapers often carried notices of patent jars for sale. One such ad boasted "Tomatoes, green corn peaches or any other fruit or vegetable may be preserved without sugar, by using Spratt's Patent Cans, which are acknowledged to be the only reliable self sealing cans to market." Immediately below this statement followed another notice that asserted, "Few things will be found more delicious in Winter than finely flavored apples and pears, kept fresh in 'Arthur's Self-sealing Cans and Jars.' Let every housekeeper try a dozen or two. . . . She will thank us for our advice next Christmas if she follows it."[23] Jars such as these were a welcome improvement for both city and rural homemakers who had to preserve nature's bounty until the next harvest season.

Urban Eating

For women who lived in city tenements, little thought was given to dietary propriety. These families were often crowded into one and two rooms with kitchen space that had to serve as workspace, sleeping quarters, and living area. Sanitation was abysmal. With no sewer systems, filthy water overflowed into pump water wells that were used for cooking. New York residents didn't receive piped water until 1842 when it was brought down from the Croton Water Works. Scavenging pigs wandered city streets and alleyways. Despite the fact that vagrant pigs were outlawed in New York in 1830, Charles Dickens noted in 1842 that pigs roamed the streets "by the scores" in the early evening "eating their way to the last" along Broadway, losing their ears and tails to derelict dogs along the way. Another writer made the observation, "I have not yet found any city, country or town where I have not found [pigs] wandering about . . . eating all types of refuse."[24] It was not unusual for some of these pigs to find their way to the tables of poor working families.

Many working women did little cooking except on Sundays, holidays, and special occasions. When they did cook, the streets and stairwells of the tenements often took on an "ethnic aroma" that matched the countries of origin of the residents. When not cooking for their families themselves, city women relied for quick and inexpensive meals on the street peddlers who sold food on street corners, from pushcarts, and from wagons that moved door to door. In New York the "hot corn women," hot potato vendors, and chestnut roasters could be found on many street corners. Philadelphia was famous for its pepper pot soup peddlers. Pepper pot soup was a mixture of tripe, vegetables, and red pepper brought to America by African slaves via the Caribbean. African American women sold the soup on street corners for pennies a bowl. An 1814 letter noted of Philadelphia "the ear is regaled with cries of 'pepper pot, right hot.'"[25]

Juliet Corson wanted to help these poor women to prepare simple and healthful meals for their families. After studying the shopping baskets of poorly dressed women in the markets, she developed a body of recipes that used as ingredients "the articles in common use among the working classes." Based on her observations, she wrote a pamphlet entitled "Fifteen Cent Dinners for Workingmen's Families." Unable to find a publisher, she raised the money herself and managed to print 50,000 copies. She then took out advertisements in newspapers, offering it for free to families earning $1.50 or less per day. The pamphlet was a tremendous success. It was reported that 200 people showed up at her door asking for a copy. One newspaper reprinted it in its entirety. Corson promised her audience that proper cooking would bring "good blood, sound bones, healthy

Street vendors working from stalls or from donkey carts like this one sold all types of items, including shellfish, vegetables, fruits, nuts, and cooked meats.

brains, strong nerves and firm flesh." She recommended breakfasts of toast and broth, or rice with scalded milk; a midday meal of baked beans, or beef and potatoes; and suppers of watery soups or stews of broth and rice. What was stew on the first day became broth for breakfast the next, and finally soup with rice. Corson's cheapest meal was a one-pot polenta dish that boasted it could feed a family for five cents. Part of her frugality was found in portion control. Her macaroni and cheese dinner was made with a "half pound of macaroni [and a] quarter pound of cheese" to feed two adults and four children.[26]

Shopping for city dwellers was done in street markets where farmers and other vendors brought their food to sell. In the days before refrigeration, women had to shop frequently. The quality of merchandise varied with the clientele of the particular market, and homemakers were warned to avoid hucksters who sold inferior goods. The *Daily Times* referred to one that served the poor of New York's Lower East Side as the "little heap of fish scales, eel heads, butcher's offal and rotting vegetables known as Catharine Market."[27] This market was quiet during the week as few people had the money to shop there daily, but, as the paper noted, "they choose one day in the hard-worked week for a feast, and on Saturday night go marketing in earnest." The crowds were "fairly wedged together" as they came to "barter with shrill eagerness for the modest luxuries they have been greedily anticipating for a week past. . . . The women who congregate here are often sharp, meager and scolding, plainly suffering from privations and excessive toil. . . . The great demand is for cheapness, and as the sidewalk vendors usually undersell the store-keepers and stall-holders, they attract the most customers." The *Daily Times* painted a picture of one of these careful shoppers, "A slight, cadaverous, slatternly woman . . . [with] a small boy clinging to her skirts thrust a bony hand into . . . the bottom of the cart. She brings out a flabby duck and submits it to a severe examination. First she pinches it; then smells it, pinches it again and throws it back into the cart bringing out another and another until her exacting taste is satisfied. . . . She has been cheated too often not to suspect such a vagabond as he."[28] The poorest shoppers arrived at the market just before closing hoping to get the cheapest prices from sellers who did not want to pack up food that had been sitting in the warm sun all day. Those in the most hopeless situations scoured the garbage after the market closed. Most urban poor subsisted on a diet of bread, potatoes, crackers, salt pork, and blood pudding.

Out of the Oven

Baking was an important part of a homemaker's weekly endeavors. Hale recommended, "when baking is done twice a week, Wednesdays and Saturdays should be chosen, if only once a week, Saturday is the best, because it allows for preparation for the Sunday dinner—a pudding can be baked—and meat, too, if the family have a real desire of keeping the day for that which it was evidently intended, rest for worldly care, as well as for moral and religious improvement."[29] One baking day per week seems to have been most common. Most women baked in brick ovens until the cookstove came into popularity and even then, many preferred the older method because they were more familiar with it. Some continued to use bake ovens for large amounts of baking into the second half of the century. Ann Howe, in her housekeeper's guide, explained, "brick ovens are . . . best for baking most things, particularly those . . . which require a long time." She admitted, however, "it is a good deal of extra trouble and expense to heat a brick oven when you have a good one attached to your cooking stove. It will generally be found preferable to use the latter."[30]

Dutch ovens were used in homes without ovens or for baking between regular baking days. These shallow, cast iron kettles with three short legs and a lid with a deep rim were a centuries-old technology. Coals were pulled out from the fire on to the hearth apron and spread beneath the oven. Additional coals were placed on top to provide even heat from above as well as beneath. Dutch ovens were excellent for making single pies or biscuits and for warming leftovers, but they could not produce a large volume of baked goods like multiple loaves of bread.

To bake in the brick oven, a woman would build a fire and let it burn down to coals. Women had various methods to test that the oven was hot enough. One common method involved thrusting the arm into the oven and counting. Catharine Beecher suggested, "[I]f you cannot hold your hand in longer than to count twenty moderately, it is hot enough. If you can count to thirty moderately, it is not hot enough for bread."[31] Some women threw in a handful of flour and waited to see how long it took to scorch. One cookbook author suggested that a properly built oven would permit the baking of successive loads of food, "the bread first—then the puddings—afterward the pastry—then cake and gingerbread—and lastly, custards, which if made with boiled milk and put in the oven hot, and allowed to stand a considerable time, will bake sufficiently with a very slight heat."[32] Sarah Bryant usually heated her oven only once each time she baked, although at times she had to "heat the oven three times" in order to finish her baking. Contrary to household advice manuals that advised designating specific days to specific chores, Sarah often combined her baking with other tasks such as washing or ironing, both of which required a fire and staying in or near the kitchen. These tended to be long days. Sarah's diary contains entries where she "baked before sunrise" and "baked pies in the evening."[33]

Many urban homemakers purchased bread from a baker. Some homemakers purchased bread during the summer rather than to go through the discomfort of building a large, hot fire at home. Hale railed against baker's bread, discounting it as tasteless and unhealthy as there was no way of knowing the quality of the flour used. She complained that "in our cities ladies marry and commence housekeeping, without knowing anything of breadmaking."[34] A Midwestern baker observed that "people who lived in the better homes . . . never thought of buying bread unless to fill in when the home baked bread ran short. They regarded baker's bread as poor-folksy: it was the working class who bought baker's bread." Commercial bakers also made crackers (sometimes called biscuits). Long used on ships and for the military, these long-lasting bread substitutes became so popular after the Civil War that large commercial bakeries were created to satisfy the demand. Cracker barrels could be found in virtually every country store.[35]

City residents had to rely on commercial bakeries for breads, baked beans, and pies. Commercial bakers heated their oven at night and baked before dawn, and children would often take a meat pie or a bean pot—filled with mother's own recipe of ingredients and sauces—to the baker in the morning for a full day of heating in the residual warmth of the baker's ovens. Those who could afford more sumptuous delights also might patronize a confectioner. One such shop owner in Portsmouth, New Hampshire, boasted that he offered "the best jelly of all kinds, Wedding cake and refreshments in general." In Salem, Massachusetts, John Remond and his wife, Nancy, advertised, "Cakes of various kinds made to order, at short notice, among which are Wedding, Plum, Pound, White, Bride, Currant, Taylor, sponge, Compositions, elections, etc."[36]

Some women aspired to the homemaker ideal found in period literature but lacked the necessary skills to follow through on a day-to-day basis. In a mobile 19th-century society with its constant evolution of domestic "appliances," young women setting up households often found themselves at great distances from family members who could give them support in ordering their households. Mary Livermore was one such new homemaker. "I had not an acquaintance in town who was a mature housewife, I was fifty miles away from my all-knowing mother." Fortunately, her "husband's good nature was unfailing, and, though he laughed over [her] 'experiments' in the culinary art which were rarely successful, he never complained." In fact, she discovered that he was "much better posted in the science and philosophy of domestic business" than was she. As the "youngest of a family of nine . . . [where] the daughters of the family were married and settled in homes of their own . . . [he] was put to the service of his mother . . . who needed him in the large dairy and in the kitchen. . . . In this way he had acquired a general knowledge of the fundamental laws which underlie good housekeeping, and knew something of the art of cooking, household sanitation, laundry work, etc." Livermore confessed to many culinary disasters, including one "fish chowder" dinner that was so bad "after dark that night, the masculine head of the house quietly buried it in the corner of the garden, that the incompetence of his wife, as cook, might never be discovered and bruited abroad."[37]

Having married in 1845, Livermore did not have the benefit of the profusion of household advice manuals that would flood the market with the next years. She complained that cookbooks "were of little value [and] were full of impossible ingredients." She proclaimed that "the less one consulted them the better!" Livermore even admitted that "I tossed the book on the table with inexpressible contempt." Finally, she decided to contact her sister whom she described as a "born housekeeper." Livermore wrote, "I engaged her to come to my relief as I would a tutor, and put myself under her instruction." She remained with the couple for months. In time Livermore was able to report, "I subordinated all other occupations to a study of domestic business, mastering the principles of cookery, and then putting them into practice, under her supervision, and always with successful results."[38]

Cheese was another commercially produced food that saved time and labor for homemakers. In 1851, near Rome, New York, Jesse Williams revolutionized commercial cheese making when he established the first factory dedicated to cheese production in the United States. Here on the banks of the Erie Canal, he made hard cheese from scratch from his own dairy herd, and ultimately he began to purchase milk from other farmers. By combining the milk and producing large cheeses, he could achieve a uniform taste and texture. Up until this time, commercial cheese makers would buy up batches of cheese curd from farmers to make into cheese, but the quality and taste varied greatly. Initially, Williams's cheese factory could produce four cheeses daily, each cheese weighing 150 pounds. "Store cheese" like cheddars quickly became popular, and central New York, Vermont, and New Hampshire all quickly became noted as cheese making regions. Commercial cheese making brought tremendous relief to farm wives. The *American Agriculturalist* proclaimed, "What the mower, reaper and thrashing machine have done for the farmer, the cheese factory has done for their wives and daughters."[39]

Home cheese making was an arduous and time-consuming job. To make cheese a housewife would heat several gallons of whole milk along with rennet, which had been dried and saved from the autumn slaughtering. Rennet is an enzyme that clots or curdles milk solids into cheese. It was obtained from the stomachs of slaughtered newborn calves. The inner membrane was kept in salt and dried. When the rennet was needed, the membrane was soaked in water. After an hour or two in the milk, the curd would form. The homemaker would drain off the whey, break the curd, and work in some butter. At this point the cheese looked much like modern cottage cheese and could be used immediately. If the mixture was to be preserved as a hard or semi-soft cheese, it would be wrapped in cheesecloth, placed in a mold, and put in a press for an hour. During this time, the cheesecloth would have to be changed and washed as the whey dripped out. It would then be repacked in a dry cloth and set in a press for 30 to 40 hours. After one final wash in whey, it would be dried and placed on a shelf in the dairy to age. The cheese would then have to be turned and rubbed daily with finely ground salt. Sarah Emery recalled that, in her home, "After dinner, the cheeses were turned and rubbed."[40]

Following the Civil War, the commercial cheese factory began a boom removing the task from the home. By 1875 there were more than 500 cheese factories in New York state alone. In those days before refrigeration, the factory had to be within a half-hour drive of the dairy because the milk had to be transported by wagon. In 1878, a German immigrant named Julius Wettstein started a cheese factory in Monroe, New York, where he produced a fine line of German, French, and Swiss types that were traded over the entire length of the Erie Canal. He sold these quality cheeses at a high price, and also taught the cheese making arts to locals for $3.00 per day. He returned to Germany a rich man after only a few years. In 1881, John Balderson, a retired sergeant from the British Army, began a cheddar factory in Balderson Corners, New York, with the support of a group of local dairy farmers. The Balderson factory was one of ten in the area. Mrs. E. P. Allerton in her essay "Dairy Factory System—A Blessing to the Farmer's Wife" wrote, "In many farmhouses, the dairy work loomed up every year, a mountain that took all summer to scale. But the mountain is removed; it has been handed over to the cheese factory, and let us be thankful."[41]

A period cheese safe made of wood and fine wire screening that kept out the flies and rodents and let in the air. Many 19th-century kitchens were supplied with "safes" for pies, bread, meats, etc.

The Icebox

Food preservation had always been a problem, especially for meat and dairy products. It was not a major problem during the winter months with their low temperatures and low relative humidity, but hot and humid weather posed a significant problem, especially in the South with its difficult climate. One of the earliest solutions to keeping food from spoiling during warm weather was the icehouse. By the dawn of the Civil War, the icehouse had become an indispensable component on the rural farm. Originally, ice was harvested by farmers using axes and long saws. The ice was cut from frozen ponds or lakes in large blocks. This could be an individual or community operation in rural regions, but there were a number of ice companies that hired large crews to cut ice and transport it to the cities and commercial storage facilities. In 1825 Frederick Tudor and Nathaniel Wyeth solved the problems of preserving ice throughout the year and made ice harvesting a commercial interest. Licenses were issued to remove ice from the Erie Canal, the Great Lakes, Lake Champlain, and other freshwater bodies for commercial purposes. Ice was not only provided to city residents in the North, it was also shipped to Southern cities and even to the West Indies. By the 1830s ice was readily available to everyone. Between 1825 and 1860, New Orleans alone increased its demand for ice seventy-fold.[42]

Thomas Moore patented the first domestic icebox in 1803. Household iceboxes, many of which were homemade, consisted of a wooden box, inside another separated by some insulating material, with a tin container at the top of the interior box. The exterior of the boxes were made of oak, pine, or ash wood; and they were lined with zinc, slate, porcelain, galvanized metal, or wood. Charcoal, cork, flax straw, ashes, or mineral wool provided the insulation between the walls.

The icebox gave individual homes and city residences a means of keeping food cold. Fresh meat, dairy products, and perishable fruit could be kept in good condition for much longer if kept cool. Irregularly shaped ice blocks were sold to consumers in baskets. Even with the icebox, the frozen blocks would only last for about a day. Boston families could obtain 15 pounds of ice per day from an ice man for $2.00 a month just prior to the Civil War. By 1850, *Godey's Lady's Book* called the icebox a "necessity of life." An early system for refrigeration was patented in 1834 by Jacob Perkins, but a practical system did not become common until the 1870s. Domestic refrigeration awaited the extension of electric power to the family kitchen, and iceboxes served most households into the first half of the 20th century.

Food Diversity

By mid-century the railroads had become a key factor in increasing the diversity of food available to the middle-class homemaker, widening the nutritional gap between classes. Perishables such as milk, oysters, and lobsters were transported by rail to urban areas in large cars filled with ice. After the construction of the Erie Railroad, milk consumption in New York City more than tripled. The railroad not only augmented the diet, it served to improve the quality of the food that was eaten. In the 1870s America went on a beef-eating binge. Railroads made beef fatter, more tender, more tasty, and less expensive. The cattle no longer were driven to market on the hoof, and hence, they developed less muscle and lost less weight. The cattle were fed on grain that was also shipped via the railroad, thus improving the flavor. Finally, the cost of an individual cut of meat was reduced because there was less loss between pasture and market. A similar situation arose with pork. Prior to railroad transportation, a desirable breeding characteristic among hogs was their ability to walk to market. This made long-legged varieties superior to short-legged ones. With the advent of rail shipping, breeders began to focus on more portly hogs and tastier meat. Railroads also increased the number of small farms outside cities. Hundreds of acres in upstate New York, Long Island, New Jersey, Delaware, Maryland, and eastern Virginia yielded produce for the cities kept in a fresh state by speedy rail transportation. Foreign visitors commented on the "almost endless variety of the choicest articles of food—meat, poultry, fish, vegetables, and fruits from all parts."[43]

Into the Fire

One of the most dramatic improvements in the 19th-century kitchen was the cast iron cookstove. Although six-plate iron stoves had been invented in the 1700s, it wasn't until the 1830s when mass production made purpose-built cookstoves more affordable that their use became more widespread. Cooking on a cookstove offered many advantages. The raised cooking surface required less bending and heavy lifting than cooking at a hearth. It also only required one fire for any number of cooking tasks, including baking and heating water. Hearth cooking often required a cook to tend several fires, in the fireplace, on the hearth apron, and possibly in the oven. The cookstove usually worked from a single firebox, and many could accommodate the use of coal—an important feature of urban environments where firewood was at a premium. Grime-faced colliers could be seen carrying loads of black coal into tenement houses on their backs or dumping whole wagon loads down coal chutes into the basement coal bins. Thereafter, the coal scuttle became a common feature of the kitchen environment. Ten to fifteen minutes after starting a fire, the cookstove oven was ready for use, whereas a brick oven might take an hour or two to heat up.

Cookstoves were also safer than open hearth fires that often sent cinders sputtering into the room or caught long skirts afire. Small children were less likely to tumble into the fire—a circumstance more common than one would expect; and since colonial times, fire had been the second-leading cause—behind childbirth—of death among young women. House fires decreased as cookstove implementation increased. Yet accidents persisted although they were different from those at the fireside. Superficial burns from the hot metal stove were frequent. The build up of carbon monoxide in an enclosed space was a great danger especially if the chimney became clogged. Stove legs could also occasion a tragedy. There were reports of legs suddenly giving way, sending the hot-water reservoir tumbling over, sometimes scalding a child or the cook.

The cookstove became the center of domestic homemaking—literally displacing the fireplace grate in the hearth; and it earned praise in many women's diaries. Charlotte Haven noted, "Our spider is now cast into the shade by a Yankee Norton cooking stove."[44] Mary Palmer Tyler acquired a stove in 1822 after she "traded away [her] chaise for a cooking stove." Forty years later she quipped that she was "disposed to vote a monument to the memory of the first inventor of family stoves."[45] Mollie Dorsey, having grown up in an area where cookstoves were common, was surprised to see women cooking in fireplaces when she moved to Nebraska in 1857. She wrote, "Mrs. Blake gave us a splendid dinner . . . however she

The modern 19th-century kitchen had its cookstove, running water, and convenient pantry.

got up such a variety puzzled me, as she cooks by the fireplace and does her baking in a small skillet."[46] Haven had a similar experience when she moved from the East to the Midwest and found that the kitchen had only a fireplace. "Mrs. C. kindly offered to get dinner . . . a Herculean task it seemed to me, with the fire-place and such cooking utensils . . . we had a nice dinner . . . venison, hot biscuits, potatoes roasted in the ashes." A few weeks later the Havens had a family party that "was pronounced excellent by all."[47] By the 1870s cookstoves had become standard household equipment even in rural areas.

Cookstoves required less fuel than fireplaces because the damper could control the draft. On the other hand, cookstoves did require extensive tending in order to properly control the heat. Anne Ellis expressed frustration with her stove, "the usual discouragements of a smoky stove and an oven which refused to bake on the bottom."[48] Carrie Young recalled her mother's efforts with an oven that "didn't bake evenly, so she had to keep turning the pans and trading them off from the top shelf to the bottom shelf."[49] Dampers required a great deal of adjustment and the more sophisticated the stove, the more complex was the damper system. The level of heat could change as the wind played across an improperly damped stovepipe, and some stoves were notorious for heating unevenly. Harriet Beecher Stowe, sister of household advice guru, Catharine, wrote her husband complaining that their stove "draws so poorly that we can't bake in it at all."[50]

Stoves had to be emptied of ashes quite frequently. Hazel Webb Dalziel recalled, "Ashes were taken out every day or so through the door at the bottom of the stove. This was a horrible messy job. . . . No one could prevent the . . . ashes from covering everything. Mother came nearest. One of my dearest recollections is seeing her . . . with the coal bucket on one side ladling them out, a shovel full at a time, and easing them into the bucket more easily than if they were eggs."[51] Flues also became blocked or coated with a dangerously flammable layer of creosote. Every six months the stovepipe had to be taken down and thoroughly cleaned to prevent chimney fires. Emily French noted in her diary, "I got up early determined to clean the stove in the kitchen, it don't burn good. I took the pipe off, cleaned it out. . . . It was an ugly job."[52] Ultimately with all iron stoves, rust became a problem. To prevent it and to keep the stove looking good, it had to be blackened and polished with regularity. Dalziel reported, "It was always Mother who polished the stove . . . every inch black & shining." Commercial stove blacking preparations quickly flooded the market. Some of these chemical combinations were particularly noxious smelling, and others proved to be little more than black paint.[53]

The cookstove created some controversy in culinary circles. Cast iron cookstoves had no broilers. Cooks tried to duplicate the open hearth flavor of broiled meat using the cookstove ovens with little success. Certain cookbook authors charged that meat roasted in cookstove ovens could never match the flavor and texture of meat roasted by the fireside. One 1885 cookbook distinguished between roast beef made at the fireside and what was called "baked beef" roasted in the cookstove oven.[54] Baking bread and pies in the cookstove oven was also called into question. Catharine Beecher, a strong supporter of the cookstove for its convenience, economy, and efficiency, grieved, "We cannot but regret for the sake of bread, that our old steady brick ovens have been almost universally superseded by these ranges and cooking stoves, which are infinite in their caprices, and forbid all general rules."[55]

Canned Food

For middle-class women industrialization brought totally novel technologies that were to lead to the mass production of commercially produced foods. The processing and preservation of food had always been a domestic activity, until vacuum packed, hermetically sealed glass jars were invented by Frenchman Nicholas Appert early in the 19th century. This set off a long history of home canning and of "putting up" of preserves that has continued into recent times. In 1818 Peter Durand followed Appert with the tin-plated vacuum can. Lobster and salmon were the first foods to be commercially canned in this manner. These were rapidly followed by corn, tomatoes, peas, and additional varieties of fish. The following year Thomas Kensett and Ezra Daggert began canning

Air-tights were the first tinned iron containers for home food preservation. The commercial production of vacuum-sealed tinned cans closely followed their general acceptance.

oysters, fruits, meats, and vegetables in New York. Peaches and pears were great favorites.[56] William Underwood—famous today for canned meat spreads and deviled ham—established a canning plant in Boston in 1821. He canned a variety of vegetables, fruits, and condiments, producing grape and mushroom catsups, jams and jellies, and several mustards. In 1849 Henry Evans was granted a patent for a machine that limited the amount of hand labor needed to produce tin cans. This increased worker production from 5 or 6 cans an hour to 50 or 60 per hour, stimulating the processing of canned food as a commercial endeavor. Gail Borden obtained a patent for canned condensed milk in 1856. Although his earlier attempts at canning were less successful, the condensed milk met with great success because he received contracts to produce it for Federal forces during the Civil War.[57]

By 1860 five million cans a year were being produced. Canned foods were welcomed because not only did they permit consumers to eat out-of-season products, but they provided a certain consistent quality. Americans living in isolated Western territories particularly welcomed the profusion of canned foods. Families living on the fringes of civilization and in the mining districts paid from $1.00 to $2.25 per can. The line from the song "My Darling Clementine" that describes Clementine's footwear as "herring boxes without topses" refers to the oval-shaped fish tins that were plentiful in mining towns.

Water

Getting the water necessary to cook and clean was a laborious task for the homemaker. Most households had to haul or pump water from a cistern or well until the 1830s or 1840s when municipal water systems began to pipe water into city homes under pressure. At a North Carolina Farmer's Alliance meeting, a discussion ensued about the mileage a woman covered hauling water to her home. The classic example was of a woman whose spring was 60 yards from the house. It was decided, for the purposes of estimation, to use six trips daily to the spring, rather than the eight or ten times she sometimes made. "Sixty yards at six times a day is 720 yards—in one year it amounts to 148 miles." In the 41 years she had been living there, it was conservatively estimated that she had hauled the water 6,068 miles. Before concluding, it was added, "Remember too that half the distance is up hill with the water."[58] Rural families continued to haul and pump water throughout the century. Some homes had a wind-mill that could pump water to the attic and distribute it to various parts of the house through pipes by the action of gravity. Naturally, whatever water was brought into the house also had to be carried out, although it was not carried as far away.

Water conservation helped ease the burden somewhat. Dishwater was reused by washing progressively dirtier and greasier items. The nicest articles were done first followed by milk pans, utensils, and finally the pots, roasters, and kettles. Fresh hot water was added at each new load. Doing the dishes required a great amount of hauled water. The cold water had to be carried to the stove to be heated, then the heated water had to be carried to the dishpans, and finally the soiled water carried outside to be dumped—often into the garden or the outhouse. As the century pro-gressed, a wide variety of indoor and outdoor water pumps were made available, and this eased the burden of carrying water from a natural source somewhat.[59]

During the beginning of the century, women made soap at home using waste grease and lye coaxed from hardwood ashes. It was also avail-able from farm women who made large quantities of it and sold it in bar form. The soap would be scraped from the bar in order to use it for dishwashing. Initially, commercially produced soap was a strictly urban product. However, after the Civil War, its availability increased and few housekeeping manuals thereafter included instructions for making soap at home.

Doing the laundry required a great deal of water. Rachel Haskell referred to it as "the Herculean task which all women dread."[60] Household manu-als instructed women to sort laundry according to type and the degree of soil and to soak them overnight. In the morning the homemaker would drain off the water and pour hot suds on to the items to be washed. She would then place the laundry in another tub of hot suds and each article was scrubbed on a washboard. She would then wring out the laundry and apply soap to the most soiled spots. Next, the homemaker would cover the laundry with water and boil it, while stirring it with a stick. She would then remove the laundry from the tub. If soil remained, she would rub the spots again. The homemaker would rinse the laundry in plain water, wring it out, and rinse it again in water with bluing. Lastly, she would wring it out once again, this time, very dry. If the items were to be starched, she would dip them in starch and wring them once more. One wash, one boiling, and one rinse required approximately 50 gallons of water. It was not surprising that Haskell complained of her aching back and "hands too tender to sew."[61]

Many of the fabrics and dyes used at this time did not hold up to frequent laundering. Garments were often taken apart and resewn after being cleaned. *The Housekeeper's Encyclopedia* provided nine pages of instructions for washing various fabrics such as, "Take rice-water, and wash them quickly, without soap."[62] Other methods employed included the use of bran, ox-gall, salt, elixir of vitriol, and egg yolk. Laundry day was traditionally on Monday, and Tuesday was ironing day. In preparation, items were dampened and rolled in a cloth to await ironing. A homemaker needed to manage from three to six irons at a time so that as one cooled, it could be replaced by another hotter iron. She would rub the sole plate of each iron with beeswax and wipe it before each use so that it would glide over the fabric. She would heat the irons by the fire or on the stove, and test each one as it was taken from the heat to make sure that it would not scorch the cloth. Irons varied in weight, but heavier irons weighing eight or ten pounds were most effective, especially with heavier fabrics. As the homemaker needed to be near her heat source—usually the cookstove or fireplace—ironing was a hot and fatiguing job. If a homemaker had any discretionary money to spend on domestic help, she hired a washerwoman to take care of the laundry.

Novel Gadgets

Nineteenth-century America was enamored with new laborsaving inventions. A superfluity of patents for gadgets created a number of new kitchen tools and appliances. Maria Parloa in her cookbook and marketing guide recommended a minimum of 139 utensils to properly outfit a kitchen, suggesting that "the homemaker will find there is continually something new to be bought."[63] Foot-peddle butter churns, mechanical apple peelers, food choppers, and egg beaters made their way into the kitchens of middle- and upper-class women. Yet, for the majority of women, such conveniences were cost prohibitive. Hannah Lamberton recalled when her family acquired a mechanical butter churn. She had been making butter using a dasher churn when her father returned from the fields. "Dad," she said, "suppose you churn awhile." He did. A few days later, after a trip to town, "he came back with a barrel churn."[64]

Helen Campbell, writing for a rural audience in 1881, listed what she felt was essential for the well-fitted kitchen. She named custard cups, cake tins, sieves, wire baskets, pots, and pans, but the only mechanical device she identified was the Dover eggbeater. She cautioned, "Many complicated patent arrangements are hindrances rather than helps."[65] It was not until the mass production and national distribution systems of the following century took hold that mechanical household implements were truly available. With the exception of the cookstove and the eggbeater, food production at the end of the 19th century looked much as it had in 1800.

All the new innovations may have reduced some of the labor that kept women busy from sunup to sunset, but, at the same time, the standards of proper housekeeping were also on the rise. With the new cookstoves with multiple burners, women could bake and boil or stew at the same time. The one-pot meals of the open hearth were replaced by more complex meals requiring a variety of cooking techniques. The availability of merchant-milled flour produced a fine white flour once only available to affluent households, raising the bar for bread making. Home baked bread became even more accessible once chemical yeast became available in the late 1860s. Homemakers expended considerable time and effort into luxury baking, making little cakes and cookies that now were available to the middle class. Even the wonderful eggbeater where, by a "thousand of cross currents the eggs are cut and aerated in a few seconds," may have saved many a sore arm, but the homemaker was now expected to make cakes, including the demanding Angel cake that required intense beating in order to achieve the proper airiness.

Sewing

Mastery of the needle was an essential skill for all women. *The Young Ladies Friend* proffered, "A woman who does not know how to sew is as deficient in her education as a man who cannot read."[66] Although the ready-made clothing industry was growing rapidly, as late as 1890 women's wear accounted for less than one-fourth of all factory-made clothing.[67] Women who could afford it had their dresses made by a dressmaker. The majority of women, however, were responsible for tending to their family's clothing needs. Clothing required mending and growing children always needed something larger. Laura Higginson reported in a letter, "Engaged in making my little boy's clothes all day, while he by my side reading or playing, has been my comfort and delight."[68] Ruth Anna Abrams, a mother of nine, made the following notations in her diary over the course of a dozen days. "I have sewed hard all day. I made

Charlie Megill a calico shirt. . . . I cut out Alice's dress skirt. I am weary."
Five days later she noted, "I worked on Adda's and Alice's dresses, they
both think theirs ought to be made first. I will make them both at once."
A week later she wrote, "This afternoon I finished Adda's dress and fixed
Lafe's bed tick. I have finished fourteen garments this week big and little.
I have kept busy all day and sewed some after night." A month later
she made the following melancholy entry. "I cut the skirt of Dorca's red
brocaded dress but I fear my eyes are too weary to finish it. I am hardly
stout enough to do all the work for so large a family and take care of the
little ones."[69] Little girls were taught to sew early so that they could help
their mothers with the ever-present task of mending and sewing. "Mother
always brought needles and thread and dry goods, and put them to good
use making clothes for the family, and teaching my sister and me to sew,"
recalled Edith White. "Before I was five years old I had pieced one side of
a quilt, sitting at her knee half an hour a day."[70]

Some women employed a seamstress who might take on the bulk of
the sewing weekly or seasonally. Seamstresses were independent crafts-
women who worked for a number of families weekly or several times
a year. They were not considered domestic help in the sense of being a
servant. If they did reside with a family, they retained their independence,
commanding respect and decent accommodations. Some opened their
own shops, often employing assistants, to help make fashionable attire
for the custom trade.

The invention of the sewing machine during the 1850s was a tremendous help to women who had to sew for themselves. Anne Whitwell's
daughter wrote her mother declaring, "Didn't this sewing machine help
me along fast. I never mean to sew by hand any more if I can help it."[71]
Unfortunately, when they first appeared on the market, sewing machines
were expensive and often out of the reach of the women who needed
them most. *Godey's Lady's Book* suggested that 10 families in each country
village could share the cost of purchasing a machine and then devise a
plan wherein each would get to use it for a specified period of time. In
time creative marketing strategies and improved production techniques
halved the cost by the end of the decade, allowing more women to acquire
them.

Plain sewing, which included stitching seams, hems, buttonholes, and
marking clothing and household linens, encompassed most of a woman's sewing tasks. Many women found it a respite from the physically
demanding chores that embodied the majority of their day. "The plain
seam is a sedative," wrote one woman, "thoughts can go ambling off into
fields of imagination as she sits over a bit of plain work! She can plan a
charming romance or lay down the project of some helpful reform, as she
draws her needle mechanically in and out of her seam."[72]

Sewing also provided a social outlet for women. Women gathered
together to use their needlework talents to raise money for social causes

The milliner was often the source of ribbons, bonnets, and fine dresses. Her shop was often a part-time business located in a spare room of her home.

such as foreign missions, abolition, the relief of soldiers' families, as well as other community needs. They also came together for quilting bees. The chance to chat and work with other women was as much of the attraction as the chance to demonstrate their needle skills. Women met more informally to learn new techniques and to get help. Rachel Haskell wrote, "Called on Mrs. Mack. Learned a new way of making a tidy serpentine braid and cotton thread. Enjoyed talking with a lady."[73] Elizabeth Hosack Martin noted in her diary, "Got some help with my quilt. Had a real good time."[74] In a time when married women spent much of their time isolated in the home, these gatherings allowed them to build friendships they would not ordinarily have a chance to develop.

Nineteenth-century women prided themselves on being thrifty and practical. Household advice manuals capitalized on flaunting titles such as *The American Frugal Housewife* and *Treatise on Domestic Economy*. They offered advice such as, "After old coats, pantaloons, &c. have been cut up for boys, and are no longer capable of being converted into strips, and employ the leisure moments of children, or domestics, in sewing and braiding them for doormats."[75] Perhaps such advice helped fuel the passion for patchwork quilting that flourished between the 1820s and 1880s. Patchwork quilts were made from scrap pieces of cloth, bits of clothing no longer wearable, and fabric that was specifically purchased for the project. Perhaps it was the opportunity to strike a balance between the practical use of remnants and the artistic expression of creativity. Whatever the inspiration, for some, quilts were a labor of love. Martha Haggard left the following inscription on her quilt, "This quilt contains 62,948 separate pieces . . . completed in two years. It took 36 yards of cloth and 24 spools of thread to make it."[76]

Women came together for other activities that grew from their scrap bags. Store-bought carpets were costly for the average family and many women, particularly in New England and the West, recycled old, worn-out clothing and leftover fabric to make rag rugs. Collected rags were cut into narrow bands and sewn together into long strips that were then rolled into balls before being loom woven. Most were a mismatch of different types, weights, and colors of fabric, although some rags were dyed first to provide some uniformity or desired color pattern. It was not unusual for a new rug to be made each year with the older rug being moved to a less important location, and the one it replaced to an even less valued place until strips of the most worn of the rugs ended up on the back doorstep or in the garden. Rag rugs were made in strips that were used either as stair-runners or in hallways. The strips were also pieced and sewn together to make a room-sized carpet. Women sometimes came together to help with this daunting endeavor. About a dozen women came to assist Susan Evans with her installation. She wrote to her sister, "W e were not very experienced hands and consequently the carpet was cut wrong, or rather one breadth fell short."[77] After spreading hay over the dirt floor, Emma Hill laid down a rag rug in her Kansas home. She "put the tool chest, trunks, the goods box made into a cupboard and the beds all around the wall to hold down the carpet as there was nothing to tack it to. . . . We were real cozy and comfortable."[78]

Scrap fabric was used for other types of rugs as well. Braided rugs were relatively easy to make. Three or more narrow strips of heavy scrap fabric or worn-out clothing, were braided and then attached to other braids in succession to form one long strip. As the braid lengthened, it was wound around itself to form a circle or oval. *Godey's Lady's Book* and *Peterson's Magazine* featured detailed instructions with suggestions for all sorts of area rugs during the second half of the century. Penny or button rugs, which were made by assembling three graduated layers of concentric circles that had been bound by buttonhole stitch into a geometric design and securing them to a plain foundation, became quite the fashion in the 1850s. *Godey's Lady's Book* gave instructions for a rug using small scraps of fabric. "Hearth rugs are sometimes made by cutting cloth into strips ½ an inch long and 2 [inches] long, and knitting them together with string . . . this sort of rug will in winter form a very comfortable addition to a poor man's fireplace. Or the bits may be knitted into smaller pieces for door mats."[79]

During the 1840s women in New England, especially those in New Hampshire and Maine, began to make hooked rugs. Woolen fabric scraps were cut into thin strips that were then worked, by means of a hooked tool, between the fibers of the rug backing. It is believed that this technique evolved from mats sailors made aboard ship. Hooked rugs became very popular during the 1850s when burlap began to be imported into the United States. The loose weave of the burlap proved to be the perfect backing for rug hooking. When slit open and laid flat, used burlap grain sacks were an ideal size for area rugs. Hooked rugs were truly an opportunity for women to express their creativity—even more so than with quilt making with its pattern restrictions. Hooked rugs were like blank canvases. Women hooked geometric designs, landscapes, and even depictions of a favorite pet. Already popular, the introduction of pre-stenciled patterns increased the number of women who took up the craft. Because of their involved designs, hooked rugs were more likely to be done by middle-class women who were interested in their decorative value as well as their practicality.

Knitting was another activity that women could engage in during the evenings or as a break from more physical activity. "After dark, when one could not see to sew . . . was usually the time devoted to knitting and crocheting, which sometimes lasted until midnight. Capes, sacks, vandykes, gloves, socks and stockings, shawls, underclothes and men's suspenders were knitted."[80] Like plain sewing it was something that could be done while conversing or listening to someone read while still allowing for productivity. Hilda Faunce described a women with whom she was visiting, "Right then she took a half-knit sock out of her apron and, stopping only for a breath between needles, she worked as fast as she talked."[81]

The invention of commercial knitting machines made ready-made knit items more readily available, but women in rural areas continued to knit items for themselves and their families. As the century progressed, knitting became less utilitarian and more artistic, particularly for middle-class women. Periodicals abounded with patterns for personal and household knit items. Many proved the inspiration for gifts. Clarissa Young Spencer recalled, "Our newest supplies in winter clothing were usually given as Christmas gifts. Among them were pretty knitted gaiters and stockings, mittens and waistbands, also neck pieces."[82]

Women of greater affluence had the opportunity to spend a good deal of time doing fancywork, which demonstrated their needle skills in decorative projects. Crochet became popular around mid-century. One of the first American booklets featuring crochet patterns explained, "It is customary among German ladies to have at hand some light piece of work, with which they can at any time be employed.—Our American ladies will doubtless find the custom worthy of imitation." Many did. Some ladies' magazines devoted two pages each month to intricate crochet patterns. Items included accessories such as purses, hair nets, collars, slippers, infant's caps, and mittens and children's hoods as well as decorative items for the home such as antimacassars, tidies, and crochet lace trim for petticoats and linens. While the items were useful, they were highly decorative and more a show of a woman's skills than a provision of necessities.[83]

Housekeeping

New demands for domestic privacy resulted in homes with an increased number of rooms that required cleaning. Architectural pattern books containing a wide variety of house plans of different sizes and prices abounded. Even periodicals carried house plans. The typical middle-class home could be divided into three classifications of rooms. There were public rooms such as the hall, parlor, dining room, and library. Bed chambers were considered private rooms and were almost exclusively located on the second floor. The mere placement of a bedroom on the first floor of a two-story home other than in the event of sickness was considered risqué in many circles. The final category of rooms included workrooms such as the kitchen, pantry, laundry, scullery, and cellar.

Home ownership and its appearance were important status symbols for the Victorian middle-class family. "The greatest art that the world has ever produced is the art of beautifying and making home attractive. . . . [T]he grandest and noblest motives that can stir the heart are those awakened within the pale of domestic life. Beautiful art can only be inspired by pure and beautiful thoughts, and unless some elements of taste and beauty are provided for the leisure hours at home, how can it be expected that the young may find their homes more attractive than places of sin and amusement, and have pure thoughts, pure hearts, and a love of refinement."[84]

Standards of cleanliness were on the rise. It was assumed that homes would be clean, neat, and orderly. Women were advised, "A snug, clean home no matter how tiny it may be, so that it is wholesome, windows into which the sun can shine cheerily, a few good books . . . the cupboard well supplied, and a flower of some kind in the room—surely none need deny themselves these elements of pleasure because of poverty."[85] Middle-class women were now expected to present tables once only attainable by the upper class. Table linens, candelabras, fancy serving pieces, and plates specific to certain courses of a meal created more pressure for the socially conscious homemaker. Gone were the simple one-pot meals simmered for hours over the fire. Cookstoves allowed women to cook a number of dishes simultaneously. Writing about "Woman's Servitude," Dr. J. H. Hanaford acknowledged that "women's labor is sufficiently onerous . . . [however] not a few of our housekeepers, for the sake of . . . setting as good a table as their neighbors . . . are wasting the energies which might otherwise be better employed."[86]

Homemakers found that, as the century progressed, more and more of their labors were becoming repetitive tasks of household management. In previous centuries homemakers spent much of their time in production activities such as candle making, soap making, textile production, and the processing of agricultural products that were important to the economic life of the family. This shift of labors created a certain amount of stress in middle-class homes and rural areas where some of this type of labor continued. These women were aspiring to the new ideals of the home but were still obliged to execute some of the production activities of the past. Susan Lesly recalled her mother rising at dawn to begin housecleaning. She would have the "two parlors, dining room, entry and stair case . . . all carefully and thoroughly swept before six o'clock."[87] Ruth Henshaw Bascom noted in her diary, "Began to wash at half past 4 this morning."[88] Even Catharine Beecher, who prescribed all the details of household management and economy in her books, acknowledged, "There is no doubt of the fact that the American housekeepers have far greater trials and difficulties to meet than those of any other nation."[89]

Notes

1. Catharine E. Beecher and Harriet Beecher Stowe, *The American Woman's Home* (New York: J. B. Ford & Co., 1869), 163.

2. Samantha Barrett, "Diary of Samantha Barrett, New Hartford, Connecticut, 1811 to 1829," Connecticut Historical Society, http://www.osv.org/education/LessonPlans/ShowLessons.php?PageID_P&LessonID_34 (accessed December 2006).

3. Laura Schenone, *A Thousand Years over a Hot Stove* (New York: W. W. Norton & Co., 2003), 116.

4. Ibid., 113.

5. Ibid., 114.

6. Catharine E. Beecher, *Miss Beecher's Domestic Receipt Book* (New York: Harper & Brothers, 1850), 183.

7. Schenone, *Thousand Years,* 116.

8. Beecher, *Domestic Receipt Book,* 13.

9. Schenone, *Thousand Years,* 116.

10. Beecher and Beecher Stowe, *American Woman's Home,* 105.

11. Ibid., 103.

12. Frances Trollope, *Domestic Manners of the Americans* (1832; repr., Mineola, N.Y.: Dover Publications, 2003), 183.

13. Marc McCutcheon, *Everyday Life in the 1800's* (Cincinnati, Ohio: Writer's Digest Books, 1993), 180.

14. For more information on Southern cooking, see James M. Volo and Dorothy Denneen Volo, *The Encyclopedia of the Antebellum South* (Westport, Conn.: Greenwood Press, 2000).

15. Jane C. Nylander, *Our Own Snug Fireside: Images of the New England Home 1760–1860* (New Haven, Conn.: Yale University Press, 1993), 192.

16. Ibid.

17. Susan Strasser, *Never Done: A History of American Housework* (New York: Henry Holt & Co., 1982), 29.

18. Beecher, *Domestic Receipt Book,* 224.

19. Ibid., 153.

20. Eliza Leslie, *Miss Leslie's Directions for Cookery* (Mineola, N.Y.: Dover Publications, 1999), 264.

21. Ibid., 238.

22. Ibid., 405–406.

23. *New York Times*, September 14, 1857, 5.

24. McCutcheon, *Everyday Life,* 99.

25. Ibid., 183.

26. Schenone, *Thousand Years,* 181–182.

27. Ibid., 178.

28. Ibid., 178–179.

29. Nylander, *Our Own Snug Fireside,* 198–199.

30. Priscilla J. Brewer, *From Fireplace to Cookstove: Technology and the Domestic Ideal in America* (Syracuse, N.Y.: Syracuse University Press, 2000), 210.

31. Beecher, *Domestic Receipt Book,* 64.

32. Mary H. Cornelius, *The Young Housekeeper's Friend; or, A Guide to Domestic Economy and Comfort* (Boston: John M. Whittemore, 1848), 19.

33. Nylander, *Our Own Snug Fireside,* 197–198.

34. Strasser, *Never Done,* 23.

35. Ibid., 24.

36. Nylander, *Our Own Snug Fireside,* 199.

37. Mary Livermore, *The Story of My Life* (Hartford, Conn.: A. D. Worthington & Co., 1899), 401–408.

38. Ibid.

39. Schenone, *Thousand Years,* 189.

40. Nylander, *Our Own Snug Fireside,* 200.

41. Schenone, *Thousand Years,* 197.

42. Waverly Root and Richard de Rouchemont, *Eating in America* (New York: William Morrow, 1976), 148.

43. Strasser, *Never Done,* 18.

44. Brewer, *From Fireplace to Cookstove,* 142.

45. Ibid., 81.

46. Ibid., 142.

47. Ibid.

48. Ibid., 175.

49. Ibid.

50. Ibid., 147.

51. Ibid., 177.

52. Ibid., 174.

53. Ibid., 177.

54. Strasser, *Never Done,* 36.

55. Ibid., 37.

56. In 1825 Kensett filed the first American patent for tin cans, but it was not until 1839 that tin cans came into widespread use.

57. James M. Volo and Dorothy Denneen Volo, *The Antebellum Period* (Westport, Conn.: Greenwood Press, 2004), 167–168.

58. Strasser, *Never Done,* 86.

59. The authors' own home, built in 1854, has an original working hand pump just a few steps outside the kitchen door, but they choose to use city water.

60. Strasser, *Never Done*, 104.

61. Ibid.

62. Mrs. E. F. Haskell, *The Housekeeper's Encyclopedia* (Mendocino: R. L. Shep, 1992), 15–23.

63. Schenone, *Thousand Years*, 184–185.

64. Strasser, *Never Done*, 46.

65. Ibid., 44–45.

66. Ibid., 132.

67. Ibid., 134.

68. Roderick Kiracofe, *Cloth & Comfort: Pieces of Women's Lives from Their Quilts and Diaries* (New York: Clarkson Potter, 1994), 24.

69. Ibid., 20.

70. Ibid., 28.

71. Ibid., 14.

72. Judith Reiter Weissman and Wendy Lavitt, *Labors of Love: America's Textiles and Needlework, 1630–1930* (New York: Wings Books, 1994), 170.

73. Strasser, *Never Done*, 134.

74. Kiracofe, *Cloth & Comfort*, 11.

75. Lydia Marie Child, *The American Frugal Housewife* (Mineola, N.Y.: Dover Publications, 1999), 13.

76. Kiracofe, *Cloth & Comfort*, 47.

77. Shirley Blotnick Moskow, *Emma's World: An Intimate Look at Lives Touched by the Civil War Era* (Far Hills, N.J.: New Horizon Press, 1990), 68.

78. Weissman and Lavitt, *Labors of Love*, 151.

79. Ibid., 163.

80. Ibid., 184.

81. Ibid., 178.

82. Ibid., 181.

83. Ibid., 184.

84. Anonymous, *Treasures of Use and Beauty: Epitome of the Choicest Gems of Wisdom, History, Reference and Recreation* (Chicago: F. B. Dickerson & Co., 1883), 280.

85. Ibid., 283.

86. Brewer, *From Fireplace to Cookstove*, 151.

87. Nylander, *Our Own Snug Fireside*, 106.

88. Ibid.

89. Beecher, *Domestic Receipt Book*, 276.

13

Children as Family

When Charlie has done reading
His book every day,
Then he goes with his hoop in the garden to play,
Or his whip in his hand,
Quickly mounts across,
And then gallops away
On his fine rocking horse.

—Little Rhymes for Little Folks, 1823

The Dawn of Innocence

Childhood has not always been viewed as the carefree stage of life during which youngsters were allowed to develop their individual personalities. Puritans in early America believed that children were born empty of knowledge and goodness and were full of willfulness. Parents were charged with the responsibility of breaking this willful spirit in their children and hastening their transition to the adult world. Children were even dressed as miniature adults. This "breaking down" was generally achieved through harsh and restrictive supervision. Toward the middle of the 18th century, this austere attitude began to soften and children were coming to be regarded as innocent, fragile beings. This enlightened view continued to expand into the 19th century and was embraced by the middle class. Children were viewed as raw material that could be shaped and molded into good citizens of the young nation. Horace Mann cautioned, "[I]f we do not prepare children to become good citizens,—if we do not develop their capacities, if we do not enrich their minds with knowledge, imbue their hearts with love of the truth and duty, and a reverence for all things sacred and holy, then our republic must go down to destruction as others have gone before it."[1]

Although children were viewed as guileless creatures with a propensity to mischief, parents were told that with discipline, reason, and love, they could produce a child of good character. Thereby parenting became a very conscious process. Parents were encouraged to toilet train their children early for if children learned control of their bodies, they would achieve discipline of mind and spirit. Self-discipline was an important characteristic at this time, and children were expected to develop an active conscience and a propensity for introspection. After recording a tale of misadventure from her mother's childhood, 10-year-old Catharine Elizabeth Havens wrote in her diary, "I am afraid I should have forgotten it was wrong, but I don't know, for we all have an inward monitor, my sister says."[2]

Childhood was seen as a period of guardianship—free from the harsh realities of the world and increasingly devoted to training, schooling, and preparation for life. Children were protected from the adult worlds of death, profanity, and sexuality. This attitude grew out of evangelical changes that called upon parents to take the innocent souls of their children and turn them toward God. The June 1833 issue of *The Ladies Magazine* described childhood "as a state which speaks to us of Heaven, which tells us of those pure angelic beings which surround the throne of God, untouched by sin, untainted by the breath of corruption."[3] It was further enhanced by a growing spirit of romanticism that viewed children as symbols of purity and innocence. They were seen as fonts of spontaneity, expressiveness, and intuition. This idealization of childhood could be seen in John Greenleaf Whittier's nostalgic poem "The Barefoot Boy," in Winslow Homer's playful painting "Snap the Whip," and in Mark Twain's popular novel *Huckleberry Finn*. Describing the child, Bronson Alcott wrote, "Herein is our nature yet despoiled of none of its glory."[4]

The bond between siblings was idealized as well. This relationship was seen as the most innocent and longest lasting of all social relationships. With birth rates declining among the middle and upper classes, children were closer in age, and they remained home longer, thus giving sibling relationships time to develop more intensely than in the previous century. Same sex siblings commonly slept in the same room and frequently in the same bed. Parents encouraged strong sibling bonds, instilling in their children the belief that they had an obligation to look out for their brothers and sisters. Children were encouraged to play with their siblings or with other cousins. Catherine Elizabeth Havens's diary makes little mention of her school mates outside of the schoolroom, yet she frequently writes of a cousin "nearly [the same] age" who is described as "my dearest friend." Catherine's diary is also filled with her escapades with Ellen, whom she introduces as "a little niece, nearly as old as I am, and she lives in the country. Her mother is my sister, and her father is a clergyman, and I go there in the summer, and she comes here in the winter, and we have things together, like whooping cough and scarlatina."[5]

Childhood was coming to be recognized as its own separate stage of life with clothing, furniture, literature, and social activities developed specifically for children. Small children were placed in specially designed high chairs that could be brought to the table so that they might comfortably dine with the rest of the family. Urban middle-class mothers began to assume the exclusive responsibility for raising their children as fathers spent a large portion of the day away from the home while at work. It was up to her to provide the proper environment during the child's early years. The family circle provided children with the nurturing and protection they required. Children were often affectionately referred to in such endearingly innocent terms as "kitten," "lamb," or "pet." Baby talk—frowned upon in former times as damaging to proper child development—not only became acceptable, it was thought to be endearing. Female educator Amira Phelps declared in her 1835 diary that she would not let her child "learn to creep" but by the time her son was between six and nine months, she altered her opinion to accept crawling as "nature's way."[6]

Children's birthdays began to be celebrated as a special event. While notations were often made in period diaries of birthdays, they were not generally celebrated with parties and gift giving in the early 19th century. By the 1830s this seems to have changed. In 1833 Louisa Jane Trumbull noted in her diary that her family had pooled its money together to buy her sister, Susan, a pair of shoes for her first birthday. She also reported that "Mother has made her a couple of gowns for her birthday present." Birthday gifts tended to be few in number and were often composed of very practical items. Merchants and publishers were most supportive of this growing custom. Books were printed with titles such as *The Birth-Day Gift* and *The Birth-Day Present* expressly for the purpose of promoting gift giving. Celebrations of the event were often simple. A story in an 1839 children's magazine entitled "The Birthday" begins, "When Mary was seven years old, her mother told her she might ask some little girls to come and see her on her birthday." At the gathering, Mary told her friends about her "birthday present" and after playing outside, "they went into the house where there was a nice birth-day cake."[7]

Childhood dependency became prolonged, and children often remained in the parental home until their 20s. Child-rearing became a more conscious and intensive activity. Instructional books such as Lydia Marie Child's *The Mother's Book* became popular guides for mothers who wanted to do the best job of raising their children. In 1860 the first outpatient clinic for children was established. Doctors began to specialize in the care of children. Dr. Abraham Jacobi, considered the father of pediatrics in America, was the first physician in the United States to devote his practice solely to the care of children. He performed emergency surgery on more than 2,500 children dying of a blocked windpipe, a complication of diphtheria. By 1880 the American Medical Association (founded in 1847) recognized pediatrics as a specialized branch of medicine, and a number of medical schools offered it as a field of study.[8]

Not everyone approved of these new attitudes toward childhood in the early decades of the century. Timothy Dwight in his 1822 *Travels in New England* denounced American parents, saying that they did not teach their children to be useful and that they preferred to make their children "objects of admiration" for visitors. "They are taught music, dancing, embroidery, ease and confidence and graceful manners," he complained. Dwight also noted that too much emphasis was placed on appearance, clothing, behavior in company, and fashionable conversation for the purpose of admiration, "not for thinking."[9]

Good Behavior

Despite the indulgences some parents may have bestowed upon their progeny, children were always expected to exhibit good behavior, to display profound respect for their parents, and to respond with prompt obedience. Jesse Cochron, a publisher from Vermont reprinted *The School of Good Manners* in 1815, which repeated for children many of the century-old puritanical maxims of child-rearing, including those admonishing that children "Speak not at the table. . . . Sing not, hum not, wriggle not."[10] In the reminiscences of her mid-19th-century childhood, Emily Wilson wrote, "Children were kept in the background to be seen and not heard. We were early taught implicit obedience, honesty and truthfulness."[11] Child cautioned her readers, "Whatever a mother says, always must be done;. . . . The necessity of obedience early instilled is the foundation of all good management;. . . . [and] Willful disobedience should never go unpunished."[12] A writer in an 1865 newspaper was even stronger, "First and most important of all lessons to be taught is obedience. On the success in inculcating this lesson depends the future character of the child. Without obedience to authority no moral virtue can be secured."[13] In a letter Betsey Reynolds Voorhees wrote, "Let them ever bear in remembrance that next to their duty to God, a cheerful and ready obedience to the wishes of their parents is the only road to happiness and respectability." In the 1870s and 1880s parents became somewhat more permissive, affecting a kind of openly loving government.[14]

From a very young age children were encouraged to participate in the popular social causes of the period. Children's books contained messages such as, "Children too, might gladden the hearts and the homes of widows and little orphans. The money which they spend for useless toys might be given to the poor, and many a tear be dried up for it."[15] Children were involved in helping the poor, and during the Civil War they were encouraged to bring comfort to soldiers. They collected books for soldiers and raised money for soldier's homes and hospitals. Girls knitted mittens and rolled bandages for soldiers. Clara Lenroot recalled scraping "away at the linen, making fluffy piles of the soft lint" that was used to pack the soldiers' wounds.[16] Reform newspapers like the *Advocate and Family Guardian* carried letters from children who donated money to a children's home. Many children donated like the two children who sent the money they were awarded by their "foster parents for going without butter for one hundred days."[17] Another sent a dollar saying, "I do not wish to spend it for candy or playthings when there are so many little children who have no food to eat or clothes to wear."[18] One little girl earned a dollar for "rising promptly in the morning, dressing and preparing herself in readiness for breakfast without any assistance for two months." She rejoiced that she had "something of her own" that she might send "for the comfort of poor little ones for whom her sympathy [had] always been deeply enlisted."[19]

Some of the donations came as commodities. One child wrote, "Last summer our father gave us the privilege of working as much of his garden as we would work well for ourselves. Our mother suggested, that we raise something to send to the Home, and here it is; dried corn, pop corn and beans." She also noted "two little girls" who said that if our mother would give them pieces, they would "piece some crib-quilts [that] are now finished, and we hope they and the other things will do somebody some good."[20]

Children also executed fairs for good causes. Catherine Elizabeth Havens wrote of several charitable efforts in which she was involved between the ages of 6 and 11. "[T]here was a dreadful famine in Ireland, and we gave up our parlor and library and dining room for two evenings for a fair for them, and all my schoolmates and our friends made things, and we sent the poor Irish people over three hundred dollars. My brothers made pictures in pen and ink, and called them charades, and they sold for fifty cents apiece, like this: a pen, and a man, and a ship, and called it, 'a desirable art'—Penmanship."[21] She also participated in another fair at the parsonage. "We worked very hard for it, and we made bookmarks and little thimble boxes of cardboard and bachelor's pin cushions and we sold apples and some candy."[22] Catherine also noted that she and three of her friends had "a sewing society, and we sew for a fair, but we don't make much money."[23]

Children's Dress

The 19th century saw the arrival of clothing that was specifically designed for children. A girl's skirts were considerably shorter than those of a woman, ending about mid-calf with pantalets that hung just below the edge of the dress. By age seven a girl would have begun to wear a hoop, although it would likely have only one hoop ring at this time. Such gradual changes in dress were acknowledgments of the child's advancement to maturity. Lucy Larcom recalled her first "grown up" outfit. "I was tall as a woman at thirteen, and my older sisters insisted upon lengthening my dresses, and putting up my hair in a comb. I felt injured, almost outraged, because my protestations against this treatment were unheeded; and when the transformation in my visible appearance was effected, I went away by myself and had a good cry. . . . I felt like a child, but considered it my duty to think and behave like a woman."[24]

Children's clothing rivaled women's fashions both in a complexity and an ornamentation that typified the period. These also served as conspicuous displays of a family's financial success. Consequently some middle- and upper-class children were dressed in layers of clothing constructed of impractical fabrics. *Godey's Lady's Book* carried the following description and accompanying picture, "Child's dress of green silk with narrow pinked ruffles, corselet of green silk, white muslin gimp, white felt hat with white wing." Ornate as it sounds, this outfit was considered not a "party dress" but a simple day dress. Gauze, silk, wool, and taffeta were common fabric suggestions for children's dress in ladies' magazines. Obsession with fashion was common in certain circles. *The Mother's Book* cautioned, "A love of finery and display is a much more common fault than neglect of personal appearance. . . . Extravagance in dress does great mischief both to fortune and character."[25]

Nonetheless, there were some concessions to practicality in children's dress. Little girls wore undersleeves, chemisettes, and tuckers. These items were accessories that were worn under a dress to create the illusion of a layered underblouse. Their purpose was to save wear on the more expensive fabric. These individual pieces could be removed and laundered separately from the entire garment. Blouses and skirts were not popular for toddlers, but they were worn by (older) young girls. Fancy aprons, both practical and ornamental, were popular for little girls. These tied around the waist and covered almost the entire skirt portion of a dress. The top covered only part of the dress front and commonly crossed over both shoulders on top. These were often decorated with flounces, bows, or other decorative details. Pinafores, which covered almost the entire dress, were more practical and much more common across all economic and social classes. They were constructed in such fabrics as muslin, calico, or linen. The pinafore fit closely to the chest and hung down loosely to the hem.

In rural areas, children's clothing was considerably more practical. Muslin and cotton were the fabrics of choice for country and poorer folk. In order to allow for growth, it was common for seams at the shoulders and under the arms to be folded in an inch each, so that they could be let out as the child grew. Sometimes a waistband was added, as the child grew, to add length to skirts and trousers. Several tucks, of an inch or so,

The dress of the children in this period illustration seems impractical to modern eyes.

were often made near the hems of skirts and trousers. These created an attractive detail that could later be let down to accommodate growth.

A boy's progress to maturity was much more marked by fashion than that of a girl's. Boys wore a series of different age-specific styles of outfits as they grew older. From age one to four, boys wore a Nankeen suit. This was a dress-like costume worn over white underdrawers not unlike the girl's pantalets, although they were likely to be less fancy. The top portion of the suit was a blousy sack, often with a large sash or a cord tied around the waist. Very young boys often had shirts that buttoned to the waistband of their pants and provided a neater look than loose shirttails.

Between the ages of four and seven, there was the French Blouse. Essentially, it was a loose, dress-like tunic secured at the waist by a belt and large buckle or sash. This would have been worn over loose knee pants, although, it was also worn over skirts for very young boys. An alternative was a loose jacket and waistcoat once again with loose, knee pants. Some boys wore a suit-like outfit with a slightly cut away jacket, gently rounded in front, and very loose trousers that extended to about mid-calf.

From 7 to 12 a boy may have worn what would be thought of as a suit-like outfit composed of a loose, ankle-length trouser and waist-length sack coat with a ribbon tie fashioned into a bow. The pants might have "box plaits." Suspenders could be introduced at this point. Sailor suits were also popular for young boys aged 7 up to 14. Some boys in certain areas did not wear long pants until 14 or 15 years of age.

It is no wonder that the Knickerbocker suit was welcomed by older boys who were as yet considered too young for trousers. Knickerbocker suits consisted of a button-faced jacket that fastened with a hook and eye at the top; a 10-buttoned waistcoat with small slits at the sides to allow for ease of movement and better fit; and knickerbockers, which were loose-fitting pants that came tight against the leg just below the knee and gave the style its name. Mrs. Emily May proclaimed in *Peterson's Magazine*, "The Knickerbocker costume is now the favorite style of dress for boys, when they are of that awkward age, too young to be breeched, and too old to wear frocks and pinafores. This costume has a great many recommendations: it can be made in almost any material; it always looks neat and tidy; and for the play-ground is particularly suitable, as it leaves boys the free use of their limbs, besides being rather more manly than petticoats, which used to be (particularly at school) a boy's abhorrence." As older teens, boys dressed much as adult men. They wore pants, vests, and jackets. Jacket types included sack, frock, and a short, military style. The change to "adult attire" was taken quite seriously, and it was a meaningful step in his social development toward being accepted as a man.[26]

Hair Styles

Older boys cut and parted their hair in much the same fashion as men, and few, if any, went about with flowing locks into adolescence. Little girls generally wore their hair in a short, ear-length blunt cut that was pushed behind the ears. Some wore their hair in long finger curls. This latter style seems to have been more popular among girls of higher economic status. As girls grew older, they let their hair grow longer. Sarah Morgan, aged 19, wrote in her diary, "The net I had gathered my hair in fell in my descent and my hair swept down half way between my knee and my ankle in one stream."[27] For much of the century, the hairstyles for small children of different genders were almost identical. The sole noticeable difference was that little girls' hair was center-parted while the boys had theirs parted to one side. Due to the gender-neutral clothing in which very young boys were attired, the hair part is often the only clue to the sex of a child when looking at period photographs.

Nurseries

Parents wanted to protect their children from the temptations and contaminations of the outside world. They wanted to provide their children with a safe, pure, and nurturing environment in which to grow. Under the growing influence of the *Cult of Domesticity*, the home was symbolically elevated to that of a familial temple. Hartford minister, Horace Bushnell, in a sermon entitled "The Organic Unity of the Family" proffered that the child "breathes the atmosphere of the house. He sees the world through his parents' eyes. Their objects become his. Their life and spirit mold him."[28] Housing designers were quick to respond. "We are in no little danger," wrote one housing planner, "of losing sight of the importance which God has attached to the family relation."[29] Rooms were specifically designed to be devoted to the nurturing and raising of children. Housing plan book author, William Ranlett, wrote, "There is so intimate a connection between taste and morals that they in each instance mutually modify each other; hence whatever serves to cultivate the taste of the community . . . will give to Christianity increased opportunity and means of charming the heart and governing the life."[30]

Families who could afford it had a nursery for the children. The dedication of a room or rooms for children reflected the importance placed upon childhood. The nursery provided a retreat where children could be protected and where they would receive a controlled exposure to the world. It could limit the stimulations a child received and might hopefully protect him or her from the accidents and disease that claimed so many children. Modest households had a single nursery room often found on the third floor of the home. Although children of the same sex often shared a bedroom in their early years, the plan book ideal was that, if possible, children should have their own rooms. Affluent households could afford both day nurseries for play and night nurseries for slumber. Furniture, painted in pastels and decorated with baby animals and characters from nursery rhymes, was produced in child-sized proportions.

Day nurseries were playrooms that also often doubled as schoolrooms for those children who were taught by the governess. In such cases they would also contain globes, maps, and perhaps a blackboard as needed for instruction. These rooms were designed to withstand the abuse that children can sometimes inflict on furnishings. Walls were often whitewashed. Curtains were simple. There would be a table with several chairs. These might be simple pine furniture bought for the purpose or cast-off furniture from other rooms. There were shelves and cupboards for books and toys and perhaps an armchair or two. The children of more affluent families enjoyed a greater degree of privacy in the home than their farming- or working-class counterparts. They spent most of their time in their nursery away from their parents but kept safe by their isolation. Poorer children, on the other hand, enjoyed more parental supervision and interaction inside the home, but they also had a great deal more autonomy outside where much of their play took place.

Toys and Diversions

Once lessons were done and chores completed, children's remaining hours were free to be devoted to play and exploration of the world around them. Once seen as a youthful manifestation of innate wicked-ness, vigorous play was now viewed as a natural part of childhood and a vehicle to help children develop skills and to teach them usefulness and virtue. Writing about creating a happy home for children, C. C. North advised the employment of a series of items set to warm the heart of any child, "Little children cease to be troublesome when amply supplied with toys, pictures, drawing-books, slates, hobby-horses, etc. indoor; and hoops, jumping-ropes, swings, etc. outdoor. And if one lives in the coun-try, nothing can equal little spades, hoes, barrows, rakes, etc."[31]

The availability of playthings varied widely with social class, however. Manufacturing increased the number of store-bought toys and board games that were available to those who could afford them. By the 1870s middle-class children had many commercially produced toys. Board games, alphabet blocks, and jigsaw puzzles were colorfully adorned with stunning chromolithographic prints. Brightly painted cast metal soldiers allowed boys to replay real and imagined battles. Doll making achieved a high level of sophistication during this period. Dolls had quasi-realistic faces, hands, and feet made of porcelain. Some had glass eyes and "real" rather than yarn hair. Rocking horses, too, reached new heights of decora-tion and realism. Horses with finely carved heads, painted bodies, flow-ing manes, and tails also sported miniature saddles and bridles. They were often presented as galloping steeds with outstretched legs fixed upon turned rockers.

Working-class and farm children played with simple, homemade toys—usually whatever a loving father might carve from a piece of wood by a winter's fire or what a mother might fashion from her bag of material scraps. Children, too, were resourceful. Jacks might be made from corn kernels, dolls from corn husks, a tea set from discarded pieces of crockery. Lucy A. Weed and her sister collected acorns, the caps of which made remarkably tiny bowls and dishes. She detailed their play in a letter, "We have spent a great many pleasant hours playing with them; we lay out our farms, and divide them into lots and lanes, and sometimes we build houses with them."[32] Lydia Child observed, "I do not believe any expensive rocking-horse ever gave so much satisfaction, as I have seen a child in the country take a long necked squash, which he had bridled and placed on four sticks."[33] Even children from the lower rung of economic success had some exposure to simple commercially produced toys. Dolls with papier-mâché heads or those made from the same fabric as their bodies were affordable for even poorer children. Emily Wilson recalled, "My sister and I had the regulation rag dolls with long curls and club feet."[34]

A number of gender-specific concepts about behavioral expectations, emotional sensitivity, and educational expectations came to govern the kinds of games played and chores performed in the home. Boys and

This grouping illustrates an American family with its playthings, including balls, hoops, teeter-totters, and, oddly, a cricket paddle.

girls were presumed to have different constitutions, temperaments, and deportment. Girls were defined in terms of delicacy and dependence while boys were portrayed as rugged and aggressive. Period portraits show boys with swords, drums, bugles, cannons, rocking horses. Girls were portrayed with dolls, miniature sets of china, and books. Nonetheless, several items seem to have escaped the cloak of gender-specificity. These included drawing, the use of balls of many sizes, play with wooden hoops and wands, manipulating stilts, making soap bubbles, forming collections, and playing board games, and playing with yo-yos and other simple mechanical toys. "We had many house games," wrote Wilson, "backgammon, checkers, fox and geese, jack straws, and stage coach, in which nonsensical jingles . . . played an important part."[35]

Mary Livermore writing in 1899 remembered her childhood in an 1820s New England kitchen. "My chief delight in the spacious room was the freedom I found there. We could play, shout, run, jump, stand on the substantial chairs to look out the windows, play housekeeping, and set out the kitchen table with our little pewter and tiny porringers, bring in our individual chairs, stools, and crickets, and build up establishments in every corner of the room, and then inaugurate a series of calls and visits to one another, take our rag-babies to ride in our overturned chair [serving as a carriage], which we dragged over the floor, sing to no tune ever written, or dreamed of, till my patient mother would beg for a respite from the ear-splitting discord."[36]

The American boy was seen as adventurous and independent like the fictional characters Tom Sawyer or Huck Finn. He was portrayed as fun-loving and impish, sometimes cruel to small animals and girls, yet ultimately noble and heroic. Boys were expected to play pranks as a means of channeling their natural aggression and of challenging authority. They formed closed associations, teams, and clubs to which they felt tremendous loyalty. Hazing, teasing, and name-calling helped to delineate the boundaries of such groups. Boys were given more freedom and less supervision in accomplishing their chores, and many took place outside the home, such as tending the livestock or running errands. Boy's games were more physical and were often highly competitive, including a field-hockey-like game called Bandy or Shinny that was characterized by a good deal of roughhousing. The prosecution of those pastimes favored by boys usually took place outside the home more often than those pursued by girls.

The *American Boy's Handy Book,* published in the latter quarter of the century, suggested numerous seasonal activities for young boys. In spring there was kiting, fishing, and stocking or maintaining a fresh-water aquarium. Summer was a time for homemade boats, camping, making objects by knotting, collecting and preserving birds' nests and eggs, making blow guns and squirt guns, producing paper fireworks, and making musical instruments from found materials. Autumn brought the trapping of small animal pests, drawing, woodcarving, and taxidermy. In winter there was snowball battles, snow forts, snow sculpture, sledding, snowshoeing, ice skating, ice sailing, ice fishing, puppets, homemade masquerades and theaters, and indoor crafts. The book encouraged boys to develop self-reliance by making all their own equipment for whatever their adventure and included detailed plans for building a number of styles of small boats, fishing equipment, sleds, winged skaters, an ice fishing shanty, and countless small toys and amusements.

Universally, though, boys played with marbles, balls, whistles, tops, small boats, toy soldiers, wooden animals, popguns, and kites. One boy wrote in a letter, "My large top will spin four minutes; I have got an India-rubber ball, and a boat that I made myself with a man on it. . . . I have got a kite and a windmill, besides a good many other playthings. . . . I have got a large, nice sled. . . . What good times we had sliding down hill last winter."[37] Urban residents had fewer chores and therefore more free time to devote to play. They also tended to have greater time to spend in concert with a wider number of other boys, and they often played in the streets or in empty fields in large groups. Such peer contact differed very dramatically from the previous century when young boys entered apprenticeships and spent much of their time working with adults in the grown-up world. Transition from the world of childhood to that of young manhood was more gradual in the 19th century. One young man summed it up, writing, "Suddenly marbles became a childish game which made knuckles grimy and chapped."[38]

The indoctrination of girls into their gender role came early. Farm girls were expected to assist their mothers with household chores as young as five or six. Middle-class girls made up the beds, sewed, and cared for younger siblings. Even girls from wealthy homes were expected to spend time knitting, sewing, or engaging in decorative needlework. Household chores took up much of a girl's time, leaving far less leisure time than was afforded to boys. What play time they did have was often devoted to vocational pursuits. The Alcott girls of literary fame, Anna, Louisa May, Elizabeth, and Anna May, played Going to Boston, Sick Lady, and School, all situations drawn from their personal experience, yet such play prepared them for the adult roles they would eventually assume.[39] Many of the toys that girls were given, such as dolls, tea sets, and needlebooks, were geared to fostering the nurturing and social skills they would need in later life. Girls mimicked their mothers' activities by playing with dolls, dressing up, and keeping house. Ten-year-old Catherine Elizabeth Havens reflected in her diary, "I don't think grown-up people understand what children like—we love to dress up in long frocks, and I guess all little girls like it for my mother did. When she was about twelve years old she put on her mother's black lace shawl and walked out on Broadway in it. . . . The shawl [was] dragging on the sidewalk and my mother looking behind to see if it dragged. . . . I know it was wrong, but it must have been lovely to think that it really dragged and that people were looking at it."[40]

There were physical activities for girls also, including tossing the Graces, swinging, shuttlecock and battledore, and jump rope. Havens wrote in her diary, "I roll my hoop and jump rope in the afternoon."[41] *The Girl's Own Book* touted jump rope as a "healthy form of exercise which tends to make the form graceful," but cautioned that it should be used in moderation. "I have known instances of blood vessels burst by young ladies, who . . . persevered in jumping after their strength was exhausted."[42] *The Mother's Book* directed mothers, "amusements and employments which lead to exercise in the open air . . . gardening, sliding, skating and snow-balling are all as good for girls as for boys."[43] Acknowledging that people would think such physical play would make little girls "rude and noisy," Child qualified her endorsement with the following. "When I say that skating and sliding are proper amusements for girls, I do not, of course, mean that they should mix in a public crowd. Such sports, when girls unite in them, should be confined to the inmates of the house."[44] *The Girl's Own Book* counseled, "Little girls should not be afraid of being well tired . . . but excessive fatigue should be avoided, especially where it is quite unnecessary."[45]

As might be expected, some girls enjoyed physical activity and the outdoors while others preferred quieter pastimes. Mrs. Alcott wrote in her diary, "My girls are doing well, Louisa enjoys the season—weeds with her father like a Trojan—Anna sticks to the books."[46] Rural girls would have had greater freedom to explore the woods and play more active games than their urban counterparts, but few would have joined males in physical activities such as swimming. Group play included such games as Blindman's Bluff; Shuttlecock; Thread the Needle; Hop, Skip and Jump; Trap Ball; Follow My Lead; I Spy; Hunt the Slipper; Flying Feather; Puss in the Corner; and Leap Frog.

Gardening was a popular activity for young village and country children. *The Girl's Own Book* advised, "Perhaps there is no amusement in the world that combines health, instruction and pleasure than gardening."[47] It was looked upon as a good way to combine fresh air and exercise while teaching horticulture. Winter always brought "coasting on single or double sleds" and ice skating. In the summer, rural boys enjoyed fishing and swimming.[48]

Both boys and girls enjoyed making hand shadows, which were quite the rage in the years before the Civil War. Making shadows figures against a blank wall using one's fingers and hands was entertainment for children and whole families alike. Children used their imaginations and nature's playthings to fashion garlands of flowers, small boats of leaves and pods, and whistles from blades of grass. Wilson wrote, "For amusements we were dependent on our own ingenuity."[49] She fondly recalled playing outdoors, "There was the never failing swing. When put to our wits' end for amusement we would sit down side by side, with our hands clasped say: 'Now let's laugh.'" The Alcott children often played out scenes that they read in their books. One of their favorite characters was "Christian," a character in *Pilgrim's Progress*.[50]

The Civil War involved the entire population in a way paralleled by no other conflict since the Revolution. Photographs of war dead and almost instantaneous reports from the front by telegraph made the war years difficult for both parents and children. In imitation of the news headlines, children played at soldiers and held mock parades, drills, and skirmishes. Margaret Junkin Preston, a Virginia mother, wrote that her children's "entire set of plays have reference to a state of war." Five-year-old George "gets sticks and hobbles about, saying that he lost a leg at the second battle of Manassas; tells wonderful stories of how he cut off Yankees' heads, bayoneted them, & etc." Seven-year-old Theodore Roosevelt—a future president who had two uncles who fought for the Confederacy when he was young—enjoyed playing "Running the Blockade."[51] Lilly Martin Spencer's painting, "War Spirit at Home," shows three children marching about while beating a pot and blowing a horn as their mother reads to them the newspaper account of the battle of Vicksburg.[52]

Play was forbidden between Sabbath service and Sunday school almost everywhere and especially in New England. Dwight observed that New England observed the Sabbath "with greater sobriety and strictness than in any other part of the world."[53] The day was particularly rigorous for children. Emily Wilson recalled, "Sunday was not like any other day. We did not play games nor read the same books and the long church services with Sunday School between were inevitable. We did not take long walks nor use the family horse and carriage except to visit the graveyard . . . or occasionally to attend a prayer meeting at the Poor House."[54]

Children were only allowed to read or to listen to the Bible or other religious literature on the Sabbath. All toys were put away except those that were considered of a religious or moral nature, and these were called Sabbath toys. One such plaything was a Noah's Ark. Sets varied, but they all contained a boat, Noah and his wife, an assortment of pairs of animals, and a dove. More extensive sets included Ham, Shem, Japheth, and their wives. Some had scores of animal pairs numbering as many as 100. Noah's Ark toys date back to the late 17th century but reached a peak during the Victorian era. Bible stories inspired other toys as well. Jacob's Ladder, made of six thin wooden rectangles connected by a cloth tape, was roughly reminiscent of a ladder. When held vertically and released, it created the illusion of tumbling blocks. The blocks were often covered with Biblical scenes. The Wolf in Sheep's Clothing was a small wooden wolf hidden within a removable fleece. The Pillars of Solomon had two pillars connected with a string, which when cut, maintained the illusion that the pillars were still attached. Some doll play was permitted. Termed "church dolls," these figures could be assembled as a congregation to whom the child delivered a sermon. Some came with tiny carved coffins in which the "corpse" could be placed. Puzzle maps of Palestine (the Holy Land) were also considered appropriate .

Many commercially produced toys were designed as educational aids, which would serve to amuse the children while helping them learn their alphabet or numbers. Of these, alphabet blocks were the most ubiquitous. Word-making tiles contained letters that children could use to build words. Expensive sets were made from bone or ivory, but cardboard letters were available at the lower end of the market. A popular and comical alphabet set from early in the century featured a very limber posture master who contorted himself into positions to form each of the letters of the alphabet. Some alphabets were capable of being projected on the wall through a Magic Lantern and provided entertainment for the entire family. Numeracy aids included Domino-Spel, a set of engraved cards with humorous scenes that incorporated spots as an aid to learning. Tangrams or Chinese Puzzles were sets of thin wooden triangles, squares, and rectangles that children were asked to arrange into various patterns contained on the accompanying cards. Board games commonly used teetotums, small multi-sided tops marked by a number or set of dots rather than dice. Dice had the negative association of being the "devil's bones" and were not considered appropriate for children.

Some games were designed to instill moral values and reinforce gender roles. "The Mansion of Happiness" was a popular board game that taught children the importance of a virtuous life. The instructions contained the following poem:

> At this amusement each will find
> A moral fit to improve the mind;
> It gives to those their proper due,
> Who various paths of vice pursue.[55]

The object of the game was to reach the Mansion of Happiness. If players were just, pious, honest, temperate, grateful, prudent, truthful, chaste, sincere, humble, industrious, charitable, humane, or generous, they would "move closer to Happiness." Vices such as audacity, cheating, cruelty, dissipation, drunkenness, folly, idleness, immodesty, ingratitude, passion, perjury, robbery, or Sabbath breaking caused the player to "move away from Happiness" or to be punished at the House of Correction, set in the pillory or in the stocks, or sent to prison. In this game Sabbath breakers were often taken to the whipping post and appropriately chastised. The illustrations accompanying the game further reinforced desired behaviors, and derided evil ones. Generosity portrayed a man who has given away a bag of money. Audacity pictured boys who recklessly started a fire, and then laughed about the danger. Cruelty depicted boys hurting a cat. The Mansion of Happiness itself was shown as a garden around a fine house where joyous men and women were dancing and making music. In liberal households, this game would have been permitted on the Sabbath because of its highly moral content.

Children's Literature

Children's reading material at the beginning of the century was limited to little chapbooks with simple woodcut illustrations. They were entertaining but there was always a moral urging children to be good and obedient. The good child was always rewarded and the disobedient child met with a troubled and even fatal end. Havens had "a little bit of a hymn book" that was given to her by one of her stepsisters. *The Children's Hymn Book*, printed in 1811, contained a hymn that she copied into her diary called, "The Sin and Punishment of Children Who Sleep in the House of God." One verse warned,

> Jehovah speaks, then why should you
> Shut your eyes and hearing too?

In anger He might stop your breath,
And make you sleep the sleep of death.[56]

The Taylor sisters, Ann and Jane, wrote books of poems and although they were not exclusively religious, many featured an avenging God. Less intrusive was the message in the stories of Maria Edgeworth, an Irish novelist at the beginning of the 19th century. Her goal was to teach practical ideas about proper behavior to children. Her astute understanding of the psychology of the child enabled her to create engaging stories that delivered a moral with grace and tender humor. There was always a gracious lady who appeared to give an award or to point out the virtuous response. Authors often used an "aunt" or a "friend to children" to help deliver a message. *Bound Out; or, Abby on the Farm* was written by "Aunt Friendly."

As the century progressed, romanticism ushered in a trend toward a body of children's literature that was less morbid and contained fantasy and realism. Washington Irving's *Sketch Book of 1819* drew upon the legends of the Dutch settlers of New York. James Fennimore Cooper wrote about early frontier life in his series, the *Leather-Stocking Tales.* Nathaniel Hawthorne retold classic Greek myths in *A Wonder Book for Girls and Boys* and *The Tanglewood Tales for Girls and Boys.* While not written primarily for children, these works were very popular with young readers. While fantasy and adventure literature drew a sizable audience, didactic works did not disappear. In the 1820s the American Tract Society began publishing a number of children's books. With titles such as *Honesty Is the Best Policy; Active Benevolence or Lucy Careful;* and *Good Boys and Chastised*, it was clear that the object of such stories was to present a moral lesson. Less obvious, with gentler, more sentimental messages, were books like *Aunt Rose and Her Little Nieces* that contained little stories of interest to children but included words of wisdom for the young readers. Aunt Rose (the nom de plume of the author) cautioned, "When young people do as they are bid, every one is glad to see them; but when they behave ill, every body wishes them far off." She also cautioned, "If ever you do wrong, my dear little ones, be sure you own your fault." Finally, she advised, "Riches take away the heart from God. Never desire to be rich."[57]

This evolved into a trend where children were the protagonists who, through indomitable morality or outstanding example, affect the lives of others by persuading them to take the higher road. Orphaned Abby, in *Bound Out; or, Abby on the Farm,* typifies this story line. Abby was a model child who accepted her hardships, answered the call to duty, and trusted in the Lord. When Mrs. Potter, the mistress to whom Abby had been bound, cut off Abby's braids so that she would take less time getting ready in the morning, Abby reflected that "she had perhaps been foolishly vain of her hair, and it would be better for her to be without it. [She] did not feel angry with Mrs. Potter [and] believed the farmer's wife meant to be kind to her."[58] The writer moralized, "Abby had much of that charity which thinketh no evil, and it kept her out of a great deal of mischief."[59] Abby had tremendous influence on the family. She was responsible for Mr. Porter's desisting to serve whiskey to his reapers during the harvest, for the spoiled son, Bubby, to want to go to Sunday School, and for Mrs. Porter's becoming more clement. "Day by day [Abby] had seen some new proof that the master was trying to walk in the heavenly path; and latterly her mistress had spoken less harshly, and had listened at the daily reading of God's word in the family."[60] All of this, of course, was because Abby "had but loved and lived as a Christian; and others had been led by her to seek the better way."[61]

The flowering of children's literature initiated a surfeit of children's periodicals. Between 1789 and 1879 almost 340 youth magazines were published in the United States. Some publications folded after only a few issues but many enjoyed success. Most were intended for 10- to 18-year-olds but publications like *The Nursery* were intended for the very young. Through these periodicals, the nation's youth were introduced to some of the country's most influential writers of the day, including Jacob Abbott, Louisa May Alcott, Samuel Goodrich, Sarah Josepha Hale, and John Townsend Trowbridge, and delighted by the illustrations of Mary Ann Hallock, Winslow Homer, and Thomas Nast. These magazines reflected virtually all of the attitudes and concerns that enveloped the nation at the time. There were educational magazines such as *Clark's School Visitor* and *The Schoolfellow,* temperance periodicals like *The Youth's Temperance Banner* and *Juvenile Temperance Watchman,* and antislavery publications included the *Youth's Cabinet* and the *Slave's Friend.* Some magazines were purely literary such as *Our Young Folks* and *Riverside Magazine for Young People.* Religious publications were extremely plentiful, and Protestant denominations were joined by Catholic, Jewish, and Mormon sects in trying to spread their message to the nation's youth through the use of the press. During the Civil War Southern children were cut off from their favorite Northern periodicals, but Southern publications such as *The Child's Index, Children's Guide,* and *Youth's Banner* filled the void.

Despite the movement away from dark, heavily moralistic tales, much of children's literature emphasized intellectual and moral education beneath a cloak of juvenile entertainment. Even children's periodicals embraced this format. The prospectus for *Youth's Companion* stated that the magazine's contents would be "miscellaneous, though articles of a religious character will be most numerous. . . . Its several departments will comprise [sic] religion, morals, manners, habits, filial duties, books, amusements, schools and whatever may be thought truly useful, either in this life or the life to come."[62] Parents would have found this very appealing. *The Mother's Book* advised, "The books chosen for young people should as far as possible combine amusement with instruction; but it is very important that amusement should not become a necessary inducement."[63] Author and founder of the children's magazine *Merry's Museum*, Samuel G. Goodrich cautioned parents about the influence of fiction, "[T]here is a magic in print which gives it great authority over the mind of the reader." He suggested that they restrict their children's reading of fiction and encourage instead "those works which deal in facts, as geographies, histories, biographies, travels & etc. [as they] are the safest for young readers."[64]

The Rev. Dr. Joel Hawes warned that a juvenile mind could be "ruined by reading a single [ill-advised] volume" while "one book, wisely selected and properly studied, can do more to improve the mind, and enrich the understanding, than skimming over the surface of an entire library."[65] Lydia Marie Child agreed, "I know that new novels are very generally read; but this springs from the same love of pleasing excitement, which leads people to the theater; it does not proceed from a thirst for information. For this reason, it has a bad effect to encourage an early love for works of fiction; particularly such as contain romantic incidents."[66]

Families commonly gathered together in the parlor in the evening. The women of the family would attend to sewing, knitting, crocheting, or decorative needlework while small children played, a practice encouraged in *The Mother's Book*, which advised, make "a habit of having the different members of the family take turns to read aloud, while others are at work."[67] Literary selections, therefore, had to entertain a wide audience and writers, like Mark Twain, wrote for this wide-ranging audience. An orphan who stayed with the Alcotts for several summers recalled, "One of our number, usually myself, would read aloud, while the mother and the two elder daughters engaged in the family sewing. They read Scott, Dickens, Cooper, Hawthorne, Shakespeare and the British poets, and George Sand's 'Consuelo.' Mrs. Alcott's comments upon and explanations of our reading, when we questioned, were most instructive to us."[68] In a letter to the editor of *Merry's Museum*, R.A.P. Jr. painted the picture of a typical middle-class family evening, "This is a wintry night. . . . Father is lying down with his gown and slippers on, and mother is lying upon the couch, reading the December number of the 'Museum,' and has just commanded us little ones to be silent, while she reads 'Billy Bump's letter from California.'"[69]

Mid-century saw a gender segmentation of the market that generated adventure stories for boys that fostered manly independence like Richard Henry Dana's *Two Years before the Mast*. Putting a new twist on this theme in 1867, Horatio Alger created a different kind of boy's adventure story that centered on the upward struggle to economic success. *Ragged Dick; or, Street Life in New York* commenced a series of rags-to-riches tales focusing on the rewards of hard work, perseverance, and concern for others. Stories targeting the female audience were mainly sentimental domestic novels with a young female protagonist, usually orphaned, who had to make her way in an often unkind world. Among these were Sophie May's

Little Prudy series, Martha Finley's 28-volume saga *Elsie Dinsmore,* and Susan Warner's *The Wide, Wide World.*

Children's literature entered a "Golden Age" following the Civil War. The market was flooded with stories that were no longer moralistic tales veiled as entertainment. These tales were designed to excite a child's imagination and to provide them with fantasies of escape. These stories were devoured by middle-class children who lived in the highly protected world of the Victorian era. Mark Twain's *Tom Sawyer* and *The Adventures of Huckleberry Finn* provided heroes who were free of parental control and who moved from one adventure to another, confounding accepted standards of behavior, but coming ultimately to a just and moral end. Besides dealing with the effects of the war on average families, Louisa May Alcott's *Little Women* addressed many of the family issues and emotions that young middle-class girls were expected to suppress. In an age of childhood regimentation and control, novels such as these established a romantic picture of childhood and young adulthood as a time of adventure, exploration, and fulfillment.

Children as Diarists

Maintaining a diary was popular with adults throughout the 19th century, and many of the children of upper-middle-class and affluent families kept diaries. Often the children were given the diaries as gifts from adults who believed that the process would encourage the children to be reflective and to reinforce a sense of order in their lives. Louisa Jane Trumbull promised to respect her mother's desire, "I am going to write in this journal every day—Aged 10 years 4 months."[70] Some must have found dedication to a similar charge challenging, but tried to comply nonetheless. Grenville Norcross reported four consecutive entries as, "Nothing important. Nothing Important. Nothing of consequence. Small doings." In another week he wrote "went to school" for each weekday followed on Sunday by "Nothing worth describing."[71]

Some children used their journals for purposes other than those expressed by their parents. Harriet Appleton used hers to write stories, to pen poems, and to make sketches. Some, like Louisa Jane Trumbull, kept track of all the books that they read. Many copied passages from things they read or parts of letters they received. Catherine Elizabeth Havens's mother recited a poem to the children "about a little girl who was cross with her sister and the sister died." Catherine copied the poem into her diary in its entirety—four pages long. She prefaced the entry with, "We cannot help crying when she tells it to us. I will copy it down. It may help some little sisters not to quarrel."[72] She also copied a valentine's poem she "teased" from one of her brothers, explaining, "I don't know all it means, but it sounds tinkly [sic], like music."[73]

Mostly, children filled their journals with brief glimpses into their lives like Sam Bigelow's "I went out and took George's sled and coasted down the hill."[74] Catherine Elizabeth Havens wrote, "Yesterday was New Year's Day, and I had lovely presents. We had 139 callers, I have an ivory tablet, and I write all their names down on it."[75] As might be expected, school figured prominently in many entries. "I hate my history lessons," wrote Catherine Elizabeth Havens. Louis Pope Gratacap likely shared the feelings of many youngsters when he wrote, "I got up this morning feeling very miserable because it was so near Monday when I would have to go to school."[76]

The children's journals often record a certain frustration with the physical process of writing. Louisa Trumbull complained, "I never knew such awful horr'd pens as these sticks, but I am in hopes that the rest of this page—in fact the rest of the book—will look better and be written as well if not better than the rest that is written in this book."[77] Sam Bigelow offered the following apology for a blot, "While writing yesterday's journal, John tripped over the ink box and spilled the ink."[78] This desire for perfection was likely due to the fact that adults often reviewed these journals. Catherine Elizabeth Havens's journal contained the following note, "My mother has read my diary and corrected the spelling, and says that it is very good for a little girl."[79] Under one of her poems Harriet Appleton requested her reader to "please give me two marks for this one."[80] Louis Pope Gratacap received an apple from a neighbor who listened to his entries from his journal. The journaling process was a vehicle that helped the child to develop into the precise, reflective, and moral adult that 19th-century society expected.

Notes

1. Mary L. Heininger, *A Century of Childhood, 1820–1920* (Rochester, N.Y.: Margaret Woodbury Strong Museum, 1984), 10.

2. Catherine Elizabeth Havens, *Diary of a Little Girl in Old New York* (New York: Henry Collins Brown, 1920), 58.

3. Sally Kevill-Davies, *Yesterday's Children: The Antiques and History of Childcare* (Woodbridge, England: Antique Collector's Club, 1991), 10.

4. Steven Mintz, *Huck's Raft: A History of American Childhood* (Cambridge, Mass.: Belknap Press/Harvard University Press, 2004), 77.

5. Havens, *Diary of a Little Girl*, 16–19.

6. Mintz, *Huck's Raft*, 80.

7. Tom Kelleher, "Happy Birthday (or not!) 1830s Style," *Old Sturbridge Visitor* (Summer 2001): 6; http://www.osv.org/education/OSVisitor/HappyBirthday.html (accessed October 2006).

8. Tragically, Jacobi was unable to save his own son.

9. Katherine Morrison McClinton, *Antiques of American Childhood* (New York: Bramhall House, 1970), 16.

10. Ibid.

11. Ibid., 18.

12. Lydia Marie Child, *The Mother's Book* (Cambridge, Mass.: Applewood Books, 1989), 26–27. Boston: Carter & Hendee, 1831.

13. "Extracts from Correspondence," *Advocate and Family Guardian* 31, no. 8, No. 716, April 15, 1865, 89.

14. Mary Antoine de Julio, *What a Rich Reward: Betsey Reynolds Voorhees and the Collection of Her Handiwork* (Fort Johnson, N.Y.: Montgomery County Historical Society, 1986), 16.

15. A Lady, *The Factory Boy; or, The Child of Providence Illustrated* (Philadelphia: American Baptist Publication Society, 1839), 64.

16. James Marten, *The Children's Civil War* (Chapel Hill: University of North Carolina Press, 1998), 179.

17. "Extracts from Correspondence," 26.

18. Ibid., 98.

19. Ibid.

20. Ibid., 120.

21. Havens, *Diary of a Little Girl*, 84.

22. Ibid.

23. Ibid.

24. Lucy Larcom, *A New England Girlhood* (Boston: Northeastern University Press, 1986), 166.

25. Child, *Mother's Book*, 125.

26. Mrs. Emily May, "The Knickerbocker Suit," *Peterson's Magazine* (November 1861), 184.

27. Charles East, ed., *Sarah Morgan: The Diary of a Southern Woman* (New York: Simon & Schuster, 1991), 102.

28. Clifford Edward Clark, Jr., *The American Family Home, 1800–1860* (Chapel Hill: University of North Carolina Press, 1986), 25.

29. Ibid.

30. William Ranlett, *The Architect: A Series of Original Designs for Domestic and Ornamental Villas* (New York: William H. Grahm, 1847), 14.

31. C. C. North, "Happy Homes for Children," *Advocate and Family Guardian* 31, no. 4, Whole No. 719 n, February 16, 1865, 43.

32. Lucy A. Weed, "Extracts from Correspondence," *Advocate and Family Guardian* 29, no. 16, Whole No. 676, August 15, 1863, 156.

33. Child, *Mother's Book*, 58.

34. McClinton, *Antiques of American Childhood*, 19.

35. Ibid.

36. Mary Livermore, *The Story of My Life* (Hartford, Conn.: A. D. Worthington & Co., 1899), 45–46.

37. Karen Sanchez-Eppler, *Dependent States: The Child's Part in Nineteenth Century American Culture* (Chicago: University of Chicago Press, 2005), 182.

38. Mintz, *Huck's Raft*, 83–84.

39. Margaret M. Lothrop, *The Wayside: Home of Authors* (New York: American Book Co., 1968), 58.

40. Havens, *Diary of a Little Girl*, 57–58.

41. Ibid., 62.

42. Lydia Marie Child, *The Girl's Own Book* (Cambridge, Mass.: Applewood Books, 1992), 103.

43. Child, *Mother's Book,* 58.

44. Ibid., 59.

45. Child, *Girl's Own Book,* 107.

46. Lothrop, *Wayside,* 49.

47. Child, *Girl's Own Book,* 246.

48. McClinton, *Antiques of American Childhood,* 19.

49. Ibid.

50. Ibid.

51. Marten, *Children's Civil War,* 118.

52. Lothrop, *Wayside,* 51.

53. McClinton, *Antiques of American Childhood,* 16.

54. Ibid., 18.

55. Taken from a game in the collection of the authors.

56. Havens, *Diary of a Little Girl,* 68–69.

57. Aunt Rose (pseudonym), *Aunt Rose and Her Little Nieces* (n.p., 1842), 4, 18, 20.

58. Aunt Friendly (pseudonym), *Bound Out; or, Abby on the Farm* (New York: Anson D. F. Randolph & Co., n.d.), 24–25.

59. Ibid.

60. Ibid., 73.

61. Ibid., 89.

62. Pat Pflieger, "A Visit to *Merry's Museum;* or, Social Values in a 19th Century American Periodical for Children" (PhD diss., University of Minnesota, 1987); http://www.merrycoz.org/papers/diss/mmoo.htm (accessed December, 2006).

63. Child, *Mother's Book,* 86.

64. Pflieger, "Visit to *Merry's Museum.*"

65. Joel Hawes, *Lectures to Young Men on the Formation of Character* (Hartford, Conn.: n.p., 1835), 144.

66. Child, *Mother's Book,* 86.

67. Ibid., 88.

68. Lothrop, *Wayside,* 74–75.

69. Pflieger, "Visit to *Merry's Museum.*"

70. Sanchez-Eppler, *Dependent States,* 31.

71. Ibid., 32.

72. Havens, *Diary of a Little Girl,* 146.

73. Ibid., 76–77.

74. Sanchez-Eppler, *Dependent States,* 35.

75. Havens, *Diary of a Little Girl,* 64.

76. Sanchez-Eppler, *Dependent States,* 25.

77. Ibid., 22.

78. Ibid., 21.

79. Havens, *Diary of a Little Girl,* 150.

80. Sanchez-Eppler, *Dependent States,* 30.

14

Children as Learners

Parents, give your children good education and they will bless you when old.

—Henry Hobart, schoolmaster
His journal, November 19, 1863

Beginnings

The early years of the New Republic saw the development of an American culture that identified itself with democracy, optimism, and self-reliance. The impact of Jacksonian Democracy during the 1820s and 1830s ushered in an age of the common man in which education came to be viewed as a basic right and universal opportunity. Many believed that if all citizens were to be equal, then everyone should be able to read in order to fully participate in government. A demand for schools that provided a general education became widespread as the urban working class grew. Economic opportunities abounded and combined with an education a person could quickly climb the social ladder. Many people saw education as means of providing opportunity to their children that they themselves had not been offered.

The U.S. Constitution is silent with regard to government involvement in education, leaving its prosecution to the states or the people under the catch-all provisions of the Tenth Amendment. Many state constitutions, adopted prior to 1800, cited the importance of education, and several called for the establishment of schools in every county. However, few provided for government funding of schools. Broad provisions for the establish-ment of common schools were made in the constitutions of Pennsylvania (1776), North Carolina (1776), Georgia (1777), Massachusetts (1780), New Hampshire (1784), and Delaware (1792). Other former colonies, like Connecticut, continued the practices in force before the Revolution. As new states entered the Union, they generally followed the tradition of including educational provisions in their constitutions. While states empowered interested local groups to do whatever was necessary to set up schools, they moved more slowly to actually set up school systems. There was no enforcement of these regulations, and children's attendance was largely dependent upon the commitment of their parents to formal-ized education.

A new period of education began in 1795 when the state of Connecticut sold off to private purchasers areas of the Western Reserves in the Ohio Territory and set aside the funds for the perpetual use of education. Three years later, the state transferred control of the public schools from the ecclesiastical authorities of the towns, who had ruled them since the 1650s, to the civil authority of a board of managers who stressed the importance of keeping records concerning school performance. It soon became obvious, however, that the towns were relying solely on the state fund to meet their educational needs. A group of School Visitors was established to uncover the conditions in the classroom in 1827, but they were underpaid and largely ineffective.

In the 1830s and 1840s Henry Barnard in Connecticut, Horace Mann in Massachusetts, and John Pierce in Michigan began a crusade for public education for all children. Through the efforts of such leading educational reformers, Common Schools, as they were called, became firmly established in the Northeast and Midwest. These schools were designed to teach a common body of knowledge and to provide each student with an equal chance in life. Mann was known for his relentless work to advance the common school movement in the United States. He served for 12 years as Secretary for the Board of Education in Massachusetts, and during his tenure he became the acknowledged leader of school organization in the country. The concepts Mann developed for the Massachusetts system were widely copied by other developing systems throughout the nation. Pierce helped to create a separate department of education in Michigan under the control of a state superintendent. He was the first to hold such a position anywhere in America, and adopted a plan of using state funds for ailing schools that helped the growth of education in frontier areas. Barnard played roles similar to Mann's and Pierce's in both Connecticut and Rhode Island, and he was very effective in mounting a national interest in education. He is often called the "Father of American School Administration."

A number of educational journals and magazines were established at this time in support of public education. These included Albert Prickett's groundbreaking *Academician* (1818); William Russell's *American Journal of Education* (1826); Mann's *Common School Journal* (1838); Barnard's *Connecticut Common School Journal* (1838); and Calvin Wiley's *North Carolina Journal of Education* (1843). These publications used the power of inexpensive printing to pursue the establishment of an American system of free public schools by reporting on similar schools in Europe and by promoting the establishment of normal schools for teacher training.

The condition of elementary education at the beginning of the 19th century was meager at best. A child's introduction to school often came in the form of a dame school. Both boys and girls were welcome, and some children began as little more than toddlers while others might be as old as ten. Lucy Larcom recalled her early learning in this type of school. "I began to go to school when I was about two years old. . . . The school was kept by a neighbor who everybody called Aunt Hannah. It took in all the little ones about us, no matter how young they were, provided they could walk and talk, and were considered capable of learning their letters." Classes such as these were held in the school mistress's house. This enabled her to attend to her household chores as well as her students. The mistress was literate but generally unschooled. She heard her students recite their prayers or the alphabet while she sewed, spun, or prepared the day's meals. "I learned my letters . . . standing at Aunt Hannah's knee while she pointed them out in the spelling-book with a pin." Instruction was extremely basic. The children were taught some reading and writing and possibly some "figuring." The girls would have learned simple sewing and knitting, skills they would have been learning from their mothers at home. "Not much more than that sort of temporary guardianship was expected of the good dame."[1]

Between 1810 and 1860 there was a great variety of elementary school organizations. Many schools in New England were organized into two parts, the primary school of six grades and the grammar (classical secondary) school. After 1848 the nine-year elementary school was typical of New England, while the rest of the country organized under an eight-year system. Nonetheless, in rural communities most children continued to attend ungraded, poorly equipped and understaffed one-room schools. The development of the high school was slowed largely by the lack of development of elementary schools, the popularity of academies, and a lack of funding in the form of tax support. The first formal schools in many communities were usually funded by subscription or tuition. Teachers received a dollar or two per student per month. Sometimes teachers would "board around," living with the families of their students for several weeks at a time, a situation likely to be awkward at best. The classroom situations the teachers found were as varied as the students they taught.[2]

The forces enlisted to establish tax-supported public schools were aided by the importation of a number of reports that lauded similar systems being used in Prussia. Among these were the reports by Victor Cousin (1832), Barnard (1835), and Mann (1843) that were widely circulated and cited in the wave of educational journals and magazines that supported free public education. Unfortunately, the Prussian system highly valued extremes of austerity and conformity as foundations of proper education. By the end of the 19th century, a rigid uniformity among elementary schools that valued the content and coverage of subjects rather than the development of children as creative learners had taken hold. This rigidity quickly spread to all levels of public education.

The Board of Education

Even as organized community support became more common, schools varied tremendously from community to community. Schools were supervised by a group of designated citizens who oversaw operations as a board of education. Their duties included "the levying of tax, the location of school houses, the purchase and sale of school property, the appointment and dismissal of teachers, and the selection of studies and textbooks." The dedication and expertise of these directors was limited, however, and their decisions and abilities were often called into question.[3]

A major difficulty in defining the responsibilities of the local board of education on the district level was the lack of an equally comprehensive statewide system of control. State boards and superintendents of schools had their origin in the committees set up for the disposition of funds from the sale of public lands that were earmarked for education in the Northwest Ordinance of 1785. At this time the legislature of New York established the University of the State of New York to act as a state board of education. This was the first of its kind. New York also set up a fund for state schools and established the post of state school superintendent. Yet in many cities school districts chartered their schools to avoid state control. Philadelphia and Baltimore organized their schools in this manner to avoid being hindered by the backwardness of the rural regions of their respective states.[4]

Infrastructure

School revenue for independent school districts was directly tied to the success or failure of local commerce and agriculture. In an 1861 report, numerous county superintendents in Pennsylvania reported frosts of June and early July. The resulting loss of the wheat crop caused not only "more than ordinary pecuniary embarrassment," but, as a result, teaching time was shortened, and in some communities the wages of the teachers were reduced. More than one superintendent lamented a false system of economy that reduced teachers' wages so much that some of the best teachers left the county or became engaged in "other pursuits." The solution for some districts was to suspend school for the entire year. Those teachers who chose to remain were applauded for their self-denial and the manner in which they bore up during a difficult time. In the same year, where lumbering was favored in some districts by high water, there was increased prosperity that made more money available for education.[5]

School buildings were constructed in a number of ways, including brick, frame, log, and stone. In the 1861 state report, 58 percent of the Pennsylvanian superintendents responding used negative terms to describe their schools. It was not unusual to see claims that the schools were "less fit for the purpose of schooling, than would be many modern out houses for sheltering cattle." One schoolhouse was described as "a crumbling, dilapidated, damp, unwholesome stone building with a ceiling eight feet high, room about twenty-six by thirty feet into which one hundred and seventeen are crowded, and placed at long, old fashioned desks, with permanent seats, without backs." Additional complaints included a lack of "out-houses and other appliances necessary for comfort and convenience." Concern was expressed over the fact that schoolhouses were "placed far off the road and buried in the wildest forest."[6]

An 1830 study of schoolhouses in one Connecticut county determined that the average size of the building was 18½ feet by 7½ feet and 7 feet high and that only one had any ventilation. A later study in 1848 reported that only about half of the schools had an outhouse.[7] Michigan schoolmaster Henry Hobart wrote in his 1863 diary, "The schoolhouses throughout the country are poorly adapted for the grand object for which they are made. It is a rare thing to find a good well-ventilated, well-arranged, well-furnished schoolroom."[8] He complained that his schoolhouse was "very wet . . . and should be moved to a better place" but was discouraged because "the District [was] not willing to incur the expense of placing it in a better place."[9]

An 1838 report concerning 3,000 school buildings in Massachusetts said, "[T]here is no other class of buildings within our limits, erected for the permanent or temporary residence of our native population, so inconvenient, so uncomfortable, so dangerous to health by their construction within, or without, abandoned to cheerlessness and dilapidation."[10] After touring schoolhouses through the state, Horace Mann wrote, "The schoolhouse in District No 3. How shall we speak of that?. . . . Already aware of the danger, the mice have forsaken it."[11]

Even in frontier regions, keeping the schoolroom warm was an almost universal problem. Firewood, cut, split, and stacked for a season, was an expensive commodity that reflected the labor required to produce it. Teachers, ministers, and other public servants were often paid in quantities of seasoned firewood, usually measured out in cords. Nonetheless, the community was not always willing to provide appropriate fuel for the schoolhouse stove. A school superintendent reported finding "the teacher and pupils huddled together, shivering with cold, and striving to warm themselves by the little heat generated from a quantity of green wood in the stove."[12] While teaching in Kentucky, Elizabeth Blackwell noted that at times she had to wear gloves, a blanket shawl, and a hood over her head. A young teacher in Iowa recorded, "Went over to make my fire, and the wood was all wet and unchopped except a couple which lay under the stove . . . as I puffed away to make the wet mass burn I found myself all at once crying like a child."[13]

Recalling his schoolhouse in early 19th-century Ridgefield, Connecticut, Samuel G. Goodrich wrote, "The schoolhouse chimney was of stone, and the fireplace was six feet wide and four feet deep. The flue was so ample and perpendicular that the rain, sleet and snow fell directly to the hearth. In the winter the battle for life with green fizzling fuel, which was bought in lengths and cut up by the scholars, was a stern one. Not unfrequently [*sic*] the wood, gushing with sap as it was, chanced to let the fire go out, and as there was no living without fire, the school was dismissed, whereat all the scholars rejoiced."[14]

Nonetheless, the Pennsylvania superintendents' report of 1861 described a number of new schools in more favorable terms. One statement described a "tasteful brick building 30 x 45 . . . furnished with first class iron frame furniture for 62 pupils." Other new buildings were constructed of milled wood, and one was "24 x 36 with four tiers of seats for 2 pupils each accommodating 64 pupils." One superintendent boasted, "All the rooms are warmed by coal stoves, most of them have ceilings of proper height, windows adapted to ventilation; plenty of black-board surface; and they are tolerably well seated." Another new schoolhouse was proudly described as having an "anti-room, closets and platform and in every respect is superior to most of the other houses."[15]

The Local Schoolhouse

With extremes at both ends of the spectrum eliminated, a typical one-room schoolhouse was a large rectangular room with a single door. A small vestibule was partitioned off from the main room. This area contained rows of peg hooks upon which students could hang their belongings while they were in class. The schoolroom would have a cast iron stove in the center to provide heat. Light was provided by the sunlight that came in the two or three windows on each side of the building. The teacher's desk was commonly on a raised platform. In the most primitive schools, students sat on long plank benches and worked on their laps. Other schools had long boards attached to the walls along the perimeter of the room to create desks upon which students, seated on benches, could write. This arrangement made the most of the light coming in through the windows, although students were positioned facing away from the teacher. In some schools students were fortunate to be furnished with rows of double desks and benches facing the teacher.

Furniture was, at best, sparse in most classrooms. "It is useless to complain of school furniture," lamented one superintendent. "It seems that people would sooner see their children have spinal or pulmonary affliction, than furnish the school room with proper desks and seats." A York County, Pennsylvania, superintendent noted, "I witnessed a great deal of uneasiness, amounting in many instances to intense suffering, among the small children, from . . . being seated too high. In some instances, the desks are still attached to the wall, the scholars with their backs to the teacher."[16] Goodrich wrote, "We were all seated upon benches made of slabs-boards having the exterior or rounded part of the log on one side, as they were useless for other purposes, they were converted into school benches, the rounded part down. They had four supports, consisting of straddling wooden legs set into auger holes."[17] Hobart complained that "most of the schoolhouses are fitted to torture the children rather than add to the comfort and ease. Under such circumstances they dislike to go to school or when they are so uncomfortable that they cannot learn. . . . People are very indifferent to the education of their children."[18] Sarah Stuart Robbins wrote in her later years, "Was it necessary that we should sit on straight wooden benches, brown and knife-chopped, with straight desks, brown and more knife-chopped, before us?"[19] Schools in larger population centers typically had better furniture and conditions, but rural schools lagged far behind throughout the century.

Schools were often crowded. Hobart reported that he had "one hundred and thirty scholars in a schoolroom large enough to accommodate seventy-five."[20] For his annual report he calculated that he "had two hundred and twenty-eight different pupils & the school averaged eighty for nine months of twenty-six days each . . . [some months] went far above one hundred."[21] Mann noted the illogic of the situation found in many schools. "You crowd 40 to 60 children into that ill constructed shell of a building, there to sit in the most uncomfortable seats that could be constructed expecting that with the occasional application of the birch [the children] will come out educated for manhood or womanhood."[22]

In many schools sufficient blackboards were also wanting. In the absence of expensive slate, blackboards were often made by taking smooth boards that were painted black and covering them with a chalk dust, which provided a fairly erasable surface.[23] Well-supported schools had not only slate blackboards but also outline maps, spelling and reading cards, charts, and globes. The average school had only one or two of these instructional materials. Paper was scarce in rural schools. Students commonly wrote on wood-framed slates, although these were initially "confined to such as had made advancement in arithmetic; but now we find the smallest scholars engaged with their slates."[24]

Textbooks

In the rapidly changing atmosphere of the 19th century, schoolbook publishing thrived, and every publisher with sufficient capital tried to market at least one reader, speller, grammar, or arithmetic. Some Eastern publishing houses had several successful texts, such as Samuel Worcester's *Reader* or Noah Webster's *Old Blue-Back Speller.* With advances in economical printing processes becoming available, the business environment was ripe for textbook publishing, especially in the Midwest where the distribution system for schoolbooks printed in the East was slow and expensive. In 1826, the presses in Cincinnati, Ohio, turned out almost 100,000 schoolbooks, not counting Bibles, music books, hymnals, mathematical tables, and almanacs. By the 1840s there were at least 40 booksellers in that city, whereas two decades earlier there was only one.

The variety and diversity of texts used during this period is remarkable, but no series of schoolbooks by a single author was more successful than the *Eclectic Readers* established by William Holmes McGuffey. The initial success of the McGuffey *Reader* was largely due to the aggressive and revolutionary sales promotion practices of the publishers, Truman and Smith of Cincinnati; but their continued use and domination of the schoolbook market was due to their high quality and matchless content. For a long time the terms *school reader* and *McGuffey* were synonymous. From 1836 until 1920 more than 120 million copies of the *Eclectic Reader* were sold in the United States.[25]

William McGuffey, described as a prim professor of language (Latin, Greek, and Hebrew), a minister, and a humanitarian, began his career as a teacher at an early age (16 or 17) in a "subscription" school in Greersburg, Ohio, but in 1826 at age 18, he failed the test administered by the local board of education for the position of headmaster in the town of Warren. Even though he had completed a college degree at Washington College in Pennsylvania, this failure spurred McGuffey to try to further establish his credentials as an educator. This he accomplished in 1833 with the publication in London of his *Treatise on Methods of Reading,* which was well received by the proponents of public education.

About this time, McGuffey joined with Dr. Daniel Drake and other educators in Ohio in forming the College of Teachers, the first real teachers' association founded in America. His connection with these educators helped to confirm his reputation. More to the point of his career as an author however, McGuffey—ordained a minister in 1833—became acquainted with Dr. Lyman Beecher, the president of Lane Theological Seminary and a prominent abolitionist. He befriended Beecher's son-in-law, Calvin E. Stowe, whose wife, Harriet Beecher Stowe, would write *Uncle Tom's Cabin* (1849). In 1835, Calvin Stowe suggested McGuffey to Winthrop Smith (of Truman and Smith) as a possible author for the firm's newest reader project. It has been said that "on this simple fact turns much of America's educational history." The first reader of the series was published in 1836. Thereafter, Winthrop and McGuffey formed a long and financially rewarding relationship.[26]

In 1851, McGuffey married Laura Howard and moved to Charlottesville, Virginia, to teach at the university there. Although married to a Southern woman who was scandalized by the radical actions of the abolitionists, McGuffey remained an anti-slavery advocate; and he supported his young daughter, Mary, when she violated Virginia state law by teaching black children to read and write. He remained in Virginia during the Civil War, but the slaughter sickened him both because he was a pacifist and because he saw his own students going off to war one by one and in groups to die or to return dismembered. His *Readers,* while approving of the fight for liberty and unity, made it quite clear that McGuffey "abhorred war and all its works," even describing (in 1866) one battle of the war as the murder of 20,000 people by another 30,000 calling themselves soldiers. McGuffey was also sickened by the post-war deterioration he saw about him. He remained at the university serving as a popular lecturer and speaker as the institution slowly recovered its prewar levels of scholarship and attendance. He died in 1873, but his *Eclectic Readers* remained in publication for another half century.[27]

Teachers

Teachers' credentials varied greatly and even those teachers who were college graduates often had received no specific teacher training. Some academies and female seminaries offered programs that included a review of elementary subjects and some lectures on "keeping school." An early text widely used for teacher preparation was Samuel Hall's *Lectures on Schoolkeeping* (1829). Some teachers were graduates of normal schools that focused on teacher preparation. First founded in 1839, until the postwar period, these schools remained largely low-level academic institutions that offered some practice teaching and some exposure to educational philosophy. Yet there was little in the way of sound theoretical foundation for a teaching career. Often comprised of a two-year program, some normal schools did have higher academic standards, but generally they were taught on the secondary rather than the college level. In the 1870s there was a trend toward three- and four-year programs at the normal school. Nonetheless, college programs for teacher preparation did not come into evidence until the last quarter of the century, and few specialized courses on methodology were made available before 1900. Generally, all that was required to teach on any level during the 19th century was a strong knowledge of the subject matter.[28]

So common was the lack or expertise that Hobart felt compelled to condemn all ill-prepared teachers. "A self-conceited young man says he thinks he can do all the examples in the Common School Arithmetic and therefore concludes that he is fitted to impart instruction to others. He applies for a School and perhaps on the committee is a relative which of course gives him the place. Now such a teacher is worthless. He knows nothing about the correct method of explaining an example or how to convey correct impressions in simple and proper language. To work an example is one thing, to explain it so that the young mind will comprehend it is another. A teacher must be experienced and make his profession a study."[29]

Such advanced thinking and genuine concern became more widespread in the postwar years. In 1866, Edward Sheldon, Secretary of the Board of Education of Oswego, New York, developed a teacher training program that taught techniques of pedagogy and fostered an understanding of and respect for the child. One strategy was "object teaching" that began by discussing simple objects with which the child was familiar and then moving on to more abstract concepts. The state legislature made Oswego a state normal school, and soon it was the most celebrated teacher training school in the nation. People flocked to the school and teachers from Oswego spread these concepts across the country.

School districts in urban areas established examinations to certify that teachers were competent to assume their duties. Most exams were a combination of written and oral questions. "They were held publicly, and attended by numbers of citizens, who had a desire to see and hear for themselves."[30]

Emma Sargent Barbour's sister, Maria, wrote about the examination process in Washington, D.C. "[Hattie accompanied] me as far as City Hall where I was to be examined, when she remarked that she had a good mind to try just for fun. She went in and passed an excellent examination and next Monday will take a position at my school."[31] Not all examinations were quite as simple as Maria implies. Many superintendents in Pennsylvania reported having to turn away applicants who had failed while others indicated that, considering the rural nature of their district, they were lucky to find teachers at all. "Parents prefer to have their children work in the mines or learn a trade, and thus but few become qualified to teach school."[32]

Institutes were held periodically to help teachers to improve their skills. Some occurred only once a year, often during the summer, while others were held semimonthly on alternate Saturdays. Naturally, not all teachers performed to the satisfaction of the districts. (See Table 14.1 for rules teachers were expected to obey in one district.) A Wayne County, Pennsylvania, superintendent wrote of his teachers, "Two last winter had the reputation of being of intemperate habits, and some few are rough and rowdyish in their manner."[33] John Pierce complained of the abominable habit of some teachers in Michigan striking their students on the head or body with rulers, books, and rods, often leaving painful welts.

Moreover, he found great injustice in the fact that many teachers—unable to prove the guilt of a particular student—proceeded with a punishment, nonetheless, assured that the pupil had gotten away with something else deserving of the rod.

Rural districts were often unsuccessful in obtaining a normal school graduate and had to settle for whatever reasonably well-educated person they could find. Goodrich wrote of his teacher, "Lewis Olmstead [was] a man who made a business of ploughing, mowing, carting manure, etc. in the summer, and of teaching school in the winter. He was a celebrity in ciphering, and Squire Seymore declared that he was the greatest 'arithmeticker' in Fairfield County."[34] Certainly, some teachers strove to do their best. One Oregon teacher confessed, "Of my sixteen pupils, there were three who were more advanced than myself, but I took their books with me at nights, and with the help of my brother-in-law, I managed to prepare my lessons beforehand, and they never suspected my incompetency [*sic*]."[35] Another would-be educator from Pennsylvania, upon learning that he had been selected for a teaching position, recorded in his diary, "I shall give myself regular lessons and I am going to study a great deal this winter. I am studying algebra and grammar at present."[36]

Table 14.1 Rules for Teachers, Kansas, 1872

1. Teachers each day will fill lamps, clean chimneys.

2. Each teacher will bring a bucket of water and a scuttle of coal for the day's session.

3. Make your pens carefully. You may whittle nibs to the individual taste of the pupil.

4. Men teachers may take one evening each week for courting purposes, or two evenings a week if they go to church regularly.

5. After ten hours in school, the teachers may spend the remaining time reading the Bible or other good books.

6. Women teachers who marry or engage in unseemly conduct will be dismissed.

7. Every teacher should lay aside from each pay a goodly sum of his earnings for his benefit during his declining years so that he will not become a burden on society.

8. Any teacher who smokes, uses liquor in any form, frequents pool or public baths, or gets shaved in a barber shop will give good reason to suspect his worth, intention, integrity, and honesty.

9. The teacher who performs his labor faithfully and without fault for five years will be given an increase of twenty-five cents per week in his pay, providing the Board of Education approves.

Gender Discrimination

Although both men and women taught, a male teacher was preferred in order to maintain good discipline. One superintendent explained that women were unsuitable for teaching "for the same reason that [they] cannot so well manage a vicious horse or other animal, as a man may do."[37] Lack of control over a population of naturally exuberant children was not the only criticism leveled against female instructors. An Ohio educator complained that his older students read with "extreme faintness of voice that some of them have acquired by going to female teachers. This is a fault that seems to be hardest to eradicate of any that I have had to contend with."[38] Most women who did teach taught in the summer schools, which were generally held for the younger children. Hobart wrote that he had a "good assistant who takes care of the primary department. . . . She is a lady of determination and aims to have everything conducted with a regard to order & discipline. It requires such a person to manage these small scholars who are not aware of what it is to mind."[39] Winter school was usually taught by men who would have been otherwise unemployed during the slowest of agricultural seasons. Records from the Turner, Maine, schools showed that in summer school, the district employed 18 female teachers and 1 male. In winter they employed 16 male teachers and 4 females.

As the public school movement grew, it became clear that there would not be enough men to satisfy the need for male instructors. This shortfall became most dramatic during the Civil War years when many young men left the schoolroom to serve in the army or to fill better-paying jobs in the mills and offices made available by the call-up of military forces. This dearth of educated male candidates finally kicked open the schoolroom doors for women in education. A county superintendent of schools at the time reassessed his former poor opinion of female instructors. "The employment of female teachers caused some dissatisfaction, as they were believed inadequate to the task of controlling a winter school. But superior cleanliness and arrangement of their rooms, the effect of their natural gentleness and goodness on the scholars . . . amply compensated for their want of physical force."[40] In congratulating his teachers, one superintendent stated, "Many of our teachers especially the ladies, deserve special mention for having their school-rooms ornamented—the walls with mottoes, handsome chromos neatly framed, and the windows made attractive with flowers, hanging baskets, and trailing vines artistically arranged, all of which tend to exert a salutary influence upon pupils in developing the finer sensibilities of character."[41] A female educator, advocating the place of women as teachers, conjectured that the male student "who would be constantly plotting mischief against a schoolmaster . . . becomes mild and gentle, considerate and well behaved towards a little woman, simply because she is a little woman, whose gentle voice and lady-like manners have fascinated him."[42] Catharine Beecher advocated the hiring of female teachers as a civilizing agent for Western settlements, submitting that "God designed women to be the chief educators of our race. . . . It is woman who is fitted by disposition and habits and circumstances to such duties."[43]

These supposed female qualities of character were appreciated even more when it was realized that the generally younger women who entered the teaching field could be paid considerably lower salaries than the male instructors. The school district committee in Turner, Maine, made the following observation. "[I]t is better for those districts now in the habit of employing young male teachers, to employ old experienced female teachers, for you can hire female teachers for less money, and have longer, and we believe better, schools." The average salary reported in 1869 for a male teacher in Turner was $29.82 per month excluding room and board. Women were paid less than half this fee.[44] The Superintendent of Common Schools in Ohio encouraged the hiring of female teachers, boasting that districts were "able to do twice as much with the same money as in counties where female teachers are excluded." By 1870 female teachers outnumbered male instructors two to one in settled areas.[45]

"The majority of teachers are between eighteen and twenty-five, and are spending a part of the year in attending academies and Normal School," wrote one superintendent in 1860.[46] Yet some of the grammar school teachers were little more than children themselves. After only one year of formal schooling, Delia Bacon began teaching in Hartford at the age of 15. Two years later she started a school of her own. One superintendent complained, "It is to be regretted, however, that parents will urge their sons and daughters to seek to become teachers at so early an age; and it is a great error in directors, as a general rule, to employ such young persons. Men engage persons of mature age and experience on the farm, in the shop or store, in the kitchen or dairy room; but they hire girls or boys of 15 or 16 to train up and educate their offspring."[47]

School Days, School Days

There were few, if any, educational standards at this time. The length of the school day and year varied as the individual community saw fit. The average length of the school term in 1860 was 5 months and 5 ½ days. Children from rural communities generally attended school for shorter periods of time than those from urban areas. Teacher John M. Roberts noted an 1859 meeting of the board of education for his Ohio township that decided "[a]fter considerable debating on the question of 65 days for a quarter, the board finally passed a resolution in favor of the 65 day plan, resolving that each and every district should make this the standing rule of action." A typical school day ran from nine to four with an hour for recess and dinner at noon. Students may have eaten lunch outside on mild days, but inclement weather forced them inside.[48]

Sarah Stuart Robbins attended a small village school for girls, all of whom lived nearby and likely returned home for the midday meal. She fondly remembered those exceptional days. "Sent to school in all weathers, on stormy days we carried our lunch, and no royal tables ever gave half the enjoyment we experienced when, upon our well-worn and not immaculate desks we spread our rows of doughnuts, biscuits, bread, cheese, cold meats, fried apple pies, nuts and pop-corn."[49]

The school day often commenced with a scripture reading followed by a patriotic song. Emma Barbour received a letter from her sister, Maria, discussing her teaching duties. "I am a regular schoolmarm. School commences every day at nine o'clock when they write a half hour and the lessons follow."[50] A subsequent letter from Maria provides more details concerning a teacher's daily routine. "School! School!—is the cry, my daily life may almost be embraced in the following program; rise at seven, breakfast at half past, practice my little singing lesson and ready to start for school at half past eight. Direct the youths how to behave and hear lessons until twelve, then from twenty minutes to a half an hour, hear missed lessons and eat lunch, chat with the boys until one o'clock, then proceed as before until three; prepare for dinner and sometimes attend receptions or receive company in the evening."[51]

Most learning was done via rote memorization and recitation. Elizabeth Buffin Chace recalled that by the time she was twelve she "had recited Murray's Grammar through perhaps a dozen times without a word of explanation or application from the book or the teacher."[52] Much to their dismay, older students were often required to memorize extensive passages from famous orations such as "Webster's Reply to Hayne." As an adult, one gentleman vividly recalled being called upon for such an assignment. "I rose in my seat with a spring like Jack from his box. My limbs were numb, so numb that I could scarcely feel the floor beneath my feet and the windows were only faint gray glares of light. My head oscillated like a toy balloon, seemed indeed to be floating in the air, and my heart beat like a pounding drum."[53]

In 1859 an Ohio educator lamented the lack of a phonetic system for the teaching of reading and spelling. "I hope that the system will be introduced into the school system of Ohio by law. Then those tedious, unmeaning spelling classes will be dispensed with. . . . Let us have a thorough set of scientific readers, real orators. More than ¾ of the time spent in school is spent in learning to spell and read. This ought not to be so, and the worst of it is that not one in ten ever acquire a decent knowledge of either of these important branches."[54]

To stimulate student motivation, less interesting material such as geographic facts were sung to popular tunes like "Yankee Doodle." After observing a geography lesson at another school, a teacher reported that the other instructor "teaches it by singing, & I am of the opinion that it is a very good plan."[55] Multiplication tables were often taught in verse, such as, "Twice 11 are 22. Mister can you mend my shoe?" or "9 times 12 are 108. See what I've drawn upon my slate."[56] Henry Hobart complained that he "found very few Scholars who could give a proper explanation of the various principles that are brought out in the various steps in arithmetic or in fact any study. It is certainly true that most Scholars go over the pages of the book and yet know very little of the truths that lie at the base."[57] Mental arithmetic was still an innovative technique in 1860, but it was all the rage in educational journals. More than one district reveled in the fact that it was taught in their schools. "Mental arithmetic has been extensively introduced during the past two years and will soon be considered an indispensable item even in our primary schools."[58]

Popular instructional materials included McGuffey's *Eclectic Reader,* Ray's *Arithmetic,* and Webster's *Old Blue-Back Speller.* Thanks to the work of etymologists like Noah Webster, spelling was just becoming standardized. *Leach's Complete Spelling Book* of 1859 contained a "Collection of Words of Various Orthography," which included words of "common use, which are spelled differently by the three most eminent Lexicographers. . . . Webster, Worcester and Smart."[59] Barbour's letter from her young cousin, Mary, gives additional insight into period texts, "I am getting along first rate, at school. I don't always get 10 though by any means. I always get 9 in writing. I study Robinson's Arithmetic, it is a very hard one. Frost's United States History, Towen's speller, Weld's Grammar, the same almost exactly like the one I studied on east, but the Grammar is not at all like it. I read out of Sargent's Reader."[60] In this regard students were not graded by the year of school attendance but rather by the standard reader from which they read. Many schools suffered from a lack of uniform class sets of texts, although the adoption of this practice was frequently a goal. "In time, however, as the old books, (some of which, carefully preserved, have descended from grand-fathers) are worn out, uniform class-books will be used, much to the advantage of teachers and pupils."[61]

In Connecticut, towns with 80 families were required to have a single school for young children that taught English grammar, reading, writing, geography, and arithmetic. Towns with 500 families added a school for older students that offered algebra, American history, geometry, and surveying, and those places with larger populations offered a study of Greek, Latin, and the physical sciences—referred to as "the natural or revealed philosophies" because of the combination of scientific fact and Biblical study. The subjects that were taught—and the depth to which students were taken therein—depended on the competency of the teacher and varied greatly from school to school. In the annual school report of Armstrong County, Pennsylvania, the superintendent boasted, "The number of schools in which geography and grammar are not taught is steadily diminishing. There is a considerable increase in the number in which mental arithmetic is taught. Algebra was taught in 11 schools; history in 4; natural philosophy in 2; Latin in 1; composition in 5, and in several there were exercises in declamation and vocal music."[62]

In the same state report, Beaver County noted, "The Bible is read in 140 schools; not read in 17. I trust that all our teachers may become so deeply impressed with a sense of their duty, in the moral education of their pupils, that we may soon report the Bible read in every school."[63] In a section of his diary subtitled, "Teach the Bible to Children Early," Hobart asserted that "the first impressions of youth are lasting . . . for if his proper training is neglected his mind will receive evil impressions and his life will be spent in ignorance or sin . . . causing his parents trouble and injuring society."[64] This need to incorporate the Bible into everyday instruction was a common attitude held since colonial times. In addition to the three Rs, schools were expected to infuse a strong moral sense, foster polite behavior, and inspire good character. Education was not only for the individual, it was also for the benefit of society as a whole. A teacher from Minnesota told a friend, "Let us not only strive to teach thoroughly the several studies which they [the students] may pursue but to instill into their minds and hearts those principles which will make them noble men and women."[65]

Moral and religious inculcation was not limited to Bible readings. An introductory geography book contained the following extraordinary attestation in its preface, "The introduction of moral and religious sentiments into books designed for the instruction of young persons, is calculated to improve the heart, and elevate and expand the youthful mind; accordingly, whenever the subject has admitted of it, such obser-vations have made as tend to illustrate the excellence of Christian religion, the advantages of correct moral principles, and the superiority of enlightened institutions."[66]

The following lesson seems more likely to be found in a religious instruction manual than in a *First Reader*.

> If God is with me, and knows all that I do,
> he must hear what I say. O, let me not, then, speak
> bad words; for if I do, God will not love me.[67]

Readers contained lessons entitled "The First Falsehood," the "Effects of Evil Company," a "Contrast Between Industry and Idleness," and a "Dialogue Between Mr. Punctual and Mr. Tardy." Stories, poems, and essays used in instruction drilled the message that good triumphed over evil, frugality surpassed extravagance, obedience superseded willfulness, and family always came first. Lesson IX in McGuffey's *First Reader* typifies this practice.

> Boys love to run and play but they must not be rude.
> Good boys do not play in a rude way, but take care not to hurt anyone.

You must not lie. Bad boys lie, and swear and steal.
When boys are at play they must be kind and not feel cross.
If you are cross, good boys will not like to play with you.[68]

Further inculcation of values can be seen even in brief multiplication rhymes, "5 times 10 are 50. My Rose is very thrifty,"[69] or beneath a picture of two boys fighting, "4 times 10 are 40. Those boys are very naughty."[70] Not even word problems neglected the chance to deliver a moral message as can be seen in Emerson's *The North American Arithmetic.* "There were 7 farmers, 3 of whom drank rum and whiskey, and became miserable; the rest drank water, and were healthy and happy. How many drank water?"[71] Robbins mused, "It is a wonder that with such a ponderous load of theology to carry, we children were yet light-hearted enough to amuse ourselves with regular [amusements.]"[72]

Another instructional objective, presented in a reading text, was "a desire to improve the literary taste to the learner, to impress correct moral principles, and augment his fund of knowledge."[73] Lesson I in McGuffey's *First Reader* sets a definite tone.

Here is John.
And there are Ann and Jane.
Ann has got a new book.
It is her first Book.
Ann must keep it nice and clean.
John must not tear the book.
But he may see how fast he can learn.[74]

Some texts published in Northern communities during the Civil War contained distinctly pro-Union sentiments. *Hillard's Fifth Reader,* printed in 1863, contained such readings as "Liberty and Union" and "The Religious Character of President Lincoln," as well as the "Song of the Union," the poem "Barbara Frietchie," and an essay on the "Duty of American Citizens," among many similar patriotic themes. Caroline Cowles Richards wrote in her 1861 diary, " I recited 'Scott and the Veteran' today at school, and Mary Field recited, 'To Drum Beat and Heart Beat a Soldier Marches By.' Anna recited 'The Virginia Mother.' Everyone learns war poems now-a-days."[75]

Discipline and Deportment

Despite being deluged with lessons on morality and deportment, students often failed to internalize these messages when it came to behavior. A student journal reported, "Just after dinner a smart skirmish . . . took place between James Neff & Robert Heazlitt. . . . [S]ticks of fire wood & stones were the missiles freely used by both parties, to which James added a draw knife."[76] Parents and school boards alike expected strict discipline, and it was considered a necessity in a school where a lone teacher was the sole source of authority. Most disciplinary actions took the form of corporal punishment. An 1802 *Primer* gave the counsel, "The idle fool is whipt at school."[77] One man recalled his school days in a rural school, "On the first day of school teachers regularly brought either a strap or a yardstick and as a preliminary explained its uses."[78] Lucy Larcom admitted that she was afraid of her schoolmaster, explaining, "Once, having caught a boy annoying a seat-mate with a pin, he punished the offender by pursuing him around the school-room, sticking a pin into his shoulder whenever he would overtake him. And he had a fearful leather strap, which was something used even upon the shrinking palm of a little girl."[79]

The student journalist who had formerly captured the antics of James and Robert again noted, "In the afternoon at recess James Neff and R. Heazlitt were running over the benches, trying to kick each other. When our teacher came in the regulator told him what they had been doing; to which Mr. Andrews applied the ruler very smart to each of them but more so to R. Heazlitt because he had boasted that Mr. Andrews could not hurt him.[80] But he did have to acknowledge to his teacher that he did hurt him."[81] Older boys often tried to intimidate female teachers and male teachers of limited physical stature but many overcame this perception of weakness. Remembering "Miss Lou," a student from Kentucky reported, "We were all dreadfully afraid of her. She ruled despotically; to cross her meant one certain thing—a thrashing, tho' you might be the biggest fellow in the school."[82]

Even girls were not spared the rod. Recalling her schooldays in a school for young girls, Sarah Stuart Robbins wrote, "The ferule, and steel thimble without a top, though never indiscriminatingly used, were conspicuous on the desk before us, ready for emergencies. The thimble was a unique help in teaching, graduating the required punishment in a droll way. For serious offense we received so many blows with the ferrule—never hard ones, for Miss Davis had a tender heart. . . . For a lesser offense, two or three snaps of the thimble, innocuous but salutary, were administered upon some part of the child's head. That the teacher would have liked to kiss away the tears that followed the snaps there is no doubt; but she was too much of a martinet for that, so she contented herself with sniffs so loud and peculiar that we came to consider them a natural and necessary part of the proceeding."[83]

Some teachers were less compassionate than the sensitive Miss Davis when it came to dispensing discipline. In 1867 one Connecticut teacher's punishment of a habitually disobedient girl left her with "black marks across her hand, a bunch on her head, and one of her ear rings tore out."[84] Nonetheless, Robbins also noted that she and the children of her acquaintance in Miss Davis's schoolroom sat "not daring to move our tired limbs, not daring to whisper, rigid little automatons, every one of us."[85]

The following selection entitled "An Appeal to Scholars," while an extreme case, appeared in an 1855 student text, and it gives the reader reason to pause even today. "I am afraid that your minds have been prejudiced against the school. I am afraid that your good old nurse, or the silly housemaid has told you some dreadful stories about the school and the teachers, and that . . . your mamma has threatened to send you to school as punishment, and that you have been taught to consider the teachers as persons employed merely to inflict pain and torment upon the children in their care. . . . Those children who go to school impressed with the idea that it is a prison, in which they are to be shut up for a certain time, and that the teacher is no other than a tormentor whose business it is to inflict pain upon the little prisoners, might as well be kept at home. . . . But you who have been long at school know that none need be afraid who are disposed to do well: and that good scholars will be both praised and esteemed."[86]

John Roberts wrote frequently about his students' behavior and the stress it caused him as their teacher. He complained that the girls were "continually lugging one another by the ears, or to speak plainer, they are continually fomenting quarrels amongst themselves. Tattling is so common here that I am nearly falling into the practice myself."[87] He worried about his reaction to the persistence of this poor behavior. "My school was very noisy this afternoon, & I am afraid that I will lose my patience if [I] do not watch myself. No one knows the trials of the teacher until they try this business themselves."[88] When "two of the little girls got the mule into them and were not going to spell" (for a spelling demonstration for visitors), Roberts "had to send out for a stick before [he] could get them to come to terms."[89] At other times the man worried that he was not being strict enough. "I am afraid that I talk too much to my scholars. I must be a little more strict with them hereafter. I do not believe in being tyrannical or harsh. I think that school government should be mild but firm."[90] He later explained the reasons for his ambiguous position on discipline. "The teacher cannot then establish a strict discipline, for if he does he will soon find himself in an empty classroom, monarch of all he surveys. And if he does not keep good order, he is of no account. If he whips, he is too severe. If he does not, he is too lax. If he listens to the tales told by his pupils, he is partial; and if he dont [sic], he is of no account. If he scolds a young woman for disobeying orders, he just does it to show off big. If he lets her go, he is partial."[91]

Fortunately, others shared the more enlightened view expressed by instructors like Roberts. Despite the application of ferule and thimble, Robbins's recollections of Miss Davis were tender and obviously the product of a respectful relationship between student and teacher. "I do not know that any child gave her a flower, or even an apple; yet we valued her smile or word of approbation above rubies."[92] Hobart reported, "I have so got control of my Scholars by mild means that everyone is free from whispering without leave. I present them a handsome ticket every four weeks for being perfect. It works fine and is the best course for governing school."[93]

Hobart later expounded on this practice at length. "It is false that [students] will learn through fear or that success is found where the teacher exercises a tyrannical power and every pupil is afraid of him."[94] He noted, "I gave out the tickets in school this morning to all the scholars who had not whispered without leave. This is a system I have hit upon myself after trying the usual means to overcome the wholesale whispering that is the main feature of too many schools. By this course there is not half as much trouble and my mind is relieved from much of the care, and anxiety of any other course. I have become a disbeliever in punishment in the school room. I believe in mild means for I have found it the best. I have not been governed by anyone's theory—it is a result of my own experience and I can show as fine a school as anyone. I have no rulers or whips. I have scholars who love me and who are willing to act as I desire. How pleasant."[95]

Hobart noted that his students brought him grapes and apples. "They all like me," he wrote, "and speak well of me. This is pleasant & right. I hold that there should be good feeling and perfect love between pupil and teacher. The scholar should love and respect his instructor."[96] Yet even Hobart had some difficult students, and he was greatly distressed when he wrote, "School has not been as pleasant today as usual for I had to punish a scholar harder than I ever did before. I done it in Yankee style over the 'tail of 'im.'"[97] Hobart went on to become a district Superintendent of Schools in 1872 in Wisconsin, where he stressed that "thorough discipline and order was of great importance, and the methods pursued should be of the kind to prepare the pupil to become a law abiding citizen." He encouraged scholars "to be held to an account for their conduct during the day and be required to give a truthful report of the same."[98]

Attendance

Between 1800 and 1825 a number of free school societies were established to relieve the plight of poor urban children for whom no educational facilities existed. These private organizations collected funds through donations and opened schools for the poor. The New York Free School Society was founded by DeWitt Clinton in 1805, and it became the Public School Society in 1826. By the outbreak of the Civil War, only about 50 percent of children outside the South attended school with some regularity. Not everyone was convinced that public education was beneficial, but public sentiment was gradually becoming more favorable to the system. "People are beginning to see that their children can get a sound practical . . . education in our common schools." Some areas of the Midwest and New England had enrollments as high as 90 percent. Attendance in rural areas, however, continued to suffer from the fact that many parents "task their children heavily with farm labor, and [not] until such tasks are finished are they allowed to start school."[99] Observers noted that the students "[did] not come half of the time," and that the parents of these pupils "never [thought] of the time lost by the pupils."[100] Many educators noted that truancy was often the direct fault of the parents. "Their neglect of their own little concerns until they are so much behind hand as to have to stop their children from school to help them up . . . to their business."[101]

Progress

While schools in larger towns and cities offered periodic report cards and held more formal ceremonies awarding diplomas, rural schools were often ungraded and had no standard final examinations, report cards, or documents of completion. Although students were often grouped according to the level of reader that they were using, ability in terms of performance was the sole indicator of progress. In many boarding schools, it was the practice of the headmistress to evaluate each student's progress in front of the class. Lucy Sheldon attended Miss Pierce's School in Litchfield, Connecticut, and recorded the comments she received in her diary. One week she wrote that Miss Pierce "had seen no fault in me except holding my arms stiff, which made me appear awkward." The following week she was able to proudly report that Miss Pierce "found no fault."[102] Finding this a most disagreeable process, another student at the school, Betsey Reynolds, wrote, "I have missed one lesson this week, it is not very pleasing to tell our own faults—but Miss Pierce requires it of us. I hope to get my lessons perfect next week, as not to be under the obligation necessary of publishing it in my journal."[103]

Scholastic success was commonly given a showcase via exhibition bees and quizzes held for parents. Students demonstrated their expertise in spelling, arithmetic, geography, and history during these presentations. In addition to adulation, winners were given merit cards, certificates, and prizes such as books or prints. Hobart scheduled spelling competitions with regularity. While planning one such event he wrote, " I intend to have some pieces spoken and shall give each scholar a ticket who can spell the last six pages in the book. It is amusing to see what an interest is created by offering them some little inducement. I see them carry their books home at night and at noon they are studying the speller."[104] Some teachers disliked the reward concept. "I have offered no rewards of merit this term, and in fact I do not know as I shall ever adopt that plan again, as I think if a teacher can infuse the right kind of spirit into his pupils he will succeed better without rewards of merit."[105] Such spectacles were as much to impress the parents and school board as to evaluate the students. One teacher observed, "The parents who attended these exhibitions of stuffed memories were struck at the proficiency of their progeny, and retired with the impression that their children knew a great deal because they had parroted off so much that was all Greek to them."[106] Gifted students could pass through the entire local system of schools by age 14 or 15, but only the most well heeled could move on to college or university. A foreign visitor to New England found that most men had a basic education that stressed reading and writing, but that few exhibited the fine formal education available in Europe.

Academies and Boarding Schools

This age of common schools also saw an expansion of academies. By 1860 there were 250,000 students enrolled in 6,000 academies. Developed during the colonial era, academies were private schools with practical programs to teach specific skills. Many offered college preparatory courses. Some were run by local boards or city governments, others by religious denominations, but many small academies were run by individuals, or family pairs. In the early years of the 19th century, most towns in the North and East had some type of private school or academy. Some saw these

A public school class in sewing for girls. The layout of the room, with its rows of desks firmly secured to the floor, was a product of 19th-century efficiency in education. Inset are period examples of cards of merit.

institutions as a detriment to the common school. A letter written for the *American Traveler* in 1836 included the following, "There is scarcely a town or village, on the borders of the Hudson, that is not provided with one or more Academies, High Schools, and other institutions of learning, which are liberally supported, and generally well managed. It is in the common school system that we are deficient. The rich and middling classes are provided for while the poor are passed by, or almost entirely neglected. In New England, and particularly in Massachusetts, the common schools are of an elevated character, and are attended by all classes. The children of the rich and the poor meet together; they enjoy similar privileges and advantages. In New York, no person of ordinary means would think of sending his children to a free school. The number is small in proportion to the population; and were he ever so republican in his views, he would feel that he was depriving others, less able than himself, of the means of education. He therefore sends them to an Academy, and takes little or no interest in the management of free schools."[107]

The Union Academy in Doylestown, Pennsylvania, first opened in 1804 and could be considered fairly typical of these institutions. In 1835 Silas M. Andrews was selected to head the Classical Department. A letter written in 1836 in response to an inquiry about the school presents a good picture of a boarding school for boys in this period. "The course of Instruction to embrace the branches of both English and Classical that are preparatory to admission into college. As the pupils will be boarded, lodged and taught in my family dwelling and as I do not contemplate employing an assistant, but will act myself as sole Instructor, the number must of necessity be very limited." Andrews then added some of the more mundane details, including that there would be two vacations in the year, one in April, and one in October. The financial terms per quarter of 12 weeks was set at $50, while the full year of 44 weeks would require $183. "This includes all charges for Tuition, board, Washing, Lights, Fuel, use of Books, etc.," noted Andrews, "Students that remain during the vacation will be charged $2.50 per week for Board, Washing, etc. The students will be required to attend Bible Class and Public Worship on the Sabbath with my family, where Pews will be provided for them."[108]

Female Education

Boarding schools for girls were popular, but their course content was often neither rigorous nor academic. As the 18th century had drawn to a close, boarding schools for girls that taught only needlework and other decorative arts (along with some French) became the objects of ridicule for many observers. Nonetheless, while visiting from Sweden in 1849, the novelist Fredrika Bremer wrote from Philadelphia that she "was delighted with the drawing academy for young girls [where they] receive instruction . . . in drawing, painting, composition; in the making of designs for woven fabrics, carpets, or paper-hangings; in wood engraving, lithography, &c." The products of these students and their teachers were of such quality that "all the girls are able to already make considerable earnings" from the "numerous orders for designs, wood engravings, &c."[109]

Parents sent their young daughters to these institutions primarily to hone their social skills. Criticism of simple boarding schools for girls, however, led to the establishment of academies or seminaries for young ladies. For some institutions the changes were in name only, but the Female Seminary Movement, which began around 1815, established schools for girls that offered the same kind of intellectually challenging curriculum that was offered to boys. A girls' academy that opened in Petersburg, Virginia, in 1817 offered, "orthography [spelling], reading, writing, grammar, composition, belles-letters, geography, natural history, history of nations, chronology, natural philosophy and chemistry."[110] A male visitor to the Female Academy in Albany, New York, in 1836 noted that the course of studies included "French and Spanish languages, Natural History, Chemistry, and Botany." After meeting with the instructors and pupils, he concluded, "It appears to be of a useful and practical character . . . as the proficiency of the great number of young ladies demonstrates."[111]

Catharine Beecher, Emma Willard, and Mary Lyon were all leaders in the movement to improve secondary education for young women. Beecher was a prodigious writer on the subject throughout the century. Willard opened the Troy Female Seminary in 1821, and Lyon founded Mount Holyoke Seminary in 1837. Fifteen-year-old Elizabeth Rogers wrote in her 1849 diary, "Education is as important to women as to men. It cannot be expected that a mind that has been left to itself should be equal to one that has been highly cultivated. I am glad that they do teach such things now as found in public schools for girls. There is no reason why the minds of girls should not be cultivated as well as boy's."[112]

Rogers has provided great detail into her later education as a young woman of wealth in her late teens. Believing that she was needed at home to assist her fragile mother, she arranged a schedule that allowed her to continue her education while meeting her familial duties. The program she followed (given below) might not seem rigorous but it had merit in that Rogers was responsible for obtaining the required information herself by visiting libraries and museums or consulting with informed adults.

Mondays and Thursdays at half past nine in the morning I go to Mrs. Hodges . . . for a little more than an hour, when I read the lesson I have completed, and take those for the next time. Mondays are devoted to English history, Biography and a Question. For the history Mrs. H gives us notes one Monday for the next . . . [we] write an abstract of it . . . in a common blank book. This when carried to her next Monday is read aloud, and the composition and facts revised and corrected. Besides this book we keep what is called a book of key words. . . . Once in four weeks the study is reviewed. . . . We also keep another book called a chart, where in eight divisions one by the side of the other, we put down the name of the king, his death, etc. For Biography we select a particular man and write from any good authority we can obtain an abstract of his life. . . . Her third lesson is a question she gives us to look out on any subject such as . . . a list of important minerals, [or] a list of important treaties. . . . Everything is reviewed at certain intervals. . . . On Thursdays we learn French history in the same way [as English history]. . . . For the second lesson we have Geography . . . [and] another question. Besides this . . . we have to write a description of certain places in the form of a letter called a Tour, and to read any piece of prose or poetry we particularly like. Also to read at home the works and life of any author and give our opinion upon his character and works, and lastly to write a theme on any subject appointed. I take a lesson in French twice a week . . . for which I have written exercises.[113]

Frances Trollope toured the United States in 1827 and recorded her observations on American life. After attending the annual public exhibition at a school for young ladies in Cincinnati, she noted "with some surprise, that the higher branches of science were among the studies." Skeptical of the quality and depth of the knowledge, she reported, "One lovely girl took her degree in mathematics, and another was examined in moral philosophy. . . . I should fear that the time allowed to the fair graduates . . . for the acquirement of these various branches of education would seldom be sufficient to permit their reaching the eminence in each which their enlightened instructor anticipates. 'A quarter's' mathematics, or 'two quarters' political economy, moral philosophy, algebra and quadratic equations, would seldom, I should think, enable the teacher and the scholar, by their joint efforts to lay in such a stock of these sciences."[114] While in New York, however, Trollope was given a prospectus for the Brooklyn Collegiate Institute and was favorably impressed with the "enlarged scale of instruction proposed for young females."[115]

Despite advancements in curriculum, many young women attended schools with the goal of becoming an "accomplished miss" capable of attracting a husband and being a good wife. *Godey's Lady's Book* carried this parody:

> I've called for the purpose of placing my daughter at school.
> She's only thirteen I assure you,
> And remarkably easy to rule.
> I'd have her learn painting and music
> Gymnastics and dancing pray do,
> Philosophy, grammar and logic.
> You'll teach her to read of course too.[116]

Elizabeth Rogers wrote further of her school days in this regard. "A schoolgirl's life, although a happy one as a general rule, and full of interest, is nonetheless often a very weary one. To rise in the morning and hurry down and breakfast and hasten to school at nine o'clock; to study from that time till two, recess and all; and never be allowed to open your lips or move from your seat unless in a recitation; to come home, swallow down dinner, and seat yourself at the piano for an hour and a half; and then if the weather be too unpleasant to walk, to sit down to write a composition or learn some lesson that must be done during the week; and then to spend the whole evening in studying for the next day: to do this, I say, is enough to weary most anyone. And yet often and often do schoolgirls have to do so; and I sometimes feel, as I do tonight, as if I shall drop down dead with the fatigue of sitting still."[117]

As she entered her last year of school in 1853, Mary Service Steen of Philadelphia wrote, "[T]o think of leaving school is the thing I like least of all. This happens to be my last year as a school girl. I suppose I will have to become very prim & precise; and in case I should not recollect or indeed not know anything about what a person is saying, I will have to appear as if I did, because I am a 'finished lady' while now I am still a school girl I can show my ignorance if I choose."[118]

Free Public Education

The Infant School was largely imported from ideas formed in England. This form of institution provided rudimentary education to children between the ages of four and eight. In 1818 Boston appropriated money for the establishment of Infant Schools, and in 1827 an Infant School Society was founded in New York. The movement was later incorporated into the public school system. Also originating in England was the Monitorial School, an idea brought to America by Joseph Lancaster in 1806. Under the monitorial system, a headmaster taught the brighter students, who then as monitors or pupil-teachers taught small groups of other students. This system was widely used in the typical one-room schoolhouse common to many rural communities.

Common schools were well established by the 1860s, and the notion of free, tax-supported grammar school education was generally gaining acceptance. The concept of high schools, however, faced more resistance. In addition to the academies, much of secondary education was provided by Latin grammar schools, which were largely elite institutions for the college-bound. High schools were essentially an urban institution, founded with the intention of providing opportunity for boys who wished to become merchants or mechanics. Many schools had programs of manual or commercial training that were seen as terminal. Some students did pursue an English classical course even though they were not college-bound. The English classical school was established in Boston in 1821. It altered its program away from the Latin focus of the Latin grammar schools and toward English literature and practical and vocational courses. Through the efforts of James G. Carter, Massachusetts passed legislation providing for public secondary education in 1827.[119]

Northern cities began to see the need for serious mechanic's institutes and vocational training to replace the apprenticeships of the prior century. In 1841 the city of Middletown, Connecticut, forcibly removed all the students aged 9 to 16 from the district academies and placed them in the state's first public high school. In 1847 Hartford followed with a similar program, and in 1859 New Haven opened Hillhouse High School for both general studies and college preparation. Worcester Polytechnic Institute opened in 1868 in Massachusetts. Although some Northern states required larger cities to establish high schools, most people felt that this was a form of higher education and should not be part of the legal public school system. Nonetheless, by 1890 a number of cities throughout the nation had manual and vocational courses in high schools. Public secondary education for girls was even slower to develop. Boston, a leader in educational matters, did not open a high school for girls until 1855. In 1860 there were 300 high schools in the United States, 100 of which were in Massachusetts. By 1876 all states had public elementary school systems, and public high schools were steadily replacing private academies.

The school reformers and educational advocates of the 1840s were mostly Northerners. This contributed to a certain skepticism on the part of Southerners, who felt the public school systems of the North were at least partially responsible for anti-Southern attitudes in the decade preceding the war. The concept of free public education for whites was framed by educational leaders such as Horace Mann and Henry Barnard and became well established in principle by the Civil War. Following the conflict, it came into practice in most of the nation with the Northern cities leading the way. Immigrants saw education as a vehicle to "Americanize" their children. Laboring and middle-class families began to demand high-quality schools for their children so that they could advance economically and socially. Social architects saw it as a means of producing moral and self-sufficient citizens.

Most Southerners were opposed to tax supported public education. They preferred to send their children to private institutions. By 1860, only four Southern states and a few isolated communities had common school systems. Many children of plantation owners were taught by tutors. As sectional tensions increased, many Southerners regretted having allowed in Northerner tutors to teach their children. With the outbreak of hostilities, the distaste for Northern teachers spread rapidly. Advertisements for teachers soon came to request that applicants be natives of Dixie or from Europe. Although teaching was a respectable vocation, women who taught in the South were often pitied for the obvious dire financial situations into which such employment placed them. Wartime dangers eventually suspended many Southern schools, and the task of educating youngsters fell to their mothers. The war left the South in physical and economic ruin. Public education was given little attention in light of the myriad problems posed by Reconstruction. For the duration of the century, beleaguered Southern schools were marked by short terms, poorly trained teachers, limited resources, and scant tax support.

Gifted students could pass through the entire local system of schools by age 14 or 15, but only the most well-heeled could move on the college or university. A high school education was seen as terminal at this time. Although college enrollments grew throughout the antebellum period, the slow development of high schools provided for a less-expensive educational opportunity than the college or the academy for boys who wished to become mechanics or merchants. Most people felt that this level of education need not be funded by the public. Almost all high schools were located in urban areas until after the Civil War. In the decade after the war, only 2 percent of the 17-year-old population had graduated from high school.[120]

Parochial Education

Religious revival led to the establishment of Sunday Schools as a means of teaching the rudimentary principles of education to working children during their free time on the Sabbath. The idea is generally attributed to an Englishman, Robert Raikes, and it was promoted by Methodists and other religious groups. A Sunday School Society was organized in Philadelphia in 1791, and Sunday Schools were opened in most of the larger cities for the benefit of poor children. The Sunday School Society was prominent as a supporter of the public education movement in its earliest stages.

With the huge immigration of Irish Catholics during the first half of the 19th century, interest developed in parochial schools. The First Amendment to the Federal Constitution generally removed the possibility of an alliance between religious groups and the state or Federal governments with regard to education. Gradually, sectarian control over education in Virginia, Maryland, and Massachusetts (in operation from colonial times) declined. However, the development of free public schools under state control caused a continuing controversy over questions of state aid for religious programs that were a common feature of 19th-century education.

A number of parochial schools had been operated under Catholic auspices in the 17th and 18th centuries, but the large-scale development of a parochial school system took place in the 19th century. Many Catholic children attended public schools, but their parents were often concerned because of the systematic use of King James version of the Bible in lessons, the singing of Protestant hymns, and most distressingly, the anti-Catholic slant that was prevalent in textbooks. Bishop John Hughes of New York protested to the New York Public School Society, demanding that they make funds available for Catholic schools. When Jewish and Presbyterian leaders also began to request funds for the establishment of parochial schools, city leaders held a public debate concerning the dispute that arose concerning the idea of public funds being used by clearly religious institutions.

The great school debates of 1840 were one of New York City's major events. Discussions were carried over into the press and even received national attention. Citizens packed the galleries to hear Bishop Hughes rebut his attackers. "We cannot send our children where they will . . . lose respect for their parents and the faith of their fathers, and come out turning their noses up at the name of Catholic," declared Hughes. Following the debates, public school principals were charged by the New York Board of Education with removing by hand all passages from textbooks thought to be offensive to sectarian groups.[121]

In October 1841, Hughes made what his opponents considered an "inflammatory speech" supporting the alteration of school funding in favor of parochial education and attempting "to mix up religion with politics—an unpalatable dish." Philip Hone was in New York in 1841 when Governor William Seward authorized the use of state money "for the establishment of separate schools for the children of foreigners, and their instruction by teachers of their own faith and language." The public outcry that followed was as immediate as it was massive. Seward was faced with the partisan charge of trying to curry favor with the Irish Catholics, and it was alleged that he was in a conspiracy with Hughes. The final result of the New York controversy was the elimination of all Bibles and Bible reading from the tax-supported schools. Hone observed, "Bishop Hughes . . . deserves a cardinal's hat at least for what he has done in placing Irish Catholics upon the necks of native New Yorkers."[122]

In 1829 the Plenary Council of Baltimore had promulgated the establishment of a system of Catholic schools. These began as parish elementary schools in many cities and developed into a system of regional high schools. In both 1854 and 1884 the council at Baltimore again charged all parishes with the task of providing sectarian schools for their young. By the end of the 1880s, Catholic schools numbered almost 3,000. Parish high schools offered relatively narrow coursework, consisting mainly of Latin, literature, grammar, and religion. Some secondary schools were established to train young men for the priesthood. Lutheran, Quaker, and Jewish schools were also established but none nearly in the same numbers as the Catholic schools.

This struggle was important because it was the denomination colleges and universities that became the focus of cultural advancement in much of America at the time. Although many were short-lived, more than 500 denominational colleges were founded in the 19th century, evidencing the continued importance of religion in American life.[123] Hughes, although controversial and lacking in restraint, was later made archbishop, and he used his power to create a privately funded Catholic school system in New York. The leading figure in Catholic education at this time, however, was the more pragmatic Bishop John L. Spaulding, who emphasized the Americanization of Catholic educational thought and also recommended a denominational public school system.

Higher Education

Post-secondary education grew slowly prior to 1880. Professions such as teaching, law, and even medicine were often taught in a manner similar to an apprenticeship and remained open to people who had not completed college. There were 11 major colleges established during the colonial period: Harvard (1636), William and Mary (1693), Yale (1701), Princeton (1746), University of Pennsylvania (1751), Columbia (King's College, 1754), Brown (1764), Rutgers (1766), Dartmouth (1770), Hampton-Sydney (1776), and Transylvania (1780). Twelve more colleges were formed from the end of the Revolution to 1800; 33 from 1800 to 1830; and 180 from 1830 to 1865. Mount Holyoke Seminary (1837) in Massachusetts, and Elmira College (1855) and Vassar (1865) in New York were established solely for women. Other colleges were established for women, and some Midwestern state universities admitted both genders. By 1870 there were approximately 500 colleges and universities nationwide, but they served only 50,000 students.

College studies were heavily classical in their content. Students read Latin and Greek from Livy, Cicero, Homer, Plato, and others. As with primary instruction, recitation was the most common form of instruction. Work in the sciences, which covered physics and astronomy with some chemistry and geology, consisted mostly of lectures with occasional laboratory demonstrations. Mathematics explored geometry, trigonometry, and calculus and encompassed memorization of rules with some effort to apply them to practical problems. Rhetoric students studied composition as well as public speaking and formal oratory. Other studies included philosophy and formal logic. The last quarter of the century saw some expansion of college offerings to include economics, history, literature, and modern language. Entrance requirements became more rigorous and graduate schools first appeared.

The year 1862 was an important year for higher education, even amid the turmoil of civil war. The Morrill Act passed through Congress, establishing a system of land-grant colleges that provided funds for state institutions of learning. It was also the year in which the Federal government at Washington made the first provisions for the schooling of blacks. The involvement of Federal authorities in education was clearly extra-constitutional, but it was not unequivocally prohibited. The earmarking of Federal funds for education was only possible at this time because the Southern delegates to Congress had largely abandoned their seats in the House and Senate in favor of places in the Confederate government. While the effect of both pieces of legislation may have been felt more after the war, they nonetheless showed a positive attitude toward a role for the Federal government in education.

College instruction was based on the same methods of memorization and oral recitation fundamental to the 17th century. In much the same way that physical activity was thought to be preparation for the life of a laborer, the function of higher education was thought to be the training of the mind through mental discipline rather than instruction in specific course content. As late as the 1850s, an observer noted the system used at Yale: "The professor or tutor sat in a box, with his students before and beneath him, and the so-called education consisted of questions upon a textbook. Not questions to elicit thought, but simply questions to find out how nearly the students could repeat the words of the book, or, if it were a classic, to find out how little they knew of Latin or Greek grammar."[124]

The first attempt to establish a college curriculum based on subject area content was made in the 1820s at Harvard, but other colleges were slow to adopt the idea. By the 1840s medicine and law—the two most commonly pursued professions at college—were being taught in many places as separate curricula. The editor of the *American Journal of Education* wrote in 1862 the following description of college education: "All branches of human learning may be embraced in the proper schedule of university instruction; but has any university given equal attention to all branches of education? What are called colleges in our country, all aim at fitting young men for the civil professions—Law, Medicine, and Theology."[125]

Alden Partridge, an educator and Superintendent of the U.S. Military Academy at West Point, was very concerned about the deficiencies of the college curriculum, which seemingly prepared students only "to become members of the college or university." After four years of study at college, he asked if the student "had been sufficiently directed to those great and important branches of national industry and sources of wealth—agriculture, commerce, and manufactures." He further denounced the large amounts of idle time afforded students away from their studies, the quantities of disposable money available to them, and the single-minded course of study to which each was put.[126]

Unfortunately, the lack of restraint so obvious in politics and reform movements was also characteristic of college life. In general, student manners were good with boys doffing their caps to faculty and attending early morning religious services. Yet there were long periods when the relations among administration, faculty, community, and student body were strained at the very least. Many disagreements escalated beyond the resort to fisticuffs and resulted in smashed furniture and windows, the use of guns and explosives, and the effusion of blood. One college in New York found it necessary to specifically forbid blasphemy, robbery, fornication, theft, forging, and dueling among the students, as well as the assaulting, wounding, or striking of the members of the faculty or the president of the college.

Rioting among the students was somewhat of a tradition at many colleges that were considered very good institutions of learning. In 1807, Harvard students protested the quality of the food; in 1823 more than half the senior class of 70 was expelled; and in 1834, the entire sophomore class was dismissed for the remainder of the year. At Yale in 1830, Professor Benjamin Silliman attended his laboratory with two loaded pistols during a period of student unrest, and in 1834, a tutor was fatally stabbed when he tried to subdue a window-breaking rioter. In both 1841 and 1858, Yale students brawled with the New Haven fire brigade, and a student shot and killed a fireman. At Princeton in 1817, of the entire student body of 200 scholars, 125 were expelled after a pistol was shot through the door of a tutor's room and a bomb exploded in Nassau Hall. Three years later, a Princeton student was stabbed by his fellows in a riot between the sons of working-class and upper-class families.

The students at Amherst became involved in local Massachusetts politics, voting themselves en masse into control of the city government in 1827. In 1831 they seized a Revolutionary War cannon and threatened to loose it upon the members of the faculty and the constables that had come to their protection. In 1835, a Southern sympathizer caned a member of the antislavery element among the Amherst graduating class and disrupted the commencement. Students at South Carolina College in 1856 surged into the town and fought with police for days. Many of these were cadets armed with muskets taken from the military program; only the arrival of the local militia ended the engagement.

The records of most colleges were filled with incidents of students apprehended for violating campus rules, and most infractions were punished by small fines, demerits, or dismissal. Yet it was a fortunate institution that did not record a more serious uprising of the entire student body. With few exceptions these disturbances had no ideological or political basis, but stemmed rather from some specific campus problem, usually with roots in eating, drinking, wenching, or simple boredom. When the students were not in disagreement among themselves, they found enemies in the town or among the faculty. The problems that bedeviled higher education may have merely reflected the degree to which violence had become a part of American life. The Civil War dispelled much of the on-campus violence as students with belligerent intent joined the armies North and South. The post-war colleges enjoyed an unusually quiet century of peace.

Education for Blacks

As far back as the colonial era, many slaveholders felt it a duty to teach slaves about the Bible and even permitted them to read. As the abolitionist movement grew and tensions increased between slaveholders and abolitionists, many Southerners turned away from this practice and actually discouraged teaching slaves to read. Following Nat Turner's rebellion in 1831, most Southern states prohibited the teaching of blacks, fearing that the written word could be used as a mechanism for spreading further slave insurrections. At the outbreak of the Civil War, only about 5 percent of slaves could read. After the Emancipation Proclamation of 1863, Federal troops set the slaves free as they occupied areas of the Confederacy. Many white reformers and many of the former slaves attempted to establish schools for blacks to help others prepare for freedom. Often, Union commanders occupying an area mandated the creation of such schools or allowed their creation by Northern missionaries. These practices led to the creation of the Freeman's Bureau in 1865, through which the Federal government took a formal stance toward the education of former slaves.

Northern teachers who traveled to the South during the war suffered tremendous physical and emotional hardships. Southerners deeply resented them and commonly refused them any accommodations. The Northern agencies that sent them generally overworked and underpaid them. Moreover, the condition of blacks in the South after years or decades of privation—at least some of which was due to the shortages brought on by the length of the war—greatly distressed most of the teachers, who were generally unrealistically idealistic rather than pragmatic in their expectations. What passed for schoolrooms were often worse than the most desolate of Northern facilities, and textbooks and instructional materials were all but nonexistent.

The abolitionists in the North had provided for the education of some free blacks. Some common school systems established schools for minority groups such as Amerindians, and free blacks. Yet in Boston, the cradle of the abolitionist movement, there were only two primary schools for black children in the 1840s. Considering the support that many regular schools were given, one can imagine the facilities that would have been provided when a separate school was established for a minority group. An observer of a "Colored School" remarked that although the black pupils "were not so far advanced . . . if the same facilities be afforded to them, which are given to the children in other schools in the borough, they will soon compare favorably with them, not only in the lower branches, but also in the more advanced departments."[127]

Moreover, the idea of racially integrated schools was vehemently opposed almost everywhere. When Prudence Crandall attempted to integrate her fashionable Connecticut school for girls in 1831, the white students were quickly withdrawn by outraged parents. Miss Crandall, herself, was insulted, threatened, and stoned. In the interest of the safety of her students, she ultimately acquiesced by closing the school and disbanding the student body in 1833. In 1846 a group of black citizens petitioned the Boston School Committee to cease the practice of segregation. While an investigation found the black schools were substandard, no action was taken. Shortly thereafter, Benjamin Roberts attempted to enroll his five-year-old daughter, Sarah, in a neighborhood school closer to her home than the one designated for black children. Sarah was turned away from that school and several others as well. Roberts filed suit on his daughter's behalf in 1849. The case advanced to the Massachusetts State Supreme Court, but Sarah's petition was denied. Her father and a group known as the Negro School Abolition Society took their concerns to the state legislature. In 1855 Massachusetts was the first state in the nation to pass a law preventing discrimination in schools, but most schools prior to the Civil War continued to reject the registration of black students.

Notes

1. Lucy Larcom, *A New England Girlhood* (Boston: Northeastern University Press, 1986), 39, 44.

2. Francesco Cordasco, *A Brief History of Education* (Totowa, N.J.: Littlefield, Adams & Co., 1970), 124–125.

3. Thomas H. Burrowes, *Report of the Superintendent of Common Schools of Pennsylvania* (Harrisburg: A. Boyd Hamilton, 1861), 14.

4. Cordasco, *Brief History*, 120–121.

5. Burrowes, *Report of the Superintendent*, 24, 20.

6. Ibid., 20–21.

7. Gail Collins, *America's Women* (New York: Perennial, 2004), 108.

8. Philip P. Mason, ed., *Copper Country Journal: The Diary of Schoolmaster Henry Hobart, 1863–1864* (Detroit: Wayne State University Press, 1991), 143.

9. Ibid., 117.

10. Clifton Johnson, *Old Time Schools and School–books* (New York: Dover Publications, 1963), 130–131.

11. Sarah Mondale and Sarah B. Patton, ed., *School: The Story of American Public Education* (Boston: Beacon Press, 2001), 28.

12. Burrowes, *Report of the Superintendent*, 81.

13. Collins, *America's Women*, 109.

14. Johnson, *Old Time Schools*, 116.

15. Burrowes, *Report of the Superintendent*, 20–97.

16. Ibid., 81, 97.

17. Johnson, *Old Time Schools*, 117.

18. Mason, *Copper Country Journal*, 143.

19. Sarah Stuart Robbins, *Old Andover Days: Memories of a Puritan Childhood* (Boston: Pilgrim Press, 1908), 61.

20. Mason, *Copper Country Journal*, 159.

21. Ibid., 203.

22. Mondale and Patton, *School*, 28–29.

23. Blackboards were not common until 1820. An early reference to a blackboard can be found in an arithmetic book published in 1809, where the method of creating this innovative teaching aid is explained in a footnote.

24. Burrowes, *Report of the Superintendent*, 80.

25. Ralph Walker, "America's Schoolmaster: McGuffey and His Readers," *American History Illustrated* (May 1973): 14–25, 19.

26. Ibid., 19.

27. Ibid., 23–24.

28. Cordasco, *Brief History*, 133–134.

29. Mason, *Copper Country Journal*, 232–233.

30. Burrowes, *Report of the Superintendent*, 40.

31. Shirley Blotnick Moskow, *Emma's World: An Intimate Look at Lives Touched by the Civil War Era* (Far Hills, N.J.: New Horizon Press, 1990), 193.

32. Burrowes, *Report of the Superintendent*, 83.

33. Ibid., 91.

34. Johnson, *Old Time Schools*, 117.

35. Daniel E. Sutherland, *The Expansion of Everyday Life, 1860–1876* (Fayetteville: University of Arkansas Press, 2000), 98.

36. Ibid.

37. Collins, *America's Women*, 107.

38. J. Merton England, ed., *Buckeye Schoolmaster: A Chronicle of Midwestern Rural Life, 1852–1865* (Bowling Green, Ohio: Bowling Green State University Popular Press, 1996), 182.

39. Mason, *Copper Country Journal*, 217.

40. Burrowes, *Report of the Superintendent*, 33.

41. J. P. Wickersham, *Report of the Superintendent of Public Instruction of the Commonwealth of Pennsylvania for the Year Ending June 3, 1878* (Harrisburg, Pa.: Lane S. Hart, State Printer, 1878), 116.

42. Steven Mintz, *Huck's Raft: A History of American Childhood* (Cambridge, Mass.: Belknap Press/Harvard University Press, 2004), 91.

43. Mondale and Patton, ed., *School*, 52–53.

44. Charlotte Haven, "A Girl's Letter from Nauvoo," *The Overland Monthly* Vol. xvi Dec. 1890 No. 96, 621. http://www.state.me.us/sos/arc/edu/turner/72repl.htm (accessed October 2006).

45. Collins, *America's Women*, 107.

46. Burrowes, *Report of the Superintendent*, 43.

47. Ibid., 27.

48. England, *Buckeye Schoolmaster*, 229.

49. Robbins, *Old Andover Days*, 63.

50. Moskow, *Emma's World*, 122.

51. Ibid., 139.

52. Collins, *America's Women*, 106.

53. Sutherland, *Expansion of Everyday Life*, 99.

54. England, *Buckeye Schoolmaster*, 199.

55. Ibid., 178.

56. Anonymous Author, *Marmaduke Multiply's Merry Method of Making Minor Mathematicians* (1841; repr., New York: Dover Publications, 1971), 13, 65.

57. Mason, *Copper Country Journal*, 220.

58. Burrowes, *Report of the Superintendent*, 42.

59. Daniel Leach, *Leach's Complete Spelling Book* (Philadelphia: H. Cowperthwait & Co., 1859), 140.

60. Moskow, *Emma's World*, 99.

61. Burrowes, *Report of the Superintendent*, 36.

62. Ibid., 21.

63. Ibid., 22.

64. Mason, *Copper Country Journal*, 137.

65. Sutherland, *Expansion of Everyday Life*, 101.

66. S. Augustus Mitchell, *An Easy Introduction to the Study of Geography* (Philadelphia: Thomas Cowperthwait & Co., 1852), 5.

67. W. H. McGuffey, *Eclectic First Reader for Children with Pictures* (Cincinnati: Truman & Smith Publishing, 1836), 15.

68. Ibid., 16–17.

69. *Marmaduke Multiply's Merry Method*, 41.

70. Ibid., 33.

71. Johnson, *Old Time Schools*, 317.

72. Robbins, *Old Andover Days*, 69.

73. Salem Town, A.M., *The Fourth Reader or Exercises in Reading and Speaking* (Cooperstown, N.Y.: H. & E. Phinney, 1849), iv.

74. McGuffey, *Eclectic First Reader*, 5.

75. Caroline Cowles Richards, *Village Life in America, 1852–1872* (New York: Corner House Historical Publications, 1997), 132.

76. Ellen Swartzlander, *Mister Andrew's School, 1837–1842: The Students' Journal* (Doylestown, Pa.: Bucks County Historical Society, 1958), 19.

77. Johnson, *Old Time Schools*, 80.

78. Sutherland, *Expansion of Everyday Life*, 100.

79. Larcom, *New England Girlhood*, 151.

80. Students at the Doylestown Grammar School were elected by their classmates to certain roles in order to assist the teacher. Titled positions included a Regulator and Deputy, a Monitor and Deputy, a Committee of Two, and a Journalist. The Regulator saw that school was called at the appointed hours, announced the time for Rhetorical Reading, gave notice of recess and the return to study.

81. Swartzlander, *Mister Andrew's School*, 89.

82. Sutherland, *Expansion of Everyday Life*, 100.

83. Robbins, *Old Andover Days*, 61–62.

84. Sutherland, *Expansion of Everyday Life*, 100.

85. Robbins, *Old Andover Days*, 61.

86. Oliver Angell, *Angell's Fifth Reader: Containing Lessons in Reading and Spelling* (Philadelphia: E. H. Butler & Co., 1855), 246–247.

87. England, *Buckeye Schoolmaster*, 171.

88. Ibid..

89. Ibid., 172.

90. Ibid., 191.

91. Ibid., 177.

92. Robbins, *Old Andover Days*, 58.

93. Mason, *Copper Country Journal*, 218.

94. Ibid., 212.

95. Ibid., 230–231.

96. Ibid., 212.

97. Ibid., 216.F

98. Ibid., 323.

99. Burrowes, *Report of the Superintendent*, 27.

100. England, *Buckeye Schoolmaster*, 163.

101. Burrowes, *Report of the Superintendent*, 51–52.

102. Susan Burrows Swan, *Plain & Fancy: American Women and Their Needlework, 1650–1850* (Austin, Tex.: Curious Works Press, 1977), 71.

103. Mary Antoine de Julio, *What a Rich Reward: Betsey Reynolds Voorhees and the Collection of Her Handiwork* (Fort Johnson, N.Y.: Montgomery County Historical Society, 1986), 8.

104. Mason, *Copper Country Journal*, 253.

105. England, *Buckeye Schoolmaster*, 151.

106. Sutherland, *Expansion of Everyday Life*, 102.

107. Anonymous, *Letters about the Hudson River, and Its Vicinity Written in 1835–1837* (New York: Freeman Hunt & Co., 1837), 134–135.

108. Swartzlander, *Mister Andrew's School*, 5.

109. Marion Tinling, ed., *With Women's Eyes: Visitors to the New World, 1775–1918* (Norman: University of Oklahoma Press, 1993), 64.

110. Collins, *America's Women*, 108.

111. *Letters about the Hudson River*, 136–137.

112. P.A.M. Taylor, ed., *More than Common Powers of Perception: The Diary of Elizabeth Rogers Mason Cabot* (Boston: Beacon Press, 1991), 68–69.

113. Ibid., 89–91.

114. Frances Trollope, *Domestic Manners of the Americans* (1832; repr., Mineola, N.Y.: Dover Publications, 2003), 49.

115. Ibid., 210.

116. Collins, *America's Women*, 108.

117. Taylor, *More than Common Powers*, 63–64.

118. Swan, *Plain & Fancy*, 77.

119. James G. Carter is called the "Father of the Massachusetts School System" because of his efforts to bring about free public secondary education. Carter wrote numerous essays against private education, which he feared would give rise to a class culture. He also labored to establish Normal Schools to better train common school teachers.

120. Carroll C. Calkins, ed., *The Story of America* (Pleasantville, N.Y.: Reader's Digest Association, 1975), 127.

121. Mondale and Patton, *School*, 36.

122. Allan Nevins, ed., *The Diary of Phillip Hone, 1828–1851*, vols. 1 and 2 (New York: Dodd, Mead & Co., 1927), 570.

123. Cordasco, *Brief History*, 131.

124. Morris Bishop, "The Lower Depths of Higher Education," *American Heritage* 22, no. 1 (December 1969): 59.

125. Henry Barnard, *Military Schools and Courses of Instruction in the Science and Art of War, in France, Prussia, Austria, Russia, Sweden, Switzerland, Sardinia, England, and the United States* (1872), The West Point Military Library Series (Westport, Conn.: Greenwood Press, 1969), 739.

126. Ibid., 840.

127. Burrowes, *Report of the Superintendent*, 67.

15

Children as Workers

Now isn't it a pity,
That a girl as pretty as I,
Should be sent to a factory
To pine away and die.
—"Letters from Susan," *The Lowell Offering*, 1844

Among the Sheaves

The expansion of a market economy and an industrial manufacturing base had dramatic effects on the children of the 19th century. Growing consumerism and mass production made middle-class children, in particular, the direct beneficiaries of their family's more privileged social position, and they were the first generation outside the social elite to enjoy mass-produced toys and games. Unlike children from earlier times, they were largely protected from the outside world and kept secure in a home where childhood was celebrated as a stage of life full of innocence and purity. In these homes, children's labor was not a necessity. Although they were expected to be of assistance to their family, the purpose of their household chores was to instill good habits and to teach lessons of personal responsibility. Girls were expected to sew and mend for practical purposes, but they were also expected to practice embroidery and other decorative needle arts. Catherine Elizabeth Havens wrote in her diary, "[M]y sister taught me to sew when I was five years old, and to darn little holes in a stocking, and she thought I was funny to want to do the biggest hole first, but I did, so as to get done with it. She gives me the skeins of sewing silk to wind, and I love to get the knots out."[1] Girls assisted their mothers with housework and sometimes with cooking; and both young boys and girls helped in the garden. Boys also ran errands, brought in firewood and water, and tended the horse if a family had one.

For farming and working-class families, however, the situation regarding child labor was very different. The growing market economy put tremendous stress on both groups. Farmers—fathers, mothers, and children—worked together through necessity, and most boys from mining, lumbering, and seafaring communities followed their fathers into the mines, the forests, or aboard ship. They had done so for generations. What was new was that many children from manufacturing regions now entered the impersonal environment of the factory rather than an apprenticeship with a local master. The factory, unlike the shop, left the child with no skill, no trade, no place in the community—only the memory of mind-numbing hours of repetitive drudgery. Yet by comparison the factory or mill paid well for youthful labor, and the value of the income of even young children (8-, 10-, or 12-year-old boys and girls) was often an essential part of a family's economic health. Children's earnings often amounted to 20 percent of the family's total income, and it was not unusual for teenage boys to earn more than their fathers.

Children who grew up on farms had always been expected to contribute to the family's productivity. A children's story about a 10-year-old farm girl has her "beating up the beds and making tidy the upper rooms . . . scouring the knives . . . darning great holes in stockings . . . digging for parsnips . . . sewing . . . learning to milk [cows], [feed] chickens, and doing just things that were disagreeable to an older person."[2] Small children helped with simple, unskilled tasks and their work increased in difficulty as they grew in size and skill. Ellen Chapman Rollins remembered that in mid-century New England, "the driving of cows to pasture passed by rotation from one child to another" and that both boys and girls worked "among the sheaves" in the field.[3]

Labor's Age

Girls were often employed in tasks related to the production and mending of clothing. They were taught the carding and spinning of wool at a young age and took up knitting as soon as they could hold and manipulate the needles. Children as young as four could knit stockings. By six, girls, and some boys as well, were making important contributions to the family's supply of stockings and mittens. Girls also helped to process food for either immediate consumption or preservation. Even very young children could snap the ends off beans or husk corn. Churning butter was another task that could be performed by children. The process was uncomplicated but boring. To help pass the time and to maintain a good rhythm, children were taught to sing to the rhyme, "Come, Butter, Come."

> Come, Butter, Come.
> Come, Butter, Come.
> Johnny's waiting at the gate.
> He wants a piece of butter cake.
> Come, Butter, Come.[4]

Louisa May Alcott described the scene of a household preparing for Thanksgiving with the help of its children. "Four young girls stood . . . busily chopping meat, pounding spice, and slicing apples, and [their] tongues . . . went as fast of their hands. . . . Two small boys sat on the wooden settle shelling corn for popping, and picking out the biggest nuts from the goodly store their own hands had gathered in October."[5] Zadoc Long observed his five-year-old son, John, as he shelled corn. "He has an old box with an iron rod laid lengthwise upon it, which is held in place with an old day book and by seating himself upon it a straddle the iron. He shells fast the ears of corn by holding them with one hand against the sharp edge of the iron, while with the other he turns them first one way, then the other—very sociable all the while."[6]

Boys were never without work due to the endless need for firewood and water, and they were expected to give regular care to the livestock. Many of their duties were outdoors. "Help was needed with farm chores in any season. Work continued throughout the cold weeks of winter with the gathering of logs for firewood and fencing materials."[7] Feeding and watering the animals generally fell to the boys of the household. They were also expected to guard the livestock in the pasture. They helped with preparing the fields for planting and sewing the seeds in the furrows. At harvest they helped gather in the crops. Boys hunted and fished; and, while this may have some recreational value for them, the food these activities provided was a welcome and, sometimes, necessary addition to the table or the larder.

Maple sugaring heralded the arrival of spring and all hands were needed to execute this great labor. Boys joined adult males as they spent several nights in the sugar camp set up in the woods among the last of the winter snows. Surely this must have been an exciting time for the boys, with the teams dragging the sugar sledge from tree to tree and the maple-scented smoke of the fires filling the forests. The boys collected sap buckets and helped to process the tremendous volume of wood needed to maintain the fires under the huge sugar pots as they boiled off the syrup. Remembering his youth, Horace Greeley wrote, "Being the older son of a poor and hard-working farmer, struggling to pay off the debt he had incurred in buying his farm, and to support his increasing family, I was early made aquatinted with labor."[8]

All farm children were engaged in harvesting and weeding the household or kitchen garden, gathering nuts, collecting eggs, and picking berries. Even the very young were given pails or baskets and were taken by older siblings to gather berries. Some entrepreneurial youngsters would gather wild cherries, known as choke cherries, and sell them. These were used for making cherry rum or cherry bounce. A good-sized tree would yield approximately six bushels. Young boys often used spare time, particularly in winter, to make birch splinter brooms that could be sold to storekeepers. Older children would lend a hand in making hay—gathering and collecting the bundles of sweet-smelling grass into stacks or driving the hay wagon from field to barn.

When families had a surfeit of children in the home, one or two of the children, especially young girls, might be hired out to assist with housework for other families. Often such placement was done in the community by word of mouth, but some families resorted to advertisements like this one that ran in a local newspaper in 1837, "A place in the country wanted for a smart active girl 11 years of age, in a small family where her services would be useful. All of her clothing would be furnished."[9]

The expanding market economy also had its influence on country towns. Some household activities expanded to such an extent that they became manufacturing workplaces. Farm families from Philadelphia produced four times as much cloth for sale as did the area's textile mills in 1809. More shoes were produced by Massachusetts farm households than by all the professional shoemakers in the country in the early decades of the century. Enterprising businessmen like country store owner, Dexter Whittemore, provided palm leaves to local families who braided them into hats in exchange for store credits. Children were expected to contribute to these endeavors as well. Girls assisted their mothers in braiding straw. They also would stitch shoe uppers for their brothers and fathers to finish. As manufacturing increased after 1820, such domestic commercial production in rural areas decreased sharply and the production of the factories and mills rose sharply.

Employing children in laborious tasks was a necessity in a time when farm families had to compete in an increasingly industrialized economy. After her father died, Lucy Larcom's mother decided to move to the city and set up a boarding house. Lucy wrote, "The change involved a great deal of work. 'Boarders' signified a large house, [and] many beds. . . . Such piles of sewing accumulated before us! [O]ur little child-fingers had to take their part. But the seams of those sheets did look to me as if they were miles long!"[10] Describing a New Hampshire farm family, Alcott wrote, "There were no servants, for the little daughters were Mrs. Bassett's only maids, and the stout boys helped their father, all working happily together with no wages but love, learning in the best manner the use of the heads and hands with which they were to make their own way in the world."[11] Many rural parents believed that it was these life skills that the children would need in order to maintain their own families and that they were more important than reading and writing. Rural children attended school for shorter periods of time during the year and for fewer years than urban children. One rural Pennsylvania superintendent complained in 1878, "The remarkably mild weather of the past winter operated to keep many of the older pupils out of school, at work, and very materially shortened the time of attendance of many others."[12]

The loss of male family members and farm workers to the Civil War increased the burdens already sustained by the farming families. The Confederacy was the first to initiate a mandatory draft that removed many poor white farm workers from the soil, but exempted many of the trades and slaveowners with more than 20 slaves. The Federal government followed with its own draft that also exempted tradesmen and mechanics. Yet the North filled its ranks largely from the unemployed immigrant populations of the cities. This left lower-class farm families at a distinct manpower disadvantage, and brought forth in many quarters accusations of "Rich man's war, Poor man's fight!" Children were forced to fill the need for labor. At age 12 Marion Drury had "to assume the work and responsibilities of a man because most of the farmhands had gone into the army." Anna Shaw was only 14 when she took on her father's and brothers' jobs, clearing fields and teaching school in addition to her sewing, cleaning, and tending boarders. At 15 Helen Brock was branding calves and erecting fences, and Fannie Eisele began to plow the family fields when she was only 10 years old.[13]

Frontier life often blurred labor's age and gender distinctions. Children cared for the livestock, hunted, fished, hauled water, collected wood and buffalo chips, cooked, cared for the sick, and attended their younger siblings. They were impressed into service as soon as they could handle the task. One Kansas father bragged that his two-year-old son could "fetch up cows out of the stock fields . . . carry in stove wood and . . . feed the hogs."[14] Children who lived near Western mining towns found there were many opportunities to earn money for the family. Enterprising youngsters sold butter, bacon, and wild game. Others offered their services cooking, cleaning, and doing odd jobs. Laura Ingalls Wilder's popular *Little House* books recount her childhood on the frontier. As a young child, she helped with housework, cared for her siblings, tended the animals, and helped with the crops. As she got older, she sewed shirts in town to bring cash into the family. She also took employment as a waitress and maid in a hotel in town, and when only 15, she began teaching school.

The Mills

The textile mills of New England offered employment to boys and girls as well as young adults. At the end of the 18th century, Samuel Slater built the first successful water-powered textile mill in the United States. With a staff of children aged 7 to 12, he successfully demonstrated the profitability of spinning yarn while utilizing youthful labor. He divided the factory work into such simple steps that even very young children could do the work. Jobs ranged from picking foreign matter (leaves, pods, and dirt) from the cotton to operating the carding and spinning machines. The children proved to be good workers who produced a quality product under Slater's supervision. As mills continued to expand, so did the need for children to work in them. By 1830, 55 percent of the mill workers in Rhode Island were children. In order to avoid accusations of alienating children from their homes, Slater often hired entire families to work for him, a method that came to be known as the Rhode Island system. "A few sober and industrious families of at least five children each, over the age of eight are wanted," advertised a newspaper in 1831.[15] A mutual dependence developed as the mill relied on the children and the families relied upon the money the children earned from the mill.

With the 1823 opening of the first factory in Lowell, Massachusetts, a new system of hiring factory workers developed. The Boston Associates, who owned the mill, recruited young girls from farms and rural areas to live and work in the cotton mills under paternalistic supervision designed to protect their respectability and optimize their productivity. The mill advertised for girls between 15 and 30, but some younger girls were

A period illustration of the workers coming to their shift at the mills at Lowell (background). Mixed in among the adult workers are young women and boys.

accepted. In the factories the overseers were responsible for maintaining work discipline and high moral standards. All unmarried girls not living with their families were required to "board in one of the boarding houses belonging to the Company, and conform to the regulations of the house where they board."[16] The boarding house keepers enforced strict curfews and codes of conduct. Boarders were "considered answerable for any improper conduct in their houses."[17] In addition to behavior, "regular attendance on public worship on the Sabbath was required for all workers." The company would "not employ any person who [was] habitually absent."[18]

The boarding houses were well maintained and served three substantial meals daily. One girl reported, "for dinner, meat, potatoes, with vegetables, tomatoes and pickles, pudding or pie, with bread coffee or tea."[19] The girls received good care. "Let no one suppose that the 'factory girls' are without guardian. We are placed in the care of overseers who feel under moral obligations to look after our interests."[20] Overcrowding, however, was a problem. Observers reported, "The young women sleep upon an average six to a room; three beds to a room. There is no privacy . . . it is almost impossible to read or write alone."[21]

The mill girls seem to have shared a passion for self-improvement. They attended evening school, pooled their coins to engage music and language teachers, attended lyceum lectures, and were reputed to be avid readers. Harriet Hanson Robinson claimed that "the circulating libraries, that were soon opened drew them [the mill girls] and kept them there, when no other inducement would have been sufficient." She wrote of a "farmer's daughter from the 'State of Maine' who had come to Lowell for the express purpose of getting books . . . that she could not find in her native place."[22] Young Lucy Larcom recalled, "The printed regulations forbade us to bring books into the mill, so I made my window-seat into a small library of poetry, pasting its side all over with newspaper clippings."[23]

Some of the girls who were attracted to Lowell had previously worked in small mills or had done work for local merchants in their homes. Many farmers' daughters moved to the city with the hope of finding better economic opportunities for themselves or their families. Generally, the girls worked from nine to ten months per year. Many returned home during the summer months when their labor on the farm was required. Lucy Larcom recalled overhearing a family discussion about finances during which one of her parents said, "The children will have to leave school and go into the mill." Lucy later reported, "The mill-agent did not want to take us two little girls, but consented on condition we should be sure to attend school the full number of months prescribed each year. I, the younger one, was then between eleven and twelve."[24] Lucy's reaction to her new situation was positive. " I thought it would be a pleasure to feel that I was not a trouble or burden or expense to anybody. . . . So I went to my first day's work in the mill with a light heart. The novelty of it made it seem easy, and it really was not hard, just to change the bobbins on the spinning-frames every three quarters of an hour or so, with half a dozen other little girls who were doing the same thing."[25]

Factory work could be dangerous, however. A sleepy or inattentive child could easily lose a finger, arm, or scalp to the unforgiving machinery. Mill girls were required to keep their hair contained in a hair net; but vanity often prevailed and many of them were injured or killed when their long hair caught in theunforgiving apparatus. Deafness or partial loss of hearing often resulted from the tremendous noise of the looms—a phenomenon, until the advent of industrialization, uncommon to ears attuned to the quiet passing of the agricultural day. An 1848 report on factory life described the Amoskeag Mills at Manchester, "The din and clatter of these five hundred looms under full operation, struck us on first entering as something frightful and infernal, for it seemed such an atrocious violation of one of the faculties of the human soul, the sense of hearing."[26] One mill girl wrote that upon leaving work "the sound of the mill was in my ears, as of crickets, frogs, and Jews harps all mingled together with a strange discord. After that it seemed as though cotton-wool was in my ears."[27]

Pulmonary ailments also abound in the mills. The mill inspectors noted, "The atmosphere of the room . . . is charged with cotton filaments and dust [and] the windows were down; we asked the reason, and a young woman answered naively, and without seeming to be in the least aware that this privation of fresh air was anything else than perfectly natural, that 'when the wind blew, the threads did not work so well.' After we had been in the room for fifteen or twenty minutes, we found ourselves . . . in quite a perspiration, produced by a certain moisture which we observed in the air, as well as the heat." Added to the normal humidity of the day, steam was regularly sprayed into the air to maintain its moisture content. This was thought to keep the threads from drying out and snapping on the looms. Having breathed in all these fibers for so many hours each day, many girls left the mills with a cough never again to return.[28]

Child Labor

The high rate of illiteracy among child laborers was of great concern to many community leaders. Massachusetts took the first step to protect children in 1835 by passing a law prohibiting the employment of any child under 15 years of age who received less than three months of schooling in the previous year. In 1846 Pennsylvania established 12 as the minimum age at which a child could be employed in silk, cotton, or woolen mills. Other states enacted minimum age requirements for work but none made provision for establishing proof of age for the enforcement of the law. Most textile workers worked a 12- to 14-hour day and half a day on Saturday. These hours were considered excessive for children. In 1842 Connecticut and Massachusetts led the reform in this area by passing laws prohibiting children from working more than 10 hours per day. By 1853 several states had established a 10-hour workday for children under 12 years old.

Child labor in New York City tenements was widespread. Young children were often sent to scavenge the streets for rope, cinders, metal, or anything that could be resold to junk dealers or neighbors. Older children were put to work as street peddlers. Young boys shined shoes and little girls sold apples or pencils. Manufacturers and contractors gave unfinished garments or materials to make artificial flowers to families who would finish or assemble these items at home. Children were often seen transporting large bundles of these materials in the streets. Once home, the children helped fell seams, sew linings and hems, finish gloves, card buttons, fasten cords to pencils for souvenir cards, assemble artificial flowers, and whatever else their age and skill allowed them to do. In his study of New York tenements, Jacob Riis reported that "the child works unchallenged from the day he is old enough to pull a thread." In a fourth-floor tenement he witnessed the following scene. "Five men and a woman, two young girls, not fifteen, and a boy who says unasked that he is fifteen, and

A late period photograph of a young girl at work in the mills checking and maintaining the hundreds of thread spindles that fed the looms.

lies in saying it, are at the machines sewing knickerbockers. . . . The floor is littered ankle-deep with half-sewn garments. In the alcove, on a couch are many dozens of 'pants' ready for the finisher, a bare-legged baby with pinched face is asleep. A fence of piled-up clothing keeps him from rolling off on the floor. The faces, hands and arms to the elbows of everyone in the room are black with the color of the cloth on which they are working. . . . The girls shoot sidelong glances but at a warning look from the man with the bundle they tread their machines more energetically than ever." On the next floor Riis found another family who had hired "an old man as an ironer" and a "sweet-faced little Italian girl as a finisher. She is twelve, she says and can neither read nor write, [and she] probably never will."[29]

Other children did not take part in the actual manufacture of the items but they bore the burden of the home-work system by having to care for younger siblings and do housework while their mothers were engaged in various types of home manufacture. Children were prohibited from working during the hours they were supposed to be in school, but there were no legal restrictions to keep families from having their children work from the three o'clock in the afternoon dismissal until well into the night. Some teachers complained that their students fell asleep in class, having worked until nine or ten o'clock at night in some form of home manufacture, but there was nothing they could legally do to remedy the situation. During autumn, when the flower-making season was at its height, it was not unusual for families to keep school-aged children home for days at a time, sending them to school just enough to show that they were complying with compulsory attendance regulations. Unfortunately, when truant school-aged children were discovered and forced to attend school, all that the law was doing was adding school work to the ceaseless toil in which the children had spent their days since early childhood.

Some families relied on the assistance of their preschool children as they were too young to be affected by compulsory attendance laws. Children as young as three were taught to pull bastings and sew buttons for garments made by their mothers. These younger children were put to work pulling apart the petals that came from the factory stuck together, thus enabling the flower assemblers to work more rapidly.

Once beyond the age of 14, young tenement girls were free to seek employment outside of the home. Many of these girls became shop girls. In New York the Women's Investigating Committee found "the majority of the children employed in the stores to be under age" but reported that they knew of only one time when a truant officer inquired at a shop. In that instance he "sent the youngest children home, but in a month's time they were all back in their places." An investigation by the Working Women's Society documented the injustices that these young girls faced. Sales girls were fined for a number of offenses, including sitting down, despite the fact that a law existed requiring stores to supply seats for saleswomen. "A little girl, who received only two dollars a week, made cash-sales amounting to $167 in a single day, while the receipts of a fifteen-dollar male clerk in the same department footed up only $125; yet for some trivial mistake the girl was fined sixty cents out of her two dollars." Superintendents and timekeepers commonly shared the revenue generated by these spurious fines. During busy seasons the girls were required to work 16 hours a day or face dismissal, and pressure was exerted on the time clerk to be very strict and exacting concerning violations. Oppressive heat and poor ventilation created a situation where "girls fainted day after day and came out looking like corpses."[30]

Many young boys were employed in coal mines. Coal mining was a dangerous and arduous means of making a living. Pay was low and, in order for many families to reach even a subsistence level of earnings, sons were sent to work in the mines as young as nine or as soon as they were physically able. Some served as door boys who sat in the dark mines waiting to open and close the doors that permitted the mine cars to pass. Others were driver boys who dumped coal from the cars so that it could advance to the processing machines. The breaker boys—covered in dust and sitting knee-to-back in long lines above the coal chutes—cleaned and inspected the material from the mine, separating the rock and slate from the coal. A 1877 report described a breaker room in St. Clair, Pennsylvania, "These little fellows go to work in this cold dreary room at seven o'clock in the morning and work until it is too dark to see any longer. For this they get $1 to $3 a week. Not three boys in this roomful could read or write. Shut in from everything that is pleasant, with no chance to learn, with no knowledge of what is going on about them, with nothing to do but work. . . . They had no games; when their day's work is done they are too tired for that. They know nothing but the difference between slate and coal."[31] Nine-year-old Joseph Miliauska, who earned 70 cents for a 10-hour day as a breaker boy, recalled, "You'd get it in the back with a broom" if you were caught letting a piece of slate slip by.[32] A Luzerne County, Pennsylvania, school superintendent addressed the problem of breaker boys in his annual report. "Something must be done to educate this important element in our community, now numbering five thousand souls. . . . These boys are not now receiving an education. They are doing but little for themselves, and their occasional attendance interferes materially with the grading of the schools. We must educate these boys or accept the consequences. The following suggestion is again offered: Establish a school in every mining district under the care of the best man that can be secured for the position. Supply the pupils with books, paper, slates, pencils, in short, everything they require. Keep it open as a night school during the entire school year, except when there is no work at the mines, and then let it be conducted as a day school. Let the course of study be reading, writing, spelling, the business operations of arithmetic, with oral instruction in civil government and the duties of citizens, not omitting moral instruction."[33]

Streetwise Beyond Their Years

Newspapers offered employment to many city boys. Newsboys were first employed in 1833 to hawk the penny paper dailies, whose low price made selling them through traditional adult conduits financially unfeasible. Newsboys bought papers at a small discount early in the morning and were unable to return unsold copies. Johnny Morrow's memoirs give insight to the finances of the trade. "I had fifty-six papers for my morning's stock, for which I paid eighty-four cents. For the sale of these I have received one dollar and twelve cents, leaving me a profit of twenty-eight cents, nine of these I am going to spend for my breakfast, and I shall then have nineteen to spare."[34] As profits accrued only after they had covered their initial investment, successful newsboys turned into clever businessmen who assessed the weather and the events of the day prior to purchasing their day's stock. The First Annual Report of the Children's Aid Society in 1860 called them the "shrewdest and sharpest" of street children.[35] Fredrick Richford Starr, in his book on newsboys, said, "A lad of mere ordinary capacity would starve at the business."[36] The headline cries of the newspaper boys soon became an integral part of the sounds of the city.

Lydia Marie Child presents a very sensitive picture of the news crier. "I had not gone far when I met a little ragged urchin, about four years old, with a heap of newspapers, 'more big than he could carry,' under his little arm, and another clinched in his small red fist. The sweet voice of childhood was prematurely cracked into shrillness, by screaming street cries at the top of his lungs; and he looked blue, cold and disconsolate."[37] The vulnerability of the newsboy and his precarious economic situation moved Louisa May Alcott to make this imploration to middle-class men whose own children were nestled in their nurseries, sheltered from the cares of the world. "When busy fathers hurry home at night I hope they'll buy their papers of the small boys. . . . For love of the little sons and daughters safe at home, say a kind word, buy a paper, even if you don't want it; and never pass by, leaving them to sleep forgotten in the streets at midnight, with no pillow but a stone."[38]

While some of these streetwise entrepreneurs had families, many newsboys were orphans, actually or in effect, having been abandoned by their parents. Riis detailed the situation, "Many were thrown upon the world when their parents were 'sent up' to the island or to Sing-Sing. . . . Sickness in the house, [or] too many mouths to feed" sent others out into the streets. When asked how he came to live ruff, a twelve year old boy offered the following, 'We wuz six. . . . Some of us had to go'. . . . Grinding poverty and hard work beyond the years of the lad: blows and curses for breakfast, dinner, and supper: all these [were] recruiting agents for the homeless army." Those who had no homes found shelter in the alleys and back streets. "In warm weather a truck [flatbed wagon] in the street, a convenient out-house, or a dug-out in a hay-barge at the wharf [made] good bunks. Two [boys] were found making their nest in the end of a big iron pipe up by the Harlem Bridge, and an old boiler at the East River served as an elegant flat for another [pair] in winter . . . fighting for warm spots around grated vent-holes that let out the heat and steam from the underground press-rooms" near Printing House Square. Others went to live in one of a number of Newsboys' Lodging Houses that were set up in several cities to provide shelter and safety for the lads. Additionally, they offered the lads classes in reading and writing and "pains [were] taken gradually to refine their tastes by entertaining lectures, readings, dramatic or otherwise and innocent games."[39] The path to refinement by this method was likely to have been a difficult one.

The Second Annual Report on the Children's Aid Society reported, "The class of newsboys were then apparently the most wild and vicious set of lads in the city. . . . Their money, which was easily earned, was more quickly spent in gambling, theaters and low pleasures, for which, though children, they had a man's aptitude."[40] The superintendent of the Newsboys' Lodging House in New York acknowledged that although "its arrangements [were] popular with the boys . . . the temptations of a street life to such boys, and its excitements [were] so strong, that it [was] exceedingly difficult to get them in . . . and induce them to stay."[41] The boys were free to come and go in the lodging houses as long as they behaved. It was like a hotel and, as such, the boys were asked to pay a small amount for their bed and their meals. "Six cents for his bed, six cents for his breakfast of bread and coffee, and six cents for his supper of pork and beans, as much as he can eat." Nonetheless, for a newsboy earning less than 50 cents a day, even these rates were exorbitant.[42]

The industrial expansion following the Civil War created an unprecedented demand for workers. In this age of increasingly commercial commodities, many families came to depend on the money that children could bring into the home. By the end of the century, nearly one-fifth of the nation's children between 10 and 16 were part of the workforce.

Notes

1. Catherine Elizabeth Havens, *Diary of a Little Girl in Old New York* (New York: Henry Collins Brown, 1920), 89.

2. Aunt Friendly (pseudonym), *Bound Out; or, Abby on the Farm* (New York: Anson D. F. Randolph & Co., n.d.), 42–44, 53.

3. Sally McMurray, *Families & Farmhouses in Nineteenth-Century America: Vernacular Design and Social Change* (Knoxville: University of Tennessee Press, 1997), 184.

4. James M. Volo and Dorothy Denneen Volo, *Family Life in 17th- and 18th-Century America* (Westport, Conn.: Greenwood Press, 2006), 264.

5. Louisa May Alcott, *An Old Fashioned Thanksgiving* (repr., Bedford, Mass.: Applewood Books, 1990), 8–9.

6. Jack Larkin, *Children Everywhere: Dimensions of Childhood in Early 19th-Century New England* (Sturbridge, Mass.: Davis Press, 1987), 16.

7. Ibid., 19.

8. Ibid., 16.

9. Jane C. Nylander, *Our Own Snug Fireside: Images of the New England Home, 1760–1860* (New Haven, Conn.: Yale University Press, 1993), 48.

10. Lucy Larcom, *A New England Girlhood* (Boston: Northeastern University Press, 1986), 146.

11. Alcott, *An Old Fashioned Thanksgiving*, 18.

12. J. P Wickersham, *Report of the Superintendent of Public Instruction of the Commonwealth of Pennsylvania for the Year Ending June 3, 1878* (Harrisburg, Pa.: Lane S. Hart, State Printer, 1878), 56.

13. Steven Mintz, *Huck's Raft: A History of American Childhood* (Cambridge, Mass.: Belknap Press/Harvard University Press, 2004), 126–127.

14. Ibid., 150.

15. "Mills of New York," http://www.nymills.com/History/Did_you_know/did_you_know.htm (accessed October 2006).

16. One of the regulations from the Appleton Company, Lowell, Massachusetts, dated 1833, illustrated in Benita Eisler, ed., *The Lowell Offering: Writings by New England Mill Women, 1840–1845* (New York: W. W. Norton & Co., 1977), 25.

17. One of the regulations of the boarding houses for the Middlesex Company, circa 1850, illustrated in Eisler, *Lowell Offering*, 27.

18. One of the regulations from the Appleton Company illustrated in Eisler, *Lowell Offering*, 25.

19. Eisler, *Lowell Offering*, 24.

20. Ibid., 64.

21. "A Description of Factory Life by an Associationist in 1848," http:teach.lanece.edu/martinezp/250%20CRG/laborhist.htm (accessed October 2006).

22. Eisler, *Lowell Offering*, 31.

23. Larcom, *New England Childhood*, 175–176.

24. Ibid., 153.

25. Ibid., 153–154.

26. "Description of Factory Life."

27. Eisler, *Lowell Offering*, 52.

28. "Description of Factory Life."

29. Jacob A. Riis, *How the Other Half Lives: Studies among the Tenements of New York* (New York: Charles Scribner's Sons, 1890), 131–133.

30. Ibid., 232–234.

31. Kirk Bane, "Remembering Child Labor in America," http://www.freezer-box.com/archive/article.php?id = 135 (accessed October 2006).

32. Mintz, *Huck's Raft*, 145.

33. Wickersham, *Report of the Superintendent*, 109.

34. Karen Sanchez-Eppler, *Dependent States: The Child's Part in Nineteenth Century American Culture* (Chicago: University of Chicago Press, 2005), 156.

35. Ibid., 154.

36. Frederick Richford Starr, *John Ellard: The Newsboy* (Philadelphia: William S. and Alfred Martien, 1860), 7.

37. Lydia Marie Child, *Letters from New York* (Athens: University of Georgia Press, 1999) 83.

38. Louisa May Alcott, "Our Little Newsboy," *Merry's Museum*, April 1868, 191–192.

39. Rachford Starr, *John Ellard*, 39.

40. Sanchez-Eppler, *Dependent States*, 172.

41. Ibid., 174.

42. Riis, *How the Other Half Lives*, 211.

16

Independent Living

The sparsely furnished rooms . . . where one lives as in state, solitary and alone, is of all places the most dreary. Better . . . after all, the crowded attic, for that at least furnishes companionship.

—A 19th-century woman boarder

Boarding

One of the unique features of the 19th century was the appearance of private and public boarding houses and commercial hotels. This was largely fueled by the change from a work-for-work or work-for-trade economy to one that was based on wages. The reason that even middle-class families took in boarders was to make extra money while providing a home-like atmosphere to strangers. A successful commercial boarding establishment could continue to exist only because its residents or guests paid in cash, and boarding from the perspective of the boarder only made sense in the context of nearby wage-paying opportunities. Setting up a commercial boarding house required a great deal of risk such as buying or renting a large house, and furnishing and staffing it for the purpose, but many homeowners had some extra rooms and could take in boarders without unreasonable additional expense. Nonetheless, bedrooms and parlors often required additional furniture; dining rooms extra tables or chairs; kitchens extra dishes, flatware, and pots; and the privy or bathroom might need expansion or duplication. Certainly many genteel people sought lodgings in a decent home-like environment with pleasant furnished rooms and good cooking.[1]

In the 18th century such conveniences did not exist. Of course there were private homes, inns, and taverns that accepted overnight travelers, but they rarely offered long-term living accommodations to their guests. Colonial establishments were patterned after their British counterparts, and customers were usually asked to share rooms or even beds. Moreover, there were very few rooms—sometimes with beds, sometimes with nothing more than straw-filled ticking on the floor in a corridor—and no promise of privacy. Services were limited to generally clean linens, the freedom to spend money at the bar until the owner retired for the night, the use of the outhouse or a chamber pot, and a single evening meal—usually pot luck. Stabling and feeding of horses cost extra. Servants, apprentices, and slaves found accommodations where they could—in the garret, the basement, the barn, or under a wagon in the street.

In the 19th century this pattern changed, to one that was more home-like and domestically oriented. The offer of long-term residence to strangers in one's home—loosely known as "boarding" or "taking in lodgers"—quickly became part of the regular process of individual and family life. It is likely that one-third of all family homes took in boarders or kept unrelated lodgers at some time during the life cycle of the family. "Boarding offered inexpensive housing space in a surrogate family setting. It provided the comforts of home without the accompanying familial obligations and parental controls. For the heads of households, taking in boarders augmented [the] family budget and [often] provided surrogate children after their own sons and daughters had left home."[2]

Becoming a boarder was a common residential alternative for men who, due to business or work constraints, needed to stay away from their family home for long periods of time, or for those single men who wished to live independently from their parents. Young married couples sometimes boarded rather than taking residence with their relations, but this circumstance was considered a great disadvantage to the development of a strong marital unit—particularly difficult on the woman who would have no household of her own in which to be mistress. However, the most remarkable development with regard to 19th-century boarding was its extension to unescorted women, even young single women.

In the 18th century few women traveled alone, and they rarely stayed in commercial establishments. Instead they arranged, usually through the local parson or minister, to stay with a good family in town if no relatives lived nearby. With the changes affecting a woman's place in 19th-century society, this living pattern changed also. In 1871 a working woman noted of her experiences, "I have known . . . what it is to be an inmate of a [boarding] house where I was received as a member of the family, regarded and guarded as a daughter, where I found pleasant companions of my own age, protectors and advisors in those older than myself; where our relationship was not one of dollars and cents, of value given and received, but of earnest, tender friendship, friendship that thus found will be as lasting as life itself."[3]

Many women ran boarding establishments as a financial expedient for their own families. They were "usually widows or single women from the country; and many questions are always asked, and references required, before a house is given to a new applicant. It is true that mistakes are sometimes made, and the wrong person gets into the pew," wrote one woman boarder in 1844. "I think it requires a compilation of good qualities to make up a good boarding woman. She looks well to the ways of her household and must be even more than all that King Solomon describes. . . . She openth her mouth with wisdom, and in her tongue is the law of kindness . . . counsel and sympathy."[4]

Accommodations for boarding varied. A New England boarder described the interior of a boarding establishment this way, "The rooms are high, very light, kept nicely whitewashed, and extremely neat: with many plants in the window seats, and white cotton curtains to the windows."[5] A woman from New York had a different experience. She wrote, "The sparsely furnished rooms . . . where one lives as in state, solitary and alone, is of all places the most dreary. Better . . . after all, the crowded attic, for that at least furnishes companionship." Some public boarding houses were described as "gregarious . . . like street-cars and omnibuses, having always room for one more [but] not professing to look after their inmates."[6]

Most boarding residences were converted from private homes and limited the occupants to their own rooms, the parlor, and the dining room. A single multi-course, family-style meal was served at a specific time each evening, usually in the dining room. The open use of alcohol was prohibited in most cases, and its covert use "in-room" was usually grounds for eviction. Smoking may, or may not, have been tolerated among male boarders, depending on the wishes of the homeowner. Of course, women were prohibited from drinking and smoking in all but the least respectable boarding houses.

Usually every class of potential boarder could find a place suitable to his own calling and means. Some boarding houses specialized in serving specific types of boarders like office workers, bargemen, railroad personnel, or factory workers. The technicians and inventors who worked at Thomas Edison's Menlo Park Wizard's Factory in the 1870s stayed at Sarah Jordan's middle-class boarding house in New Jersey. The Tremont House and the Franklin House in New York City were fashionable boarding houses for the well-to-do, while the less elegant, but clean, corporation houses in Lowell, Massachusetts, were intended for the working-class employees of the nearby textile mills.

A good deal of detail is known about the boarding houses used by the working girls at Lowell because so many of the mill women wrote letters to friends and relatives describing them. One inmate arriving in 1844 wrote, "I had expected coldness, or at least indifference, in this city, and the cordiality of the good landlady filled my heart with gratitude. I have since inquired if she was not unusually kind; but, though she is a very good woman, the girls here say that she is not more so to me than to any other new boarder; and that the boarding-woman are always dreadfully good to a new boarder." The dining room of this house had three "common-sized dining tables" about which all the girls sat, and the writer's first breakfast meal was "tea, flapjacks, and plum-cake" as well as "bread, butter, and crackers, upon the table." After evening supper the tables were cleared, and "some of the girls came in with their sewing, some went to their own rooms, and some went out upon the street . . . some to meetings, or evening school, or they were shopping, or visiting upon some other corporation [boarding house], all of which is going upon the street in factory parlance." Another young woman noted, "Since I have wrote you, another pay day has come around. I earned 14 dollars and a half, nine and a half dollars, beside my board ($5). The folks think I get along just first-rate."[7]

Charles Dickens, during his visit to America in 1842, came to observe the residences and factories at Lowell to see how the girls lived and worked in a "modern" manufacturing setting. He found that many of the young women workers came in from the country to find jobs away from the farm, while others were unemployed school teachers filling in during the long school breaks of summer. There was a seemingly unending supply of young women willing to work, and most had homes and families to which they could return. Remarkably, many of the mill girls were well educated. In his *American Notes,* written upon his return to England, Dickens left a generally stark and unsatisfactory verbal description of many American cities as they appeared to him, but he was pleasantly surprised by the home-like atmosphere afforded the mill girls at the boarding houses. He wrote, "There is a piano in a great many of the boarding houses, and nearly all the young ladies subscribe to circulating libraries." Dickens found them "omnivorous readers of books" and subscribers to newspapers and literary magazines. "It was their habit, after reading their copies, to send them by mail or stage-coach to their widely scattered homes, where they were read all over a village or a neighborhood; and thus was current literature introduced into lonely places." There was always a best room in the boarding house in which to entertain callers, and it had the finest furniture and appointments in the building. Many of the girls with regular gentlemen callers needed to reserve this room ahead of time. Nonetheless, segregated from male workers by division of labor and removed from the patriarchal protection of their family homes, mill girls were allowed little interaction with men who were not their blood relations.[8]

On the other hand the *Home for Young Working-Women*—an institutionalized public facility in New York City for 1,500 residents—was designed "with mathematical exactitude" by a well-intentioned, but misdirected, philanthropist named Alexander. T. Stewart. Having parlayed a tiny dry goods store in Manhattan into a multimillion-dollar personal fortune, Stewart—an Irish immigrant—was a department store tycoon and early supporter of the photographer Mathew Brady. His Broadway store was a marble-faced, steel-and-concrete edifice that spanned 9th and 10th streets. In 1862 this store took in an amazing $23,000 in a single day.

Stewart's *Home,* however, was the antithesis of the Lowell Houses. The solitary rooms were each 9 feet by 7 feet with a bed that was 4 feet by 7 feet, leaving little space for anything else. "Put in this space a chair, a table, a trunk or a wardrobe, and a washstand—the barest necessities in the way of furnishings—and how much space is left? Scarcely enough to stand a cat in, still less to swing one," wrote one woman. "Where are to be the pictures, the flowers, the bookcase, the birdcage; whence the rocking-chair, the work-basket, the stand for books and papers, the plain and cheaply-made but comfortable lounges; where the room for the entertainment of friends and neighbors? Yet these are all requisites of a home, and of just as vital importance as a place to eat or sleep. . . . Will some one with the brain of a man, the heart of a woman, and the instincts of a mother devise a boarding-house . . . that shall meet these wants?"[9]

In sharp contrast to such institutional living were the residences erected by the Young Men's Christian Association (YMCA) and Young Women's Christian Association (YWCA). The residential wings of these institutions, and similar residences developed by other religious groups, provided decent housing in a moral atmosphere for persons who did not want to live with a family and wanted to avoid the sinful pitfalls thought to be associated with common boarding and lodging houses. The buildings usually had toilet facilities on each floor and a large common room furnished with a fireplace, wood paneling, modest fixtures and accents, comfortable furniture, and often a small reading library filled with morally inspiring texts or religious tracts. Rooms cost about $3.00 a week for members. Food was usually not included, but many residents cooked in their rooms on small gas-fired hot plates.

For those who wished similar lodgings in a non-sectarian environment, there were many other non-profit hotels, clubs, and rooming houses set up by philanthropic agencies. Among them were the Junior League Hotel for Women, established in Manhattan, and the Jane's Clubs, also for women, founded in Chicago. In the latter the residents did a little light housework, and hired servants did the cooking and heavy cleaning. The fees charged by the non-profits varied, and they just covered the operation of the establishment and the salary of a resident matron, steward, or caretaker. All of these establishments were racially restricted to whites, but in New York, near the end of the 19th century, the Tuskegee Hotel and the Hampton Hotel were opened for use solely by black women.

Establishments that rented rooms for the night, week, or month and served no meals were considered *rooming houses* rather than *boarding houses* in both Chicago and New York. In Philadelphia, similar establishments operated under the title of *furnished rooms,* and in San Francisco, they were known as *lodging houses.* A room rented for a dollar or two each week (payment in advance), but the residents were usually forced to share toilet and bathing facilities and to seek their meals outside the dwelling. At the seamier end of the lodging spectrum was the *flophouse.* A small cubicle with a cot and a chair could be had for between "two and four bits" (25 to 50 cents) a night; for a dime (10 cents), the lodger could choose among a row of cots, hammocks, or a mattress; and for a nickel (5 cents), a pile of newspapers and a space on the floor could be had. Although they rarely had toilet facilities or heat, flophouses found their greatest trade in winter when the underemployed or unemployed were driven in by the cold from living in the streets and alleys. The residents often included a large number of drunks and itinerates of questionable character.

The city of Buffalo, New York, can serve as an example with regard to boarding and lodging as it might be found at mid-century. As the western terminus of the Erie Canal and a portal to the Midwest, Buffalo was a city with a large portion of its population continually in flux. The city had grown so rapidly after the opening of the Erie Canal in 1825 that, with a lack of individual housing structures, more than 50 percent of unmarried men and women living there did so either as boarders or lodgers. One of the most consistent findings of studies done on the residence patterns of the people in Buffalo in mid-century was that young unmarried migrants, men and women, were most likely to take up temporary living arrangements in a private household. "Many girls would a great deal rather board [*sic*] in the plainest three-roomed cottage where she could be one of the family."[10]

Among men recently arrived in Buffalo in 1855, data suggest that 39 percent took up residence in private homes and 57 percent lived in public boarding houses or hotels. Additionally, 40 percent of these men were self-identified as skilled workmen, 22 percent as white-collar workers, and 15 percent as clerks. Their average age was 24 years. For women boarding in private homes (52 percent), unraveling the situation is more complicated statistically because many in the sample may have been domestics or wards of the unrelated families owning the homes. Only 47 percent of women in Buffalo stayed in public accommodations. Although the women's occupations (if any) were not recorded, their average age was a mere 21 years.[11]

Among both boarders and lodgers 81 percent of men and 62 percent of women were noted as being single. Most of the young women were probably working girls, yet many women boarders considered as single in the data may simply have been accompanying their parents or other relatives. Virtually all boarders, men and women, who considered themselves married were either accompanied by a spouse or indicated that they were widowed. Commonly these boarders changed residence after about one year. Longer-term residents tended to marry and form their own independent households in the city. The data samples are just not precise enough to make additional distinctions. Nonetheless, because city business records were kept, data concerning boarding and lodging establishments in Buffalo can be broken down statistically: private homes (43 percent), public boarding/rooming houses (36 percent), and commercial hotels (21 percent).[12]

An unidentified woman writing in 1871 in *Arthur's Lady's Home Magazine* described the plight of a young working girl trying to find "a boarding-place within her means" in New York City. This was difficult because the residence fee had to be deducted from an average wage for women that rarely exceeded $10.00 a week and was often as little as $5.00. "The city was scoured, friends and strangers alike appealed to for suitable accommodations . . . but all to no purpose. The comforts of a home commanded a price that would more than swallow up her modest wages. And a board within her means meant a cold, cheerless, scantily furnished fourth or fifth story, with three or four roommates—just a place to sleep in with the privilege of coming to the table—nothing more. And this with winter just setting in, and four or five cold months in prospect." The author, considering herself a successful and experienced "working-women," nonetheless confessed that she was not a member of the "strong-minded sisterhood." She questioned how any girl could live on $5.00 a week "as the inmate of a house, no matter how genteel, whose only interest in its boarders is that they pay their boarding-bills regularly and not have too good an appetite."[13]

Commercial Living

Within the growing cities, a whole new business emerged, that of the commercial hotel. The City Hotel in New York was the first American

The Lowell boarding houses as they appeared in mid-century.

structure allegedly designed and built as a commercial hotel in 1794. It had 73 private rooms that were considered immense by contemporary standards. It also had accommodations for meetings and meals. Although the lodgings were generally functional and impersonal, the hotel became a center for Manhattan society. Chronologically, the Adelphi Hotel (1827) of New York City (not the one in Saratoga Springs) was the first major hotel to open in the 19th century, and the concept was quickly copied in Boston, Baltimore, and Philadelphia. The Adelphi was a six-story building often considered Manhattan's first skyscraper. However, it was the Tremont House opened in 1829 in Boston that set the standards for America's first-class commercial hotels. Its 170 rooms featured door locks, a wash basin, and pitcher of water. A free cake of soap was given to each guest. There were eight indoor toilets and bathrooms distributed throughout the building. The Tremont had a highly trained staff that included the first bellboys and 24-hour hotel desk clerks. The hotel was noted for the fine French cuisine to be found in its restaurant. In 1830 the Boston Exchange opened. Eight stories tall and sporting 300 rooms, the Exchange offered food, drink, and accommodations in a grand style. In 1844 the New York Hotel in Manhattan offered a number of rooms with private baths for the first time; in 1859 the Fifth Avenue Hotel installed an elevator to carry guests between its six floors; and in 1881 the Prospect House in Blue Mountain Lake, New York, installed electric lights in all its rooms.

Hotels became a gathering place for men of politics and business, and the lobbies, salons, and dining areas became places of public and private business. The hotel concept also moved west with the railroads and the expanding nation. When Abraham Lincoln made his one and only trip to Kansas as a presidential candidate in December 1859, he crossed the Missouri River at St. Joseph and made his way to Elwood, Kansas, and the 75-room, three-story Great Western Hotel. Elwood was important as the first Kansas station on the Pony Express route and the beginning of the Missouri to California railway line. In the 1850s scores of river barges had crossed the river at Elwood, and thousands of emigrants had outfitted their wagons there for the trip to Oregon or California. At the Great Western Hotel, Lincoln made his first speech of the election tour, condemning slavery and blaming the violence in "Bloody Kansas" on the policy of popular sovereignty favored by the Northern Democrats. The next day he moved on to Ashel Lowe's imposing hotel known as the Doniphan Guest House, then to the Massasoit House in Atchison, where he received word of John Brown's execution for leading the Harper's Ferry anti-slavery raid earlier that year. He then moved on to the Mansion House in Fort Leavenworth before ending his tour. Ironically, no Kansas newspaper bothered to make a record of his appearances at any of these establishments.

One of the best-known hotels in Washington, D.C., was Willard's Hotel, which served during the Civil War as a meeting place of politicians, generals, and presidents. Lincoln first came to Willard's as a congressman in 1849 to attend a meeting of the supporters of President Zachary Taylor, and he stayed there rather than at a rented house for 10 days prior to his own inauguration in 1861. The First Family occupied Parlor No. 6, a pricey corner suite of rooms on the second floor. The bill for the stay was more than $770. Diarist George B. Loring spotted Lincoln at Willard's when the president-elect made his first public appearance in the nation's capital. "I was standing in the upper hall of Willard's hotel, conversing with a friend and listening to the confused talk of the crowded drawing-room adjoining. As we stood there, a tall and awkward form appeared above the stairs, especially conspicuous, as it came into view, for a new and stylish hat. It was evidently President Lincoln, whom neither of us had seen before. As soon as his presence was known, the hall was thronged from the drawing rooms. He seemed somewhat startled by the crowd, did not remove his hat, wended his way somewhat rapidly and with mere passing recognition, and took shelter in his room."[14]

Lincoln departed from Willard's for his inauguration and returned there afterward for a luncheon consisting of Mock Turtle soup, corned beef and cabbage, parsley potatoes, and blackberry pie. While president, he conducted official business at Willard's many times, and he entertained visitors in Willard's wide variety of suites and public rooms. All three defeated presidential candidates from the 1860 election called on Lincoln there in the first days of his presidency—Stephen Douglas, John Bell, and John C. Breckinridge. Shortly thereafter the president met with delegates from 21 of the 34 states in one of Willard's drawing rooms in an unsuccessful attempt to avoid civil war through negotiation. During the conflict in 1861, he and the First Lady, Mary Todd Lincoln, attended a concert there given by Meda Blanchard, and they stopped to review General Ambrose Burnside's troops from the entranceway steps in 1864. Also among the hotel's luminary guests were Julia Ward Howe, who wrote the words to "The Battle Hymn of the Republic" in her hotel room one morning in 1861; Phineas T. Barnum's diminutive General Tom Thumb and his tiny bride, who stayed over in 1863; and General Ulysses S. Grant, who stayed there in 1864 and later again many times as president. Grant was so often accosted by political favor-seekers when going in and out of Willard's reception area that he coined the term *lobbyist* in reference to them—a word still used today for these denizens of the halls of Congress.

Many single or widowed men and women of sufficient financial means took up permanent residence in hotels, utilizing the staff and accommodations as if they owed them. Yet American-style hotels initially shocked many European visitors by giving lodging to traveling salesmen and beardless youths seeking business connections at the same time and in the same manner as international dignitaries, eminent industrialists, and the socially prominent. The democratic mingling of people of all kinds—as long as they were white and could pay—was in stark contrast to the strict

European practice of separating accommodations by social class. Under the American style, there were different rates for better accommodations, but everybody paid for their meals, ate in the same dining room, and shared equally the other common facilities of the establishment.

The photographer Mathew Brady made his permanent residence at the Astor House, one of New York's most elegant and popular residence hotels. Built in 1836 on Broadway, the Astor House was an imposing building of white granite with a façade of white Corinthian columns forming a portico over the main entrance. Also resident there was Thurlow Weed, the New York politician, and Daniel Webster, secretary of state in the Tyler administration, had a standing order for a room there at a "moment's notice." The Astor's owner, Charles A. Stetson, was the city's unofficial dinner host. Somewhat of a social personality himself, Stetson was a close friend of Senator Daniel Webster, but he was most famous for the sumptuous meals that he offered in the Astor's dinning room.[15]

With time, hotel lodging became fancier and more expensive. St. Louis had the Planters Hotel, Omaha the Paxton, San Francisco the Palace, and Chicago both the Sherman and the Grand Pacific. One of the fanciest of the post-war hotels was the Palmer House in Chicago. Built in 1873, its amenities included oversized rooms, luxurious decor, sumptuous meals, and a hotel barber shop with a floor tiled in a mosaic of real silver dollars. The service staff was made up solely of members of Chicago's small black community, who were generally treated by both the "white only" management and the "white only" customers as if they were house slaves on a plantation from an earlier decade and region. Notwithstanding its elegance, British author Rudyard Kipling was unimpressed by his stay there in 1890. "The Palmer House . . . is a gilded and mirrored rabbit-warren, and there I found a huge hall of tessellated marble, crammed with people talking about money and spitting about everywhere. Other barbarians charged in and out of this inferno with letters and telegrams in their hands, and yet others shouted at each other."[16]

Many smaller hotels, of the mom-and-pop variety, imitated the grand hotels and offered lodgings in smaller cities and larger towns with varying degrees of success. Strawberry Flat Hotel in Nevada, for instance, was a well-known stopping point for traveling miners moving between the gold fields of California and the Comstock Lode in 1859. One of these, J. Ross Browne, described the scene as hundreds of miners flooded the barroom and jostled each other for a place in the dining room. "At the first tinkle of the bell the door was burst open with a tremendous crash . . . [and] the whole house actually tottered and trembled at the concussion, as if shaken by an earthquake. Long before the main body had assaulted the table the din of arms was heard above the general uproar; the deafening clatter of plates, knives, and forks and the dreadful battle-cry of Waiter! Waiter!"[17]

With the acceptance of American hotels by the elite came the return of European-style social restrictions. Lodging, which had been affordable for everyone, was thereafter divided by classes into hotels for the rich and those for regular people. Commercial lodgings specifically designed for the latter group did not take hold until late in the century. In the early 20th century, Ellsworth Statler created the first chain of middle-class hotels that mirrored many of the best features of the smaller hotels developed decades earlier. Although servantless and virtually serviceless, the Statler Hotels set the standard for comfort, cleanliness, and moderate prices (a room and a bath for a dollar and a half) for businessmen and other travelers throughout America.

The Hotel Pelham built in Boston in 1855 and the Stuyvesant Flats of New York established in 1869 were among the first residences to appeal to well-to-do, but socially inferior clients. The buildings contained many of the elite amenities of the Grand Style, but their lodgers lived as permanent residents in rooms and suites of various sizes, many with their own cooking and toilet facilities. The Dakota—established in New York City in the 1880s by Edward S. Clark of the Singer Sewing Machine Company—had high roofs, gables, dormers, balconies, and balustrades reminiscent of a German town hall. The building surrounded a central courtyard accessible through a high arched passage capable of admitting a horse-drawn carriage and team. The suites were divided into street-side rooms (parlor and master bedroom) and courtyard rooms (dining room, kitchen, and ancillary spaces). Some suites had drawing rooms 50 feet long with 14-foot-high ceilings. Many of the residents of the Dakota maintained their own staff of servants (a maid, butler, or cook) within their apartments. This style of commercial residence was also popular in Paris during the same period.

Vacation Hotels

The vacation hotel rose to prominence during the 19th century. (See Table 16.1 for a listing of popular mid-century vacation spots.) Throughout the South it was the habit of the plantation families to remove themselves inland to a seasonal cottage, a resort, or a city with a finer climate than that of the miasmic swamps of the tidewater in summer. It has been estimated that the gentry of South Carolina alone spent more than a half-million dollars a year outside the state on such trips. Moreover, upper-class families throughout the nation frequently tried to absent themselves from the cities during the fever seasons that came with the intolerably hot and humid weather of summer. Cape May in New Jersey became the summer destination for a wide variety of upper- and middle-class families from both the North and the South because of its central location on the Atlantic coast at the entrance to Delaware Bay. Families from New York, Philadelphia, Washington, Baltimore, Wilmington, and Norfolk made the Jersey shore their summer destination. John Hayward, contemporary author and gazetteer, wrote that Cape May "situated at the mouth of Delaware Bay . . . [had] become an attractive watering-place, much frequented by the citizens of Philadelphia and other [cities]. During the summer season, a steamboat runs from the city to the cape, and affords a pleasant trip. The beach is unsurpassed as a bathing place."[18]

Abraham Lincoln vacationed in Cape May at the seaside Congress Hotel, which exhibited all the services of a world-class residence during the summer months. The Congress was (and is) a massive structure for a seaside building with its high exterior porticos and towering exterior pillars. The interior ceilings of the ground floor were high, the marble floors were pleasantly cool, and the double-hung windows were large and numerous. The interior appointments were appropriately ornate for a seaside establishment, and the layout of the building allowed for cross ventilation from almost every direction. The majority of the rooms had ocean views, and the seaside boardwalk was only a few yards from the front entrance. It was remarkable that a seasonal clientele could support such an enterprise, but they paid willingly because the sea breezes and salt air were thought to be therapeutic as well as invigorating.

Nineteenth-century medical experts also suggested that the taking of mineral waters had beneficial effects on the health of those who could afford a month at the many vacation spots noted for their springs. The mineral-laden waters, filled with sulfates and salts of many types, were commonly taken internally to correct real or supposed intestinal ailments, dyspepsia, or general aches and pains. The warm and hot springs of these vacation destinations were commonly fitted with pools or tubs for soaking and fountains for drinking. Doctors and chemists often charted a particular itinerary or regimen for their patients that would, in their opinion, provide the proper "cure" by alternate soakings and imbibings of the mineral-laden liquid, but many happy travelers followed their own designs in the hope of stumbling upon Nature's own antidote.

From the 1830s to the mid-1850s a particularly popular and affordable trip for Southern families was a "Springs Tour." The city of Chattanooga in the hill country of Tennessee, for instance, was known for its sulfur springs and attracted a good deal of patronage among the gentry. The region of western Virginia that straddles the Alleghenies also abounded in various natural springs. Around these a number of fashionable resort hotels were to be found, connected by good turnpikes and dependable stagecoach lines. These locations were convenient to the best families of the South and within the financial means of the moderately well-off. The best-known springs at the time were all located in a 75-mile square within a respectable distance of many coastal plantations.

The hotels and cottages that served this clientele varied in their appointments and level of hospitality. As an example, besides well-appointed rooms for his guests, the resort of Colonel John Fry at Warm Springs, for example, featured a large ballroom, a stag-horn bar, and chilled wines—with a black bartender to serve them. While the women gossiped and loitered, the men talked politics, played chess, billiards, or cards, and smoked and drank prodigiously. Young unmarried men and women were expected to be polite and openly socialize, but they were warned to avoided any lasting attachments. Many places on the Springs Tour became disgracefully overcrowded, with insufficient blankets, and two people to a bed. So many private carriages entered the area that there was often insufficient space in the barns; and coaches, teams, coachmen, and servants often were left about to fend for themselves and find shelter under the coaches or under trees almost completely open to the weather.

The United States Hotel at Saratoga Springs in New York was one of America's most popular luxury hotels and a favorite destination of many wealthy families. The city of Saratoga also boasted the palatial Adelphi Hotel (not the one in New York City) with its three mineral baths and its fountain of youth. At the time these were two of the largest hotels in the world, but the upstate region of central New York also had dozens of smaller hotels and hostelries. The mineral springs, particularly those of Balston and Saratoga, were made more accessible by the growing system of canals and railroads throughout the region. The visitors were offered lodgings in a grand style, and many spent the entire summer taking the waters, attending the horse races, and enjoying a country village life filled with boating, canoeing, and fishing on the many local lakes. Most travelers, however, invested only about six weeks of their time in gossiping, socializing, and soaking while having consumed brandy juleps, ham, mutton, ice cream, and many gallons of mineral spring water.

At the springs of central New York were found rich merchants from New Orleans, wealthy planters from Arkansas, Alabama, and Tennessee, and the more haughty and polished landowners from Georgia, North Carolina, South Carolina, and Virginia, all mixed together with New Yorkers, Bostonians, Philadelphians, and other members of the Northern elite. Famous names from all over the nation can be found on the old hotel registers, including Daniel Webster, Martin Van Buren, Washington Irving, Andrew Jackson, and Franklin Pierce. The springs also became a magnet for many common families trying to emulate fashionable society.

Nineteenth-century vacationers were drawn to visit the many natural wonders of America. Cave tours were considered "agreeable and instructive" with a "pleasant sensation of refreshing coolness," especially in summer. Nonetheless, caving could be physically difficult for some visitors. Mammoth Cave in Kentucky catered to its visitors by supplying "a large and commodious hotel . . . two or three hundred paces from the mouth of the cave . . . with lights, guides, and whatever else may be required for their expeditions." This afforded the visitors to the cave a view of "its vast dimensions, its great heights and depths in different apartments, and of the singularity and beauty of the natural decoration they contain."[19]

The Pavilion Hotel opened in 1883 served visitors to Howe's Caves in central New York, a wonderful cavern first discovered by Lester Howe in

1842 and a great favorite as a touring destination for young adults. The cave was advertised as one of the most remarkable curiosities in the United States. A newspaper description of the new hotel noted, "The rooms are large, well ventilated, handsomely furnished, and en suite or single. It has accommodations for 200 guests. It has all the modern improvements of a First-Class Hotel. Our Patrons will find the Cuisine, style and management unsurpassed. It is located on the brow of the mountain commanding one of the most picturesque and beautiful views to be found in the state; has fine shade trees, and pure water; no mosquitoes or Malaria. There is good livery connected with the Hotel, and the Cobleskill and Schoharie Valleys afford the finest scenery and drives in the country. . . . The Pavilion Hotel [is] 39 miles from Albany, on the Albany and Susquehanna R.R., only five minutes walk from the depot."[20]

Also in this area, made famous as the setting for many of the popular frontier novels of James Fennimore Cooper, were a number of smaller establishments, including the Mineral Springs Hotel in Cobleskill, the Parrot House Hotel in Schoharie, the American Hotel and Rose Hotel in Sharon Springs, the fully electrified Sagamore Hotel on Lake George, and the gracious Hotel Fennimore on Lake Otsego in Cooperstown at the headwaters of the Susquehanna River. All boasted the good effects of their sulfated water, moderate summer temperatures, and clean air; and each was located on first-class plank roads serviced by daily stagecoaches that connected to the historical sites from the American Revolution, the natural wonders and rock outcroppings, and the romantic fresh-water lakes of the region.

Tours of the ruins of the French and English forts from the era of the colonial wars at Lake George, Crown Point, and Ticonderoga in New York were very popular and could be reached after a revitalizing steamboat cruise on the lake. Of course, at the time, the sites were just battlefields and outlines in ruin. It would take another century before full-scale re-creations of historic places would become common. Yet the ruins had a certain romantic and Gothic quality that fit the period. From New York City by steamer up the Hudson River and through the Champlain Canal, "passengers leave the Champlain boat [at Whitehall, New York] for stage coaches by which they are conveyed over a hilly but romantic road about three miles to Ticonderoga, at the head of Lake George, and thence down the lake, 36 miles, by steamboat, to the Lake House [Hotel], at its southern extremity [Lake George Village, site of Fort William Henry] . . . and from thence to Saratoga Springs."[21]

Natural cataracts like Bellows Falls in Vermont, Catawba Falls in North Carolina, and St. Anthony's Falls on the faraway Upper Mississippi River were considered great natural wonders. "The river seems to stop for a moment [before] it encounters the fall; then, breaking through every obstacle, it plunges on, its huge billows breaking on the rocks, and throwing a shower of spray [with] great grandeur and beauty." Niagara Falls, the outlet of one-half of all the fresh water on earth flowing from the Great Lakes, was "justly regarded as one of the most sublime and imposing spectacles in nature." The volume of falling water, estimated at more than half a million tons per minute, the precipitous heights, and tremendous roar were amazing. "It is the vastness of elements like these, entering into the conception of this stupendous natural phenomenon, which carries the emotions of wonder and sublimity with which it strikes the outward senses to their highest bounds."[22]

While Southerners abandoned their own beaches as pestilential and unhealthy in summer, New England beaches—particularly those within easy access of large cities—were considered a "delightful retreat in the summer months, for those who wish to enjoy the luxuries of sea air, bathing, fishing, fowling, etc." The "constant sea breeze and convenient sea bathing" were considered to "have a fine effect in restoring the exhausted energies of the human system." The coasts of Connecticut and the rocky islands and points of Maine were particularly popular; and the shoreline and island of Rhode Island's Narragansett Bay drew the wealthy to build palatial summer residences there. The island of Newport in the center of the bay became a mecca for the wealthy after the Civil War.[23]

Good accommodations, hotels, and boarding houses "of the first order" could be found at most seaside resorts around New York City, and some places provided special services for invalids and the elderly. Rye Beach and Flushing Bay on Long Island Sound and Rockaway Beach and Coney Island on the Atlantic were all popular destinations for New York residents. Coney Island, "much resorted to by visitors for the sea air and bathing," was considered a convenient destination for New Yorkers, even though they had to pay a toll to cross the bridge over the narrow channel that separated it from the mainland.[24] Rockaway Beach was 20 miles from the city, but it could be easily approached by railroad or by coach. The Marine Pavilion at Rockaway was "a splendid establishment erected in 1834 upon the beach," while a number of boarding houses offered "invigorating ocean breezes with less cost and display than at the hotels."[25]

The Grand Tour

The epitome of touring for upper-class families at mid-century was the Grand Tour of Europe. To winter in Rome had been the fashion among Europe's social elite since the 17th century, and Americans had followed their lead and extended their trips to include their historic roots in England, cosmopolitan and modern continental cities like Paris, romantic and artistic centers like Venice or Florence, enigmatic Egypt, and the Holy Land. Many well-known Americans had toured Europe with their families or lived there for extended periods. Among them were the politicians Thomas Jefferson, James Monroe, Martin Van Buren,

John Adams, and John Quincy Adams; the writers Washington Irving, Nathaniel Hawthorne, Henry James, and James Fennimore Cooper; and the painters John Frederick Kensett, Thomas Cole, and Jaspar Francis Cropsey.

Writer and novelist Henry James visited Europe at age 24 in 1867. He wrote that Americans were "forever fighting against the superstitious valuation of Europe. We feel that whatever it is we are lacking here can be found in Europe. There one finds royalty, foreign languages, high fashion; philosophers, anarchists, and artists; Neanderthals, pagan temples, and castles. Those who read a lot can easily become infatuated with Europe, and it becomes a projection of what it is they most desire."[26] Historian Henry Adams, a grandson and great-grandson of two presidents, wrote that his father (Charles Francis Adams, U.S. Minister to London) felt that too strong a love of Europe "unfitted Americans for America," but Europe remained a pilgrimage site for many of his countrymen throughout the century. The flow of socially elite families to the Continent between 1820 and 1890 was interrupted only by the wars of European nationalism in the 1840s and America's own Civil War.[27]

Available to only the richest of the antebellum plantation aristocracy, the wealthiest of the old-money families, or the most fortunate of the *nouveau riche*, the Grand Tour could last for more than a year—sometimes several years—as families took in all of Europe's major cities, sights, museums, and vacation spots. Many fathers resorted to such once-in-a-lifetime trips in order to expose their children to the ways of the world and provide a polish that was thought to be missing from America's upper-class youth. Moreover, the stay was thought infinitely superior to an equal time spent in the colleges or female seminaries of America. The cost could run into thousands of dollars, but the tour was a priceless introduction to Europe's history, art, society, and culture for the entire family. "To lives made wealthy by the whirring wheels of northern industry or bumper harvests of southern cotton . . . the Grand Tour seemed the quickest and surest method of absorbing something which America lacked but which time-mossed Europe possessed in ample measure."[28]

As Mark Twain (Samuel Clemens) wrote in *The Innocents Abroad* (1869) of his own grand tour in 1867:

For months the great pleasure excursion to Europe and the Holy Land was chatted about in the newspapers everywhere in America and discussed at countless firesides. . . . It was to be a picnic on a gigantic scale. The participants in it . . . were to sail away in a great steamship with flags flying and cannon pealing, and take a royal holiday beyond the broad ocean in many a strange clime and in many a land renown in history! They were to sail for months over the breezy Atlantic and the sunny Mediterranean: they were to scamper about the decks by day . . . or read novels and poetry in the shade of the smokestacks, or watch for the jelly-fish and the nautilus over the side . . . and at night they were to dance in the open air, on the upper deck, in the midst of a ballroom that stretched from horizon to horizon, and was domed by the bending heavens and lighted by no meaner lamps than the stars. . . . They were to see the ships of twenty navies—the customs and costumes of twenty curious peoples—the great cities of half the world—they were to hob-nob with nobility and hold friendly converse with kings and princes, grand moguls, and the anointed lords of mighty empires![29]

The itinerary for the Grand Tour was no mean ride through the countryside. The Crystal Palace built for the Great London Exhibition of 1851; the Champs-Elysées; the battlefields of Waterloo, Crécy, and Breitenfeld; Hadrian's Forum and the Coliseum; Vesuvius and Stromboli; the Parthenon and Delphi; and the Great Pyramids with the enigmatic Sphinx were all among the popular stops on the tour. The tourists stayed in the best European-style hotels and visited foreign resorts such as mineral springs, baths, shrines, and alpine retreats, sometimes in an effort to restore a shattered health in an alternative environment. All of these were on the usual itinerary of the European upper classes, and it was partly for this reason that many Americans were sure to visit them.

Seventeen-year-old Fanny Knight of Natchez, Mississippi, traveling with her family from 1854–1859, reveled in her diary of fleeting glimpses of Queen Victoria and Prince Albert, the Emperor Louis Napoleon and Empress Eugenie, Pope Pius IX, Russia's Emperor Alexander II, and Jerome Bonaparte (émigré brother of Napoleon I) and his American wife. Also prominent on Fanny's tour were meetings with ex-President Millard Fillmore and Senator Charles Sumner of Massachusetts, who had been caned on the Senate floor by Representative Preston Brooks of South Carolina a year earlier. The Knight family remained on tour long enough to become resident members of an international colony of traveling tourists that included a young sculptor from Hartford, Connecticut; two young American girls on their way to enter a convent in Spain; and two families of their acquaintance from home passing through Egypt on their own tours. Chief among the Americans with whom Fanny had contact at this time was Thomas McDannold, a young attorney from New Orleans who was attracted to her. He became a suitor after serving in the Confederate Army and made her his wife in 1867.

Throughout the century American tourists shopped for European and ancient culture while on the Grand Tour. The families of America's robber barons, in particular, bought up all the "portable culture" they could find on the European market while on tour and shipped it or carried it home. After returning from Paris, London, Rome, Florence, or Cairo, the family could bask in the reflected glory of their journey in a home decorated with paintings, sculptures, curiosities, archaeological souvenirs, and other mementos that marked them as persons worthy of admiration and envy. In defense of the Americans, it should be noted that upper-class European families did exactly the same thing throughout the Victorian era.

Table 16.1 Mid-Century Travel Destinations: Mineral Springs, Waterfalls, Caves, Beaches, and Other Fashionable Resorts as Identified by Hayward's *Gazetteer*, 1853

Ascutney Mountain, VT	Madison's Cave, VA
Avon Springs, NY	Madison Springs, GA
Balston Spa, NY	Mammoth Cave, KY
Bellows Falls, VT	Mitchell's Peak, NC
Black Mountain, SC	Monadnock Mountain, NH
Blennerhasset's Island, OH	Montauk Point, NY
Blue Hills, MA	Montmorenci Falls, Canada
Blue Sulphur Springs, VA	Mount Everett, MA
Booth Bay, ME	Mount Holyoke, MA
Brandywine Springs, DE	Mount Hope, RI
Burning Springs, NY	Mount Vernon, VA
Cape Ann, MA	Nahant, MA
Cape May, NJ	Nantasket Beach, MA
Carrolton Gardens, LA	Natural Bridge, VA
Catawba Falls, NC	New Lebanon Springs, NY
Cohasset Rocks, MA	Newport, RI
Cohoes Falls, NY	Niagara Falls, NY
Coney Island, NY	Nicojack Cave, GA
Crown Point, NY	Old Man of the Mountain, NH
Dighton Rock, MA	Old Orchard Beach, ME
Drennon Springs, KY	Onondaga Salt Springs, NY
Flushing [Bay], NY	Passaic Falls, NJ
Fort Ticonderoga, NY	Phillip's Point, MA
Franconia Notch, NH	Pine Orchard, NY
Gingercake Rocks, NC	Pleasant Mountain, ME
Guilford Point, CT	Plum Island, MA
Hampton Beach, NH	Plymouth Rock, MA
Harper's Ferry, VA	Red Sulphur Springs, VA
Harrodsburg Springs, VA	Richfield Springs, NY
Hoboken, NJ	Roan Mountain, NC
Hopkins Springs, MA	Rockaway Beach, NY
Hot Springs, AK	Rye Beach, NY
Hot Springs, VA	Sachem's Head, CT
House of Nature, IL	Saguenay River, Canada
Indian Springs, GA	Salisbury Beach, MA
Isles of Shoals, ME	Salt Sulphur Springs, VA
Latonia Springs, KY	Saratoga Springs, NY
Long Beach, NJ	Saybrook Point, CT
Lookout Mountain, GA	Weir's Cave, VA

Among Fanny Knight's keepsakes were those minute things one might expect of a 19th-century teenager: prints, postcards, bills, and letterheads. These included colorful printed mementos from the Old Ship's Head Hotel in Brighton, the Turkshead Hotel in New Castle-on-Tine, the George Hotel in Melrose, Stringer's Hotel in Windermere Waterhead, as well as the Hotel de Flandre in Bergen, the Hotel de Russ in Brussels, the Hotel Belle Vue at The Hague, and the Eagle House in Heidelberg. There was also a chromolithograph of the *Luxor,* an Egyptian river steamer fitted with ornate furniture, beds and bedding, a coal stove, and provisions of the best quality on which the Knights traveled the Nile.

As Mark Twain pointed out, the Grand Tour was "a brave conception; it was the offspring of a most ingenious brain. It was well advertised, but it hardly needed it: the bold originality, the extraordinary character, the seductive nature, and the vastness of the enterprise provoked comment everywhere and advertised it in every household in the land."[30] The Grand Tour was, for most upper-class families, "at once the fulfillment of a lifelong ambition and a flamboyant way of letting neighbors know that they had arrived."[31]

Notes

1. Susan Strasser, *Never Done: A History of American Housework* (New York: Henry Holt & Co., 1982), 149.

2. Maris A. Vinovskis, ed., *Studies in American Historical Demography* (New York: Academic Press, 1979), 17.

3. Unidentified author, "The Needs of Working Women: Homes for Working-Girls," *Arthur's Lady's Home Magazine* 37, no. 1 (January 1871): 53–54.

4. Benita Eisler, ed., *The Lowell Offering: Writings by New England Mill Women, 1840–1845* (New York: W. W. Norton & Co., 1998), 59.

5. Ibid., 57.

6. "Needs of Working Women," 53–54.

7. Eisler, *Lowell Offering,* 46–47.

8. Dickens quoted in Harriet Robinson, *Loom and Spindle; or, Life among the Early Mill Girls* (New York: T. Y. Crowell, 1898), 34.

9. "Needs of Working Women," 53–54.

10. Ibid., 54.

11. Lawrence Glasco, "Migration and Adjustment in the Nineteenth-Century City: Occupation, Property, and Household Structure of Native-Born Whites, Buffalo, New York, 1855," in Tamara K. Hareven and Maris A. Vinovskis, ed., *Family and Population in Nineteenth Century America* (Princeton, N.J.: Princeton University Press, 1978), 165–166.

12. Ibid.

13. "Needs of Working Women," 53–54.

14. "Abraham Lincoln at the Willard Hotel," Abraham Lincoln Online, http://showcase.netins.net/web/creative/lincoln/sites/willards.htm (accessed January 2006).

15. Roy Meredith, *Mathew Brady's Portrait of an Era* (New York: W. W. Norton & Co., 1982), 34–35.

16. Rudyard Kipling, *American Notes* (1891), http://www.chicagohs.org/fire/queen/pic0521.html (accessed October 2006).

17. Quoted in Remi Nadeau, "Go It, Washoe!," *American Heritage* 10, no. 3 (April 1959): 39.

18. John Hayward, *Gazetteer of the United States* (Hartford, Conn.: Case, Tiffant & Co., 1853), 667.

19. Ibid., 650.

20. Quoted from a newspaper advertisement clipping in the authors' collection printed in June 1883.

21. Hayward, *Gazetteer of the United States,* 646.

22. Ibid., 657.

23. Ibid., 655.

24. Ibid., 184.

25. Ibid., 667.

26. C. Hartley Grattan, *The Three Jameses: A Family of Minds* (New York: New York University Press, 1962), 239.

27. Henry Adams, *The Education of Henry Adams* (New York: Modern Library, 1999), 70.

28. Alexandra Lee Levin, "Miss Knight Abroad," *American Heritage* 11, no. 3 (April 1960): 15.

29. Mark Twain, *The Innocents Abroad* (New York: Penguin Putnam, 1980), 2–3.

30. Ibid.

31. Levin, "Miss Knight Abroad," 15.

17

Domestic Servants

The prevailing popular image of a precious and charming Victorian past
is built upon the repression of the harsh lives of laboring women.[1]
—Patricia West, Historian, 1992

Domesticity and the True Woman

The relationship between the house servants, or domestics, and the family
for whom they worked is largely obscured by a lack of documentary
evidence. The written sources regarding domestic service were largely
done from the perspective of upper- and middle-class employers whose
unbiased judgment of the situation is often considered questionable.
Many employers failed utterly to record anything about their domestic
servants. The house servants themselves generally lacked the leisure
time or the ability to write beyond the occasional letter or diary entry.
Moreover, the material resources of the domestics—their work dress,
their tools, their keepsakes, the sparse furnishings of their rooms—have
seldom survived. Indeed, the Victoriana of the upper classes, which furnishes many museum houses today, was carefully tended in its time and
was later collected by dedicated but somewhat shortsighted antiquarians
and curators, who were all but contemptuous of the role played by the
domestic servants that cared for them.

This form of institutionalized "selective memory" has worked against
those who would write an accurate history of domestic service, and rein-
forces the 19th-century concept of the *Cult of Domesticity,* a term regularly

used in historical studies to describe the ideology of a woman's role in 19th-century society. The *Cult of Domesticity* did not apply to all classes of women in America, and its advantages would not have been available to most upper-class women except for the leisure provided to them by the labor of the army of domestic servants. A *true woman* was expected to be domestic (involved in her home), as well as pure, pious, and submissive. Yet she was also expected to develop herself intellectually to be reflective, analytical, rational, cultured, and socially aware. "The result of an exclusive use of the brain and a neglect of the muscular system" had created, according to Catharine Beecher and Harriet Beecher Stowe, a "great inefficiency in practical domestic duties" and a "race of . . . fragile, easily fatigued, languid girls of a modern age, drilled in book-learning [and] ignorant of common things." In 1869, the sisters authored the following. "So much has been said of the higher sphere of woman, and so much has been done to find some better work for her that, insensibly, almost everybody begins to feel that it is rather degrading for a woman in good society to be much tied down to family affairs; especially since in these Woman's Right's Conventions there is so much dissatisfaction expressed at those who would confine her ideas to the kitchen and nursery. . . . Still, *per contra,* there has been a great deal of crude, disagreeable talk in these conventions, and too great tendency of the age to make education of women anti-domestic . . . to the entire neglect of that learning which belongs distinctively to woman."[2]

This last sentiment sounds more like Catharine Beecher, who unlike her sister Harriet, did not stand against slavery nor support the vote for women. She believed in the subordination of women to men as part of the natural order of society, but strove rather, to reduce women's household drudgery through the development of "rationalized" housekeeping. While both sisters were of a class that would have employed domestic servants in their own households, writers of "Home Economics" like Catharine Beecher, Sarah Josepha Hale, and others chided the women of their own class as "frivolous, superficial, [or] showy" because they so despised and neglected "the ordinary duties of life" and "shirked the primary responsibility of their sex." Beecher's major goal was to redeem personal housekeeping from dishonor as a vocation and to break the pattern common among the well-to-do of leaving housework to domestics. This writers' campaign generally failed to curb the use of domestic servants among the upper classes.[3]

Servitude

The upper classes had always had servants, among them both freemen and bondsmen, male and female. There were servants among the original colonists at Jamestown in 1607 and at Plymouth in 1623. The Hudson Valley Dutch in New York owned black slaves and established tenants on their lands who were little less than serfs. In colonial and revolutionary times indentured servants, apprentices, and slaves were available to do odious or heavy tasks around the house.

However, beginning in the second decade of the 19th century, there was a sharp decline in the use of apprenticeships (a form of personal service), and many among the immigrants who came to America did not come as indentures but rather as redemptioners, who could buy off their passage with cash instead of time. As the decades passed, there grew among the class of immigrants those with a growing network of family and friends already established in America who were willing to aid those who wished to emigrate from their native lands. It is also generally true that decreases in the cost of passage across the Atlantic allowed many more immigrants to pay for their fares from their own resources without encumbering themselves as servants. By the 1830s indentured servitude among European immigrants had almost entirely ended. Yet personal service contracts could still be found among immigrants from Asia, largely confined to California and the West; and the use of slaves increased many-fold, mostly in the South.

As indentured servitude grew more rare and the number of persons willing to work for a wage increased, the relative cost of employing indentures rose. This contributed to the end of the practice in the United States by about 1840. Many employers, however, continued to consider wage labor and abject servitude interchangeable—a development much despised by white workers living in the slaveowning South. The lack of indentures and the increased pool of young women willing to work for wages tended to augment the development of paid domestic service as an alternative to forced service. Yet, contemporary observers noted that "in the present state of prices [1869], the board of a domestic costs double her wages, and the waste she makes is a more serious matter still."[4]

The mistresses of colonial households had often relied on temporary, short-term paid "help" from among the young women of the neighborhood. These were often the supernumery daughters of local families from the middle range of the local social hierarchy. The vast majority of these part-time servants were single women between 15 and 25 years of age who fully expected to become mistresses of their own homes in the fullness of time. They often alternated work in their family home with that in the homes of their neighbors. They were usually of the same class as the mistress of the house and expected to work beside her in doing the normal tasks required of proper housewifery. "Such shuffling and reshuffling of workers was part of a larger system of neighborly exchange that sustained male as well as female economics in the period." In the 19th century this common feature of domestic service changed.[5]

Getting Help

The redistribution of wealth due to industrialization, the availability of wage-paying non-domestic employment for women, and the resulting growth of the middle classes caused a great decrease in the number of young women from good families who were willing to take up domestic service. Frances Trollope, a British visitor to America, wrote, "The greatest difficulty in organizing a family establishment in Ohio, is getting servants, or, as it is there called, 'getting help,' for it is more than petty treason to the Republic, to call a free citizen a servant. The whole class of young women, whose bread depends on their labor, are taught to believe that the most abject poverty is preferable to domestic service. Hundreds of half-naked girls work in the paper mills, or in any other manufactory, for less than half the wages they would receive in service; but they think their equality is compromised by the latter, and nothing but the wish to obtain some particular article of finery will ever induce them to submit to it."[6]

Beecher and Stowe—veterans of the crusades against slavery and a civil war—made the following remarkable notion concerning their own class of women just four years after the close of hostilities, "Domestic service is the great problem of life here in America: the happiness of families, their thrift, well-being, and comfort, are more affected by this than by any one thing else. The modern girls, as they have been brought up, can not perform the labor of their own families as in those simpler, old-fashioned days: and what is worse, they have no practical skill with which to instruct servants, who come to us, as a class, raw and untrained."[7]

American-born, non-immigrant women particularly resented working as domestics. "A sore, angry and even wakeful pride . . . seemed to torment [them]. In many of them it was so excessive, that all feeling of displeasure, or even of ridicule, was lost in pity," noted Trollope. "One of these was a pretty girl, whose natural disposition must have been gentle and kind; but her good feelings were soured, and her gentleness turned to morbid sensitiveness, by having heard a thousand and a thousand times that she was as good as any lady, that all men were equal, and women too, and that it was a sin and a shame for a free-born American to be treated like a servant."[8] Beecher and Stowe noted the story of "an energetic matron" who refused to allow her daughters to serve as domestics in the summer vacation household of her neighbor saying, "If you hadn't daughters of your own, may be I would; but my girls are not going to work so that your girls may live in idleness."[9]

Although it had been shown that young women could be successfully integrated into a work setting outside the home, the general employment of women in the male-dominated surroundings of factories and office buildings remained controversial right through the Civil War years. Factories that successfully attracted women employees were often run like corporate convents in order to reassure parents that their daughters' reputations would be safe. Such male condensation was not so much a contempt for the ability or value of women as workers, but rather a proclamation of men's own strongly felt social duty to support and protect their wives, daughter, mothers, and sisters. Even those men with liberal attitudes toward the rights of labor spoke of "being sickened by the spectacle of wives and daughters—and, even worse, single girls—leaving their preordained positions as homemakers" to take jobs outside the *Cult of Domesticity*. The duties performed while in domestic service were considered to be among the "normal womanly obligations" surrounding home care, even if they were carried out in someone else's home. The picture of a woman cleaning and cooking for others seemingly relieved some of the cultural distress associated with females working among machines, drive belts, and smokestacks.[10]

The quickening tempo of trade and finance during the 1840s and 1850s greatly enlarged the number of white-collar jobs available to Americans, and the resultant increase in middle-class status and wealth widened the demand for domestic servants. Although many women expressed a desire to go to work, few wished to fill positions as servants. As an example, a Brooklyn gentleman advertised for a lady copyist at a salary of $7 a week, and his wife advertised for a cook at $10. Although the wages offered were close to the average expected for such work, they were much higher than those paid for factory work—then at about $5 per day. Yet there was "only one applicant for the cook's place, while 456 ladies were anxious to secure the post of copyist."[11]

"No honest work was as derogatory as idleness," but service as a domestic was never considered "a reasonable channel for the employment of educated ladies." Some 19th-century social observers considered domestic service appropriate only for "redundant women" or those without husbands or families with the means to support them.[12] Many men feared that "once out of the household, women were subject to the whims of greedy and, sometimes literally rapacious overseers and masters, who would treat them like slaves."[13] A female supporter of maintaining the gender distinctions among the classes of society noted, "Who would not smile if the proposition were advanced of clergymen's and physicians' sons going out as valets, footman, and butlers? Classes and sexes must sink or swim together; that which is impossible for the man can not be made available—speaking for the class point of view—for the woman."[14]

Ultimately, such thinking caused society to turn more and more for domestic service to women who would not have been considered appropriate as "help" in the 1790s. These included blacks and immigrant women (predominantly Asians in the West after 1850, and the Irish in the East after 1820). Black "house slaves," both male and female, had sufficed as domestics for generations on Southern plantations, and they continued to do so right through the Civil War and up to the end of the century. Even the Presidential Mansion proudly employed an army of black domestics as butlers, doormen, servers, and maids. Chinese men and women in the West willingly worked for negligible wages as cooks and laundresses; and many established Americans hired the Irish even though they viewed them only in prejudicial terms. At the end of the century, a study of

Irish immigrant women—"Bridget and her sisters"—usually
made up the domestic staff of upper-class homes.

domestics found that 60 percent were foreign-born, 17 percent black, and
24 percent native-born whites.[15]

The Irish came to be the group most closely associated with urban
domestics outside the South. In 1825 in New York, 59 percent of women
employed through the Society for the Encouragement of Faithful Domestic
Servants were identified as Irish. Yet the Irish as a group were not only the
victims of social and religious prejudice, they were also accused of voting
illegally, of selling their votes to unscrupulous politicians, of undermin-
ing the wages and employment opportunities of other Americans, and of
engendering crime and immorality. Irish servants were hotly derided in a
series of cartoons that appeared in *Harper's* in 1856 and 1857 under the title
of "The Miseries of Mistresses." However, the Irish, being white, were less
visibly offensive to the social and political sensibilities of the sometimes
hypocritical upper-class Protestant households that employed domestics
but did not want to interact with persons of another race. Even if the Irish
were mostly Papists, Catholicism didn't show through a service uniform;
and the Irish, unlike other immigrant groups, could speak and take directions in English. Nonetheless, some of the discrimination toward domestics came to be identified with "Bridget" and her Irish sisters who became
characters in popular discussions of the "servant problem."[16]

It has been pointed out that "Irish culture fostered female self-assertion
and social independence." By way of contrast to other European women
who usually came as part of family groups where the men were the primary wage earners, many single Irish women came to America alone or
in small groups of females. This was part of a desperate economic strategy

that required that they send money home to their starving relatives still in Ireland. The tendency toward delayed marriage or non-marriage among Irish women under these circumstances made them prime candidates for domestic service, and in Eastern cities such employment paid fairly well—sometimes nearly twice that of factory work. It has been estimated that the Irish in New York City alone sent home more than $20 million to their families in Ireland in the single decade before the Civil War.[17]

Black domestics could prove an embarrassment for some white families. For example, George and Elizabeth Custer were usually accompanied by their cook, Eliza, a former slave who had served them since the second year of the Civil War. The Custers were post-war Democrats, and they had made many friends during their residence in the South. George Custer, like many whites, regarded the granting of suffrage to blacks as absurd, and he did not hesitate to say so publicly. Regardless of any other feelings they may have had about the black race, however, the Custers were very affectionate toward their black cook. On a trip through Louisiana after the war, the proprietor of a lunchroom tried to banish Eliza from the Custers' dining table because of her color; but the general insisted that she stay because "no other table had been provided for servants." At another time, General Custer succeeded in having Eliza wear a colorful turban when accompanying him in public. It was one of the fads of the day to have black servants dress in Turkish or Hindustani costume.[18]

Elizabeth, "Libbie," Custer had lost her mother as a child, and was the product of a woman's boarding school education. In her diary she freely admitted a "deficiency in housekeeping skills, possibly because of the overindulgence of her stepmother." Her husband, too, did not highly value these skills, and because he was demanding of her time and attention, he saw no reason for her to do tasks that could be turned over to others. Consequently, in addition to Eliza, George Custer hired additional domestic help whenever possible.[19]

In New York City at mid-century, Irish domestics composed the largest recognizable group of female workers, which suggests the extent of the demand for such workers and the Irish response to it.[20] Moreover, domestic service in general was the leading occupation in the city, employing 15 percent of the total male and female working population.[21] The 1870 census—the first to break down occupation for women by age and race—found that there was one female domestic for every 8.4 families. These were most prevalent in urban areas and in the South. Half of all working women were employed in private or public housekeeping in 1870. By 1890 this proportion had fallen to one-third, and by 1920 to one-sixth. Nonetheless, domestic service remained the largest occupation for women in every census until 1940.[22]

Domestic Order

In Europe, the persons who went into service did so as a class, and the service was considered a profession of sorts marked with customs and defined by well-established and well-understood requirements regarding the positions of the employed and the employer. Masters and mistresses there had no fear of being compromised by condensation and had no need to raise their voices or assume airs of authority. In 19th-century America, domestic service was clearly not so well defined, and those in service were "universally expectant" that their condition was a "stepping-stone to something higher . . . some form of independence which shall give them a home of their own. . . . Your seamstress intends to become a dressmaker, and take in work at her own home; your cook is pondering a marriage with the baker, which shall transfer her toils from your cook-stove to her own. . . . Your carpenter . . . is your fellow citizen, you treat him with respect. . . . You have a claim on him that he shall do your work according to your directions—no more."[23] Nonetheless, Beecher and Stowe noted that "the condition of domestic service [in America] . . . still retain[ed] about it something from the influences of feudal times, and from the near presence of slavery."[24]

In homes with several domestics under the direction of a housekeeper, there seems to have been formed among them a formal hierarchy—almost a family within a family. The housekeeper was probably an older female worker or the worker whose residence in America was the longest. She usually ran the service-side of the household as a manager with all the other servants reporting to her. The housekeeper was probably the only domestic to interface with the mistress. All the other servants would have been ignored by the employer's family except when being given commands, and many homes were built with hidden stairwells and passages to keep the servants out of sight. The cook, whose experience, quality, and skill were most important to the family, ran the kitchen and usually had a scullery maid or two to help her. In addition there may have been parlor maids, chambermaids, waitresses, laundresses, and a seamstress. In smaller establishments many tasks were incorporated into a single person. While the vast majority of domestic laborers were female, male domestics such as butlers, valets, gardeners, stable help, footmen, and coachmen may also have been part of the domestic household. In no case were governesses or tutors considered in the same class as the domestic help.

A domestic servant's hours of work were long and somewhat irregular because they were always on call. Most worked from sunrise to sunset, averaging about 12 hours a day with a half-day off per week. This serf-like circumstance needs to be viewed in a 19th-century perspective, however. Most farmers worked equally long or longer hours, and factory workers often complained about 14-hour workdays during which they were under constant supervision. At the end of the day the service staff generally retired to rooms in the attic, garret, or basement where a bed, a washstand, and a chair might be made available to them. Pegs on the wall served as substitutes for a wardrobe or chest of drawers, but most domestics came with a trunk or footlocker for storage. The rooms were usually shared with other servants, and they lacked the privacy afforded to the employer and her family. Nonetheless, they were generally better than the accommodations afforded to slaves or indentures in the previous century.

Domestic work could be physically demanding. Since commercial cleaning products were virtually unknown, sand, salt, camphor, lye, vinegar, and various homemade concoctions were used, but the application of good old-fashioned elbow grease seems to have been the most common method used in cleaning. The servants tended to labor in their own sections of the house when not cleaning or arranging the family's quarters. Depending on their responsibilities, they spent a great deal of their working time in the yards, the cellars, the pantry, the larder, the laundry, the linen closet, or the kitchen. The industrial economy of the nation made many goods and comforts available to the wealthy, but the servants seem to have worked in generally hot, crowded rooms, dirty and sooty by modern standards, and furnished with standard worktables, cupboards, cabinets, and perhaps a chair or two.

The kitchen was the domain of the cook, her scullions, and the waitress if there was one. The cook dealt with tradesmen, deliverymen, and suppliers, and she directed the preparation or preservation of raw foodstuffs and the butchering of meats into manageable cuts. In an era that lacked refrigeration, it required an enormous amount of care and attention to detail to safely prepare food for consumption. Besides the repetitive cycle of dishwashing, advice manuals from the period suggested the establishment of a daily cleaning regime, and a complete scrubbing of the kitchen environs was required twice a week. Sinks were scalded with a lye solution, cutting surfaces were scraped down, work surfaces scrubbed with bristle brushes, floors mopped, tools cleaned, silver polished, and fireplaces and stoves swept of ashes and cinders.

The parlor maid cleaned and maintained the main floor rooms such as the hallways, library, drawing room, and, of course, the parlors. There may have been both a public and a family parlor in some great houses. Victorian-era furniture was generally heavy, bulky, and ornately carved, suggesting a great deal of dusting, polishing, and heavy moving. Carpets, rugs, and draperies required daily sweeping or brushing, and they were removed seasonally and cleaned at least twice a year. In most homes all the carpets were removed during summer and replaced by reed mats. This probably required a combined effort among the servants due to the heavy lifting required.

The upstairs maid was commonly known as the chambermaid. As the name suggests, it was her task to air, dust, and sweep the family sleeping chambers and dump and clean any of the chamberpots, commodes, or washbasins that had been used in the night. The bed linens were arranged or changed; soap, towels, candles, and tapers replaced; fireplaces swept, and wood or coal replenished; and drinking and washing water put in pitchers. In many households the water for all this cleaning, and all the water used in the home, was drawn from a single source and had to be carried to other parts of the building. The same was true of any coal or firewood delivered in one place and used in another, but the kitchen fuel supply was usually located nearby to the kitchen service door.

Of all the tasks to be done in the household, the one most hated was found in the laundry. Although there were technological advances available to aid the processing of clothing and linens such as pumps, wash-boilers, hand-cranked wringers, and sinks with drains, the job was relentless and the work heavy. Water was fetched and heated on the stove or in the boiler, and the washing was done in a tub with a paddle and a washboard. The lye soap used at the time was very harsh on the skin. Pressing was done with a series of heavy irons heated on a stove or on an oil-fired heater. Fine fabrics and woolen outerwear were often sponged clean and brushed rather than washed.

The stables, stable-yards, lawns, and ornamental gardens were almost solely staffed by men and older boys. Work in the stables around large animals was dangerous; hay bales and grain sacks were heavy; and manure was difficult to remove. Harness, saddles, and tack needed constant attention, oiling, and repair. Northern city dwellers rarely rode on horseback except for amusement or exercise, but they did own carriage horses. In the South and Midwest, on the other hand, men were particularly fond of riding astride and could not be made to dispense with their horses even under the most trying of economic or meteorological conditions. Moreover, they often provided their servants with four-footed transportation in order to provide care for their own mounts when away from home.

Both the male and female gentry traveled mostly by carriage or chaise, and well-heeled city dwellers sometimes supported a coach as a sign of their affluence, even though they never left the urban districts in it. The gentry would go into debt in order to maintain their own carriage and team; and great pride was taken in being seen in a fine conveyance, pulled by matched horses, and manned by a properly attired driver and footman. The social elite considered the use of rented vehicles and teams an embarrassment to those who could not afford the ownership of a team and carriage, or the servants needed to maintain them.

Notes

1. Patricia West, "Irish Immigrant Workers in Antebellum New York: The Experience of Domestic Servants at Van Buren's Lindenwald," *The Hudson Valley Regional Review: A Journal of Regional Studies* 9, no. 2 (September 1992): 9.

2. Catharine E. Beecher and Harriet Beecher Stowe, *The American Woman's Home* (1869; repr., New Brunswick, N.J.: Rutgers University Press, 2002), 234.

3. Susan Strasser, *Never Done: A History of American Housework* (New York: Henry Holt & Co., 1982), 167.

4. Beecher and Stowe, *American Woman's Home*, 235.

5. Laurel Thatcher Ulrich, *A Midwife's Tale: The Life of Martha Ballard, Based on Her Diary, 1785–1812* (New York: Vintage Books, 1990), 82.

6. Frances Trollope, *Domestic Manners of the Americans* (1832; repr., Mineola, N.Y.: Dover Publications, 2003), 32. Mrs. Trollope was the mother of the Victorian novelist Anthony Trollope. She traveled in America in the early part of the century and wrote convincingly of the society and culture she found there. She was a woman of intelligence and keen perception, and her writing is regarded as honest and without malice or hate.

7. Beecher and Stowe, *American Woman's Home*, 235.

8. Trollope, *Domestic Manners*, 33.

9. Beecher and Stowe, *American Woman's Home*, 236.

10. Sean Wilentz, *Chants Democratic: New York City and the Rise of the American Working Class, 1788–1850* (New York: Oxford University Press, 1984), 249.

11. Faithful quoted in Marion Tinling, ed., *With Women's Eyes: Visitors to the New World, 1775–1918* (Norman: University of Oklahoma Press, 1993), 122.

12. Wilentz, *Chants Democratic*, 249.

13. Ibid.

14. Faithful quoted in Tinling, *With Women's Eyes*, 122.

15. Strasser, *Never Done*, 165.

16. Ibid., 166.

17. West, "Irish Immigrant Workers," 4.

18. Elizabeth Bacon Custer, *Tenting on the Plains; or, General Custer in Kansas and Texas* (Norman: University of Oklahoma Press, 1971), xiv.

19. Ibid., xxiii.

20. Wilentz, *Chants Democratic*, 110.

21. Ibid., 403.

22. Strasser, *Never Done*, 167.

23. Beecher and Stowe, *American Woman's Home*, 237.

24. Ibid., 235.

18

Slaves

Slavery

The continuation of slavery was one of the pivotal questions in dispute throughout the antebellum period. History inexplicably continues to blame the English for creating a system of "American" plantation slavery when the system is documented to have existed before the New World was discovered and more than a century before the English set foot in any colony of their own. Moreover, although a court-imposed sentence of indenture for life was recognized by the courts, there was no provision in English law for making a person a slave through the mechanism of birth regardless of his race. The African slave trade was begun by Arab and Muslim traders in the 15th century, and the Portuguese adapted slavery to their immensely profitable sugar plantations in the islands of the eastern Atlantic before the discovery of the New World. Three-quarters of all the Africans brought to the New World were imported by Spain or Portugal.

Unfortunately, the early history of slavery in North America is poorly documented and inconclusive. It seems certain that none of the founders of the first English colonies anticipated a dependence on black slaves. While the first Negroes brought to the English colonies were formerly thought to have been exclusively slaves, recent research suggests that many of them were actually indentured servants or free craftsmen. It is equally clear, however, that there were distinctions made between black and white laborers as well as slaves and servants in even the earliest

English colonies. Throughout the 17th and 18th centuries colonial laws and procedures progressively abandoned the common-law precedents of English jurisprudence in order to control the bound population of the colonies and appease both the employers of indentures and slaveowners. The distinction between free blacks, black indentured servants, and black slaves quickly blurred into a system of race-based perpetual servitude.

By the beginning of the 18th century, race-based slavery had firmly established itself in place of indentured service wherever large numbers of agricultural workers or menial laborers were needed. During the 18th century slave labor had proved profitable only on large-scale plantations that produced a cash crop. Historians have been hard pressed to explain the sudden shift from white indentured labor to black slavery as indentures were less expensive to maintain and generally proved more tractable workers. The absurd theory that the dark-skinned races were better suited to the hot climate of the South than whites was put to rest by John Quincy Adams when he noted that white Europeans successfully cultivated the land in hotter climates in Greece and in Sicily than those found in Virginia or the Carolinas.

In the decades before the Civil War there was a substantial population of free blacks living mostly in the Northern and Midwestern states. These free blacks seem to have preferred to live in an urban setting where they found jobs as household servants, craftsmen, and dock-side stevedores. Many owned their own businesses. They were twice as likely to live in cities than slaves, who were primarily agricultural workers. In cosmopolitan areas free blacks found opportunities for employment, exposure to black culture and religion, and the company of others of their race both free and bound. However, the majority of free blacks lived on the margins of poverty, and all blacks were subject to detention and questioning by the authorities without cause. Freemen were continually encouraged to sell themselves back into slavery or put themselves under indenture. Under the laws in force at the time, especially in the South, such a course was not as ridiculous as it sounds. Ironically—though it sounds a perversion of common sense—the laws of many states afforded legal protections to the life and limb of slaves and bondsmen through the property rights of their masters that they did not provide to private persons.

Slave Narratives

The first examples of black writing in the formal literary genres appeared in the 1820s as the work of freemen. Some early work appeared as poetry that attracted a following among positively disposed whites in the North, but certainly the slave narratives, which began to appear in the 1830s, had the greatest effect on the general population. Slave narratives sold very well to the American public, supplying sensationalism and sentimentality to an audience who relished both. Of these Frederick Douglass's *Narrative*

Slaves in the fields often worked in gangs under the supervision of other slaves who were appointed as drivers.

(1845) has perhaps garnered the most fame. Other significant works were penned by William Wells Brown—America's first black novelist—Josiah Henson, and Henry "Box" Brown. Popular narratives published during the antebellum period were not the sole domain of men, but few saw print before the Civil War. An exception to this was Harriet A. Jacobs's *Incidents in the Life of a Slave Girl*, published in 1861.

Many surviving slave biographies and narratives available today were based on oral interviews of former slaves and were taken down in the 1920s and 1930s by historians desperate to document the details of slave life before its participants faded away. Under the sponsorship of the Federal Writers Project, the Virginia Writers Project, and other agencies, these narratives were given by people who were, on the average, more than 80 years old at the time of their dispositions and had been mere children when the Civil War began. The validity of these records can be judged by contrasting them with other information found in the letters, diaries, and contemporary writings of the slaveholders; and the collections of plantation records, freeman's bureau documents, and other written material dealing with the slave trade and plantation management that survived the war. Each of these must be subjected to the same type of evaluation by which all sources of historical information are judged.

The small number of slave autobiographies from the era of slavery, in particular, has been used extensively by historians because they are few in number. Yet under close scrutiny they often turn out to be carefully crafted propaganda pieces, rooted in truth, but designed by abolitionists to appeal to all the dissimilar reform groups of the North. In the 1860s, however, there was an explosion of handwritten testimony from those slaves recently freed by Federal troops that opened a whole arena of information concerning the condition of black families under the institution of slavery. Much of the data collected took the form of anecdotal statements by former slaves recorded and assembled by well-meaning, but not unbiased, investigators. Nonetheless, the data that was compiled are useful, particularly since the testimony was timely and the slaves could not be expected to leave much in the way of other written documentation.

It is not correct to say that all the sources describing slavery are biased. Some sources suffer from other limiting characteristics beyond their obvious intent, such as the witness' selective memory, or his desire to make himself seem heroic. Furthermore, it is almost impossible to correct the data that we have for the prejudice of untrained, negligent, or incompetent 19th-century researchers. Such data have been used, perhaps too uncritically, by scholars, authors, playwrights, and screenwriters to distort the picture of slavery beyond our ability to know the truth.

The Slave Family

The slave family, by active design of the slaveowners and through no fault of its own, was an unstable institution. No Southern state recognized a marriage between slaves. Marriage was considered a legal medium by which property was handed down through white families unencumbered by indenture or sentence as a bondsman. Since slaves ostensibly had no property and could own none, the law saw no reason to recognize the union of slaves as binding. Likewise the legitimacy or illegitimacy of slave children was thought to have been equally irrelevant for any purpose outside of documenting the property rights of their owners. For this reason many plantations kept records of both births and parentage.

Nonetheless, the slaves themselves coveted marriages blessed by the presence of clergy. Some morally scrupulous planters encouraged such marriages in opposition to the immorality of open promiscuity. Others found that such a policy decreased the incidence of runaways and discouraged fighting among the slave population. A tradition of "jumping the broom" is thought to have been developed by slaves denied a legally binding wedding ceremony as a physical manifestation and finalization of their union. Female slaves did not take the name of their husbands, rather they retained the name of the slaveowner. Weddings of slaves dear to the slaveholding family were often held in the "big house" with the master and mistress supplying castoff finery to attire the couple and providing ample provisions for a celebratory feast, but this was the exception rather than the rule.

Slave courtship and marriages "abroad," as those between couples on different plantations were called, were generally discouraged due to the freedom it allowed slaves to travel beyond the owner's holdings. A dearth of available mates, however, made the practice more common among small holdings. Husbands were generally issued weekend passes that permitted them to leave after a half-day of work on Saturday and to return Monday morning in order to visit their wives and children abroad.

During the Federal occupation of New Orleans, more than 500 slave marriages were recorded as having taken place while couples had been slaves. Of these, fewer than 100 remained unbroken. While some unions lasted 20 to 40 years, the average length of a slave marriage was a mere 5.6 years. Records indicate that 70 percent of these marriages ended due to death or personal choice, and only 30 percent were broken apart by the planters. Many planters went to considerable length to avoid breaking up families because of the unrest it caused. It must be remembered that the greatest fear among Southern whites was that of a widespread slave revolt. Unfortunately, mortgage foreclosures, loan repayments, crop failures, the settlement of gambling debts, and the execution of wills brought many slaves to the auction block with no concern for the maintenance of the black family unit. Executors of estates often divided up slaves into lots of equivalent value for distribution to heirs or for sale to creditors with no notice being given to the integrity of the black family. Additionally, planters often made gifts of slaves to their children, especially as wedding presents. This almost always meant a change of residence for at least some of the slaves.

Slave children did not belong to their parents and were generally considered the property of the mother's master. The father and the father's master, should he not hold the mother, were denied any standing in regard to the offspring of slave unions. This effectively denied the father his place in the family and led to a largely matriarchal community organization. The offspring of a slave woman and a free man was, therefore, a slave. The progeny of a slave and a free woman, however, was considered to be freeborn, even if the woman were black. Even the children of a white master by a slave mother were born slaves, although the father could declare them free. This often caused great friction among the master's free-born white children who sometimes tried to reverse their father's will to the detriment of their biracial siblings after his death. In the case of a dispute in this regard, with very few exceptions, whenever a slave's human rights came into conflict with a master's property rights, Southern courts invariably sided in favor of the master.

Slave Dwellings

Slave quarters were constructed by the slaves themselves to the specifications of the plantation owner or of a person appointed by him. Accounts describe two-story as well as one-story dwellings, although many existing photographs depict single-story units similar to the

British "hall and parlor" type found in England and Northern Ireland. Another popular style was the "double pen" wherein a one-room cabin had a second room added to it. The addition was commonly done on the other side of the chimney from the hearth. In some cases, this may have accommodated a second family, although contemporary accounts clearly state that these were single-family dwellings. Average cabin size was 18 by 22 feet. This was a small space in which to house a family with five to seven children and perhaps an elderly grandparent. The interior walls of frame buildings were often lined between the wooden posts with roughly mortared bricks to provide some moderation of temperature and defend against rats. Less-affluent plantations provided only log cabins chinked with clay.

On large plantations, the slave quarters were arranged in groups with street names that reminded one English visitor of a country village. One South Carolina plantation contained three such groupings, each containing 12 dwellings. Some slave quarters had glass windows while others had only shutters. Slave dwellings often had shaded front porches—an architectural form thought to have been drawn directly from African or West Indian sources. The slaves were left pretty much to themselves in these areas, although some plantations located the overseer's house prominently at the end of the street.

The interior arrangement of slave dwellings varied widely. While appearing very European on the outside, many were adapted on the inside to resemble two-room dwellings commonly found in Africa. The main room functioned as both a kitchen and dining area, the center of which featured some type of table and chairs or benches. Cooking and eating utensils were stored in chests or sideboards. Some slave quarters were decorated with cast-off furniture from the slaveowner's home. Slaves who possessed carpentry skills generally provided their families with above-average furnishings. Walls were likely to be decorated with landscape prints obtained from traveling salesmen.

All of the rooms in slave dwellings were likely to be used as sleeping quarters at night. Some were furnished with serviceable beds, some had plank bunks, and some had nothing more than mattresses that would be rolled up out of the way during day. Children were frequently accommodated in sleeping lofts.

Slave Clothing

The clothing of slaves varied with the economic status of the slaveholder and with the tasks with which the slave was charged. Slaves who worked in the household were seen by visitors to the slaveowner's home and, therefore, their appearance was a reflection on their master, who might provide them with finer clothing than could otherwise be expected. Slaves who worked in the fields needed serviceable clothing that would survive the rigors of the work being done. These were generally sturdy garments and purely functional in nature.

Clothing was usually issued twice a year. While some plantation owners purchased clothing for the slaves ready-made, most plantation owners purchased cloth by the yard and had the clothing fashioned on site, quite a labor-intensive enterprise. Very large plantations had slave women working as full-time seamstresses who undertook most of the labor. Commonly the mistress of a small plantation oversaw the process personally, and she might even be involved in the cutting and sewing process. The work would be based on several sets of common-sized patterns with individual ones for the very tall or very broad. Other operations allocated set amounts of yardage for the garments to be made and allowed the slaves to fashion the clothing themselves. Children would be given yardage or finished clothing commensurate with their size and gender.

Plantation slaves were often clothed in coarse, but durable, "Negro-cloth" that was produced from cotton in the mills of New England or from wool broadcloth imported from England. The coarse cotton fabric was sturdy and became soft as flannel as it was washed. Wool or woolen blends were both warm and somewhat fire-retardant. Blue, red, and gray were common colors. The slaves might also dye the white suits tan or gray with willow bark or sweet gum. The cloth was fashioned into trousers and shirts for the men and boys, and dresses and skirts for the women. Slave women commonly wore calico, woolen, or linsey-woolsey dresses, head handkerchiefs, and aprons. Both sexes were provided with straw hats and handkerchiefs that were used generally as head coverings or neck cloths. Men, women, and children were not generally provided with undergarments, but flannel underwear was sometimes distributed for the winter.

Shoes for slaves were difficult to procure at a reasonable cost. In the absence of a slave trained in shoemaking from raw leather, plantation owners resorted to buying shoes in bulk. There existed an entire trade dedicated to the manufacture of cheap shoes for slaves made possible by the industrialization of the shoemaking process. These shoes—sized small, medium, and large in the same manner as military issues—were of inferior quality and rarely gave long use without the services of a cobbler. Despite the fact that some effort was made to measure at least the length of their feet, most ex-slaves complained of rarely having been the possessors of shoes that fit well. They generally preferred to go barefoot in the fields, as did their white counterparts when farming in temperate climates. Slaves who went barefoot in winter greased their feet with tallow to protect the skin.

Slave Food

Slave rations were distributed weekly, usually on Saturday. The quality and amount varied from farm to farm. Economic fluctuations often caused cotton planters to cut costs, which translated into poorer-quality rations, a pattern that those involved in the lucrative nature of rice cultivation did not experience. Some slaves cooked and ate all their meals in their cabins, but on large plantations meals were also prepared in a central kitchen. The latter was most common for midday meals because it provided the least amount of disruption in the workday. House servants often ate the same meal as the family after they had been served.

Slave narratives suggest that the quantity of food was often abundant, but there was little variety. Much of the food common to slave households was thought unwholesome or offensive to the delicate palates of whites. Whites normally did not eat chicken necks, gizzards, or feet. The small intestines of hogs were made up into chitlins; and coosh-coosh, a mixture of boiled cornmeal, syrup, and bacon fat, was considered less than appealing. Nonetheless, ham and gravy, fried chicken, sweet potatoes, ashcake, and hoecake—all Southern standards—were found in slave kitchens. To supplement their diet slaves were allowed to grow their own vegetables and to catch fish, squirrels, raccoons, ground hogs, opossums, and rabbits. They also brewed locust or persimmon beer.

Salted codfish was a staple of the slave diet as it was inexpensive and easy to store. Cod was purchased from New England fishermen who considered it a "junk" fish. Salted cod was a familiar staple item in many European communities, especially those along the Atlantic and Mediterranean coasts; and there was a worldwide market for it. Nonetheless, slavery provided a large and continuing market close to home for the American fishermen, and almost all that they caught and preserved with salt was sent south. Besides salted codfish, slaves were periodically issued molasses, salt pork, okra, peas, collard greens, turnips, and black-eyed peas. These foods supplemented their steady diet of cornmeal, fresh or dried corn, and potatoes or yams. Wheat flour, white bread, and beef were almost unknown to them.

The food provided for slaves was of poor quality by modern standards, and the diet was periodically unbalanced. Surprisingly, slaves seem to have been provided by this diet with sufficient calories and nutrients to allow for the heavy labor to which they were put.

Slave Music

Music was an integral part of slave life. It existed as spirituals, laments, work chants, secular songs, and funeral dirges. In a way, these songs provided a certain release from the dire situation of perpetual bondage. The airs established a group consciousness and provided strength to withstand oppression. The chants created rhythms for repetitive tasks, easing the physical burdens of labor and relieving the tedium. Slave music furnished an outlet for repressed anger, and served as a means of self-expression. The slaves brought songs with them from Africa, which by the 19th century had been adapted to English words and heavily influenced by the imagery of Bible stories taught to them by missionaries and evangelists.

Musical accompaniment commonly came from a banjo or fiddle. Masters would sometimes let slaves borrow these for holidays and celebrations. Some such instruments were purchased by slaves themselves with extra earnings generated by gardens or crafts. Many instruments were hand-made. A slave with particularly fine skills might carve his own fiddle, but it was more likely that ingenuity led them to improvise with materials at hand. Stringed instruments were made using horsehair and animal skins or bladders and gourds. Goat and sheep skins were stretched across a variety of objects to create drums. Other percussion instruments drafted sheep ribs, cow jaws, tree trunks, old kettles and pans into their design. Animal horns could provide the raw material for wind instruments.

Slave Patrols

Slave patrols, made up of whites, monitored the roads and periodically checked the slave quarters. Often an outgrowth of the militia, the patrol was usually composed of a captain and three others who were appointed for a period of a few months. Some states required these patrols while others merely provided the authorization for local communities to raise them. Alabama and South Carolina were more dedicated to the practice than other states, most of whom observed a degree of vigilance reflective of public sentiment at the time. All blacks were required to have a pass signed by the master or overseer when off the plantation and not accompanied by a white. A slave caught without such documentation was subject to deten-tion, immediate and sometimes vicious punishment, or even death. Twenty lashes were almost expected in such a case. Complaints against slave patrols came from masters and slaves alike. Masters who bought their way out of serving on the patrol were often replaced with poor whites who, not having a master's perspective, abused the slaves and hassled them in the slave quarters. Slaves grieved such untoward punishment, often regarding their masters as protectors from such scurrility.

Slaves instituted their own resistance measures. Warning systems were created that notified of nearby patrols. In time of turmoil masters would have all drums confiscated, believing correctly that the slaves were using them as signaling devices. Trap doors and hiding places were built into slave quarters to help unauthorized travelers hide. To protect slave meet-ing places, vine ropes were tied across access roads to trip approaching riders, thus providing additional escape time.

Slave Religion

The slaves who first were brought to the Americas came from diverse cultural and religious backgrounds. Upon arrival at a plantation, they found themselves intermingled with other Africans who held a wide range of beliefs and practiced a multiplicity of rites. The desire to hold true to ancestral customs was a strong one and some slaves would periodically steal away to neighboring farms to join with others from the same ethnic group. The diversity, nonetheless, produced an openness that transcended cultural differences and evolved into a common mystical relationship to God and the supernatural. African religious practices were marked by a communication with the natural world and a joyful expression of overt sexuality that shocked the prudish Protestants. Lacking an understanding of the African culture and having no desire to cultivate one, slaveholders did their best to strip slaves of their native religious culture. Effectively, however, these practices were merely driven underground to be practiced in secret.

As an outgrowth of the religious revival that was sweeping the country, many whites felt it their duty to bring Christianity to the slaves, and an intense commitment to conversion was focused on slave communities. Evangelical, revivalist Protestantism was thought to level all men as sinners before God, regardless of their wealth or color. The comprehensiveness of such an undertaking was facilitated by the increasing number of second-, third-, and even fourth-generation slaves who retained fewer cultural and linguistic barriers to Christian instruction. Generally, the slave community was open to this movement. The emotionalism, congregational response, and plain doctrine of revivalist preaching favorably impressed those of African religious heritage. Remnants of African dance and song found a home in the spirituals of evangelical Protestantism. The egalitarian perspective of this movement opened the way for black converts to participate actively in churches as preachers and even as founders of black congregations. Although they were required to sit in a separate section, slaves had the freedom to attend church with their owners and in some instances to worship at independent black churches. By the eve of the Civil War it was not unusual for slaves to outnumber whites at racially mixed churches. Even so, the majority of slaves who had the opportunity to become church members in the antebellum period were household servants, artisans, and urban residents rather than field hands.

In the 1830s and 1840s churchmen became increasingly committed to the idea of an aggressive program of plantation missions in order to reach the rural slave population. Planters were generally amenable to the concept of slave conversion in a theological sense, although two slave revolts led by slaves who found validation for their cause in scripture (Denmark Vesey in 1822 and Nat Turner in 1831) produced huge setbacks in any latitude afforded slaves with regard to independent religious practice. Planters were expected to join missionary societies and local churches with monetary support for the plantation missionaries, yet the distance between plantations made ordinary pastoral care virtually impossible. Proponents of the cause adopted the techniques of Bible and Temperance societies to raise Southern consciousness by printing sermons and essays, adopting resolutions, and devoting entire conferences to the topic.

As the decades advanced, growing uneasiness toward Northern abolitionists created an ambivalence in Southerners regarding slave instruction, however, the criticism of Northern churches against those of the South only made Southerners more sensitive to fulfilling their duty. Southerner slaveowners began to see that scripture could be used as a political tool to sanction a kind of Christian social order based on a mutual duty of slave to master and master to slave as found in Ephesians 6:5–9.

Supporters of plantation missions continued to encourage slaveholders to respect their Christian duty toward their slaves. Mistresses in particular were urged to take an active role in slave instruction by reading sermons to them, including them in family prayers, and conducting Sabbath schools. Some household slaves were led in prayer each morning by the mistress. Slaveholders were encouraged to allow their slaves the opportunity to garden a small plot, raise livestock, and accumulate money in the belief that as one class rose so would the other. This idea that "all boats follow a rising tide" had an economic appeal to some. The ideal of a Christian master-slave relationship fed the Southern myth of the benevolent planter-patriarch who oversaw the simple, helpless black.

This manifestation of the plantation missionaries' success was misleading and represented only one component of a slave's religious experience. In the secrecy of their cabins and amid brush or "hush arbors," slaves met free from the owner's gaze and practiced a religion that addressed issues other than a slave's subservience to his master. Freedom was often the subject of their prayer. Through prayer, song, and "feeling the spirit," slaves gained renewed strength through hope. These informal prayer meetings were filled with spirituals that perpetuated a continuity with African music and performance. The drums that had once been a vital part of their spiritual expression were replaced by rhythmic hand clapping and foot-stomping known as "shouting." Rather than truly adopting Christianity, the slaves had adapted it to themselves.

Generally, slaves faced severe punishment if they were found attending these secret prayer meetings. Gathering in deep woods, gullies, and other secluded places, they created makeshift rooms of quilts and blankets that were wetted down to inhibit the transmission of voices and singing. A common practice was to place an iron pot or kettle turned upside down in the middle of the floor to catch the sound. The roots or perhaps the symbolisms of this practice have been lost. On occasion, rags would be stuffed into the mouth of an overzealous worshiper. Slave narratives repeatedly note the uplifting nature of these meetings.

An underground culture of voodoo and conjuring were practiced in areas where there were large numbers of slaves from the Caribbean or where African snake cults that handled serpents as part of their ritual had been imported and adapted. The power of the voodoo priests or conjurers never reached the level it had in its native lands.

Slave Burial

Death rituals among slaves retained images and meanings that tied them to their African roots. In death one "went home." To a slave, this symbolized freedom and, if anything, it was a reason to rejoice rather than to mourn. While graves were marked by simple wooden markers, they were decorated, much as they were in Africa, with the last items that the deceased had used. Often these would be pottery or glass containers, medicine bottles, quilts, dolls, or toys. As a tangible symbol of the separation of the deceased from the world of the living, it was essential that these items be broken. Failure to do so was thought to invite a similar fate to the surviving family. Marble headstones, often with very fine tributes to the departed, were erected by some slaveholders for servants who were held most dear.

Slaves were buried in their own graveyards. Contemporary journals describe them as simple sites with a variety of markers and headstones. Some graves were decorated with evergreens or shrubs and on occasion, railings enclosed family lots. Funeral services required permission. It was not unusual for slaveowners to allot a portion of the workday to provide time for the funeral. Some even provided food for the celebration that followed. Others required that the funeral be held after the day's labor had been completed. The master and mistress of the plantation commonly attended the funerals of personal and household servants. If permission could be obtained, slaves from neighboring farms attended. Funeral sermons could be separated from burial by days, weeks, or months. This could be related to the African system of multiple funerals, or it could have been necessitated by slaveholder restrictions. Witnesses of night funerals described these services as solemn yet eerie, lit by pine-knot torches and filled with mournful strains of slave hymns. While slaves did not follow the mourning dress conventions of white society, some slaves were known to have had mourning attire. Such clothing was probably purchased after the death of the master and the slave was then permitted to use it for personal losses.

Slave Escapes

While the thought and planning of escapes was undoubtedly widespread, many slave escapes were prompted by the anticipation of a beating or rumors of being sold. The obligations of motherhood kept female escapes lower than those of males, but escapes were made by both sexes. Some slaves traveled via the "Underground Railroad," journeying along a variety of routes that lead north, or south to other countries. Many fugitives, however, were alone, penniless, and left largely to their own resourcefulness.

In the border states such as Maryland, Kentucky, and Tennessee, slaves were more likely to be successful in their attempt to slip away to freedom; but escape was far more difficult for those of the Deep South. These slaves often sought refuge in the wilderness, sequestered in caves for months and years, some banding together in what came to be known as maroon communities. Others secreted themselves in hiding places in sympathetic households willing to risk the conspiracy. The Seminole Indians also offered refuge to escaped slaves.

Some of the most ingenious escapes included that made by Henry "Box" Brown who was shipped by Samuel Smith in a two-foot-by-three-foot shipping crate to the office of black abolitionist William Still. Smith boxed up two additional slaves who were unsuccessful in their escape to freedom. Having initially hid under the floorboards of a house and then in a den in a bamboo swamp, Harriet Jacobs finally sought refuge in her freed grand-mother's storage shed attic. After seven years in the dark and cramped attic, friends obtained passage for Harriet on a northbound ship and she was able to complete her escape. Lear Green was a female slave who suc-cessfully traveled from Baltimore to Philadelphia inside a chest.

William Craft disguised his light-skinned wife, Ellen, as a white invalid gentleman while he acted the part of a male black servant. Ellen wore dark glasses and a poultice in a handkerchief to conceal her beardless cheeks. To avoid having to write, she kept her right arm in a sling. Ellen played the role of a sickly young man to the hilt and was befriended by fellow travelers who warned the fragile "young man" to watch his servant least he attempt escape. Successful attempts were limited. Census reports, for the 20 years prior to the Civil War, recognize 1,000 slaves as having fled. Some slaves did runaway only to hide and return after an extended period of time.

Mammyism

Prominent among the traditions associated with the Old South is the stereotypical character of Mammy, the perennially present black servant who seemingly ran the plantation house. Available records acknowledge the presence of female slaves who held positions somewhat equivalent to that of a head housekeeper or caregiver to the master's children. Yet their appearance in the record of the antebellum period is incidental, and not until after the Civil War are there a significant number of black women working in such circumstances. The secure place of the Mammy in the mythology of the plantation has been created by a combination of historic revisionism and romantic imagination.

The character of Mammy (and her male counterpart as in Harriett Beecher Stowe's character Uncle Tom) seems at first to have been a projection of the slaveowners' own delusions that their household slaves were devoted to them on a personal level—a repeated allusion found in contemporary Southern diaries, especially those of young women. Besides being characterized as benign and maternal, Mammy exhibits wisdom and "folksy" common sense. She represents a social relationship between blacks and whites that transcends the auction block, fetters, injustices, and punishments of the overseer. Mammy interacts directly with the slaveowning family in ways that no white domestic in the North would have dared, yet somehow failing to offend the traditional hierarchy of a stratified and highly race-conscious society.

No historian or revisionist cemented the image of Mammy more firmly into the mythology of Southern culture than the filmmakers of Hollywood. When author Margaret Mitchell published her novel *Gone with the Wind* (1936), she incorporated into it a large number of Southern stereotypes, including the mythological Mammy. The character of Mammy in the resulting 1939 film, ably portrayed by Hattie McDaniels, exhibits all of the characteristics of "Mammyism." She chides the debutante Scarlet in a motherly way, is concerned in family complications, weeps during its tragedies, and is aware of the most private interpersonal feelings of the family members. While Ms. McDaniels's performance as Mammy provided moving, warm moments (garnering her an Academy Award), there is no hard historical evidence that such women existed as anything other than a fictional balm for guilty Southern consciences.

Slave Labor

Gang labor was commonly used on large plantations. Plantations having of 50 or more slaves generally divided their workers into two gangs. The most able-bodied men and sometimes women were known as plow-hands. Less capable workers were designated as hoe-hands. On some plantations trash-gangs were assigned to such light work as weeding and yard cleanup. This last group often included children, those of greater age or other limiting factors. The gang was generally headed by a slave driver, usually chosen from the male slaves of that gang.

Sometimes skilled slaves were hired out to work for artisans or others who were in need of their services. This practice facilitated the labor supply and demand and generated additional income for owners who sometimes found themselves with surplus slaves. It was not uncommon for slaves to be hired out to pay for the schooling expenses of minor heirs or to meet other pecuniary needs of the surviving family. Slave hiring was more likely to occur nearer to cities, where the need was greater and better suited to the evolving industrial necessities of an urban economy.

Slaves worked in industries such as the manufacturing of textiles and iron, the processing of tobacco and mining. Most of these workers were male and the majority were owned by the companies engaged in the

Table 18.1 Slave State Statistics

Slave States	Whites	Colored	Slaves	Total
Delaware	71,169	18,073	2,290	91,532
Maryland	417,943	74,723	90,368	583,034
Virginia	895,304	53,829	472,528	1,421,661
North Carolina	553,118	27,373	288,412	868,903
South Carolina	274,023	8,900	384,984	668,907
Georgia	521,438	2,880	381,681	905,999
Alabama	426,486	2,293	342,892	771,671
Mississippi	295,758	899	309,898	606,555
Louisiana	255,416	17,537	244,786	517,739
Tennessee	756,893	6,271	239,461	1,002,625
Kentucky	761,088	9,736	210,981	981,805
Missouri	592,077	2,544	87,422	682,043
Arkansas	162,068	589	46,982	209,639
Florida	47,167	925	39,309	87,401
Texas	154,100	331	58,161	212,592
District of Columbia	38,027	9,973	3,687	51,687
Total	6,223,275	236,876	3,203,842	9,618,793

Source: John Hayward's *Gazetteer of the United States* (1853) provides this information about the Slave States in this period.

industry, but, as many as one in five were hired out by their masters on an annual basis.

Slaves were hired out to work in construction, carpentry, and masonry trades. Unskilled slaves were also hired out to work in brickyards. Due to the fact that brickyards were often situated near swamps, even the most desperate free workers were loath to work there. Risk of malaria and respiratory problems prompted masters who hired out their slaves to such facilities to demand premium compensation. Period papers indicate that slaves employed in such hazards drew double the rate for other slaves and as much as one-fourth of their value annually.

Some skilled slaves found substantial independence by offering themselves for hire. These slaves were only the most trusted. Their wages were paid to their masters. It was not without its negative aspects, however, as the person hiring the slave did not have the same personal or financial interest in the slave to temper working conditions. Hiring out also could separate a slave from his family and friends. From time to time, white artisans, resenting the competition, called for ordinances to limit the practice of hiring out, but slaveowners felt that regulation infringed on their property rights. This practice was illegal in some Southern states.

On large plantations the most common form of organized labor was that of the "gang." However, the cultivation of rice utilized a slave labor system, known as *task labor*, different from that of other Southern crops. The extensive hydraulic engineering needed to provide ditches and gates for flooding the crop did not require the labor gangs necessitated by sugar or cotton production. Slaves on rice plantations were assigned specific, individualized jobs. The task was delegated based on an average worker's ability to perform it in a single day's labor. Enterprising and skillful slaves were often able to complete their day's assignment and then apply themselves to the cultivation and marketing of their own crops or production of handicrafts. The slaves were subject to less direct supervision in this system and thus enjoyed greater independence. While the task labor system was developed on the rice plantations, it was also utilized by forward-thinking plantation owners to produce other crops throughout the South.

The Navy versus the Slavers

The role of the U.S. Navy during our nation's first tottering steps toward the abolition of race-based slavery is often overlooked. Although slavery within the United States was not abolished until Abraham Lincoln signed the Emancipation Proclamation of 1863, Jefferson had made the international trade and transportation of slaves illegal a half-century earlier in 1808 by signing the U.S. Slave Trade Act. From the start, however, the act proved unenforceable, largely because of Jefferson's opposition to an advanced program of naval shipbuilding. The lack of ships denied the U.S. government any power to halt the slave trade where it was weakest— in the Middle Passage at sea. At the same time, rising cotton production in the South was expanding the demand for slave labor, and slave ships continued to take blacks from West Africa and the Caribbean and secretly bring them in to American ports for black-market sale and trade.

The efforts of the U.S. Navy to suppress the international slave trade through cooperation with the British Royal Navy were initially hindered due to the antagonism left over from the Revolution, and all efforts were suspended during the War of 1812. Under several treaties between 1817 and 1830, the Spanish and Portuguese also made the slave trade illegal. The plantation South despised the agreements, but the U.S. Navy was, nonetheless, required to help enforce them. It was common for abolitionist forces in America to complain that the navy was not taking the law seriously. They pointed out that while the British Royal Navy went out of its way to actively patrol the west coast of Africa and the Caribbean for slavers, the Americans only seemed to enforce the restrictions when it was convenient.

In May 1820 Congress passed a new bill, which allowed severe punishment for violation of the Slave Trade Act. Slaving at sea was thereafter considered an act of piracy and any American caught could be punished with death. The navy was empowered to seize slave ships wherever they were found, and President James Monroe allocated $100,000 to enforce the act, immediately sending a flotilla of warships to the African coast. This was the first occasion on which the United States acted against slavery as an international partner with Britain. Sir George Collier, commander of the British antislavery squadron, reported that the American navy on all occasions acted with the greatest zeal and the most perfect unanimity with His Majesty's forces with respect to stopping the slavers.

Among those sent to patrol the waters of West Africa was Lt. Matthew C. Perry, whose family had been associated with the establishment of the American Colonization Society in 1816. It was he that escorted the first group of former black slaves as settlers to African Liberia in 1820. The navy captured 10 slavers in that first season of patrolling. At least six were from Baltimore, Charleston, and New York. In 1821 the 10-gun schooner *Shark* was launched from the Washington Navy Yard with the specific objective of eliminating piracy and slave trading in the reef-filled waters of the West Indies. Perry was chosen as the schooner's commander.

In the 1830s a commercial liaison formed between slavers in Cuba and the builders of quick-sailing Baltimore Clippers in the United States. It was almost impossible to prove that the Americans were in a conspiracy to trade slaves. However, Nicholas Trist, the American Consul in Havana from Virginia, was found to be deeply involved in fraudulently authenticating these sales in an effort to hide the paperwork trail from builder to slaver. Trist was removed from his post in 1841, but the trade flourished in the interim.

In June 1839 the *Amistad*, a slave ship belonging to Spanish owners, sailed from Havana for another Cuban port. On the journey the African slaves aboard, under the leadership of a warrior named Cinque, overcame the crew and took control of the ship. In the process, they killed the captain and the ship's cook. With the coerced help of the surviving crew, they proceeded to sail north along the Atlantic coast of the United States. Some months later, the navy found the vessel at anchor off the shore of Long Island, New York, and the Anti-Slavery Society brought suit in the Supreme Court, where in 1841 Justice Joseph Story claimed the freedom of the "Africans" under existing U.S. law. The court ruled that they were at liberty to return to Africa if they wished on the grounds that they had always been free men.[1] On November 27, 1841, with money raised for the purpose among interested abolitionists, 35 of the surviving Africans were returned to their homeland along with five white missionaries and teachers. A Christian mission to Africa was established there and remained prosperous for many decades.[2]

In 1843 a permanent African Squadron under Matthew C. Perry was sent to patrol all known slave harbors, but he was called away to serve with the Gulf squadron during the Mexican War in 1846. Perry had entered the navy as a midshipman in 1809 and did his first service under his brother Oliver Hazard Perry. In the War of 1812 he had been promoted to lieutenant in 1813, but had waited to receive a captaincy until 1847. From 1838 to 1840 as commander of the steam frigate *Fulton,* he had made a number of important experiments with power naval operations. In 1853 he was sent with a squadron to show the American flag in the Pacific, and with the diplomatic help of Townsend Harris, he helped to open Japanese ports to American shipping for the first time in 1854.

The U.S. Navy captured more than 100 slave ships before the start of the Civil War, yet it has been estimated that at least 50,000 Africans were smuggled into the United States pass the patrols. Nonetheless, the navy's role was invaluable in deterring the international slave trade, and it was arguably the first faltering step toward institutional racial equality in America.

The Dred Scott Decision

About 1795 Dred Scott (d.1858) was born as a slave on a Virginia plantation. He was to grow up to be the most famous slave in America. Taken to Missouri in 1827, Scott was sold to an army surgeon, who used him as a valet and barber. For four years, two in Illinois and two in Minnesota, Dred Scott lived in these free states. Upon the death of his master, Scott was passed on to the man's widow and her new husband, an abolitionist Congressman who persuaded him to sue for his freedom in the Missouri Courts on the grounds that he had lived on free soil for four years. The state courts quickly gave him his freedom; but the case was appealed and reversed by the Missouri Supreme Court.

In 1857, in a celebrated case (*Dred Scott v. Sanford*), the Federal Supreme Court decided that the Missouri Compromise was unconstitutional, and that a black slave taken to free soil "never ceased to be a slave" and so could not claim his freedom in a court because he lacked standing as a citizen with the right to sue. The 7 to 2 decision effectively denied the right of Congress to prohibit slaveowning anywhere within the United States. The opinion of Chief Justice Roger B. Taney was probably the most significant. Taney suggested that blacks could not be citizens even if they were free. The Constitution had been made by and for white men only. Moreover, Taney found that it was useless and mischievous for the opponents of slavery to quote the Declaration of Independence, for its great words were never intended to include Negroes. Slaves were articles of merchandise, and their owners could take their property with them anywhere as they pleased—in or out of slave states or free states. Not only was Scott not free, but no black, free or slave, could bring suit in a Federal court.

The decision effectively meant that Congress could do nothing about the extension of slavery into the territories. The South rejoiced that the highest court in the land had endorsed its slavery doctrine. Nonetheless, the Northern Democrats and their leader, Stephen A. Douglas, who had hoped to bury the slavery issue through the use of popular sovereignty, were embarrassed. The decision was a public relations blunder of the first magnitude. The abolitionists, who had instigated the suit in the hope of setting a precedent, were abashed by their failure. An outburst of protest greeted the Dred Scot Decision in the North, and the Republicans, who were the real winners in the case, made it a cornerstone of their successful 1860 presidential election campaign.

Dred Scott could have been freed at any point by his abolitionist owners; and he was set free by his owner soon after the Supreme Court decision. But there was little joy in this achievement for Scott. He worked for a short time as a janitor doing odd jobs and was finally given a position as a porter in Barnum's Hotel in St. Louis. He died of tuberculosis less than a year after receiving his freedom.

Notes

1. Fred J. Cook, "The Slave Ship Rebellion," *American Heritage* (February 1957): 60–64, 104–115.

2. Howard Jones, *Mutiny on the Amistad* (New York: Oxford University Press, 1987), passim.

19

The Family and Manifest Destiny

It will be something to say that I saw the first railroad train depart from St. Louis, and to add to that, the equally important fact that it was the first ever started West of the Mississippi. There are many who witnessed this event . . . who may not live to realize all the hopes and bright prospects which this commencement promises.

—*The Republican*, December 10, 1852

Manifest Destiny

In July 1845 New York newspaperman John L. O'Sullivan wrote in the *United States Magazine and Democratic Review* that it was the nation's "manifest destiny to overspread and to possess the whole continent, which Providence has given for the development of the great experiment of liberty and self-government." The phrase *Manifest Destiny* caught the imagination of the country and came, thereafter, to stand for the entire expansive movement to the West. Yet the slogan also coalesced a number of hazy images Americans already held concerning themselves, and it provided the nation with a solid purpose that carried it through civil war and reconstruction to the end of the century. *Manifest Destiny* was the one idea about the American nation on which all the sections and citizens could agree.[1]

Individual families are not normally considered powerful agents of nation building. Surely it is armies, speculators, industrialists, and railway magnets that are the impetus of national expansion. Yet this was not always the case in 19th-century America, and these tended to follow families rather than to lead them west. Calling themselves settlers and emigrants, families from across the states began a march into the vaguely empty space west of the Appalachian Mountains as soon as the Revolutionary War had ended. The simplest maps of the unknown interior spurred thousands of Americans to relocate to towns that existed nowhere except on land office surveys. With them, in many cases, came their slaves, forced to emigrate sometimes in ways that forever broke black family ties. Before them stood the Indians with their own families, aboriginal inheritors of the land, poised to be swept aside and ultimately to be dispossessed of their heritage.

Nonetheless, the exploration and domination of the North American continent was no haphazard series of fortuitous ramblings and random discoveries, but a careful process initiated by Thomas Jefferson in 1803 and programmed thereafter from the urban centers of the East and Midwest, particularly Washington, D.C., and St. Louis. Politicians, land speculators, and businessmen formulated specific instructions and sent explorers, traders, artists, photographers, and soldiers into the unfenced expanses of grass, the towering mountains, and the formidable deserts to gather information that would further the nation's plans for the development of the continent. In 1805 Merewether Lewis and William Clark returned from a two-year-long exploration of the Louisiana Purchase. Their maps, drawings, and descriptions of the territory fired the imagination of the nation concerning the West.[2]

The early life of David "Davy" Crockett in particular can be used to help illustrate the manner in which families moved west in the early decades of the 19th century. Crockett, famed as a frontiersman, Indian fighter, and founding patriot of the Republic of Texas, was born in East Tennessee in 1786. He was initially licensed to marry a young woman named Margaret Elder in 1805, but for some unrecorded reason the union was never completed. The next year at age 20 he married a local teenager named Polly Finlay. The young couple settled in a small cabin near other kinsman of the Crockett family where their two sons, John Wesley and William, were born. The growing family moved farther west twice in the space of the next seven years, and a daughter Margaret was born in middle Tennessee in 1813.

At the time of Margaret's birth Crockett was away fighting with the Tennessee Volunteer Militia in the Creek Indian War (part of the War of 1812). He participated in an indecisive battle at Tallussahatchee on November 3, 1814, and afterward was part of an attempted "walkout" of volunteers whose enlistments had expired. This mutiny was halted by the direct intervention of General Andrew Jackson, who had several ringleaders shot. At the end of the war in 1815, Crockett returned home to find that his young wife had died. The cause of Polly's early death is unrecorded, but it left the frontiersman a widower with three children to care for—one little more than a toddler. He thereafter sought out and married Elizabeth Patton, a local widow with three children of her own. The newly constituted family of eight moved to a creekside location, opened a mill using money left to Elizabeth by her first husband, and added three more children in almost as many years. The mill prospered for a time, but was destroyed in a flash flood.

The Crocketts moved again—this time onto the Mississippi River–West Tennessee border region. This area had been struck by a massive earthquake in 1811 that had changed the course of rivers, rearranged the landscape, and reportedly caused a concentration of game in the region. The quake (known as the New Madrid earthquake) was "centered on what is now the Missouri boot heel, forcing the Mississippi backward and causing church bells to ring as far east as Pennsylvania." Many lakes and ponds were dried up by the upheaval and others were formed where they had never before existed in low-lying areas. The dynamics of the catastrophe had caused many of the local Indians to relocate, leaving the region open to uncontested white encroachment. Had the Richter scale existed at the time, the quake would have registered an 8.0, making it one of the largest ever to hit the North American continent.[3]

Crockett first became involved in politics as magistrate of a frontier community and as colonel of the West Tennessee militia. In 1821 and 1823 he was elected and reelected to the state legislature. From 1827 through 1833, he served in the Congress of the United States as a representative. However, in his run for a fourth term, he was defeated by a narrow margin. Crockett had made no pretense at being a great political thinker. He rarely spoke of issues, tending rather to gain votes by personal contact, good-natured humor, and a free flow of rum. Feeling abandoned by his constituents in 1835, Crockett moved on again—this time to the Mexican state of Texas with a small band of Tennessean emigrant families.

A great deal of detail is known about Crockett from his autobiography, *A Narrative of the Life of David Crockett* (1834), most likely the actual work of Crockett edited and corrected by a fellow congressmen, Thomas Chilton. More than 30,000 copies were sold in the first year of its publication. "Bear Hunting in Tennessee," a story from the autobiography, emphasized Crockett's reputation as a hunter—one of the first great hunters in American frontier folklore and mythology. In the 19th century the "mighty hunter" was a common literary character, based on Crockett, that found its way into a number of period plays and novels. This and the popularity of his life story cemented a myth that allowed Crockett to become a legend in his lifetime. His death at the defense of the Alamo in 1836 assured his fame for years to come.

Like many other families at the time, the Crocketts responded to adversity or changes in their family circumstances by pulling up stakes and moving farther west, but they always relied upon the prospect of ultimately mapping, cultivating, and domesticating the unmanaged wilderness. Free emigrants often sought to re-create themselves physically, economically, and socially by thus moving beyond the limits of civilization. Family strategies like these and the underlying expectations that they included can be seen at work again and again among the writings of early travelers and settlers in the wilderness. In like manner the Virginia ancestors of Abraham Lincoln had moved westward to Indiana; the family of Andrew Jackson had moved from North Carolina to Tennessee; and that of Jefferson Davis had moved from Kentucky to Mississippi. This common attitude toward geographical movement was formulated as part of the "frontier thesis" of historian Frederick Jackson Turner (1890), who saw the availability of western land as a political and economic safety valve for the growing American Republic as well as a formative ingredient in the American character. Turner's work—although more than a century old—remains fundamental to formulating an understanding of the period of national expansion.[4]

By the Centennial Year of 1876, America had changed from a backwater set of fragmented British colonies hanging onto the fringe of the Atlantic coastline into a modern multi-ocean international power favored with the greatest industrial base in world history. Following its manifest destiny, the nation brought half a continent—some say the most valuable half—under its control. Only the cold wilderness expanses of Canada and the dry wastelands of Mexico remained outside its direct control, yet some Americans covetously spied even these. Although the nation was still to experience a number of setbacks such as the Plains Indian Wars and the Apache Wars of the final quarter of the century, it also developed tens of thousands of inventions, expanded its political base to include all its white male citizens, extended public education to most of its children, fought and won several minor wars with foreign powers, and became the leading maritime shipper and producer of manufactured and agricultural goods in the world.

Expansionism

The Ohio River and its tributaries initially provided the most direct route to the lands of the Midwest. The movement of emigrants usually paralleled the valleys of the Ohio or the Tennessee Rivers. Early pioneer families floated or poled their way down these waterways and their tributaries on a wide assortment of rafts, barges, and keelboats. Others moved west on overland courses parallel to the rivers where the going was easier and the topography more gently changing. The rivers wore gaps in the mountains that made their passage feasible. The Cumberland Gap is the best known of these. Formed by an ancient creek that was later redirected by geologic forces into the Cumberland River, the gap was used for centuries by Native Americans to cross the mountains. Daniel Boone was credited with opening the gap to white settlers entering Kentucky and Tennessee, and the foot trail through it was later widened to accommodate wagons.

A large area of Ohio known as the "Firelands" was quickly settled by families from coastal Connecticut who had been given government land to replace their homes burned by the British in the Revolutionary War. The Midwestern territories of Indiana and Illinois were initially settled by Southerners coming through Kentucky. Those sympathetic to the Southern way of life were quickly overwhelmed by others with Northern opinions and by immigrants with European sentiments. The Midwest attracted a significant increase in population during the 1840s from among Germans, Swedes, and other working-class Europeans who bypassed the slaveholding South to settle there.

Internal Improvements

In 1796, Congress authorized the construction of Zane's Trace, a road from western Virginia to Kentucky that became a major thoroughfare for emigrant families from the upper South to Kentucky. In 1807 the U.S. Senate instructed Secretary of the Treasury Albert Gallatin to prepare a plan for opening roads and building canals for those wishing to emigrate in order to improve the economic growth of the nation as a whole. In 1811 the First National Road from Cumberland, Maryland, across the southwestern corner of Pennsylvania to Wheeling, (West) Virginia, on the Ohio River was completed. This was the first multistate improvement project attempted by the Federal government, and a number of "pike" towns sprang up along its route. The Boonesborough Turnpike between Hagerstown and that town was paved in macadam in 1823. The National Road was paved in the 1830s. The Shenandoah Valley Pike through Maryland to the Carolinas and Georgia and the Columbia Pike south out of Nashville, Tennessee, were completed in like manner in the 1850s.

Gallatin's far-reaching plan of Federal outlays also included support for a man-made waterway across central New York State from the Hudson River to Lake Erie. In 1825 the opening of the Erie Canal formed a convenient transportation link between the cities of the Northeast, the headwaters of the Ohio River, and via the Great Lakes to all the Midwest as far away as the Indian lands in Wisconsin and Minnesota. In its first year of operation 19,000 vessels passed through the Erie Canal. Its financial success provided an impetus for imitation, and man-made watercourses soon connected separate lakes and streams into a vast and efficient waterborne transportation web. Along the riverbanks and lakeshores a mix of mostly New Yorkers, Pennsylvanians, and New Englanders created the first great urban centers of the American Midwest.

The decades before the Civil War also saw a rapid growth in the region of telegraph lines and railroads with both track mileage and usage skyrocketing. The vast interior of the country was thereby brought into unprecedented communication with the older parts of the nation. Inexpensive waterborne transportation provided the Midwest with a commercial advantage over its Southern neighbors for the sale of its agriculture produce to the urban centers of the Northeast. In response to the increasing competition, many Southern planters abandoned their worn-out coastal farmlands in Georgia and South Carolina for new fields in Mississippi and Alabama that promised to be more fertile. Yet in doing so they dispossessed the Indians of their land, threatened the spread of slavery, and inflamed the demands for both Indian removal and abolition. This circumstance was repeated in the 1840s by Southern planters moving farther west into Texas and Arkansas. In this manner Southerners settled the trans-Mississippi Southwest by attempting to enlarge the antebellum cotton kingdom.

Travel to the territory beyond the Mississippi River proved difficult and dangerous. A British pamphlet from 1820 notes of the region, "Two hundred miles west of the Mississippi River the arable soil of the country experiences a total change. Beyond that limit an extensive desert commences, which extends to the Pacific Ocean." The editors in London erroneously reported the growing city of St. Louis to be on the outermost edge of feasible development. Grasses on the plains could be taller than an adult and difficult for horses or oxen to push through with a wagon in tow. Canebrakes composed of thick native bamboo could be all but impenetrable. Travelers coming from the mountains and forests of New England would find the shifting ooze of Missouri and Arkansas bottomland unfamiliar and threatening, while former residents of the Tidewater would be equally unaccustomed to the dry prairie heat of the day and the sudden cold that froze the ground in a single night.[5]

For three decades after the Lewis and Clark Expedition the trans-Mississippi region of the Great Plains remained a mere wilderness tempting only to adventurers, land speculators, and fur traders. The 19th-century explorations of men like Merewether Lewis, William Clark, Zebulon Pike, John C. Fremont, and others hinted at the richness of the interior West. Only the Indian nations of the eastern woodlands, driven from their native lands by white encroachment, settled there. Yet even these were greeted with the armed resistance of the Plains Indian tribes.[6]

The Emigrant Train

A contemporary observer noted that "pioneers are never satisfied, no matter where they are. They always want to be somewhere else." In the 1840s and 1850s that "somewhere else" was increasingly identified as the Far West of Oregon or California.[7] Nineteenth-century farm families often sought to change where they lived, and two or three families in a community might get together and decide to set out together. Like little streams, forming rivulets, and rivulets adding together to create a surge, small groups of families joined others to create mighty emigrant trains whose mutual goal was to cross the continent and find a more successful life. At the peak of emigration almost 50,000 persons may have moved West annually.

Francis Marion Watkins was a 10-year-old boy when his father and two neighbor families decided to go to California in 1865. Greatly aged when relating the story, Watkins noted, "It was no easy matter when I was a boy in Iowa seventy years ago to get to California. There were only three ways to get there. One was to take a steamer in New York and go by way of the Isthmus of Panama. Another was to cross the plains as a passenger on the Overland Stages, the third was to come in an emigrant train. That is the way, in the summer of 1865, that I arrived in California."[8]

Besides his mother and father, young Francis was accompanied by an eight-year-old sister, three unmarried brothers (aged 13, 20, and 22), two married brothers and their families that included a four-year-old girl and a two-year old boy (Francis's niece and nephew). Added to the five wagons that would move his relatives were five more belonging to their neighbors. These included a couple with three children, the older girl 15, and a second couple with five older children, three girls and two boys who Francis deemed "already grown up." Francis's father also hired two additional drivers for each of his five wagons, 10 young men in all, who "were tickled to death to get the chance" to move west. The elder Watkins, seemingly a thoughtful and sensible man, "knew that when we got out in

Captain Marcy noted the strain placed upon emigrants, "Sometimes men . . . upon trial, do not come up to anticipation."

the Indian country we would have to take turns standing guard at night and he wanted to make it as easy as possible for the drivers."[9]

Emigration entailed no small expense in those days of national crisis and civil strife. Consumer prices were near their wartime peak in 1865. Although the drivers agreed to serve for the food they would receive, the elder Watkins sold his Iowa farm for $12,000 and had a mere $3,000 left after fitting out his traveling establishment. Some of the mule teams cost $700 a pair, but horses were slightly less. Twenty riding horses and harness mules were purchased so that they could be rested alternately. Three large new wagons—two heavy wagons each with four-mule teams for equipment and provisions and one lighter one with a two-horse team for carrying the family—were purchased. Francis's married brothers provided their own wagons and kit.

There were without doubt endless arguments about the comparative qualities of mules and oxen, not only for use on the emigrant trail but also for everyday farm use. In 1843 Peter H. Burnett, an oxen fancier, wrote, "The ox is a most noble animal, patient, thrifty, durable, gentle, and easily driven." Burnett, later governor of California, found oxen "greatly superior to mules." In 1849 James Stewart, a mule proponent, expressed the following sentiment on the subject, "It is a noble sight to see those small, tough, earnest, honest Spanish mules, every nerve strained to the utmost, examples of obedience, and of duty performed under trying circumstances." A period price list from 1850 shows a pair of oxen for $50, while a single mule cost $75—a great deal less expensive than they were to be found 15 years later, but an extravagance when compared to their bovine counterparts.[10]

A best-selling informational handbook for prospective emigrants to the West was Capt. Randolph B. Marcy's *The Prairie Traveler* (1859). With regard to wagon teams, Marcy advised, "There has been much discussion regarding the relative merits of mules and oxen for prairie traveling. . . . Upon good firm roads, in a populated country, where grain can be procured, I should unquestionably give the preference to mules, as they travel faster, and endure the heat of summer much better than oxen . . . if the journey be not over 1000 miles. . . . But when the march is to extend 1500 or 2000 miles, or over a rough, sandy or muddy road, I believe young oxen will endure better than mules." Marcy also suggested that oxen teams were less expensive, less likely to be stampeded by Indians, and more likely (because of their slow speed) to be recovered if stolen.[11]

The senior Watkins was obviously a mule fancier, but Watkins, the younger, noted that his father was careful that no one wagon was loaded so heavily that just two mules could not pull it. "Father took along enough provisions to last four months. We had at least fifteen hundred pounds of flour alone. Bacon and hams and lard were brought along in large quantifies as were also dried apples, peaches and pears. Father even had the family doctor fix up a box of medicines, such as quinine, etc., that we might need on the trip." Each of the married Watkins brothers had his own wagon, and the neighbors had a total of five more. The small group of 10 wagons, with close to 40 persons, was heavily armed with revolvers, rifles, and shotguns to provide their own protection on the first leg of the journey. They traveled 125 miles to cross the Missouri River at Omaha, where they expected to join a larger train that would cross the Great Plains.[12]

The peak of emigration by wagon train had taken place about 1850, and most families moving in the 1860s understood the potential hardships of the trip. The emigrants had many trails to follow to their new homes. Chief among these was the Oregon Trail, beginning in Independence, Missouri, and ending in Portland in Oregon Territory. The first stop on the Oregon Trail was Fort Leavenworth, Kansas, which also served those planning to take the Santa Fe Trail to the south. An offshoot, the California Trail, climbed the Sierras and ended in Sacramento. Along these routes emigrants stopped at one of the many recognizable landmarks, such as Chimney Rock. Near the Sweetwater River many children and young adults climbed Independence Rock in order to etch their names among the others left by previous passersby. Seventeen-year-old Jenny Scott noted that climbers had to be careful to skirt the rattlesnakes nestled among the prairie grasses, "but this didn't faze the boys and girls who were busy devising ways to ascend to seemingly unreachable heights to find blank spots where they could write their names."[13]

Seemingly more bothersome than rattlesnakes, which could be avoided with care, were the insects. "One teamster died," reported a desert traveler, "from a scorpion's bite." Yet even fatalities were less "aggravating" for the survivors than the seed-ticks and chiggers. "The latter bury their heads under the skin, and when they are swollen with blood, it is almost impossible to extract them without leaving the head imbedded. This festers, and the irritation is almost unbearable."[14]

Another route, pioneered by the Mormons and used by others, entered Salt Lake and made a side connection with the California Trail. It was appropriately called the Mormon Trail. There were also a number of other "short-cuts" and "cut-offs" proposed by various wagon guides, but some of these like Meck's or Hasting's proved dangerous or even deadly. It was on Hasting's cut-off that the Donner party became stranded and was forced to resort to cannibalism to survive; while Meck's short-cut proved hundreds of miles longer than staying on the original trail. The main artery to the southwest was the Santa Fe Trail, which split after entering the mountains into the Gila Trail and the Old Spanish Trail.

The western regions were vast, but they were not devoid of white contact. Francis Parkman, recording his observations along the Arkansas River in 1845, noted, "When we had stopped to rest at noon, a long train of Santa Fe wagons came up and trailed slowly past us in their picturesque procession."[15] The emigrant trains on the Oregon Trail followed the same road along the Platte River that was used by the Overland Stage Lines. Slow-moving emigrant wagons were often overtaken by fast coaches that moved between stations and forts at the gallop in stages of 12 to 15 miles—hence the terms *stage line* and *stage coach*. In Indian country groups of about two dozen soldiers were posted at these stations, and companies of 100 men or more were placed in outpost forts at 100-mile intervals to protect the stages and the emigrant trains. Squads of cavalry (usually composed of eight troopers) were sometimes set as escorts for the coaches, but the emigrants trains were usually expected to fend for themselves.

While a uniformed presence produced a certain level of optimism concerning security, small groups of soldiers were no guarantee of protection in the face of overwhelming numbers of Indian warriors. Marcy noted, "Our little army, scattered as it has been over the vast area of our possessions, in small garrisons of one or two companies each, has seldom been in a situation to act successfully on the offensive against large numbers of . . . marauders, and has often been condemned to hold itself almost exclusively upon the defensive."[16] Consequently the government ordered emigrants to form up in trains of at least 20 wagons when planning to cross hostile country, and the soldiers were very strict about stopping small groups of emigrants from traveling alone.

The 10 Watkins's wagons joined a train of more than 214 wagons at Fort Laramie led by Brad Crow and his five brothers. All the wagons of the Crow emigrant train were divided up into companies of 20 led by a wagon master, and each company rotated its position in the daily line of march so that they were not constantly "eating dust." The Crow emigrant train was one of the largest of its time, containing among its complement more than 600 men of fighting age. Small groups of emigrants often avoided the soldiers and the forts by leaving the roads and circling around them because they did not want to join big trains like the Crow train where every man did guard duty and subjected himself to military-style rule.[17]

Many wagon trains required that those joining the company sign contracts to the effect that they would follow certain rules, maintain a minimum outfit, and place themselves under the laws of a council of emigrants chosen for the purpose. Breaking the compact could be punished by banishment from the train, fines, or physical punishments like flogging. "In Indian country there was no law except what the emigrants themselves made."[18] Few trains ever knowingly abandoned a wagon, and breakdowns or sickness were usually dealt with in terms of community aid and care. "If there was any place in the world where people will stick together it was when traveling through a hostile country."[19]

Capt. Marcy advised that small groups of whites traveling on the Plains avoid any Indians that they came upon "unless able to resist attack under the most favorable circumstances . . . signal them to keep away. If they do not obey . . . make for the nearest timber [but] never draw trigger unless [you] find that your life depends on the shot; for, as soon as your shot is delivered, your sole dependence, unless you have time to reload, must be upon the speed of your horse."[20] The soldiers at the forts suggested that the emigrants shoot any Indians skulking about the camps, and that they respond immediately to any bands that appeared from the north side of the road, which was thought to be the province of hostile tribes. "On the south side of the road the government orders were to keep a sharp lookout for Indians but not to shoot them if they came up peaceably." Raiding Indians were described as rushing in on their ponies, letting fly with their arrows, and rushing back out of range of gunfire. Yet few large wagon trains were ever attacked in such a manner.[21]

As soon as the night camp was reached, the wagons would draw up in a great circle with the front wheels beside the rear wheel of the previous wagon. This was done each day, but it took a great deal of time for the whole length of the train to arrive at the same point. The wagon circle served as protection in case of attack, but its real purpose was to contain the livestock after they had been grazed and fed on the surrounding prairie until dusk. The Hollywood-style movie concept of Indians doing laps on their ponies around the outside of a wagon circle in an attack is not evident in the historical record. Stealthy infiltration of the livestock herd by Indians set on stealing a horse or a cow was a much greater threat. Accounts of Indians repeatedly detected prowling at night around the camps were considered portents of a very dangerous nature, and a single man was sometimes killed and scalped without anyone's knowledge. For this reason, "Two men were on duty from each company until midnight

Emigrant trains circled their wagons in order to protect their stock at night. Many trains may have been traveling along parallel routes at the same time.

when they were relieved by two more who stood guard until daylight. In a large train this could be a total of 20 armed men. The guards walked back and forth outside the corral."[22]

With the guards set and a frugal meal downed, all the members of the wagon train "were collected around one camp-fire for the observance of public worship, which was conducted by a clergyman present. Into that hour of earnest worship were crowded memories of the home-land and friends now forever abandoned for a settlement in the far off Southwest. There flowed and mingled the tear of regret and of hope; there and then rose the earnest prayer for Providential guidance." The hush of sleep quickly stole over the camp, broken perhaps by the growl of an ever-faithful watch dog, or the outburst of some infant appealing for a night-time meal. All, wearied by the hurry and bustle of the previous day, repaired to sleep in order to face another.[23]

Most of the women who emigrated west were competent in cooking and in making do. They seem to have been excellent managers under very trying conditions, even if they had no trouble with the Indians. One of these was Rebecca Ridgley who traveled with her husband Joshua from Wisconsin to Nevada in 1864. She was described as "an ideal helpmate for a westward bound pioneer." Rebecca seems to have been a remarkably good cook, and according to Albert Dickson, a 13-year-old bound-boy traveling with the group, they "ate well." She took along on the trip "dried apples and peaches, cereals, dried pumpkins and sweet corn, beans, some root vegetables (including onions with which one could work wonders in the limited diet), a year's supply of bacon and lard, [and] enough flour to last until the next year's wheat crop could be harvested and ground." She also packed bags of seed and cuttings for planting, a number of window sashes, and an iron cookstove, all things that were difficult to find on the frontier. Rebecca packed her glass canning jars and preserves in the barrels of flour where the temperature was uniform and the jars protected from breaking. When the wagons stopped for a layover or to rest the livestock, Rebecca put-up jams and jellies made from local chokeberries, currants, gooseberries, and wild plums. The Ridgley party expected to buy potatoes at the stepping-off place on the trail, but the wagon train ahead of them had bought up the entire supply. Joshua was able to trade 50 pounds of flour for an equal quantity of potatoes from a group he passed on the prairie.[24]

The Ridgleys were among the first families to settle in the Gallatine Valley of western Montana Territory, and it was six months before their family in Wisconsin knew they had arrived safely. With a crude cabin built of logs and a field cleared for planting, Joshua and Rebecca immediately realized a need to irrigate their crops, and they joined with 13 other families to dig a great ditch for the purpose of tapping a local creek for irrigation. Their first crops of rutabagas, cabbages, and potatoes were loaded on two wagons and headed for the goldfields near Helena (90 miles away) where they brought 28 cents a pound in gold and twice that in greenbacks in 1865.

Captives

In his Oregon Trail journal Francis Parkman noted, "Nothing excited [the Indians] so much as the wanton destruction committed among the [buffalo] cows, and in [their] view shooting a calf was a cardinal sin."[25] A great number of buffalo hunters had been active in the Great Plains region in the 1840s and 1850s, killing the herds, stripping the hides, and using the tongues for food while allowing the rest of the carcasses to rot. The extent of this wholesale slaughter exasperated the Indians to the point that the Kiowa, Comanche, Cheyenne, and Arapaho joined together determined to make war on the white intruders. Yet the Indians generally avoided attacking groups of buffalo hunters with their powerful, large caliber rifles, and they attacked instead emigrants in individual wagons or on trains that were too small to take care of themselves. These innocents were "slaughtered . . . by the hundreds."[26]

In 1851, the Mormon emigrant train of James C. Brewster headed out of Independence, Missouri, for the confluence of the Colorado and Gilla Rivers in California via the Old Santa Fe Trail. Inducements had been held out to the emigrants to establish an American settlement near the Gulf of California. The Oatman family—Royse, Mary Ann, and their seven children—foolishly abandoned the company of the other wagons just south of the Gilla River. Before two days passed, the Oatmans were attacked by Apache just inside the border of Mexican Territory (the Gadsden Purchase had not yet occurred). Every one of the family members was killed, with the exception of the son Lorenzo (age 14, mistakenly left for dead) and the two younger girls, Olive and Mary Ann (13 and 7 years old), who were taken alive. Among the dead were father, mother, and four children—from an oldest girl of 16 to a youngest son of 1 year. Lorenzo, though badly wounded, regained consciousness and found his way back to civilization. The living girls were taken into captivity, sold to Mojave Indians, and removed farther to the west.

Maj. Samuel P. Heintzelman, commanding the post at Fort Yuma, initially refused to pursue the attackers because they were in territory whose ownership was disputed with Mexico, and he was widely criticized for waiting two days before sending out a relief party. The younger girl died of starvation among the Mohave within a year, but Olive, the lower half of her face tattooed in Indian-style, was returned to Fort Yuma in 1856, having been purchased from the Mohave at a village some 400 miles away. Olive had spent almost five years in captivity. A clergyman, R. B. Stratton, became interested in the story, and after interviewing the surviving boy and girl, he penned a surprisingly successful book about their trials. The work sold 5,000 copies within two weeks of its publication in 1857. Subsequent editions sold 24,000 copies by 1859 alone. The book remained in print until 1903.[27]

Although the massacre was graphically portrayed, the focus of Stratton's book was the misery that Olive experienced "among the degraded savages" for a period of years, yet the *Los Angeles Star* carefully reported that she had not been "made a wife" even at the age of 18. The American public generally assumed the inevitable and repeated rape of women and older girls in such a defenseless situation, but this was not found to be true in most documented cases. Stratton wrote, "Let it be written . . . that one of our own race, in tender years, committed wholly to their power, passed a five-years' captivity among these savages without falling under those baser propensities." Skepticism about Olive's continued virginal state among the Indians remained active, however, into the 20th century.[28]

One of the most prominent attacks on emigrant families took place in western Kansas near Fort Hayes in 1874. The Germaine family traveling in a lone wagon from their former home in Georgia to a new life in Colorado was attacked by Indians on the banks of the Smokey Hill River in September. The family consisted of a father, mother, one son, and six daughters aged five and up. Mr. Germaine, his wife, and son were killed and scalped; one daughter was shot; and another burned to death before the eyes of her sisters. The wounded girl and her surviving sisters were carried off. It was the ultimate fate of the five young surviving sisters that caught the eye of the press and the sympathy of the American public.

The details of the rescue of these girls as recorded in 19th- and early 20th-century sources are ambiguous and sometimes contradictory. Nonetheless, the five captive sisters were seemingly separated among three different bands that made up the attackers. The wounded (eldest) girl was rescued under cover of a winter snowstorm within weeks of the attack from an Indian village on the banks of the Solomon River. It was she who provided the initial details concerning the attack to the press. The rescue was accomplished by a group of soldiers from Fort Wallace under the direction of a civilian guide named James Cannon.

Some months later (March 1875) Cannon led Lt. Frank D. Baldwin commanding a mixed force of Delaware scouts, frontiersmen, and 100 soldiers to the Cheyenne camp on Crooked River on the Texas panhandle. The two youngest girls were reportedly held there. An immediate attack was ordered, the Cheyenne retreated, and the two girls were found abandoned along with an old Indian woman. Baldwin's quick action and skillful leadership earned him his second Congressional Medal of Honor. His first had been earned during the Civil War.

Information was gleaned from Indian captives that the two eldest Germaine girls, in the middle years of their adolescence, were with another band camped south of the Red River. This proved to be the Cheyenne band led by Stone Calf, a noted warrior and troublemaker. The rescue of these girls was effected by Benjamin F. Williams, a deputy

U.S. marshal working out of the Cheyenne and Arapaho Agency at Darlington, Indian Territory. Having been informed of the presence of the girls, Williams rode boldly into Stone Calf's camp where he was accorded a cool and suspicious reception. Nonetheless, he was able to negotiate not only the release of the girls, but also the return of the band to the agency. The girls reportedly wept when they met Williams, their tears trickling through the face paint that had been smeared on them to conceal their white identities.

The newspapers had a field day with the story of the Germaine family, and everyone except the Indians tried to benefit from the publicity. *Frank Leslie's Illustrated Newspaper* ran the story and an engraved illustration of the two younger girls in its July 4, 1875 edition. All the sisters were sent to Fort Leavenworth where Gen. Nelson A. Miles volunteered to become their legal guardian. Congress, swept up in the public euphoria over the rescues, diverted $10,000 of Indian annuities for the support of Germaine sisters. The income from this amount was to be used during their minority, and the principal divided among them after they had all come of age.[29]

Seasoning

It was thought that individuals who radically changed their surroundings through emigration were obliged to pass through a period of acclimation to their new environment known as seasoning. This process was often more physically challenging than the cross-country trip. Emigrants were often seized with dangerous illnesses immediately after arriving in their new homes. Some of these sicknesses were expected because they had marked the movement of Europeans to the New World since the colonial era. Others were totally outside the experience of the emigrants. Chills and fevers, known as the "ague," stomach upsets, and bowel complaints were commonly ascribed to a lack of seasoning, but may actually have been caused by exposure to unfamiliar water and heavily salted provisions. One family member after another would fall to these illnesses in almost a mechanical sequence. For this reason common wisdom suggested that emigrants plan their arrival for autumn and past the sickly season of summer heat. They would thereby marshal their bodily reserves for the assault of winter and the starving time of early spring. Nonetheless, only after several years, or seasons, of sequential sicknesses would most emigrant families be cautiously brought back to full health. Passage through the process was commonly used to separate the established resident from the "green" one, and it was said that outsiders could separate the seasoned and unseasoned in a given locality by the very features in their faces.

The seasoning process could be prolonged and painful, and it could be as dangerous as it was inexorable. Local physicians erroneously ascribed many types of disease to a lack of seasoning and assured those with long residence in an area—sometimes incorrectly—that they were unlikely to be at risk even when sicknesses of epidemic proportions invaded the ranks of the newly arrived. "Such assessments fill guidebooks and military reports, physicians' articles and private letters; they form a little-noticed undercurrent in the flow of population . . . [and reveal] much of their everyday experience and matter-of-fact expectations of the world."[30]

Outbreaks of malaria, cholera, and other epidemic diseases were sometimes falsely assigned to a lack of seasoning, and inappropriate remedies could be as deadly as none at all. Of course, it was often insect or waterborne bacterial or viral infections that actually spread disease; but this biological reality was unknown to doctors at the time. The true mechanism behind seasoning probably came from the acquisition of natural immunities through exposure over time to a variety of local pathogens. However, changes in behavior on the part of the emigrants may have also helped the seasoning process. These came in the form of better overall nutrition as initial plantings were harvested, the development of potable water sources, improved shelter from the elements, changes to more practical and more protective clothing, or a simple return to normal periods of rest and sustainable work regimes after undergoing the stress and strain associated with cross-country travel and carving out new homesteads.[31]

In 1829 Gottfried Duden published an influential guide for German emigrants to America in which he adamantly warned of the dangers of changing environments too quickly. Sudden confrontations with a new environment could create dangerous disturbances in the health of immigrants. These were thought to involve mostly the dangers of intense heat. In 1860 a Kansas City physician, Dr. G.M.B. Maughs, published a theory that heat combined with rotting vegetation and debris of any kind—no matter how innocuous—was potentially harmful. He termed the wetlands and marshes of the South "laboratories for the production of *miasmas.*" These were vapors and odors erroneously thought for centuries to carry disease. Typhoid, typhus, cholera, malaria, and yellow fever were all ascribed to an exposure to "bad air," and the epidemics of Biblical proportions that regularly swept Southern cities seemed to verify the concept. In 1832, for example, one-sixth of the population of New Orleans died of yellow fever in just 12 days, and the next summer one-fifth succumbed. In 1853 an epidemic outbreak afflicted 40,000 persons, and two weeks later the first cases of cholera appeared. For these reasons (among others) immigrants from the colder climes of northern European countries tended to avoid settling in the American South where both intense heat and swamp-like conditions were thought to be common.[32]

Photographing America

The early history of photography in America transcends the antebellum, Civil War, and Reconstruction periods. Although daguerreotype, tintype, and wet-plate photographic portraiture had been around for decades, all these processes were ill suited to outdoor use, and the practical use of photography to record large-scale historical events was not attempted until the Crimean War of 1854. Moreover, there were no published manuals for photographers prior to that printed by George B. Coale in 1858, and it is doubtful that the pocket-sized booklet could be used to successfully teach the intricacies of the photographic art in the absence of face-to-face instruction. The domination of the complicated wet-glass plate colloid process from 1855 to 1888 helps to explain why photography remained in the hands of professionals.

Among the many brave photojournalists who recorded the battle scenes and war dead of America's Civil War were Alexander Gardner, George N. Bernard, and Capt. Andrew J. Russell. Although he limited most of his work to the studio, Matthew Brady is possibly the best-known photographer of the period, and people flocked to him to have photographic portraits and cartes de visite taken in their best clothes. Historians continue to dispute Brady's active participation on the battle-fields of the Civil War, but there is no question that the Brady studios sponsored many of the most productive photographers of the period.

In this period individual images from negatives were almost exclusively made on chloride paper, and the technology of reproducing photographs for the printing press was almost nonexistent before the end of the century. The usual way of reproducing a photograph for a newspaper, magazine, or book was to have an artist redraw it and make a woodcut or engraving as with battlefield sketches. This process neutralized most of the advantages of photography for the print medium. Moreover, Americans seem to have favored the more romanticized full-page chromolithographs and engravings over the generally small black-and-white photographs made by contact printing.

Nonetheless, hundreds of photographs of battlefields and personalities were shown in galleries in the major cities of the North during the Civil War years. The pictures, including some of the first to show war dead on the battlefield, were poignant and realistic, and may have helped to create an anti-war feeling in the North. The photographic galleries in New York and Washington, in particular, were very popular and admission was expensive. The South also had its photographers. George S. Cook, J. D. Edwards, and A. D. Lytle, among others, were able photographers committed to the Southern cause, but their work was more circumspect than that of their fellows from the North, being generally limited to portraiture. The South's limited technical facilities forced the public to be content with rough woodcuts, engravings, and paintings.

It was through the older and simpler technology of the metal-plate process, however, that photography was introduced to the rural American public. All through the last half of the 19th century itinerant photographers traveled the fairs and road shows producing tintypes (sometimes called ferrotypes). Some tintypists traveled alone, riding a regional circuit of towns and seasonal stops, and returning to them at regular intervals to update the images of children and record the likenesses of newborns or recently married couples. Beginning with the presidential election of 1860, tintype campaign pins became the single most important electioneering apparel of the period with the exception of printed ribbons. All four major candidates for president that year had their slightly out-of-focus features photographically placed on dime-sized brass buttons. These tintype pins were considered invaluable as an electioneering tool, and they remained popular with the candidates until the 1880s. One inventive photographer took out a patent on "tombstone tintypes" made to fasten an image of the dearly departed to the grave marker. Tintypes were less expensive than paper prints, but they were one-of-a-kind works unless taken with multiple lenses. There was no negative from which prints could be duplicated. The tin was itself the product of the exposure. Nonetheless, tintypes were long lasting and accurate in their portrayals. Tintype photographers could still be found working the county fairs in the 1920s.[33]

With the development of faster-acting dry-plate glass negatives by George Eastman in 1888, photographers were better able to take their instruments out-of-doors. William Kurtz was the first to specialize in night photography using flash powder, and social reformer Jacob Riis used the dry-plate system to capture the misery of slum life in New York's tenements. A young politician (then police commissioner), Teddy Roosevelt, often took Riis with him when enforcing the city's health and safety regulations in order to make a permanent record of the violations. Also noted at the time for their images of street scenes and immigrants were Percy Byron and Lewis Hines (New York), Sigmund Krausz (Chicago), and Arnold Genthe (San Francisco). The new realism of such photographs became the vogue among Americans and generated a post–Civil War generation of documentary photographers.

The Vanishing American

It was not long before the cameras were turned toward the American Indians and the West. In 1846 Thomas Easterly had made daguerreo-type portraits in his St. Louis studio of several Sauk and Fox warriors in their Indian attire and paraphernalia, and in the 1850s portraits of the Indian leaders who traveled as diplomats to the nation's capital were available for viewing in the city's galleries. Civil War photographer Alexander Gardner produced a number of these, and in 1868 he brought his camera to Fort Laramie to record the treaty negotiations with the Sioux. Joel E. Whitney used his camera in 1871 to record the drama of a Sioux rebellion in Minnesota, and in the same year Timothy O'Sullivan accompanied the Wheeler Expedition and Survey to Navajo and Mojave territory. John K. Hillers accompanied John Wesley Powell on his monumental exploration of the Colorado River, and he recorded for the first time the extraordinary beauty of the Grand Canyon. Will Soule photographically recorded life at Fort Sill deep in Indian Territory, and Frederick Monsen joined George A. Crook and Nelson A. Miles during their Apache campaigns in the Southwest, capturing some of the only images ever taken of "hostile" Indians in the field.

At age 16, David F. Barry of Wisconsin became an apprentice for an itinerant portrait photographer named O. S. Goff. By 1878 Barry and Goff had become partners in a photographic studio in Bismarck (Dakota Territory). It is unclear why Barry became interested in photographing the American Indian, but it was no whim or fancy. He supplied himself with a portable studio of his own design and traveled by wagon throughout the territory between 1878 and 1883, making stops at a number of military outposts and forts as far north as the Blackfoot country of Montana. In the process he took images of soldiers, trappers, scouts, emigrants, women, warriors, children, and chiefs. These included Sitting Bull, Rain in the Face, Gall, Red Cloud, Shooting Star, and Gen. Crook. In 1883 Barry returned to Bismarck and established a friendship with Buffalo Bill Cody. The firm of Barry and Goff took many photographs of the cast of Cody's impressive traveling Wild West Show. For a short time in 1890 Barry tried to exhibit his work for an admission fee in New York City, but with the availability of lower-cost paper prints, the time of the photographic gallery had largely passed. He returned to Wisconsin and lived there quietly, working until his death in 1934.

In the 1880s photographer John Choate took a whole series of before-and-after images of the inmates at the Carlisle Indian Industrial School in Pennsylvania meant to convince 19th-century observers of the natives' inevitable progress from "savagery to civilization." The modern eye, however, can easily discern from the images of young Native Americans—crammed into ill-fitting suits and dresses, shorn of their flowing hair, and sitting bolt upright on wooden benches—that no such transformation had actually taken place. By way of contrast to Choate's work, many men found themselves driven by the need to capture the essence of the 19th-century world of the American Indian before it disappeared through fatal contact with white civilization. It is not uncommon for the dominant culture to adopt the role of keeper or defender of the native lifestyle once the conquest of a people is seen as complete and irreversible.[34]

Photographers Roland Reed and Joseph K. Dixon were seemingly obsessed with the subject of Indian culture, and Prince Roland Bonaparte, visiting from Europe in 1887, recorded an amazing 7,000 Native American images. Many of these were housed in Europe and not made available to researchers until the 20th century. In 1892 Horace S. Poley created a major collection of images of Native Americans from the Southwest, and he remained active until 1935, serving as a photographer for several archaeological expeditions to Arizona, New Mexico, Utah, and Colorado.

Poley is best known for his hand-colored "magic lantern" slides of the West, which he used when giving travelogue lectures.

Best known among the photographers of the American West was Edward S. Curtis, who first dubbed the Indians a "vanishing race." The extent of his work made him the most influential photographer of Native American life in the period. Curtis created a vast collection of almost 40,000 images in a 30-year career, but he came to his subject late in the century and much of the uninfected Indian culture that he hoped to capture photographically had already passed. Critics of these late-century images might have preferred a more documentary and less romantic result, but the same reservations have been charged against the contemporary paintings of Fredric Remington and Charles M. Russell, who also tried to recapture the fading glory of the West.

Summary

When Thomas Jefferson was born in western Virginia in 1743, the frontier was still east of the Allegheny Mountains. Sixty years later in 1803 Jefferson purchased the rights to the vast Louisiana Territory from France, taking the frontier farther west to the Rockies. The nation had been doubled in size by the time of Jefferson's death in 1826. British pretensions to the Old Northwest of the Great Lakes region were permanently erased in the peace that ended the War of 1812; the boundary between Maine and New Brunswick was settled in 1842, and the Oregon treaty line with Canada was settled at the 49th parallel in 1846. After a successful war with Mexico in 1846, Texas had been annexed, and California and New Mexico had been added by 1848. In 1853 the Gadsden Purchase filled out most of the familiar boundaries of the continental United States. Alaska had been added by purchase from Russia in 1867. The Indians had been driven from their native lands almost everywhere, and they had been killed or confined to reservations by 1890. By the turn of the century a number of island possessions had been acquired: Hawaii in 1893; Puerto Rico, Guam, and the Philippines in 1898; and Wake Island in 1899. The nation, initially isolated on a thin strip of land along the Atlantic coast, had attained its *Manifest Destiny* by stretching from sea to sea in little more than a single century, and it had become in the process a multi-ocean colonial power.

Notes

1. William H. Goetzmann, *Exploration and Empire: The Explorer and the Scientist in the Winning of the American West* (New York: History Book Club, 1966), ascribes the slogan *Manifest Destiny* to Jane McManus Storm.

2. See ibid., v–vi.

3. Conevery Bolton Valencius, *The Health of the Country: How American Settlers Understood Themselves and Their Land* (New York: Basic Books, 2002), 21.

4. See ibid., 18–19.

5. Ibid., 16.

6. Ibid., 20–21.

7. Francis Marion Watkins, "The Story of the Crow Emigrant Train of 1865," *The Livingston Chronicle,* January 1937, 33. The original story was recorded from conversations with Watkins in Los Banos, California, in 1935 by Ralph Leroy Milliken.

8. Ibid.

9. Ibid., 6.

10. Burnett and Stewart quoted in James M. Volo and Dorothy Denneen Volo, *Encyclopedia of the Antebellum South* (Westport, Conn.: Greenwood Press, 2000), 173.

11. Randolph B. Marcy, *The Prairie Traveler: A Hand-book for Overland Expeditions* (1859; repr., La Vergne, Tenn.: Lightning Source, 2004), 28.

12. Watkins, "Story of the Crow Emigrant Train," 4–5.

13. Scott quoted in Tricia Martineau Wagner, *It Happened on the Oregon Trail* (Guilford, Conn.: Globe Pequot Press, 2005), 73.

14. Elizabeth Bacon Custer, *Tenting on the Plains; or, General Custer in Kansas and Texas* (Norman: University of Oklahoma Press, 1971), 139.

15. Francis Parkman, *The Oregon Trail* (New York: Lancer Books, 1968), 429.

16. Marcy, *Prairie Traveler,* 201.

17. Watkins, "Story of the Crow Emigrant Train," 11.

18. Ibid., 20.

19. Ibid., 19.

20. Marcy, *Prairie Traveler,* 208.

21. Watkins, "Story of the Crow Emigrant Train," 8.

22. Ibid., 19.

23. Royal B. Stratton, *Captivity of the Oatman Girls* (New York: Carlton & Porter, 1857), 24–25.

24. Dickson quoted in Dorothy M. Johnson, *The Bloody Bozeman* (New York: McGraw-Hill Book Co., 1971), 138–139.

25. Parkman, *Oregon Trail,* 406.

26. Watkins, "Story of the Crow Emigrant Train," 11.

27. Stratton, *Captivity of the Oatman Girls,* xi.

28. Ibid., xiii.

29. See Frank W. Blackmar, ed., *Kansas: A Cyclopedia of State History,* vol. 3 of 4 (Chicago: Standard Publishing Co., 1912), 746–747.

30. Valencius, *Health of the Country,* 4.

31. See ibid., 22–25.

32. See ibid.

33. Harold Holzer, "Photographs on Tin: The Ferrotype Endures," *The Antique Trader Annual of Articles* 10 (September 1979): 316.

34. Bernd C. Peyer, *The Tutor'd Mind: Indian Missionary-Writers in Antebellum America* (Amherst: University of Massachusetts Press, 1997), 5.

Selected Bibliography

Brewer, Priscilla J. *From Fireplace to Cookstove: Technology and the Domestic Ideal in America.* Syracuse, N.Y.: Syracuse University Press, 2000.

Chudacoff, Howard P., and Judith E. Smith. *The Evolution of American Urban Society.* Upper Saddle River, N.J.: Pearson-Prentice Hall, 2005.

Clark, Clifford Edward, Jr. *The American Family Home, 1800–1860.* Chapel Hill: University of North Carolina Press, 1986.

Clinton, Catherine. *The Plantation Mistress: Woman's World in the Old South.* New York: Pantheon Books, 1982.

Collins, Gail. *America's Women.* New York: Perennial, 2004.

Conner, Alvin E. *Sectarian Childrearing: The Dunkers, 1708–1900.* Gettysburg, Pa.: Brethren Heritage, 2000.

Cooper, James Fenimore. *Notions of the Americans Picked up by a Traveling Bachelor.* Albany: State University of New York Press, 1991.

Cordasco, Francesco. *A Brief History of Education.* Totowa, N.J.: Littlefield, Adams & Co., 1970.

East, Charles, ed. *Sarah Morgan: The Diary of a Southern Woman.* New York: Simon & Schuster, 1991.

Eisler, Benita, ed. *The Lowell Offering: Writings by New England Mill Women, 1840–1845.* New York: W. W. Norton & Co., 1998.

England, J. Merton, ed. *Buckeye Schoolmaster: A Chronicle of Midwestern Rural Life, 1852–1865.* Bowling Green, Ohio: Bowling Green State University Popular Press, 1996.

Faust, Drew Gilpin. *The Creation of Confederate Nationalism: Ideology and Identity in the Civil War South.* Baton Rouge: Louisiana State University Press, 1988.

Fehrenbacher, Don E. *The Era of Expansion, 1800–1848.* New York: John Wiley & Sons, 1969.

Fite, Emerson David. *Social and Industrial Conditions in the North during the Civil War.* Williamstown, N.Y.: Corner House, 1976.

Gwin, Minrose C. *A Woman's Civil War.* Madison: University of Wisconsin, 1992.

Hareven, Tamara K., and Maris A. Vinovskis, eds., *Family and Population in Nineteenth Century America.* Princeton, N.J.: Princeton University Press, 1978.

Heininger, Mary L. *A Century of Childhood, 1820–1920.* Rochester, N.Y.: Margaret Woodbury Strong Museum, 1984.

Hunt, Gaillard. *As We Were: Life in America, 1814.* 1914. Reprint, Stockbridge, Mass.: Berkshire House Publishing, 1993.

Ketchum, Richard M., ed. *The American Heritage Book of the Pioneer Spirit.* New York: American Heritage Publishing Co., 1959.

Kevill-Davies, Sally. *Yesterday's Children: The Antiques and History of Childcare.* Woodbridge, England: Antique Collector's Club, 1991.

Kiracofe, Roderick. *The American Quilt.* New York: Clarkson Potter, 1993.

Kiracofe, Roderick. *Cloth & Comfort: Pieces of Women's Lives from Their Quilts and Diaries.* New York: Clarkson Potter, 1994.

Larcom, Lucy. *A New England Girlhood.* Boston: Northeastern University Press, 1986.

Larkin, Jack. *Children Everywhere: Dimensions of Childhood in Early 19th-Century New England.* Sturbridge, Mass.: Davis Press, 1987.

Lunt, Dolly Sumner. *A Woman's Wartime Journal by Mrs. Thomas Lunt Burge.* Atlanta: Cherokee, 1994.

Lupiano, Vincent de Paul, and Ken W. Sayers. *It Was a Very Good Year: A Cultural History of the United States from 1776 to the Present.* Holbrook, Mass.: Bob Adams, 1994.

Marten, James. *The Children's Civil War.* Chapel Hill: University of North Carolina Press, 1998.

McCutcheon, Marc. *Everyday Life in the 1800's.* Cincinnati, Ohio: Writer's Digest Books, 1993.

McMurry, Sally. *Families and Farmhouses in Nineteenth Century America.* Knoxville: University of Tennessee Press, 1997.

McPherson, James M. *For Cause and Comrades: Why Men Fought in the Civil War.* New York: Oxford University Press, 1997.

Meredith, Roy. *Matthew Brady's Portrait of an Era.* New York: W. W. Norton & Co., 1982.

Mintz, Steven. *Huck's Raft: A History of American Childhood.* Cambridge, Mass.: Belknap Press/Harvard University Press, 2004.

Mitchell, Reid. *The Vacant Chair: The Northern Soldier Leaves Home.* New York: Oxford University Press, 1993.

Mitford, Jessica. *The American Way of Birth.* New York: Dutton, 1992.

Mondale, Sarah, and Sarah B. Patton, eds. *School: The Story of American Public Education.* Boston: Beacon Press, 2001.

Moskow, Shirley Blotnick. *Emma's World: An Intimate Look at Lives Touched by the Civil War Era.* Far Hills, N.J.: New Horizon Press, 1990.

Nye, Russel B. *The Cultural Life of the New Nation, 1776–1830.* New York: Harper & Row, 1960.

Nylander, Jane C. *Our Own Snug Fireside: Images of the New England Home, 1760–1860.* New Haven, Conn.: Yale University Press, 1993.

Paul, Rodman Wilson. *Mining Frontiers of the Far West, 1848–1880.* New York: Holt, Rinehart & Winston, 1963.

Peyer, Bernd C. *The Tutor'd Mind, Indian Missionary-Writers in Antebellum America.* Amherst: University of Massachusetts Press, 1997.

Pitt, Leonard, ed. *Documenting America: A Reader in United States History from Colonial Times to 1877.* Dubuque, Iowa: Kendall/Hunt Publishing Co., 1989.

Richards, Caroline C. *Village Life in America, 1852–1872.* Gansevoort, N.Y.: Corner House, 1997.

Richards, Leonard I. *Gentlemen of Property and Standing: Anti-Abolition Mobs in Jacksonian America.* New York: Oxford University Press, 1970.

Riis, Jacob A. *How the Other Half Lives: Studies among the Tenements of New York.* New York: Charles Scribner's Sons, 1890.

Robenbloom, Joshua L., and Gregory W. Stutes. *Reexamining the Distribution of Wealth in 1870.* Cambridge, Mass.: National Bureau of Economic Research, 2005.

Root, Waverly, and Richard de Rouchemont. *Eating in America.* New York: William Morrow, 1976.

Rowland, K. T. *Steam at Sea: The History of Steam Navigation.* New York: Praeger Publishing, 1970.

Sanchez-Eppler, Karen. *Dependent States: The Child's Part in Nineteenth Century American Culture.* Chicago: University of Chicago Press, 2005.

Schenone, Laura. *A Thousand Years over a Hot Stove.* New York: W. W. Norton & Co., 2003.

Sewell, Richard H. *A House Divided: Sectionalism and the Civil War, 1848–1865.* Baltimore: Johns Hopkins University Press, 1988.

Strasser, Susan. *Never Done: A History of American Housework.* New York: Henry Holt & Co., 1982.

Swan, Susan Burrows. *Plain & Fancy: American Women and Their Needlework, 1650–1850.* Austin, Tex.: Curious Works Press. 1977.

Tinling, Marion, ed., *With Women's Eyes: Visitors to the New World, 1775–1918.* Norman: University of Oklahoma Press, 1993.

Trager, James. *The Food Chronology.* New York: Henry Holt & Co., 1995.

Trollope, Frances. *Domestic Manners of the Americans.* 1832. Reprint, Mineola, N.Y.: Dover Publications, 2003.

Valencius, Conevery Bolton. *The Health of the Country: How American Settlers Understood Themselves and Their Land.* New York: Basic Books, 2002.

Vinovshkis, Maris A., ed. *Studies in American Historical Demography.* New York: Academic Press, 1979.

Volo, James M., and Dorothy Denneen Volo. *The Antebellum Period.* Westport, Conn.: Greenwood Press, 2004.

Volo, James M., and Dorothy Denneen Volo. *Encyclopedia of the Antebellum South.* Westport, Conn.: Greenwood Press, 2000.

Volo, James M., and Dorothy Denneen Volo. *Family Life in 17th- and 18th-Century America.* Westport, Conn.: Greenwood Press, 2006.

Wagner, Tricia Martineau. *It Happened on the Oregon Trail.* Guilford, Conn.: Globe Pequot Press, 2005.

Weissman, Judith Reiter, and Wendy Lavitt. *Labors of Love: America's Textiles and Needlework, 1630–1930.* New York: Wings Books, 1994.

Wilentz, Sean. *Chants Democratic: New York City and the Rise of the American Working Class, 1788–1850.* New York: Oxford University Press, 1984.

Yalom, Marilyn. *A History of the Wife.* New York: Perennial, 2002.

Index

About the Authors

JAMES M. VOLO is a science teacher at Norwalk Public Schools in Norwalk, Connecticut. He is co-author of *Family Life in 17th- and 18th-Century America* (Greenwood, 2006), *Daily Life during the American Revolution* (Greenwood, 2003), and many other Greenwood titles.

DOROTHY DENNEEN VOLO is a math teacher at Norwalk Public Schools in Norwalk, Connecticut. She is co-author of *Family Life in 17th-and 18th-Century America* (Greenwood, 2006), *Daily Life during the American Revolution* (Greenwood, 2003), and many other Greenwood titles.